C000125807

THE RUGBY LEAGUE WORLD CUP

THE RUGBY LEAGUE WORLD CUP

An illustrated history of Rugby's oldest global tournament

LEAGUE
Publications Ltd

Acknowledgements

In 2000, League Publications, publishers of Rugby Leaguer & League Express and Rugby League World magazine, decided it was time, after twelve tournaments stretching back to 1954, to record the history of the Rugby League World Cup. It would have been remiss of us therefore not to update the history to include full details of the 13th World Cup.

For some unknown reason, rugby's oldest world cup has been seen as a threat by the chattering classes, and the 13th tournament was ridiculed, not least for its predictability, at least until an unforgettable final in Brisbane, when New Zealand upset the odds to win their first World Cup. I'm sure, when the smoke has cleared and we look back on the 2008 World Cup, we will all remember it as a highly successful event.

That we are able to publish this book is down to having people on the ground to witness and record history as it happened. Without the advent of Rugby Leaguer & League Express in 1990, that might never have been possible. Records for the tournaments before that were in the main sketchy, particularly in the earlier years.

For the histories of those early tournaments we relied on the joint knowledge of the founder of Open Rugby, now Rugby League World, Harry Edgar, and Rugby Leaguer & League Express's man down under, Malcolm Andrews. Many of the original histories published in 2000, have been augmented by additional research.

Match reports from 2008 were provided by our reporters down under, Gareth Walker, Steve Mascord, Trevor Hunt, Joanna Lester, Malcolm Andrews and yours truly. Magnificent pictures throughout the tournament were provided by Col Whelan of Action Photographics and Dave Williams of RLPhotos. Design of the book once again is down to Daniel Spencer.

Lastly, thanks once again to the players and officials who made the 13th World Cup one to remember, and hopefully gave the administrators of the game the motivation and confidence to establish the tournament as one of sport's great global events.

TIM BUTCHER, League Publications

First published in Great Britain in 2009 by League Publications Ltd, Wellington House, Briggate, Brighouse, West Yorkshire, HD6 1DN.

Copyright © League Publications Ltd

A CIP catalogue record for this book is available from the British Library
ISBN 1-901347-20-3

Designed and Typeset by Daniel Spencer, League Publications Limited

Manufactured in the EU by L.P.P.S. Ltd, Wellingborough, Northants

All rights reserved. No part of this book may be reproduced or transmitted in any form or by any means, electronic or mechanical, including photocopying, recording or by any information storage and retrieval system, without prior permission in writing from the publisher.

Contents

Introduction

Paul Barrière died on May 29th, 2008, aged 87. Barrière was the founding father of the Rugby League World Cup, which first took place in his native France in 1954 with the lukewarm participation of Great Britain, New Zealand and Australia. Five months after his death, the Frenchman's vision for the world game was full vindicated by the 13th Rugby League World Cup.

Barrière was one of League's greatest administrators. A former Resistance leader, awarded the Croix de Guerre and Medaille de la Resistance, Barrière took the fight for League's reinstatement to the National Sports Committee in Paris, despite rugby union's opposition. He was 27 when elected president of the French Rugby League Federation in 1947 and presided over a golden age for rugby à treize in France during the 1950s.

If it hadn't been for the foresight of Barrière the Rugby League World Cup might never have happened.

The concept of a World Cup had its opponents back in the 1950s; administrators, sound people with the future of the game at heart, who couldn't see the merit or the potential in Rugby League as a world game. Some might say, little has changed. But in this age of global media and marketing it would be folly for administrators to sit back and not impose Rugby League on a world stage.

For many years the Rugby League World Cup was restricted to four nations – France, Great Britain, New Zealand and Australia, with England and Wales given brief appearances in one competition.

Papua New Guinea was invited to the show in 1985, when the World Cup was played over three years! – but it wasn't until the 1995 World Cup, the centrepiece of the English centenary celebrations, that Rugby League finally took the bull by the horns, with ten nations enjoying a wonderful three weeks, in unseasonably balmy October English weather.

By the year 2000 the Rugby League World Cup had expanded to 16 teams, confirming Paul Barriére's vision of League as a truly global sport.

The expanded competition gave the World Cup organisers the opportunity to showcase the game in every part of the United Kingdom, in Ireland, and in France.

How satisfying must it have been for Barrière to see his beloved France qualify for the quarter-finals of the 2000 World Cup with their win in front of a capacity crowd in Carcassonne, on the same day the Treizistes unveiled a statue of World Cup legend Puig Aubert.

The 2008 World Cup was a more conservative affair than the one eight years before, with ten teams involved in a format to suit TV broadcasters. That wasn't received well, but it did produce some fabulous events. It was a pity that Barrière couldn't have survived to see the likes of Fiji, Tonga, Samoa, Ireland and Scotland produce matches of such quality and excitement.

New legends were born in the World Cup of 2008. One was Australia's fullback Billy Slater, winner of the Golden Boot in 2008, presented by Rugby League World magazine to the best player in the world. Slater was the out-and-out player of the World Cup, and yet made the mistake that gifted New Zealand their first World Cup.

And Stanley Gene, playing in his third and last World Cup for Papua New Guinea, was carried on the shoulders of his countrymen in tears after the Kumuls' exit at the hands of Australia.

And it will be hard to forget how the Fijians celebrated their victories by joining in a circle to belt out the sweetest of hymns.

There were many more legends before. There's the story of how a Scotsman was the first to lift the great old trophy, captaining a side of British no-hopers that weren't even allowed to take their coach with them to the first World Cup in France. The star of the 1957 World Cup, who was almost prevented from representing the Kangaroos by his club committee. The Roman Catholic priest from Newcastle who featured in the infamous battle of Headingley in 1970 that led to calls for Rugby League to be banned from TV screens to protect the nation's youth. Captain Clive Sullivan, who effectively won the World Cup for Great Britain - for the third and last time – by racing 70 metres for a stunning try in Lyon. And Emperor Wally Lewis, who helped win the 1988 World Cup for Australia despite suffering a broken arm in the final.

We hope you enjoy this comprehensive record of rugby's oldest World Cup tournament, and leave you with a hope held by Paul Barrière back in 1953 when he was attempting to persuade the rest of the Rugby League world to think global: "It appears to us...that the time has now come to organise a World Cup series – indeed we feel it indispensable."

Let's hope that the spirit of Paul Barrière will always live on.

1
2008
RUGBY LEAGUE
WORLD CUP

WORLD VISION

New Zealand won a stunning World Cup victory - the first time they had ever lifted the trophy - at the 13th attempt. The tournament was held in Australia for the first time since 1977 and was judged a great success, eight years after the last one in Europe - a plan announced in 2002 to stage it in the northern hemisphere in 2005 had been scrapped.

The 2008 World Cup was officially launched on 7th November 2007 in Leeds, less than a year before it was due to kick off. The draw for the 10-team tournament had already been announced in April that year, with England, Australia, New Zealand and Papua New Guinea placed in a 'super pool', the top three teams qualifying for the semi-finals, the fourth eliminated. The other two pools were to contain three nations each, one of those able to qualify for the semi-finals.

The draw created outrage in Papua New Guinea, with the formula making the Kumuls' chances of reaching the semi-finals remote. PNG great Marcus Bai said: 'I reckon it's crap. I am furious about this. It's really rubbish. Our guys will try very hard, but if you look at results over the past ten years you could say we've got no chance. They say anything can happen, but really...'

At the launch, tournament director Colin Love defended the convoluted draw. 'The format of the competition means that we will see teams with a real chance of causing an upset in almost every game,' he said. 'It is going to provide some great television viewing, and the pleasing thing is that we are still receiving considerable interest from further prospective broadcast partners.'

TV cameras from several different broadcasters were in Australia to capture the action, with live coverage in the UK, Australia, New Zealand and the Middle East. BSkyB's live coverage attracted a peak audience of 420,000 for the England v New Zealand semi-final. Fiji's demand for World Cup matches led to the country's supply of UHF aerials selling out as people tuned into Mai TV. Special 'live sites' were arranged in Queen's Park, Suva, to allow people to see their semi-final against Australia, forcing the closure of key streets.

After the Qualifying tournament of 2007, Ireland, Scotland and

Samoa were the nations taking the last three spots in the 2008 World Cup. That meant Wales failed to win a place, despite having reached the semi-finals of the previous two World Cups in 1995 and 2000. Also eliminated in 2007 were the United States, Russia and Lebanon. England, Australia, New Zealand, Papua New Guinea and France were automatic entries and Tonga and Fiji had already qualified in 2006.

'The goal of this tournament was to re-establish the World Cup as a viable event in its own right and to raise funds to support the international game,' said Love. 'On the first count we've seen exciting and competitive matches throughout the tournament and I congratulate the players and the coaches for the spirit in which they have been played.'

A projected surplus of more than A$5million (£2million) was earmarked to help develop the international game before the next World Cup in 2013, although the venue of that tournament had not been decided as the 2008 World Cup came to a close.

New Zealand's triumph was the major story of the World Cup, but there were other significant sub-plots. All of the minor nations, including PNG, who as expected failed to win a game, came home with great credit and with great hopes of further developing the sport in their nations.

Fiji had the most success on the field with a hammering of France and progress to the semi-finals after their win in the qualifier against Ireland.

Tonga and Samoa were involved in some high-quality matches that reflected the huge number of Polynesians involved in the game in Australia. Samoa coach John Ackland and Tonga counterpart Jim Dymock both called for more matches involving the Pacific nations in the future.

Ireland and Scotland were expected to be easybeats, but both played with terrific spirit, with Ireland almost making it to the semi-finals, before going down with honour against Fiji. The prospect of clubs emerging in the two countries to capitalise on the interest generated down under moved a step closer.

The two real disappointments of the 2008 World Cup were England and France. John Monie was ditched as France's head coach following his team's bottom-place performance. The former Parramatta, Wigan and London coach was hired three years before amid high expectations and with the aim of taking France into the semi-finals of the competition, but big defeats by Fiji in their pool and Samoa in the rankings play-off spelled the end of Monie's reign.

Tony Smith's side's World Cup was equally disappointing. England were eliminated by New Zealand at the semi-final stage after a sub-standard campaign that had seen them edge past Papua New Guinea, thrashed by Australia and beaten twice by New Zealand.

After the 32-22 semi-final defeat at the hands of New Zealand in Brisbane, both the RFL's Executive Chairman Richard Lewis and England coach Tony Smith declared that there would be no changes at the top of the England international set-up, with Lewis brushing aside suggestions that Smith might lose his job.

Australia's defeat by New Zealand didn't sit too well with the host nation, and the big shock was felt most by their coach Rick Stuart.

The gloom in Australia's ranks was obvious. They'd lost the World Cup they had held since 1975. As 1-10 favourites they lost the 'unlosable' final.

In the post-match press conference, Stuart seemed to have accepted the result. 'I just feel sorry for the [Australian] players,' he said. 'Please don't make this too much about Australia. They were better than us. They [the Kiwis] have got their trophy in their shed. It's not in ours.'

But reports emerged that after the Final, Stuart had verbally attacked the ARL chief executive Geoff Carr, alleging an anti-Australian conspiracy by tournament organisers, and suggesting that an Australian defeat was favoured by them in order to give more credibility to future World Cups. 'Ricky needed to blow off some steam, he needed to get it out there,' Carr told the Sydney Morning Herald.

However, Stuart hadn't got it off his chest and on the Sunday morning was involved in another verbal attack, this time on match referee Ashley Klein in a Brisbane hotel lobby. Stuart called Klein 'a f—ing cheat' several times and RFL referee controller Stuart Cummings was manhandled by Stuart as he attempted to intervene.

The RLIF launched an independent investigation and Stuart, who apologised, was fined $20,000 for his outburst. NSW-based ARL directors publicly backed Stuart to be the Kangaroos coach in 2009, but on 8th December his resignation was made public.

Pool 1

Australia confirmed their pre-tournament favouritism with a majestic stroll through their pool games that highlighted the weakness of the World Cup's structure. To avoid one-sided romps and create better games for TV audiences, the hosts and reigning world champions met their nearest challengers in the pool games, with three out of the four teams qualifying from the group. Barring a massive shock somewhere along the way, that meant Australia, New Zealand and England would progress to the semi-finals, with Papua New Guinea eliminated.

But it meant that by the end of the second week, Australia had handsomely beaten both their closest rivals, strengthening the belief that the destiny of the 2008 World Cup was a foregone conclusion.

One could not have thought otherwise as the Kangaroo backline produced lightning-fast, attacking football that had commentators hailing it the best Australia line-up of all time.

Australia had a couple of injury withdrawals before the big kick-off, both shoulder injuries, with Brisbane's Justin Hodges replaced by clubmate Darius Boyd, and fullback Brett Stewart's withdrawal meaning a call-up for another Bronco, Karmichael Hunt. Stewart had been in great form for premiers Manly all season, but the man who stepped into his shoes, Melbourne's Billy Slater, proved untouchable in Australia's stroll to the final.

Leeds fullback Brent Webb (back) and Melbourne prop Jeff Lima (knee) withdrew from the New Zealand squad, after it was confirmed both needed off-season surgery. Roosters centre Sia Soliola was ruled out with a shoulder injury a week before kick-off, meaning a call-up for Wests Tigers second-rower Bronson Harrison.

Webb was replaced by St George Illawarra outside back Jason Nightingale and Lima by Warriors front-rower Evarn Tuimavave. Tuimavave and original selection Melbourne back-rower Sika Manu were the only uncapped players in the squad coached by Stephen Kearney, assisted by former Australia coach Wayne Bennett.

Nathan Cayless returned as captain in place of the injured Roy Asotasi. Frank Pritchard was also injured, and fellow forward Sonny Bill

Williams had made a high-profile switch that season to French rugby union. Halfback/hooker Nathan Fien was returned to the international arena two years after being ruled ineligible to play for the Kiwis after having gained two caps. The Kiwis played two warm-ups, as the All Golds against the Maori and the week after against Tonga.

Hull Kingston Rovers forward Stanley Gene was poised to line up for his third successive World Cup having played in 1995 and 2000, and was joined by fellow Super League players Makali Aizue (Hull KR) and John Wilshere (Salford) in the Papua New Guinea squad.

The Kumuls warmed up with a 54-30 defeat by the Australian PM's XIII, and an 'Origin' trial match in which a team drawn from overseas defeated a team of resident Papua New Guineans 22-12. They were widely expected to be uncompetitive despite them boasting NRL players Neville Costigan (Canberra), Paul Aiton and Keith Peters (Penrith Panthers), and young gun winger David Moore (Gold Coast Titans).

On the eve of the World Cup, it emerged that a campaign was building for a club from Papua New Guinea to play in the NRL. PNG Prime Minister Michael Somare had outlined his country's bid for inclusion in a letter sent to both the ARL and NRL.

PNG's first opponents were due to be England, who held high hopes of winning back the Cup for the first time since 1972 (as Great Britain), despite Tony Smith's squad having been hit by a number of withdrawals due to injury.

Four Bradford Bulls players had to pull out of the train-on squad that Smith gradually named as the Super League XIII play-offs unfolded. Scrum-half Paul Deacon needed surgery on his injured knee and clubmates Sam Burgess, Terry Newton and Andy Lynch withdrew with shoulder injuries; Warrington hooker Jon Clarke was out with a broken arm and Wigan Warriors loose forward Sean O'Loughlin was sidelined with a broken shoulder. Hull FC winger Gareth Raynor also pulled out with a toe injury. Wigan Warriors' Hull-bound winger Mark Calderwood was added to the train-on squad, despite having earlier been called up by Scotland.

Warrington Wolves coach James Lowes stepped down as England trainer to concentrate on his club commitments. Bradford's Steve McNamara was to continue as right-hand man to Smith.

The England train-on squad (with players from Leeds and St Helens not named until after the Grand Final) was: Martin Aspinwall (Huddersfield), Ryan Atkins (Wakefield), Shaun Briscoe (Hull KR), Mark Calderwood (Wigan), Garreth Carvell (Hull), Tony Clubb (Harlequins), Stuart Fielden (Wigan), Peter Fox (Hull KR), Martin Gleeson (Warrington), Darrell Griffin (Huddersfield), Mickey Higham (Wigan), Gareth Hock (Wigan), David Hodgson (Huddersfield), Jamie Langley (Bradford), Richie Myler (Salford), Rob Purdham (Harlequins), Adrian Morley (Warrington), Louie McCarthy-Scarsbrook (Harlequins),

Michael Shenton (Castleford), Paul Sykes (Bradford), Joe Westerman (Castleford), Ben Westwood (Warrington).

When Tony Smith named his final 24-man squad on Tuesday 7th October, 15 of the 24 players were from Leeds Rhinos and St Helens, who had contested the Super League Grand Final three days before.

Wigan prop Stuart Fielden was the most noticeable omission and there were surprise call-ups for back-row forwards Jamie Langley (Bradford Bulls) and Rob Purdham (Harlequins) while Leeds Rhinos utility back Lee Smith played his way into the squad with his match-winning Grand Final performance.

Jamie Jones-Buchanan was among eight back-row forwards, with just four specialist props in Jamie Peacock, who was to skipper the side, Adrian Morley, James Graham and Maurie Fa'asavalu. Only Calderwood, Purdham, Smith and Ben Westwood had not played a full international but all four had represented England at second-tier level, with Purdham captaining them to a Federation Shield triumph two years before.

Smith claimed that pace was a key determinant in his selection policy and experience would be vital. In contrast, Aussie coach Ricky Stuart chose seven Test debutants in his 24-man squad. 'Anthony Laffranchi, Joel Monaghan, David Williams, Terry Campese, Glenn Stewart, Josh Perry and Anthony Watmough have been chosen for a specific reason,' Stuart wrote in his Sydney Telegraph column. 'They will help eradicate my greatest World Cup fear, complacency.

'Complacency in Rugby League is for the lazy and the weak.'

ENGLAND 32 PAPUA NEW GUINEA 22

England got a winning start in a rip-roaring World Cup opener in tropical Townsville, with Leeds winger Lee Smith getting a hat-trick of tries. But it didn't come easy.

Down 16-12 at the break, England were visibly struggling against a Kumuls side brimming with enthusiasm and passion, and it was to their credit that they were able to lift themselves to take the win.

It could have been much, much worse, six minutes after the break, when PNG left winger David Moore was sent into the corner on the overlap. The Kumuls fans, and there were thousands of them, were even more delirious than after their three first-half tries, but they were aghast when Aussie referee Shayne Hayne ruled that Jason Nightingale's final pass was forward.

England had taken the lead after twelve minutes when St Helens hooker James Roby - who won the official man of the match award - went blind and put clubmate Ade Gardner in at the right corner. But PNG, on the back of a penalty against Leon Pryce for ball-stripping, hit back as Paul Aiton's flat pass sent loose forward Rod Griffin powering over a gallant Paul Wellens for a try that John Wilshere converted to level the scores.

Lee Smith's first try came after Kumuls centre Jessie Joe Parker sustained a fractured eye socket preventing Roby extending the lead, with Rob Burrow and Wellens combining to create the overlap.

But that 12-6 lead evaporated as Stanley Gene's long ball sent substitute Jason Chan racing through a huge gap in the centre channel, and then George Kepa scooped up Keith Peters' bomb to the England left corner that bamboozled Lee Smith.

It was no more than PNG deserved, as they ran with their usual vigour, with some exciting handling along the way, including an audacious pass through the legs from replacement hooker Charlie Wabo just after he entered the action.

The Kumuls had a youthful average age, but their standout was the not-so-young Gene, who had evidently found another bottle of the elixir of youth as he rolled back the years with a vintage performance at stand-off.

In the first half he was truly inspirational; either popping up passes at pivot, or charging at the line himself, and winning two goal-line drop-outs with clever sliding kicks in-goal. He didn't look any older than in the World Cup of 1995.

His compatriots responded in spades. Hull KR teammate Makali Aizue was outstanding, and a host of players from the NSW and Queensland competitions below the NRL rose to the occasion. A team of mostly part-timers more than matched their star-studded opposition.

At least for 46 minutes, after which England, led by captain Jamie Peacock and James Graham, raised their game to levels the Kumuls hadn't experienced before.

Three minutes after Moore's disallowed effort, Lee Smith went in for his second try from Jon Wilkin's long pass to the left wing to level the scores, and, as Kevin Sinfield missed a conversion attempt for the first time, it was 16-all.

Then England won the game with two huge defensive efforts that pinned PNG in their own '20' for two successive sets. They almost wasted their chance with some injudicious offloading, but a clever inside ball from Rob Burrow sent Martin Gleeson through a huge gap for the lead.

Sinfield kicked that goal to give England a six-point lead, and they looked likely to run away with the game.

Smith was denied a hat-trick try when, after a superb piece of footwork by Danny McGuire – just off the bench - referee Hayne ruled a forward pass from the Leeds stand-off.

Gene's personal performance mirrored that of his side, as he spilled the ball under pressure from Sinfield just in English territory. And, although right winger George Kepa was sent down the right wing out of his own '20', England were still in control. Their next try came after Gene sent up a bomb and obstructed Paul Wellens as he tried to catch the ball.

On the end of the next English attack, Sinfield opted to run the ball to the right, and his long pass was cleverly shipped inside by Gleeson to Leon Pryce, who sent Ade Gardner into the corner. Sinfield goaled and the lead was 12 points.

Three minutes later the points avalanche seemingly began when Lee Smith did get his hat-trick try after another beautiful McGuire shimmy down the left that sent Keith Senior on the charge. The centre - wearing a bandage after an early clash of heads with Parker - unselfishly passed to his winger. Sinfield missed the kick, and the avalanche never came, as the dead-on-their-feet Kumuls found more fuel.

With five minutes to go, Paul Aiton was the first to a kick in-goal from Penrith teammate Keith Peters, and Wilshere's conversion brought the deficit back to ten. And when Sinfield was penalised for ball-stripping a minute later, England fans began to get the jitters.

But, on the first tackle, Gene put in an aimless chip, to the astonishment of just about everyone, and the excitement was over.

AUSTRALIA 30 NEW ZEALAND 6

After the World Cup's official opening ceremony - before the third game of the tournament! - at Aussie Stadium, Australia threw down the gauntlet as the Kiwis never really looked like producing the upset that so many critics had predicted they could. Indeed, the final scoreline flattered the outclassed New Zealanders.

Early in the action the Australians showed plenty of confidence, tossing the ball around with enthusiasm. With eight minutes on the clock it almost paid dividends. A host of Aussies, including Greg Inglis, Darren Lockyer and Johnathan Thurston, flung it around as if it was a hot potato. But Thurston was caught short of the tryline.

Thurston actually opened the scoring with a penalty goal in the tenth minute. He was playing despite the fact he was grieving for his uncle, who had been murdered in a Brisbane park the previous morning. But Thurston seemed to have put the death behind him in his endeavour to give 100 per cent for his country.

New Zealand's centre Steve Matai must have been worried when he was called out three minutes later for a high tackle. A year before he had received his marching orders for a similar offence in a Test in Wellington that the Kiwis eventually lost 58-nil. There was a sigh of relief when referee Ashley Klein placed him on report, although he was subsequently banned for one game.

But the penalty gave the Australians the pitch position from which to score. Brent Tate, Petero Civoniceva and Anthony Laffranchi were all cut down by the Kiwi defence before Lockyer gave a superb pass for

Inglis to swing past a couple of would-be tacklers to score the first try of the evening.

The lead looked certain to be extended when Israel Folau charged towards the right corner. But Jerome Ropati and Manu Vatuvei crunched him into touch. Within a minute and a half, New Zealand Test debutant Sika Manu had accepted a reverse pass from Benji Marshall and charged past half-a-dozen Australians to score at the other end of the pitch.

But, from the restart, Ropati handed over the ball and gave the Australians a perfect spot from which to launch an attack on the tryline. Lockyer and Billy Slater had a hand in the subsequent try to Test debutant Joel Monaghan.

Right on half-time the Aussies were almost in again, but a long, torpedo pass to Tate was so solid that the winger could not rein it in.

Early in the second half the Australians threw everything at the Kiwis, and it seemed a miracle that that the New Zealanders were able to hold them out.

Seven minutes into the half, with the Kiwis trying to work the ball out from their own tryline, Inglis managed to get his hands on a loose ball. And within a couple of tackles Israel Folau was in for his first try of the night.

The ever reliable Tate was helped from the pitch injured in the 57th minute. Moments later a 70-metre movement started by Glenn Stewart and continued by Thurston ended with a wonderful try by Billy Slater to put the Kiwis out of contention.

Thurston seemed to have set up another try for Australia with 12 minutes remaining. Cameron Smith was over the line and claiming success. But English video referee Steve Ganson ruled otherwise.

When Ropati was close to scoring a few minutes later, Slater slid in and booted the ball out of his hands. It was a dangerous ploy – but it saved the Australians. Ganson ruled 'no try'. Slater was warned later in the week that the tactic wouldn't be allowed in future.

By this time Thurston had been rested. His had been a brave effort in the wake of the personal grief.

With only seconds remaining on the clock, Australia ground the Kiwis' noses into the turf, with Folau over for his fifth try in just three internationals, off quick hands by Paul Gallen and Slater.

There may have been some excuses for New Zealand coach Steve Kearney. He was without several stars from the team that went down to Australia in the Centenary Test in May. Captain Roy Asotasi, fullback Brent Webb, centre Sia Soliola and forward Frank Pritchard were all injured, while Sonny Bill Williams had defected to French rugby union club Toulon.

But, on the positive side, strike weapon Benji Marshall was back at stand-off and tough-tackling Matai in the centres.

Marshall was hardly sighted in attack. And Matai seemed to be carrying a shoulder injury that manifested itself late in the match. Wigan's Thomas Leuluai looked slow at scrum-half. Hooker Nathan Fien's kicking game was sub-standard.

Australian props Steve Price and Petero Civoniceva didn't need to respond to pre-match criticism by former Wigan coach Graham Lowe that they were old and out of gas. They performed their jobs in their usual competent way. The combination of Thurston, Lockyer, Inglis and Slater looked unstoppable.

AUSTRALIA 52 ENGLAND 4

England's campaign was in disarray after a record World Cup defeat at the Melbourne Telstra dome. The brilliant Greg Inglis and Billy Slater both scored dazzling hat-tricks on a night to forget for Tony Smith's side. And all this without Australia's first choice scrum-half, with Scott Prince stepping into the injured Johnathan Thurston's shoes to great effect.

Up front, England's pack matched their counterparts for spells, but once the ball went wider than Darren Lockyer, they simply couldn't handle the speed and timing of their opponents. Defensively Tony Smith's side were poor at times, while with the ball they lacked any kind of cohesion and direction for much of the game.

The Kangaroos' coach Ricky Stuart described Inglis and Slater after the game as 'special talents', and that their performances in Melbourne would go down in the history books. Australia were better in every department. Lockyer was his usual imperious self; Anthony Laffranchi capped a hard working display with two tries, while Cameron Smith was quietly effective from dummy-half.

Tony Smith tried to stay positive after the game and insisted his side would recover. He had praise for James Roby, Gareth Hock, Adrian Morley, James Graham and Jamie Peacock, with all five tellingly among the forwards. In the backs, only the hard working Mark Calderwood emerged with any kind of real credit, though even he was not mistake free.

Smith started the game with Peacock in the second row and Morley at prop, with Gareth Hock dropping down to the bench and Calderwood coming in for the injured Lee Smith. Australia had Prince in for shoulder victim Thurston, with Karmichael Hunt handed an opportunity as a substitute.

England made a decent start, with a reasonable first set being ended with a good kick and a great hit by Kevin Sinfield on Slater. It would prove to be one of the only times they got a proper hold of the Melbourne fullback, and for the next ten minutes it was all downhill, starting when Calderwood failed to collect Prince's wide kick, resulting in a goal-line drop-out.

On the last tackle of the next set, hooker Smith took on the blindside and kicked perfectly for his Melbourne teammate Slater to follow through and touch down.

Five minutes later the Australians were over again, though there was more than a touch of controversy about the try. Petero Civoniceva's knock-on three tackles before the score went unnoticed by Australian referee Tony Archer, as did the suspicion of obstruction in the build-up to Inglis' first. But the main concern for England was the way Inglis pushed off Leon Pryce with ease before touching down.

England did regroup, and gained a genuine foothold in the game. They had already gone close, with Paul Wellens just failing to hold on to a Graham pass close to the line, when Roby opened their account. The St Helens hooker remarkably grounded the ball despite five Australian defenders attempting to stop him, for a try awarded under the benefit of the doubt ruling after several viewings by video referee Ashley Klein.

Sinfield missed the conversion to leave the score at 12-4, and England continued to push forward. Rob Burrow made a half-break that resulted in Brent Tate holding him down for too long, while a Sinfield kick led to Israel Folau being trapped behind his own line by Calderwood.

But England just couldn't make the pressure tell, and the Australians punished them with two crucial tries before half-time.

For the first, Inglis squeezed over in the left corner after good work from Lockyer, a dubious grounding of the ball given the green light by Klein. Then, soon afterwards, Wellens let a Prince kick roll dead, unaware that Wilkin had got fingertips to the ball as it was punted. After the goal-line dropout, Laffranchi ran a great line to take Lockyer's pass and power past Roby for a disappointing try for England to concede.

One Prince conversion made it 22-4 at the break, and England showed their willingness to attack from the off with a short restart to the second half. But the ineptness of their attack was summed up in a shambolic set of six on the Kangaroos' line after Slater had made a rare mistake by dropping Sinfield's spiralling kick.

A Prince penalty – awarded for Danny McGuire's needless spear tackle – edged the Australians further ahead, and twice try-saving tackles were required to stop the Green and Gold machine – first by Peacock on Tate, and then by McGuire and Sinfield on Lockyer.

But the resistance could not last, and Slater soon turned creator, providing a peach of a cut-out pass to send Joel Monaghan over out wide. At that point Lockyer was withdrawn with a slight bicep problem, but, rather than signal a slowing in the scoring, it simply acted as a prelude to an even more one-sided final quarter.

First there was the try of the match, as Inglis scooped up a poor McGuire kick on his own line and showed superb awareness to immediately release Slater. He raced downfield, where Calderwood was his only obstacle, and he thrillingly turned the Hull-bound winger inside out before diving over for a 95-metre try.

The next score was arguably the worst of the whole night from England's point of view, as Wellens' short high kick-off was tapped back by Senior, only for Inglis to react the quickest, brush off Peacock, and step past the England fullback for his hat-trick try.

Slater wasn't far behind him in reaching his treble, though defensively it was another poor try to concede, as he split Leon Pryce and Martin Gleeson from close range. England's misery was then completed when another shrewd kick from Prince was touched down by second-rower Laffranchi for his second try.

NEW ZEALAND 48 PAPUA NEW GUINEA 6

New Zealand picked up their first win in the 2008 World Cup with a convincing 48-6 victory on the Gold Coast over a Papua New Guinea side that competed strongly, but which was ultimately outclassed.

The Kiwi improvement from the previous week's disappointing defeat to Australia was visible, and after England's humiliation in Melbourne on the Sunday night, they emerged from the weekend as the side with the greatest chance of pulling off an upset against the green and golds.

New Zealand took the lead in the ninth minute after the Kumuls unnecessarily conceded a goal-line drop out. Keith Peters' kick only went 25 metres, and the Papua New Guineans compounded the problem by conceding a penalty for a ruck infringement. Jeremy Smith's offload found Lance Hohaia, who shipped the ball wide to Benji Marshall. The classy stand-off got on the outside of the defence and sent Jerome Ropati to the line for a 4-0 lead. Soon afterwards the same two players combined, only for the centre to be held up.

PNG hit back with centre Jesse Joe Parker almost intercepting a Smith pass on halfway. But from the scrum Manu Vatuvei stormed down the left, and two plays later Simon Mannering crossed on the other side of the field after taking a Thomas Leuluai pass for a 17th minute try, which Krisnan Inu goaled for a ten-point lead.

There was more to come. After a strong hit-up from Melbourne prop Adam Blair, Nathan Fien opened up the Kumuls with a fine surge from dummy-half, being grounded just a yard from the line. From there, Leuluai found Mannering down the right channel, and he got on the outside of Parker to score. Inu knocked over his second goal for a 16-0 lead, and any chance of an upset was looking extremely remote.

Nevertheless, PNG were playing well, and they forced a goal-line drop out in the 32nd minute. A penalty followed, before Tu'u Maori found David Moore close to the line, but he was bundled into touch by Vatuvei.

A couple of minutes later, Stanley Gene was penalised for not being square at the play-the-ball. Greg Eastwood, David Fa'alogo and Sam Rapira drove strongly into Kumul territory, Marshall stepped and threw a spectacular long ball to Sam Perrett on the right wing, and the Sydney Roosters player had the simple task of putting the ball over the line.

On the stroke of half-time the Kumuls threatened again when Keith Peters chipped from a scrum-base ten metres from the Kiwi line, only for the bounce to beat three chasing attackers and land in the hands of a grateful Vatuvei.

The Kiwis withdrew Marshall at the break with a tight hamstring, although he was confident that he would be available for the final group game with England.

The Kumuls opened the second-half scoring with a terrific try in the 48th minute, finished off by Moore. A 20-metre restart was quickly followed by a penalty, and loose forward Rod Griffin burst through, only to slip. But with the Kiwis scrambling back, PNG moved the ball to the left, where Neville Costigan and Parker combined to set up Moore, who stepped inside for a smartly taken try. John Wilshere's conversion cut the deficit to 16 points.

The Kiwis put the kick-off out on the full, although PNG's penalty didn't find touch. But they escaped punishment when Perrett was gang-tackled into touch by four enthusiastic defenders.

On 56 minutes, impressive interchange hooker Issac Luke scored an individual try from dummy-half from 30 metres out. Good runs from Hohaia and Rapira had tested the Kumuls, and Luke exploited poor marker defence to score, although Inu missed the relatively simple conversion.

Luke then had a hand in another try three minutes later, finding Fien from dummy-half, and he gave it to David Fa'alogo close to the line for a soft try. Luke missed another very kickable goal, however.

Three minutes later Vatuvei was brought back for a harshly awarded forward pass, but the Kiwis didn't have long to wait for another score against a tiring Papuan defence, when Leuluai found Blair with a flat pass close to the line. Inu goaled for a 36-6 lead.

The now rampant New Zealanders registered two further tries - firstly, when Perrett scored after Inu challenged for a Luke high kick, and then when Eastwood burst through Rodney Pora 30 metres out, and beat Wilshere with a right-foot step to score.

ENGLAND 24 NEW ZEALAND 36

Coach Tony Smith looked thoroughly dejected as an England team without several first-choice players threw away a match-winning position in Newcastle, conceding 28-unanswered points in the process and allowing giant winger Manu Vatuvei to run free on the left touchline. Vatuvei scored four tries, though three of them came with barely a hand being laid on him during a catastrophic second half for England.

England's inability to defend out wide – so apparent in the mauling by Australia – again came to the fore as they were exposed time and time again by the clever distribution of Lance Hohaia. The talented fullback laid on three of Vatuvei's tries and scored another himself in an excellent display. But the Kiwis' key player was replacement hooker Issac Luke, who sparked Stephen Kearney's team off the bench, causing the English defence constant problems.

The match was an improvement on the horror show in Melbourne. Mickey Higham took the chance offered him with both hands, while Jamie Peacock set another terrific lead up front and Rob Burrow grabbed two trademark tries. Newcomers Ben Westwood, Jamie Jones-Buchanan and Rob Purdham also gave everything they could for the English cause.

Former Leeds coach Smith was quick to highlight his squad's 'anger', and when asked whether the Kiwi loss hurt more than the 52-4 thrashing by Australia, he answered 'absolutely'.

Bradford centre Paul Sykes copped plenty of criticism for his part in Vatuvei's second-half rampage, as he was twice caught out of position playing in the unfamiliar right wing role, and then knocked on when switched to fullback. But he was the fall guy for a confused defence.

Smith's team were due to get another chance to crack the Kiwis in the semi-final the following Saturday in Brisbane. 'This doesn't change things too much – whether we won or lost, we still have to win next week,' Smith added. 'I don't think this makes it harder next week, the scoreboard will still be 0-0 when we start.'

The main negative for Kiwi coach Stephen Kearney was a serious-looking neck injury to centre Steve Matai, which delayed the match for a significant period in the first half while he was stabilised and then stretchered from the field.

Smith made changes from the Australia defeat, handing a chance to six players yet to take part in the competition and recalling winger Lee Smith after he missed the Kangaroos clash through injury.

His side started the night by forming a closed circle while New Zealand performed their traditional haka – a move labelled 'disrespectful' by Kiwi captain Benji Marshall but defended by coach Smith.

If anything it seemed to inspire England more as they raced into a 12-0 lead inside eight minutes.

Handed field position by an early penalty awarded for offside, Higham took full advantage by burrowing his way over from close range after Purdham had gone close. Four minutes later the English were over again. Keith Senior broke the tackles of Jason Nightingale and Thomas Leuluai deep inside his own half, and found Burrow racing on his inside to take the pass and finish an outstanding try.

The Kiwis responded with a score that would signal the warning bells about England's fragility out wide. Straight from a scrum, Jerome Ropati bust three tackles before being hauled down, but on the next play Hohaia started a trend by sending Vatuvei powering over.

The almost constant scoring continued as a mistake from Matai handed Smith's side a scrum, and makeshift stand-off Martin Gleeson sliced straight through to score despite Vatuvei's last-ditch tackle.

New Zealand responded for a second time, as Hohaia stepped past Purdham and then touched down in Paul Wellens and Gareth Ellis's tackle. But England still appeared in complete control as great work from Higham secured another penalty, and on the last tackle of the resulting set Burrow stepped past Adam Blair for a terrific try.

Purdham's fourth conversion from as many attempts made it 24-8, and the game looked secure.

But crucially the Kiwis scored before the break to hand themselves a route back into the game. Great offloads from Jeremy Smith and Bronson Harrison allowed the recently-introduced Luke to lob a pass over to Nightingale, who finished in the corner. Luke added the touchline conversion for good measure to close the gap to ten points.

Within 15 minutes of the restart New Zealand were level, as they completely dominated possession and field position.

With Sykes on the right wing following a reshuffle prompted by an ankle injury to Paul Wellens, the Kiwis took full advantage.

After securing a repeat set, Marshall and Hohaia combined for Vatuvei to finish smartly for his second.

It was almost déjà vu not long after, as Marshall and Hohaia again raided England's right directly from a scrum and Vatuvei strolled over to complete his hat-trick.

The two teams were now deadlocked after Luke converted one of the winger's double, though the Kiwis were still firmly in the ascendancy.

England were handed a golden opportunity to stem the tide when Hohaia dropped a Kevin Sinfield kick deep inside his own half under no pressure, but Smith's team failed to take advantage.

Instead it was the Kiwis who edged in front, albeit in controversial circumstances. Luke took a dive when making minimal contact with Sinfield chasing a Marshall bomb, but referee Tony Archer awarded the penalty in front of the posts. Luke obliged to make it 26-24 with ten minutes remaining.

England tried to break from deep, only for Westwood's pass to Mark Calderwood to be ruled forward.

Moments later the game was over, as Marshall released Harrison, whose attempted pass was touched by Westwood. Kiwi hooker Nathan Fien reacted the quickest to dive over, and Jeremy Smith's conversion made the gap eight points.

New Zealand added further dismay to England with a seventh try three minutes from the end, with Marshall taking a turn to send Vatuvei over virtually unchallenged.

It was the story of a forgettable night for everyone connected with England.

AUSTRALIA 46 PAPUA NEW GUINEA 6

Australia ran in eight tries against the tournament's sentimental favourites to finish top of pool one undefeated. PNG fared better than England against the might of Australia, whose new winger David Williams scored a hat-trick, while fellow debutant Terry Campese's World Cup ended with an eye injury. The 40-point margin was eight better than England managed against the Cup holders and captain Cameron Smith reckoned the Kumuls were 'up there' with Tony Smith's men. Campese's replacement, Scott Prince, went on to score two tries – as did another Raider in Joel Monaghan.

PNG fans brought the house down, however, when late inclusion Menzie Yere scored off Rod Griffin's kick with eight minutes left. Kumuls skipper Stanley Gene was carried from the field in tears after his last international.

The Kumuls held the Australians to just one try in the opening 20 minutes. That came when Johnathan Thurston kicked to the right wing and Manly's Williams flew high to claim the ball. Four minutes after Campese's departure, Thurston and Karmichael Hunt combined for centre Monaghan to open his own account.

For all the good things Papua New Guinea did, they struggled at times to keep the champions out if they got close to the Kumul line. The ball was kept alive and Monaghan scored again, before play swept to the left and back to the right before Williams bagged his second to make it 22-0 at the break.

Playing his final international, Stanley Gene threw an ill-conceived pass on his own line three minutes after oranges and substitute Prince snaffled an interception for the first of his two tries.

PNG had become so frustrated by referee Steve Ganson that coach Adrian Lam sent out a trainer to ask him what the penalty count was. It was only 3-1 but Lam apparently thought it was 8-1.

The Kumuls got one two minutes after the query but it didn't stem the tide. Prince found a big gap off scrum-half Thurston for his second and Williams scooted 40 metres for the best of his threesome.

PNG fans brought the house down, however, when late inclusion Menzie Yere scored off Rod Griffin's kick with eight minutes left.

The pattern of multiple tryscorers in the Australian team was then broken with two minutes on the clock when sub Anthony Tupou galloped over.

Pool 2

Fiji were the winners of Pool Two, despite a loss to Scotland in their second game. The margin of their victory over France five days before was enough to see them through.

The RLIF had managed to get dispensation and placed home-grown players with country clubs such as Parkes, Terrigal and Fassifern to make them more competitive, and the addition of several players of Fijian heritage from NRL clubs, such as Jarryd Hayne from Parramatta, who had represented Australia in 2007, Newcastle Knights pair Wes Naiqama and Akuila Uate, and Bulldogs' Daryl Millard, plus Bradford winger Semi Tadulala, gave them a potent mix of explosive talent that eventually saw them through to the semi-finals, with two of the players from the local competition - Waisele Sukanaveita and Alipate Noilea - true stars of RLWC08.

Scotland's win over Fiji gained Steve McCormack's side a lot of credit. The withdrawal of Super League players Daniel Heckenberg and Rhys Lovegrove from their squad through injury had been a blow, and the Scots also withdrew Wigan winger Mark Calderwood after his call-up into England's train-on squad. The initial 40-strong squad was already hit by the loss of Workington back-rower Iain Marsh, with a broken arm, while Richard Fletcher (Widnes), Spencer Miller (Whitehaven) and Graeme Horne (Hull FC) all pulled out for personal reasons. They also looked like losing Michael Robertson to Australia following his hat-trick for Manly in the NRL Grand Final. He was vying with clubmate David Williams for a vacant wing position, though Williams was Australia coach Ricky Stuart's eventual choice. Former Hull FC and Wigan Warriors forward Scott Logan was the only survivor from the previous World Cup in the final 24-man squad, which was captained by Wakefield Trinity Wildcats scrum-half Danny Brough

France were a big disappointment, despite a convincing win over Scotland in Canberra. Prop David Ferriol missed the tournament with a groin tear, but France head coach John Monie was in an upbeat mood when announcing the 23 players in his World Cup squad. The former Parramatta, Wigan and London Broncos boss believed that the Catalan

Dragons' experience and the French championship players' enthusiasm would help them achieve their long-held objective of a place in the semi-finals.

FRANCE 36 SCOTLAND 18

France opened their World Cup account with a hard-fought win in Canberra over Scotland, who were on the end of three contentious calls in a match that was much closer than the scoreline suggested. Australian video referee Phil Cooley ruled out two potential Scottish scores after several viewings, while the Scots were also disappointed with John Wilson's first-half try for the French. Wilson touched down after Kiwi official Leon Williamson had allowed play to continue for three tackles with Duncan MacGillivray knocked out in back play.

The French, while disjointed at times, showed several glimpses of their potential. Captain Jerome Guisset set a big lead up front, and was well supported by Adel Fellous, while halfbacks Thomas Bosc and James Wynne, the latter off the bench, gave them a real cutting edge at times. But on the downside, Julien Rinaldi's World Cup was ended after he fractured a cheekbone in three places.

The two teams played out a scrappy opening quarter, with both sides struggling to control the ball and wasting good attacking opportunities.

Michael Robertson's early knock-on gifted the French a chance, only for Rinaldi to begin a familiar pattern by losing the ball close to the line. Scotland's first attack saw Danny Brough's high kick fall well over the dead ball line, while soon after a more accurate effort just evaded right winger Dean Colton.

French back-rower Eric Anselme was helped from the field in a neck brace in the 13th minute after being dumped to the turf in Wests Tigers centre Gavin Cowen's tackle, though he soon returned to the bench with an ice pack.

The deadlock was eventually broken in the 16th minute after the game's first moment of real fluency. French prop Fellous burst the defensive line on halfway, and then handed onto the supporting Jared Taylor, who had the pace to reach the line under the posts.

Bosc added the straight-forward conversion, but Scotland hit back almost immediately. Handed a good attacking position when Rinaldi's pass to Guisset was ruled forward, the Scots took advantage, as Lee Paterson's clever handling sent Jon Steel over in the left corner.

Brough slotted the touchline conversion, and he thought he had created a second try for his side soon afterwards.

His dangerous kick caused problems in the French defence, and MacGillivray scooped up the loose ball to touch down. But video referee Cooley ruled that Robertson had knocked on in the build-up to disallow the score, and France then dominated the remainder of the half. They regained their lead after Iain Morrison conceded a penalty on halfway to help launch a French attack. Guisset was the eventual beneficiary, beating three Scottish defenders to touch down from close range.

Then came the controversy, as Kiwi referee Williamson allowed play to continue for three tackles with MacGillivray down in back play concussed. On the final play of the set Bosc's high kick saw Wilson out-jump the defence to touch down – with the Scots still protesting in back play.

Bosc's conversion made it 18-6 at the break. But Scotland roared back into the contest straight after the restart.

They had already had two genuine attacks by the time Brough's clever pass sent Oliver Wilkes charging over from close range to close the gap to six points. And when France threatened to respond immediately, Mick Nanyn covered well to dump Teddy Sadaoui into touch.

Monie's team did temporarily re-establish their 12 point cushion on 54 minutes. A smart break from substitute Wynne set the position, while Scottish prop Scott Logan was incredibly lucky not to be penalised for holding back Bosc in back play. But France scored seconds later anyway, as Bosc's flighted kick led to a try from Sebastien Raguin.

Still the Scots came forward. Raguin blotted his copybook by throwing a pass straight into touch deep inside his own half, and Scotland capitalised fully. Brough, Ian Henderson and Duffy combined smoothly for Mick Nanyn to send Dean Colton over in the right corner.

Brough again converted from the touchline to make it 24-18, before another major turning point.

Keeping the ball alive on the last tackle, the Scots attacked France's left side defence, and Colton dumped a ball back inside to Nanyn. He caught the ball cleanly, before it appeared to be knocked out by Rinaldi, allowing Duffy to run through and touch down.

But after several viewings video referee Cooley again ruled against Steve McCormack's team, and the match finally went away from them in the closing six minutes.

The decisive try came from Guisset, who followed a Rinaldi grubber by the posts and then stole the ball from Robertson behind his own line to score. And, in the final seconds, Raguin broke from inside his own half and found the supporting Taylor, who handed on to Christophe Moly to give the scoreline a lopsided look.

FIJI 42 FRANCE 6

The match-up at a cold and chilly Wollongong on the second Saturday of the World Cup provided the first blowout of the competition, all the more surprising because France had gone into the game as strong favourites.

The Fijians were a relative unknown. But a threequarter line high on NRL experience and a typically rugged pack, mostly drawn from their homeland after some country football experience - with the exception of Ashton Sims, the Brisbane second-rower - produced a marvellous performance, full of speed and power.

Right winger Akuila Uate emerged as the first real star of the competition, with a thrilling hat-trick and a series of runs that the French found almost impossible to contain. Uate's try two minutes after the break after another piece of irresponsible handling from France was the end of the line for the out-gunned French. And the margin of the win made Fiji almost certain qualifiers. Uate had some high praise despite not being able to break into Newcastle Knights first grade, with Andrew Johns rating him one of the best athletes he had ever seen.

Not far behind Uate was Parramatta winger Jarryd Hayne, who played at fullback, scored two tries – one of them an amazing effort – and caused havoc with his kicks. Halfback Aaron Groom had one NRL game under his belt with the Bulldogs, but he too had languished in the NSW Cup. He took the official man of the match award with a tenacious display featuring some rock-solid defence on some of France's big men.

France's only injury absentee was Julien Rinaldi, who fractured his cheekbone in three places in the 36-18 defeat of Scotland the previous Sunday. James Wynne, official man of the match in that game, moved into the hooking role. But he lasted only six minutes before leaving the field with a dislocated elbow.

The Fijians didn't commence with a war dance, instead standing in a huddle and singing a song – but it did the trick. Out-muscled France were penalised twice in the opening seconds, and from the second – for offside on the middle of their own 20-metre line - Newcastle centre Wes Naiqama opened the scoring.

The big Fiji contingent had their champions fired up, and after Wynne injured himself in a tackle on France's first foray into the Fiji '20', stand-off Alipate Noilea made a lightning burst up the middle. From the play-the-ball, Hayne linked up and stepped his way through the left channel for the first try.

Naiqama missed that conversion, and the next play summed up France's night. Uate knocked on from the restart on his own line, and France had six tackles to regain parity. The ball was spread right from the scrum, and in a crunching tackle from three Fijians, John Wilson lost possession.

France's first real chance came on the twelfth minute, after Jean-Christophe Borlin had won possession with a mighty tackle on halfway. On the end of that set Thomas Bosc slid a grubber in-goal, and Daryl Millard did well to slide and touch down the ball to concede the drop-out. Olivier Elima threw away possession when, forced backwards in a tackle, he tried to offload, and the ball dribbled into touch.

Fiji extended their lead with a lucky try, Groom's flat ball ricocheting off Hayne under the French posts straight into the arms of prop Iowane Divavesi, who shot over the line. The video referee gave him the benefit of the doubt, Naiqama goaled, and it was 12-0.

Hayne kicks produced two goal-line dropouts, and France looked shot, but two quick penalties in their favour gave them position to get into the game on the half-hour, as Jared Taylor popped up the ball for Wilson to go over. Bosc converted for a 12-6 scoreline, and hope flickered for the French.

Four minutes later normal service resumed, however, as Naiqama dropped off Uate ten metres out and he went through Sebastien Raguin and Dimitri Pelo for a try on the right.

Two dropped balls in the tackle from a decidedly off-colour Jamel Fakir was France's reply, and when Maxime Greseque stopped a try from Groom in an offside position, Naiqama made it 18-6 at the break.

France needed to score first after the break, but after two minutes Fakir had a brainstorm and passed behind the runners 40 metres out. Groom scooped the ball up and raced away and, although Taylor did tremendously well to catch him, from the play-the-ball, Uate was unstoppable from dummy-half.

Naiqama kicked the goal and a penalty, before a succession of wasted attacks from the French had their fans with their heads in their hands.

Semisi Tora's try on 67 minutes, after Noilea's fine break and sharp pass, was the matinee before the top-of-the-bill acts.

First Hayne returned a Bosc kick and broke out of the stand-off's and Greg Mounis's tackles on half way to race for the left corner. Taylor again did well to cut him off, but Hayne stopped in his tracks to step inside and score the best individual try of the World Cup so far.

At least for another four minutes, as Uate stepped Wilson on his own '20', raced 80 metres and turned Taylor and then Pelo inside out for a thriller of a score.

Naiqama finished with seven goals, and the Fijians in the healthy crowd were in dreamland.

FIJI 16 SCOTLAND 18

Scotland created their own piece of World Cup history on a memorable night in Gosford, as Oliver Wilkes' late try helped them to their first ever win in the tournament. It may not have been by the 28 points necessary to reach the semi-final qualifier, but it could not in anyway detract from a magnificent performance by Steve McCormack's aptly-named Bravehearts.

McCormack had called for his side to be more physical and dominant around the ruck, and despite several of their forwards being considerably smaller than the opposition, Scotland achieved their coach's goal. No player reflected that more than Ian Henderson, who after being switched from hooker to loose forward to accommodate the loss of the injured Lee Paterson and the arrival of Ben Fisher, produced a terrific performance.

In the first half especially, Henderson constantly took the game to the Fijians at a ground just up the road from the town of Terrigal where he and brothers and teammates Andrew and Kevin grew up. Henderson had support from right across his team, with Iain Morrison another to hurl himself at the Fiji defence, and the bigger Scott Logan and Wilkes also battling away manfully.

Despite all that, the Scots still looked set for defeat when Semi Tadulala's 73rd minute try – the second of the night for the Bradford winger – gave the Batis the lead for the first time.

But, after retaining a short Danny Brough kick-off, Scotland worked the position for Wakefield prop Wilkes to power over, and Brough then held his nerve to add the extras.

Widely written off before the game against a Fijian side that had hammered France, the Scots improved markedly on their own opening-game display.

Despite falling below the form that saw them blitz the French, the Fijians, with only three days rest after their opener, still played their full part in a captivating match, with Parramatta star Jarryd Hayn magnificent in broken field.

Joe Dakuitoga's side started ominously, as, on just the fourth tackle of the game, left winger Akuila Uate – so impressive against France – launched a long-distance attack that ended when Hayne just failed to take his pass with the line open.

But instead, the Scots took the game to their opponents and ended a fiery first half 12-4 in front. They scored the opening try when winger Jon Steel – who was playing opposite the formidable Uate – took advantage of smart work from Ian Henderson down the blindside to step inside and touch down. Brough added the conversion from the touchline for an early six-point advantage. Fiji were perhaps then fortunate not to be reduced to 12 men, when prop Iowane Divavesi appeared to deliberately trip Scottish winger Wade Liddell, and escaped with only a penalty against him.

The Fijians then hit back on the scoreboard as, following a great run from Hayne, an excellent ball from Sevanaia Koroi put Tadulala over in the left-hand corner.

A half that had simmered throughout the opening 30 minutes finally boiled over when opposite numbers Jason Bukuya and Ian Henderson came to blows, with the penalty going Scotland's way.

McCormack's side appeared to be further galvanised by the incident, as they scored again right on half-time. Brough's hopeful kick struck the upright, and fullback Michael Robertson reacted the quickest to just touch down before the ball rolled dead. Brough's straightforward conversion gave his side an eight-point interval lead.

But ten minutes into the second half the Fijians were level.

They responded soon after the restart when Bukuya somehow forced the ball down, despite being surrounded by four Scottish defenders.

Newcastle Knights centre Wes Naiqama converted from the right touchline, and then added a penalty eight minutes later after Scotland's markers were caught not square.

Both sides then had the opportunity to push ahead, with the Scots having four consecutive sets on the opposition line, and Fiji's Jone Macilai seeing a try disallowed when a teammate strayed offside.

But after a period of stalemate, former London Bronco Nick Bradley-Qalilawa helped create Tadulala's second to edge the Fijians in front.

That looked to have won it – until Wilkes and Brough's dramatic late contributions.

Pool 3

Ireland were surprise winners of pool three, after they were confidently predicted to finish bottom behind Samoa and Tonga sides crammed full of NRL and Super League experience.

Andy Kelly did a magnificent job in instilling a magnificent team spirit into a mixture of Super League and National League players that took them to the cusp of the semi-finals. Two high-profile NRL players - 21-year-old Wests Tigers winger Shannon McDonnell and State of Origin prop Brett White, who played for Melbourne in the Grand Final defeat by Manly and was under consideration by the Kangaroos - withdrew with injury after being named in the final squad. Former Wigan Warriors forward Mick Cassidy, who had retired after a last season in NL2 with Barrow, and who played for England in the 1995 World Cup, was drafted in along with Treaty City Titans prop Brendon Guilfoyle. There were three other products of the Irish domestic league in Carlow trio Ross Barbour, Steve Gibbons and Wayne Kerr, with Kerr playing twice in Ireland's three games.

Also ruled out through injury were Wigan prop Paul Prescott (back) and Warrington Wolves duo Chris Bridge (Achilles) and Simon Grix (shoulder), with Sheffield Eagles' Ged Corcoran another to earn a late call-up. Simon Grix's elder brother, Wakefield utility back Scott, captained the squad. Another item to make the news was that the Ireland squad travelled to Australia in economy class while Tony Smith's England team enjoyed business class on the same flight.

Samoa's squad was a who's who of international Rugby League, and included the Wigan Warriors duo of George Carmont and Harrison Hansen, Huddersfield Giants' former Kiwi hooker David Faiumu, Leeds forwards Ali Lauitiiti and Kylie Leuluai, St Helens threequarters Francis Meli and Willie Talau and Bradford Bulls second-rower David Solomona. Captained by the experienced Nigel Vagana, they were expected to make the semi-finals.

Tonga also looked strong, dominated by NRL players, with Wakefield's Tevita Leo-Latu, Hull's Willie Manu and Castleford's Awen Guttenbeil Super League's only representatives. But a number selection confusions clouded their build-up, right up to their first game, against Ireland. When they named their 24-man squad, Warrington back-rower Louis Anderson was included, with the Tongan management having gained clearance from the RLIF for him to play. But Anderson was recovering from surgery on a broken arm suffered at the end of the domestic season and announced total surprise at his selection. The Wolves confirmed he would not be taking part in the World Cup.

Sydney Roosters back-rower Anthony Tupou was also named, but, after training with Tonga, he was then called up to the Australian squad when Hull-signing Michael Crocker withdrew through injury. Australian Rugby League boss Geoff Carr revealed Tupou had failed to lodge the necessary paperwork with the Rugby League International Federation for consideration of dual eligibility.

The efforts of two other NRL players to get back to their roots were also thwarted. Fuifui Moimoi and Taniela Tuiaki lost their bids a year after successfully switching to New Zealand for the Test series in Great Britain. The Tongan Rugby League took the RLIF to court to try and get the decision overruled, but the hearing went against them, just hours before their game with Ireland.

The Australian selectors decided to avoid further conflict with Tonga by overlooking Penrith's Michael Jennings as a replacement for injured centre Justin Hodges. 'The Australian selectors don't want to interfere with the preparations of other teams,' Geoff Carr said.

IRELAND 20 TONGA 22

The 2008 Rugby League World Cup exploded with the game of the opening weekend, with Ireland making a mockery of their 'no-hopers' tag to come within minutes of a sensational victory over much-fancied Tonga.

With disallowed tries, contentious video-refereeing decisions and two hugely partisan factions of red and green in the crowd, it was a magical Monday night at Parramatta Stadium.

Wakefield winger Damien Blanch finished with a hat-trick of tries, with Karl Fitzpatrick, Scott Grix and Simon Finnigan also impressing. Wakefield hooker Tevita Leo-Latu was magnificent for Tonga alongside former London Bronco Feleti Mateo.

The lead changed hands six times before, with seven minutes left on the clock, Mateo produced a booming 40/20 which set up the position for Esikeli Tonga's match-grabbing try in the left corner.

Tonga gave an early indication of their power with a couple of strong runs from Leo-Latu and Antonio Kaufusi, before a Mateo bomb gave Ireland their first nervous moment, when Michael Platt let the ball bounce off his chest for Blanch to clear up ahead of a posse of Tongan pursuers.

Tonga's promising centre Michael Jennings showed the frailties of the Irish defence with a blockbusting run that should have brought more than the knock-on from Etuate Uaisele.

On nine minutes, the try that had been threatened finally came. After Lopini Paea was held short of the line, the ball was whipped to the right from Joel Taufa'ao to Uaisele, who offloaded to Jennings, and his angled run back to the post wrong footed the Irish defence for the opening try that Taufa'ao goaled.

It was no more than Tonga deserved, but the Irish, helped by a flurry of penalties at the play-the-ball, started to get into the game before they were brought back by a forward pass from Bob Beswick to Platt.

Leo-Latu was causing all sorts of problems, however, and Cooper Vuna should have taken his pass for a second try.

Then Ireland got the benefit of the doubt from video-referee Paul Simpkins when Platt again spilled the high ball, and somehow Jennings knocked on when regathering to go over the line.

Winger Esi Tonga was sin-binned for lying on in the 25th minute, and within three minutes Ireland exploited the extra man when Scott Grix's cut-out pass to the right put in Blanch, too far out for Pat Richards to add the goal.

Two minutes later Ireland had the lead with a terrific try, as Grix put Gareth Haggerty away. He found Lee Doran, whose pass gave Fitzpatrick room, before he somehow put an overhead pass to the supporting Platt to score. It looked a mile forward, but the video-referee could only check the grounding. Richards goaled and Ireland had the lead.

But if Platt had been the hero, he was the villain five minutes later when he was slow to react to Taufa'ao's kick to the corner, and Vuna was able to sneak up on the blind side to get the touchdown.

Taufa'ao missed the conversion, but was able to find the mark with a penalty on the stroke of half-time, when Ireland were caught offside, giving the Tongans a 12-10 interval lead.

There was no let-up in the second half and, with English referee Steve Ganson having sin-binned Mateo for dissent, Blanch gave the Irish the lead again when Fitzpatrick, Grix, Finnigan and Sean Gleeson combined to put him in at the corner for an unconverted try.

Back roared Tonga, with a miracle pass from Mateo putting Epalahame Lauaki away, and he in turn put Uaisele in for a try goaled by Tony Williams.

The fans were on the edge of their seats, and the large Irish contingent were dancing when Liam Finn's kick to the corner was snatched out of midair by Blanch, who swung round to ground the ball before being bundled in-goal. The try stood, and Richards goaled from wide out.

It looked all set for an upset, but a '40/20' from Mateo, which Platt appeared to let go into touch, swung the game again. This time the ball was whipped wide, and Esikeli Tonga swept in at the corner.

Still the drama was not over, but when Gleeson broke clear his attempted pass to Blanch went to ground under a fearsome hit, before a scrum and kick from Grix bounced desperately from the chasing Blanch and to safety.

SAMOA 20 TONGA 12

It wasn't the all-out war predicted, but Samoa and Tonga fought out a bruising, compelling battle in Penrith. The Samoans eventually emerged victorious from a rousing clash that left Ireland with a chance of making the semi-final qualifiers, if they could manage a victory by six points or more against Samoa the following Wednesday - which looked a tall order.

There was a heroic defensive effort from Tonga, led by Tevita Leo-Latu, particularly during a second-half onslaught from the men in blue. In the end it was Samoa's Super League contingent which provided many of the telling contributions, with Francis Meli and George Carmont among the try scorers, and David Solomona producing some typical magical touches. Carmont's 53rd minute try sealed it against a tiring Tongan side.

There was certainly no lack of hype in Sydney before the game, with reports of extra security for the crowd and warnings to both teams not to cross the halfway line during their pre-match hakas.

But while passion flowed from both camps – in the stands and on the field – the atmosphere was always more carnival than menacing.

The hakas certainly provided spectacular viewing, and the fact that Samoa started first was reflected when the match kicked off, as Tonga quickly found themselves ten points behind.

Stand-off Feleti Mateo – a man who needed to shine for Tonga, but who ultimately failed to inject himself sufficiently into the game – produced the mistake that gifted Samoa field position, as his ill-advised offload was knocked back by Meli.

The big St Helens winger then found himself on the end of a try scoring move moments later, as Ben Roberts, Solomona and Carmont combined to put him over in the left corner.

Tonga did respond initially, with front-rower Antonio Kaufusi held up over the line. And they were on the attack when Samoa scored their second, as Leo-Latu made a rare mistake. His wide pass was picked off by Nigel Vagana, who just had the pace to win the 90 metre race to the line, despite his advancing years. Roberts' conversion made it 10-0.

Tonga gradually fought their way back into the contest, and they opened their account in the 20th minute after a mistake by the otherwise impressive Lagi Setu.

A superb ball from powerful substitute Tony Williams released the exciting Michael Jennings, and he grabbed his second try of the tournament by pushing off Matt Utai en route to the line. Williams converted, and then produced another telling contribution, as his desperate tackle upset Vagana sufficiently for the Samoan skipper to drop the ball over the line.

Moments later Tonga were suddenly in front, after quick thinking at dummy-half from Leo-Latu earned them a penalty.

It was the Wakefield hooker who then grabbed the try, scampering over from close range after Willie Manu had been stopped just short.

But Samoa were back in front just before half-time. Good hands from Albert Talipeau, Vagana, Joseph Paulo and Willie Talau gave Utai just enough space to dive over by the right hand corner flag, making it 14-12 at the break.

The game was firmly in the balance at that stage, but the Samoans gained control of the contest immediately after the restart.

Meli had already broken down the left once, when a brilliant offload from Solomona released Setu, who timed his inside pass perfectly for Carmont to race through and score.

Tonga would soon have been further adrift, had referee Shayne Hayne not ruled a marginal forward pass from Roberts to Carmont after Samoa had won a scrum against the head.

Fleet footed Samoan fullback Smith Samau then grounded the ball just short in a three-man tackle.

That just about kept the Tongans in the game, and they stirred again late in the contest in a bid to spark a late comeback. But, when Leo-Latu lost the ball in trying to stretch over five minutes from the end, their chances of victory had gone, and on the final hooter supporters from both teams spilled onto the pitch, something that enhanced a feeling of respect rather than bitterness between the two countries.

IRELAND 34 SAMOA 16

Ireland forced themselves into the semi-final qualifier, and into the hearts of the Australian public, with a thrilling success against Pool 3 favourites Samoa at Parramatta Stadium. All the Irish players had 'no strength without unity' tattooed in Gaelic on their bodies after the narrow defeat to Tonga, and they put those words into practice.

After a start that saw them twice get the benefit of video referee Steve Ganson's decisions Ireland took a stunning lead they never looked like losing. The indomitable Irish spirit that had almost accounted for Tonga was once more in evidence as they never took a backwards step. Liam Finn's 69th minute try opened up an 18-point gap with 11 minutes to go, and Ireland were not going to let that slip. Pat Richards collected a record Irish haul of 22 points.

It was all Samoa in the opening stages, as a spilled ball by eventual man of the match Richards gave Samoa a goal-line drop out on the first set of six. Then when Willie Talau put in a kick and Michael Platt made a hash of the take, the ball was hacked for Nigel Vagana to seemingly touch down. But the video ref correctly said no, adjudging the Samoa skipper had not got the ball down before the goal line. Terence Seuseu and Ben Roberts both went close before a second video call, this time the judgement being that Tony Puletua's driving run over the try line had been helped by an obstruction.

The Irish were defending desperately, Simon Finnigan, Ben Harrison, Bob Beswick and Eamon O'Carroll in the thick of it, with Damien Blanch and Stuart Littler being called upon too.

It looked inevitable that Ireland would succumb to the sheer power of players like Ali Lauitiiti, Tony Puletua and Lagi Setu as Roberts and Vagana sprayed the ball around, especially when Blanch took a bone-crunching tackle from Seuseu that left him poleaxed.

But on 11 minutes, on Ireland's first real attack, a Finn crossfield kick was taken by Richards and in one fell swoop he had the ball down for a try, hitting the upright with the conversion

Almost immediately from the kick-off Ireland scored again when a great dummy and break from Beswick left the Samoans flat footed and Finnigan was in support to finish from 20 metres out, incredibly Richards missing the conversion again.

But Ireland were in full flow and on 18 minutes Scott Grix's kick was lost by Francis Meli under a challenge from the recovered Blanch, and Sean Gleason was able to touch down for a try that this time Richards goaled from wide out.

On 24 minutes Vagana got the right video decision when Platt lost Roberts' kick through and Richards failed to hack dead. Roberts goaled.

The Samoan momentum built and after Vagana had been hauled down short a video decision confirmed Misi Taulapapa's try from dummy-half, Roberts again goaling, though Ireland managed to pull back a 40-metre Richards' penalty when the ball was ripped out in the tackle and nervously led 16-12 at the break.

In the second half the men in green charged down field from the off, and a superb long ball to the left from Karl Fitzpatrick created enough room for Richards to step inside two men and score wide out.

He missed the conversion but suddenly the large contingent of green-clad Irish fans, many in green wigs, were roaring their side on and a 51st minute Richards penalty for ball-stealing saw the gap widened to ten points.

Samoa piled on the pressure. Seuseu was held on his back over the Irish line unable to ground the ball, and so was Talau before Blanch was pulled back after racing 90 metres for what he thought was a touch down, for a knock-on before he got the ball. But when Solomona put an elbow to the face of Sean Gleeson, which went on report, two more points came from Richards' boot.

The Wigan Warrior's fifth goal came on 67 minutes when he was the victim a late tackle by Tony Puletua, before the gamebreaker try on 69 minutes, as Grix's kick was lost by Taulapapa and Finn snapped the ball up to score, too wide out for Richards.

Solomona kept Samoan hopes alive when taking George Carmont's pass on 74 minutes for an ungoaled try. But with two minutes remaining, Richards bagged his hat-trick try from Finn's kick and the Irish celebrations began in earnest.

Play-offs

SEMI-FINAL QUALIFIER

FIJI 30 IRELAND 14

Ireland's World Cup dream was finally ended at Skilled Park, home of the Gold Coast Titans, when the strength and the power of the Fijians provided one test too many for the battered Wolfhounds.

It was always going to be tough for the Irish, especially after their bruising win over Samoa that qualified them for the play-off, and when Simon Finnigan charged down Aaron Groom's second-minute kick it became even tougher. The scrum-half regathered the ball before darting to the right and launching captain Wes Naiqama on a 30-metre run that left three defenders in his wake for the opening touchdown after only two minutes. Newcastle Knights centre Naiqama then added the extras.

But in true Irish spirit, the large green-clad following were given plenty to cheer five minutes later when Liam Finn and Sean Gleeson quickly moved the ball to winger Damian Blanch and he sped away down the right over 40 metres for a classic winger's try. First Blanch slipped Daryl Millard's tackle and then feigned to run inside fullback Jarryd Hayne before beating him for pace on the outside for a fantastic score that Pat Richards converted to level.

Osea Sadrau was held close and Hayne lost the ball with the line begging as the Fijians piled on the pressure. Twice Michael Platt pulled off fantastic tackles on Groom and livewire hooker Waisele Sukanaveita to keep the Irish line intact.

Ireland missed a chance to take the lead when Richards pulled a 40-metre penalty shot wide - this after Ireland had spurned two other more kickable penalties - and on 29 minutes Fiji took the lead again when boom winger Akuila Uate ran across field from dummy-half and sliced through between Ryan Tandy and Lee Doran for another Naiqama-goaled try.

Yet again Ireland hit back, this time a great run from Ryan Tandy, ending with Scott Grix crashing in for a 36th minute try. Richards' shot at goal hit the post and bounced away.

Trailing 12-10 at half-time, Ireland needed a good start, but it was Fiji laying siege to their line as Groom, Jason Bukuya and Suka constantly caused problems. Substitute James Storer looked to have burrowed over for a try but the video referee ruled that Finnigan and Michael Platt had prevented him from grounding. Ireland had their moments too with a Karl Fitzpatrick break putting Ged Corcoran away, only for him to get caught, before Tandy's grubber in-goal was made safe by Naiqama.

On 55 minutes, a disallowed try and four successive penalties against them, and a couple of goal-line drops outs on the back of those, saw Ireland's energy reserves start to dwindle. When Bukuya snatched up a knocked down Alipate Noilea pass to glide through and score and Naiqama goaled, the writing was on the wall.

Liam Finn and Grix were both playing with head wounds heavily bandaged and the knocks were starting to tell. A 62nd minute Naiqama penalty from under the posts for a Platt flop on Uate opened the gap further, before a Groom kick was taken by Hayne, and although he collided with an upright, his agility saw him still ground the ball for the crucial try.

Uate made more pressure tell with his second try on 75 minutes, courtesy of a fine pass from Naiqama, who hit the post with his conversion attempt, but Ireland gave their fans something to cheer at the end when Finn, Grix and Doran combined to put Blanch in for his second try. Richards' patchy tournament with the boot continued as he failed to goal, and Ireland's dream was over.

The Irish had so many walking wounded that it was perhaps a blessing in disguise they failed to make the semi-finals, because coach Andy Kelly may have been left short of fit players to take on the reigning World Champions.

RANKING GAMES

SCOTLAND 0 TONGA 48

In the steamy heat of Rockhampton in central Queensland, Manly signing Tony Williams starred during the Mate Ma's eight-try, 48-0 pasting in the play-off for seventh, as Scotland's World Cup odyssey came to an unfortunate but inevitable end. Playing without injured skipper Danny Brough and a host of others, the Scots had little hope of backing up their historic win in Gosford just three days before.

A decision was taken before kick-off to play the game in four quarters because of the oppressive heat, but in the end the move proved unnecessary with a cool change arriving just before kick-off.

Tonga's first try came after just five minutes, scrum-half Eddie Paea kicking across the face of the goalposts and stand-off Feleti Mateo – the official man of the match - flying high to touch down.

South Sydney's Paea scored a worryingly easy try at nine minutes, accelerating through a yawning gap, and another Tongan try was called back when Michael Jennings' pass to Cooper Vuna was ruled forward.

After the first drinks break, centre Jennings looked set for a length-of-the-field try before being hauled down by Bravehearts fullback Michael Robertson. But the Scots defence was unable recover sufficiently, with the promising Etuate Uaisele crossing in the corner off Andrew Emelio's pass.

Scotland had a couple of scoring chances in the first half - notably when captain Ben Fisher lost the ball as he tried to touch down over his head in the 33rd minute - but the skipper only had himself to blame when his pass was intercepted by fullback Fetuli Talanoa just short of half-time.

South Sydney's Talanoa scooted 95 metres to the line and dead-eye Williams made it 24-0 for the break.

The second half was largely a mirror image of the first, with Penrith's Jennings getting the final try in the last minute and Williams, who insisted he never practised goal-kicking, finishing with six from six.

Centre Vuna, probably Tonga's best player of the World Cup, bagged a brace of touchdowns.

'We racked up some points and the most pleasing thing is they didn't score any points," said Tonga coach Jim Dymock. 'We left it a bit late but it was good to go out in that way.

'I feel sorry for Scotland. It was a tough ask for them. A two-day turnaround, they play Fiji, then they come up against us. It was pretty hard for them.'

Scotland coach Steve McCormack said philosophically afterwards: 'Scotland's never actually won a World Cup game before … to get a win against Fiji, I consider that a massive step forward for the game in Scotland. Nobody give us a chance of walking around at the end of a game in Rockhampton. Everybody booked us into the hotels in Penrith (where the ninth-place play-off was held) before the tournament had started."

FRANCE 10 SAMOA 42

In the fixture that many expected to see as the semi-final qualifier, rather than a battle for the tournament's ninth and tenth spots, the French were blown away from the outset by a far more enthusiastic and imaginative Samoa.

Since their win over Scotland in game two of the World Cup, France had slumped to the bottom of their pool and the foot of the rankings, leaving many questioning the wisdom of incorporating the Tricolours into an expanded Four Nations competition the following season. Even with ten Super League Catalans players on show, the French were blown away from the outset by a far more enthusiastic Samoa. Winger Dimitri Pelo's misplaced offload on the stroke of half-time which was snaffled up by Misi Taulapapa to extend Samoa's lead to 24-0 was typical of France's World Cup campaign.

With a makeshift side hit by injuries, the Pacific Islanders showed superior strength and skill, opening the scoring after five minutes as Matt Utai easily split the defence and scooted in at the corner during their first attack on the French line. Samoa's dominance in the outside backs was confirmed minutes later as Francis Meli powered through some sluggish French defence, although Ben Roberts' off-day with the boot ensured the advantage remained only eight points.

After a period of unco-ordinated attack from both sides, Samoa finally made the most of a chaotic set as Ben Te'o barged over through some lacklustre tackling for a try converted by Roberts for a 14-0 lead. Further Samoan tries followed courtesy of George Carmont and Misi Taulapapa, both of which were given the nod by the video referee, as the Pacific Islanders left the field with a seemingly unassailable 24-0 half-time lead.

Seven minutes into the second half, Te'o picked up his second try after being put into space by stand-in scrum-half Albert Talipeau.

The disparity in speed of thought within the French side was evident as passes repeatedly went to ground and they struggled to maintain any momentum in attack. Samoa also endured an error-strewn 15 minutes, until they pounced on a Jean-Phillipe Baile knock-on and Carmont sent Roberts over in the corner, with Joe Paulo adding the extras.

France finally got on the scoreboard after 63 minutes when determined skipper Jerome Guisset barged through on the back of a neat pass from Christophe Moly – France's third-choice hooker after tournament-ending injuries were suffered by Julien Rinaldi and James Wynne in the earlier matches.

Thomas Bosc converted and the Tricolours managed to build some momentum, forcing a repeat set through John Wilson's kicking, from which Sebastien Planas stretched over to take the French into double figures at 36-10.

But the revival was short-lived, as a creative Bosc effort was ruled out by the video referee for offside, and Samoa passed the 40-point mark when two consecutive penalties set up the position for a barnstorming Tony Puletua try, converted by Paulo - creating a party atmosphere to end their 2008 World Cup.

Samoa bade farewell to their fanatical supporters with a lap-of-honour of war cries, performing to each stand in turn, to great appreciation.

Semi-Finals

ENGLAND 22 NEW ZEALAND 32

England's World Cup hopes disappeared in Brisbane amid a flurry of handling errors against New Zealand.

Coach Tony Smith counted 20 errors in all and, with the familiar defensive frailties out wide again evident, England were always up against it.

They weren't without moments of hope, despite playing their way into a 16-point deficit that had threatened another capitulation like at Melbourne against Australia two weeks earlier. Three times the English closed the gap to six points, only to allow handling errors to end any genuine chances of a comeback. Even in the closing stages there was an opportunity they could force extra time, only for the all-too common knock-on to crop up again, this time in the shape of loose forward Rob Purdham. And when the Kiwis clinched victory, and their final place, via another English hand moments later, the entire match had been summed up in the space of three minutes.

Jamie Peacock and Adrian Morley once again gave their all to the cause, and centre Martin Gleeson had his best game of the tournament, while that year's Man of Steel, James Graham, never dropped his work rate during another lengthy stint on the field.

England managed to nullify the threat of New Zealand's best two players the previous week in the shape of powerhouse winger Manu Vatuvei and quickfire replacement hooker Issac Luke. Instead their main tormentors this time were Nathan Fien and Thomas Leuluai, whose positional switch between scrum-half and hooker worked to perfection.

Fien's kicking game was a key element of the Kiwis' victory, especially when compared to England's substandard effort. Leuluai had one of his best international games playing at hooker, while Bronson Harrison was the pick of a hard-working forward pack, and Benji Marshall showed plenty of glimpses of his wonderful talent.

After blitzing England in the opening 22 minutes, New Zealand wasted a number of chances to kill the game off completely.

The legacy of the two previous weeks' disheartening defeats could be felt among the hugely impressive English support prior to kick-off, with the atmosphere and enthusiasm noticeably and understandably subdued. By the 22nd minute, with Smith's side trailing 16-0 after an awful start to the game, it was even worse.

Right from the start the Kiwis made yards with ease, most notably around the play-the-ball area, where Leuluai twice poked his head through the defensive line early on. And there had already been three handling errors by the time Sam Perrett opened the scoring in the ninth minute. The latest one had come from Gleeson out wide, and New Zealand seized their chance, as Marshall scooped up Fien's lose pass and gave Perrett enough space to finish on the right-hand side.

In a rare early England attack, Ade Gardner thought he had responded soon after, only for video referee Phil Cooley to correctly rule that his foot had just touched the line in Vatuvei's tackle a split second before touching down.

As if the handling errors that were putting Smith's charges under pressure weren't enough, they then gifted the Kiwis field position through an unnecessary penalty, conceded by Ben Westwood for a late hit on Marshall. In the ensuing set Leuluai again escaped from dummy-half and sent Lance Hohaia stretching over for New Zealand's second.

Two soon became three after Purdham kicked the resulting restart out on the full. Again the Kiwis grasped their chance as Leuluai, Fien, Marshall and Hohaia combined smoothly for strong centre Jerome Ropati to get outside Danny McGuire and touch down. Two Jeremy Smith conversions from three attempts gave the Kiwis a formidable looking 16-0 lead.

It could have been more had Mark Calderwood not got back to haul down a high stepping Marshall after Rob Burrow had lost possession, and eventually England stirred into action, scoring twice before half-time.

Fittingly, the first went to Peacock, who had been battling away constantly in the face of adversity. This time it was the turn of New Zealand – in the shape of Vatuvei – to make an error in their own half, and after Gareth Ellis had offloaded to Burrow, Peacock showed sheer strength to force his way over from close range.

Soon after, Purdham broke through only for McGuire to just fail to hold his pass under pressure, but it wasn't long before the two were combining to better effect. Directly from a scrum 40 metres out, Purdham kicked beautifully for McGuire to run through, accept the favourable bounce and dive over to make it 10-16.

Remarkably, England were now in the game despite a generally poor display, but they needed to score first after the break. They almost broke clear down the right, only for a Gleeson pass to Gardner to be dubiously called forward, and then forced their only goal-line drop-out of the game, only to waste the chance.

There was no such profligacy from the Kiwis, who re-established their lead soon after against an England side now minus the injured Ellis. It was down his side of the field that Fien released the impressive Harrison, who stepped past Wellens to score.

Coach Smith then withdrew the St Helens fullback, who cut a lonely figure on the end of the substitutes' bench. Leon Pryce was deployed at fullback from the bench, and he was involved as England stirred again. It was Pryce's pass that gave Gleeson the chance to step through and reach over, closing the gap to six again.

Back came the Kiwis, as Fien's kick was missed by first McGuire and then Gardner to allow Ropati to snaffle his second.

But the English side wasn't done, and McGuire showed terrific balance to break through and touch down in Jeremy Smith's tackle.

That made it 22-28, and suddenly there was a glimmer of hope again. England poured forward, and McGuire's kick forced a mistake from Perrett to earn a full set on the Kiwis' line. But, as the ball was worked right, Purdham knocked on, and when Gardner followed suit soon after on his own line, the game was up.

New Zealand's last try epitomised so much of what had gone before, as a kick from Fien was knocked back by Vatuvei to Ropati. His pass was touched, but not held, by McGuire, and Marshall swooped on the gift to touch down and complete a miserable night for England's 5,000-strong travelling army.

AUSTRALIA 52 FIJI 0

Australia's seemingly unstoppable charge to World Cup glory continued as they steamrollered past Fiji in a ten-try victory in Sydney.

The Kangaroos had now scored 180 points and conceded only 16 in their four games so far, but coach Ricky Stuart claimed that blowouts against Papua New Guinea and Fiji were hardly the best rehearsal for the World Cup Final.

Fiji made up in passion for what they lacked in points, and some heroic defence managed to keep the Kangaroos scoreless for 20 minutes in the first half. But a knock-on in the second tackle of the game had been a sign of things to come. Fiji didn't get the ball back for ten minutes, by which time they were already 16-0 down.

When Darren Lockyer and Israel Folau put Brent Tate into space and he raced 60 metres for a converted try to take the scoring well past the point-a-minute rate at 22-0 after a quarter of an hour a century looked possible. But the Bati rallied in defence and continued to threaten in attack, though they found it impossible to break the Kangaroos down. Fiji's passion in defence never abated, and a huge hit from Jarryd Hayne on Lockyer reminded the Kangaroos that they were physically still in a contest, and prompted a series of fiery challenges from both sides.

The floodgates opened following that early error, as Paul Gallen barged over on the back of a Billy Slater offload. Johnathan Thurston added the extras and three minutes later Brent Tate strode through unopposed in the corner after quick hands from Darren Lockyer and Slater had stretched the Fiji defence beyond its limits.

The green and gold machine continued relentlessly, as a bomb from Thurston was expertly caught by Slater who planted it under the posts. Slater clearly gave Alipate Noilea a shove off the ball but was given the nod by the video referee.

Fiji finally got their hands on the ball and, with Hayne controlling matters, the adverse scoreline didn't seem to concern the large contingent of fanatical, flag-waving Fiji supporters in the 15,000-strong crowd, as the Bati tried to build some momentum in attack.

But it was Australia who extended their lead minutes later as Tate's try took the scoring well past the point-a-minute rate at 22-0 after a quarter of an hour. It was Tate's last act as he collapsed after suffering a hip injury while running the ball in shortly after.

The Bati rallied in defence and continued to threaten in attack, but found it impossible to break the Kangaroos down with any combination of kicking and passing, Slater magnificent in mopping up and clearing every kick to the goal-line.

Two minutes before the interval Slater scored his second try, dummying and grounding the ball despite some heroic Fijian tackling, and the Pacific islanders found themselves 26-0 down at the break.

Fiji began the second half with some enterprising attack but it was interrupted by an injury to Newcastle Knights winger Akuila Uate, one of the stars of the tournament.

And after the stoppage Australia were soon at it again, as quick hands sent the ball the width of the field in both directions before creating a gap for Slater to pinch his third.

Despite being 32-0 down, Fiji's passion in defence never abated, and the huge hit from Hayne on Lockyer was the tackle of the tournament.

Thurston interrupted the hit-a-thon with a hat-trick in just ten minutes, converting two of them, while Greg Inglis had the last laugh with an incredible balancing act that saw him plant the ball down for a try before his airborne feet hit the ground in touch.

Fiji continued to threaten until the very end, and looked certain to get on the scoreboard two minutes from time but for a fumble by Semisi Tora with the line begging, to universal sighs of disappointment.

Despite the unflattering scoreline, the Fijians proved themselves passionate and committed opposition and ensured a happy ending to their World Cup adventure. The entire squad and staff gathered on the field for a post-match sermon and prayer song, lasting long after the final whistle.

World Cup Final

AUSTRALIA 20 NEW ZEALAND 34

New Zealand stunned Australia in one of the greatest international upsets in the history of Rugby League, winning the World Cup for the first time in history.

The Kiwis, trailing by four points at the break, came out and posted 22 second-half points, while holding the much-vaunted Aussies to just four.

The Australians - 1-10 favourites - had only themselves to blame. Two 'brain explosions' in the second half cost them dearly. A suicidal pass by fullback Billy Slater - who had been brilliant again in the first half - gifted a try to Benji Marshall. And winger Joel Monaghan tackled Lance Hohaia when he didn't have the ball to hand him a penalty try. And the stats revealed that after completing 15 of 15 sets in the first half, Australia only completed 9 of 17 after the break.

Kiwis coach Stephen Kearney, who was appointed to the job following the previous year's disastrous tour of England, when the Kiwis stumbled to a 3-0 series defeat against Great Britain, was on top of the world.

'I am a bit numb at the moment,' admitted an elated Kearney.

'I am very pleased for the lads who played, the guys who didn't get much footy during the campaign, and all the staff who put in such a lot of hard work. I am just very pleased for those people.

'The game back home was in a bad state at this time last year, and some tough decisions had to be made. I was very fortunate to be given the opportunity to take on the coaching side.

'I am very pleased for the game back home. On the back of what the Warriors achieved this year (one game away from a Grand Final), it has been a real boost for our game.'

Before kick-off, the Australians linked arms and walked forward to stare out the Kiwis as they performed their pre-match haka. And it was explosive from the start, with no quarter given by either side.

'The haka gave a fiery start to the game,' reflected New Zealand captain Nathan Cayless. 'It was good for us, good for the TV and probably good for the crowd and the game. We can't complain that they walked away. They challenged us and that was what we wanted.'

After Benji Marshall had missed a chance to ground a Nathan Fien kick in-goal the Kangaroos seemed to have already won the Cup when Darren Lockyer looked to have given them a 16-0 lead after Slater had created two thrilling tries. But referee Ashley Klein had other ideas, and sent the decision upstairs, where video replays showed the Australian captain had lost the ball inches before he grounded.

'I have no doubt that had I scored that try it would have been a whole different ball game,' said Lockyer, who was chosen as official man of the match in defeat. 'But hindsight is a wonderful thing.'

After the no try, the momentum quickly changed, with the Kiwis exerting pressure at the other end, with loose forward Jeremy Smith powering through some weak Australian defence to score under the black spot. Issac Luke had no trouble adding the extra two points for the New Zealanders to trail by just 10-6.

Within a minute of the restart, the Kiwis were over to score again. Australian second-rower Anthony Laffranchi knocked the ball from the hands of Benji Marshall as the Kiwi stand-off raced downfield. David Fa'alogo snapped up the loose ball and raced away, drawing Slater, before sending in Jerome Ropati to score. Video referee Steve Ganson awarded the try, and suddenly, with Luke's successful conversion, the Kiwis were in front.

That stirred the Australians. In a wonderful display of quick passing they utterly bamboozled the Kiwis. Brent Kite, Lockyer, Thurston, Anthony Tupou and Anthony Watmough (with his first touch since coming off the bench) flung the ball around as if it was a hot potato, before Lockyer backed up to score his second try of the evening. It sent the Australians to the break with a 16-12 lead.

'A real important period for us was after half-time, and it was important that we kept our line intact," reflected Kearney.

'We didn't need to score, we were only six points behind or so, but we couldn't let them score either, and I think we fronted up big then. It was real gritty throughout the second half, and we dragged them into an arm wrestle. Things just flowed on from there.

'We only made two mistakes in the second half, and our completion rate in the first half was fairly handy too. We knew it was going to take that top type of performance to get the goods, and I am just so happy for the lads, the whole team, that they got the cream.'

Kearney and Wayne Bennett's wise counsel during the interval paid almost immediate dividends as Hohaia forced his way past Slater, Lockyer and Petero Civoniceva to score close to the posts, and Luke's conversion had the Kiwis back in the lead, albeit only by two.

Then came one of the defining moments of the match. Marshall put in a kick. Slater took the ball on his fingertips and started a run downfield. But when it looked as if he was going to be thrown into touch he tossed a loose pass back infield to no one. Will-o'-the-wisp Marshall calmly collected the ball and planted it behind the stripe to increase the lead to six.

The Aussies weren't yet ready to throw in the towel. They took the ball the length of the pitch. Lockyer threw a long, overhead, cut-out pass to an unmarked Greg Inglis, who was untroubled to score in the left-hand corner.

It was Australia's last hurrah.

Five minutes later Fien put in a kick. Joel Monaghan fumbled and then tackled Hohaia without the ball. Video referee Ganson ruled that Hohaia was in a better position to get to the ball than Slater, who was racing across behind the tryline, and awarded a penalty try.

Aussie forward Brent Kite disagreed: 'Of course he (Slater) could have got there,' said Kite. 'I think anyone could have seen that. Even if he wasn't there, there still has to be no doubt that he's not going to bobble the ball – how many times do you see that? That was very disappointing…but to say that Billy didn't have a very good chance of getting that ball was hard to swallow.'

'Lance didn't get an opportunity to see if he could get the try. That is the decision that had to be made,' said Kearney.

The icing on the black and white cake came with a flurry of kicks and passes near the Australian tryline five minutes from full-time, with the irrepressible Adam Blair scooping up the ball and touching down.

It was retribution for Bennett, who had been the Australians' mentor at Elland Road in 2005 and personally took all the blame for their shock flogging by the Kiwis in the final of the Gillette Tri-Nations Tournament. Now the shoe was on the other foot for Bennett.

After the match Australian coach Ricky Stuart refused to blame Billy Slater for his blunder. 'I love Billy Slater as a bloke and as a player,' Stuart said. 'I would never ever be critical of Billy. If he eliminated that part of his game, we'd be losing a great footy player's style. Look, when you touch the ball so many times in a game, whether you're Billy Slater, Darren Lockyer, Johnathan Thurston or Cameron Smith, you're going to make a mistake.

'If I ask Billy Slater to take it out of his game, it wouldn't be the Billy Slater we all love.'

The Rugby League World panel that decided the destiny of the 2008 Golden Boot agreed with Stuart. Later that week, Slater was presented with the world's most prestigious international award.

POOL 1

Saturday 25th October 2008

ENGLAND 32 PAPUA NEW GUINEA 22

ENGLAND: 1 Paul Wellens (St Helens); 2 Ade Gardner (St Helens); 3 Martin Gleeson (Warrington Wolves); 4 Keith Senior (Leeds Rhinos); 5 Lee Smith (Leeds Rhinos); 6 Leon Pryce (St Helens); 7 Rob Burrow (Leeds Rhinos); 8 Jamie Peacock (Leeds Rhinos) (C); 9 James Roby (St Helens); 10 James Graham (St Helens); 11 Gareth Hock (Wigan Warriors); 12 Gareth Ellis (Leeds Rhinos); 13 Kevin Sinfield (Leeds Rhinos). Subs (all used): 14 Danny McGuire (Leeds Rhinos); 15 Maurie Fa'asavalu (St Helens); 16 Adrian Morley (Warrington Wolves); 17 Jon Wilkin (St Helens).
Tries: Gardner (12, 69), Smith (30, 49, 72), Gleeson (57); **Goals:** Sinfield 4/6.
PAPUA NEW GUINEA: 1 John Wilshere (Salford City Reds) (C); 5 George Keppa (Brisbane Norths); 3 Tu'u Maori (Sydney Roosters); 4 Jessie Joe Parker (City Rangers); 2 David Moore (Gold Coast Titans); 6 Stanley Gene (Hull Kingston Rovers); 7 Keith Peters (Penrith Panthers); 8 Makali Aizue (Hull Kingston Rovers); 9 Paul Aiton (Penrith Panthers); 10 Trevor Exton (Ipswich Jets); 11 Neville Costigan (Canberra Raiders); 12 James Nightingale (Windsor Wolves); 13 Rod Griffin (Northern Pride). Subs (all used): 14 Rodney Pora (Mendi Muruks); 15 George Moni (Mendi Muruks); 16 Jason Chan (Windsor Wolves); 17 Charlie Wabo (Mendi Muruks).
Tries: Griffin (20), Chan (36), Keppa (40), Aiton (75); **Goals:** Wilshere 3/4.
Rugby Leaguer & League Express
Men of the Match:
England: Jamie Peacock;
Papua New Guinea: Stanley Gene.
Penalty count: 8-8; **Half-time:** 12-16; **Referee:** Shayne Hayne (Australia); **Attendance:** 10,780 *(at Dairy Farmers Stadium, Townsville).*

Sunday 26th October 2008

AUSTRALIA 30 NEW ZEALAND 6

AUSTRALIA: 1 Billy Slater (Melbourne Storm); 2 Joel Monaghan (Canberra Raiders); 3 Greg Inglis (Melbourne Storm); 4 Israel Folau (Melbourne Storm); 5 Brent Tate (New Zealand Warriors); 6 Darren Lockyer (Brisbane Broncos) (C); 7 Johnathan Thurston (North Queensland Cowboys); 8 Petero Civoniceva (Penrith Panthers); 9 Cameron Smith (Melbourne Storm); 10 Steve Price (New Zealand Warriors); 11 Glenn Stewart (Manly Sea Eagles); 12 Anthony Laffranchi (Gold Coast Titans); 13 Paul Gallen (Cronulla Sharks). Subs (all used): 14 Brent Kite (Manly Sea Eagles); 15 Josh Perry (Manly Sea Eagles); 16 Anthony Tupou (Sydney Roosters); 17 Kurt Gidley (Newcastle Knights).
Tries: Inglis (14), Monaghan (29), Folau (47, 80), Slater (59); **Goals:** Thurston 4/5, Smith 1/1.
NEW ZEALAND: 1 Lance Hohaia (New Zealand Warriors); 2 Sam Perrett (Sydney Roosters); 3 Steve Matai (Manly Sea Eagles); 4 Jerome Ropati (New Zealand Warriors); 5 Manu Vatuvei (New Zealand Warriors); 6 Benji Marshall (Wests Tigers); 7 Thomas Leuluai (Wigan Warriors); 8 Nathan Cayless (Parramatta Eels) (C); 9 Nathan Fien (New Zealand Warriors); 10 Adam Blair (Melbourne

Storm); 11 Simon Mannering (New Zealand Warriors); 12 Sika Manu (Melbourne Storm); 13 Jeremy Smith (Melbourne Storm). Subs (all used): 14 Dene Halatau (Wests Tigers); 15 Greg Eastwood (Brisbane Broncos); 16 Setaimata Sa (Sydney Roosters); 17 Sam Rapira (New Zealand Warriors).
Try: Manu (26); **Goals:** Matai 1/1.
On report: Matai (13) – alleged high tackle.
Rugby Leaguer & League Express
Men of the Match:
Australia: Johnathan Thurston;
New Zealand: Simon Mannering.
Penalty count: 7-7; **Half-time:** 14-6;
Referee: Ashley Klein (England);
Attendance: 34,157 *(at Sydney Football Stadium).*

Saturday 1st November 2008

NEW ZEALAND 48 PAPUA NEW GUINEA 6

NEW ZEALAND: 1 Lance Hohaia (New Zealand Warriors); 2 Sam Perrett (Sydney Roosters); 3 Krisnan Inu (Parramatta Eels); 4 Jerome Ropati (New Zealand Warriors); 5 Manu Vatuvei (New Zealand Warriors); 6 Benji Marshall (Wests Tigers); 7 Thomas Leuluai (Wigan Warriors); 8 Nathan Cayless (Parramatta Eels) (C); 9 Nathan Fien (New Zealand Warriors); 10 Adam Blair (Melbourne Storm); 11 Simon Mannering (New Zealand Warriors); 12 Setaimata Sa (Sydney Roosters); 13 Jeremy Smith (Melbourne Storm). Subs (all used): 14 Issac Luke (South Sydney Rabbitohs); 15 Greg Eastwood (Brisbane Broncos); 16 Sam Rapira (New Zealand Warriors); 17 David Fa'alogo (South Sydney Rabbitohs).
Tries: Ropati (9), Mannering (17, 24), Perrett (34, 71), Luke (56), Fa'alogo (59), Blair (68), Eastwood (77); **Goals:** Inu 6/8, Luke 0/1.
PAPUA NEW GUINEA: 1 John Wilshere (Salford City Reds) (C); 2 George Keppa (Brisbane Norths); 3 Jessie Joe Parker (City Rangers); 4 Tu'u Maori (Sydney Roosters); 5 David Moore (Gold Coast Titans); 6 Stanley Gene (Hull Kingston Rovers); 7 Keith Peters (Penrith Panthers); 8 Makali Aizue (Hull Kingston Rovers); 9 Paul Aiton (Penrith Panthers); 10 Trevor Exton (Ipswich Jets); 11 Neville Costigan (Canberra Raiders); 12 James Nightingale (Windsor Wolves); 13 Rod Griffin (Northern Pride). Subs (all used): 14 Rodney Pora (Mendi Muruks); 15 George Moni (Mendi Muruks); 16 Jason Chan (Windsor Wolves); 17 Charlie Wabo (Mendi Muruks).
Try: Moore (48); **Goals:** Wilshere 1/1.
Rugby Leaguer & League Express
Men of the Match:
New Zealand: Simon Mannering;
Papua New Guinea: Jessie Joe Parker.
Penalty count: 7-7; **Half-time:** 22-0;
Referee: Steve Ganson (England);
Attendance: 11,278 *(at Skilled Park, Gold Coast).*

Sunday 2nd November 2008

AUSTRALIA 52 ENGLAND 4

AUSTRALIA: 1 Billy Slater (Melbourne Storm); 2 Joel Monaghan (Canberra Raiders); 3 Greg Inglis (Melbourne Storm); 4 Israel Folau (Melbourne Storm); 5 Brent Tate (New Zealand Warriors); 6

Darren Lockyer (Brisbane Broncos) (C); 7 Scott Prince (Gold Coast Titans); 8 Steve Price (New Zealand Warriors); 9 Cameron Smith (Melbourne Storm); 10 Petero Civoniceva (Penrith Panthers); 11 Anthony Laffranchi (Gold Coast Titans); 12 Glenn Stewart (Manly Sea Eagles); 13 Paul Gallen (Cronulla Sharks). Subs (all used): 14 Karmichael Hunt (Brisbane Broncos); 15 Brent Kite (Manly Sea Eagles); 16 Anthony Tupou (Sydney Roosters); 17 Josh Perry (Manly Sea Eagles).
Tries: Slater (5, 63, 72), Inglis (10, 33, 65), Laffranchi (37, 77), Monaghan (56);
Goals: Prince 8/10.
ENGLAND: 1 Paul Wellens (St Helens); 2 Ade Gardner (St Helens); 3 Martin Gleeson (Warrington Wolves); 4 Keith Senior (Leeds Rhinos); 5 Mark Calderwood (Wigan Warriors); 6 Leon Pryce (St Helens); 7 Rob Burrow (Leeds Rhinos); 8 Adrian Morley (Warrington Wolves); 9 James Roby (St Helens); 10 James Graham (St Helens); 11 Gareth Ellis (Leeds Rhinos); 12 Jamie Peacock (Leeds Rhinos) (C); 13 Kevin Sinfield (Leeds Rhinos). Subs (all used): 14 Danny McGuire (Leeds Rhinos); 15 Maurie Fa'asavalu (St Helens); 16 Gareth Hock (Wigan Warriors); 17 Jon Wilkin (St Helens).
Try: Roby (20); **Goals:** Sinfield 0/1.
Rugby Leaguer & League Express
Men of the Match:
Australia: Greg Inglis; *England:* James Roby.
Penalty count: 6-5; **Half-time:** 22-4; **Referee:** Tony Archer (Australia); **Attendance:** 36,297
(at Telstra Stadium, Melbourne).

Saturday 8th November 2008

ENGLAND 24 NEW ZEALAND 36

ENGLAND: 1 Paul Wellens (St Helens); 2 Mark Calderwood (Wigan Warriors); 3 Paul Sykes (Bradford Bulls); 4 Keith Senior (Leeds Rhinos); 5 Lee Smith (Leeds Rhinos); 6 Martin Gleeson (Warrington Wolves); 7 Rob Burrow (Leeds Rhinos); 8 Adrian Morley (Warrington Wolves); 9 Mick Higham (Wigan Warriors); 10 Jamie Peacock (Leeds Rhinos) (C); 11 Jamie Jones-Buchanan (Leeds Rhinos); 12 Gareth Ellis (Leeds Rhinos); 13 Rob Purdham (Harlequins). Subs (all used): 14 Kevin Sinfield (Leeds Rhinos); 15 Ben Westwood (Warrington Wolves); 16 Gareth Hock (Wigan Warriors); 17 Jamie Langley (Bradford Bulls).
Tries: Higham (4), Burrow (8, 26), Gleeson (16);
Goals: Purdham 4/4.
NEW ZEALAND: 1 Lance Hohaia (New Zealand Warriors); 2 Jason Nightingale (St George-Illawarra Dragons); 3 Steve Matai (Manly Sea Eagles); 4 Jerome Ropati (New Zealand Warriors); 5 Manu Vatuvei (New Zealand Warriors); 6 Benji Marshall (Wests Tigers) (C); 7 Thomas Leuluai (Wigan Warriors); 8 Adam Blair (Melbourne Storm); 9 Nathan Fien (New Zealand Warriors); 10 Evarn Tuimavave (New Zealand Warriors); 11 Simon Mannering (New Zealand Warriors); 12 David Fa'alogo (South Sydney Rabbitohs); 13 Jeremy Smith (Melbourne Storm). Subs (all used): 14 Issac Luke (South Sydney Rabbitohs); 15 Greg Eastwood (Brisbane Broncos); 16 David Kidwell (South Sydney Rabbitohs); 17 Bronson Harrison (Wests Tigers).
Tries: Vatuvei (14, 47, 55, 78), Hohaia (20), Nightingale (36), Fien (75);

Goals: Matai 0/2, Luke 3/4, Smith 1/1, Marshall 0/1.
Rugby Leaguer & League Express
Men of the Match:
England: Mick Higham; *New Zealand:* Issac Luke.
Penalty count: 4-9; **Half-time:** 24-14; **Referee:** Tony Archer (Australia); **Attendance:** 15,145
(at EnergyAustralia Stadium, Newcastle).

Sunday 9th November 2008

AUSTRALIA 46 PAPUA NEW GUINEA 6

AUSTRALIA: 1 Karmichael Hunt (Brisbane Broncos); 2 David Williams (Manly Sea Eagles); 3 Joel Monaghan (Canberra Raiders); 4 Brent Tate (New Zealand Warriors); 5 Darius Boyd (Brisbane Broncos); 6 Terry Campese (Canberra Raiders); 7 Johnathan Thurston (North Queensland Cowboys); 8 Brent Kite (Manly Sea Eagles); 9 Cameron Smith (Melbourne Storm) (C); 10 Josh Perry (Manly Sea Eagles); 11 Anthony Watmough (Manly Sea Eagles); 12 Anthony Tupou (Sydney Roosters); 13 Craig Fitzgibbon (Sydney Roosters). Subs (all used): 14 Scott Prince (Gold Coast Titans); 15 Steve Price (New Zealand Warriors); 16 Paul Gallen (Cronulla Sharks); 17 Israel Folau (Melbourne Storm).
Tries: Williams (9, 35, 70), Monaghan (22, 30), Prince (43, 54), Tupou (78); **Goals:** Thurston 7/8.
PAPUA NEW GUINEA: 1 John Wilshere (Salford City Reds) (C); 2 Tu'u Maori (Sydney Roosters); 3 Menzie Yere (Island Gurias); 4 Anton Kui (Goroka Lahanis); 5 David Moore (Gold Coast Titans); 6 Stanley Gene (Hull Kingston Rovers); 7 Keith Peters (Penrith Panthers); 8 Jason Chan (Windsor Wolves); 9 Paul Aiton (Penrith Panthers); 10 Trevor Exton (Ipswich Jets); 11 Neville Costigan (Canberra Raiders); 12 James Nightingale (Windsor Wolves); 13 Rod Griffin (Northern Pride). Subs (all used): 14 Kevin Prior (Wentworthville); 15 Nicko Slain (Goroka Lahanis); 16 Jessie Joe Parker (City Rangers); 17 Jay Aston (Melbourne Storm).
Try: Yere (72); **Goals:** Wilshere 1/1.
Rugby Leaguer & League Express
Men of the Match:
Australia: David Williams;
Papua New Guinea: Rod Griffin.
Penalty count: 5-2; **Half-time:** 22-0; **Referee:** Steve Ganson (England); **Attendance:** 16,239
(at Dairy Farmers Stadium, Townsville).

POOL 1							
	P	W	D	L	F	A	D	Pts
Australia	3	3	0	0	128	16	112	6
New Zealand	3	2	0	1	90	60	30	4
England	3	1	0	2	60	110	-50	2
Papua New Guinea	3	0	0	3	34	126	-92	0

POOL 2

Sunday 26th October 2008

FRANCE 36 SCOTLAND 18

FRANCE: 1 Jared Taylor (Lezignan); 2 Justin Murphy (Catalans Dragons); 3 John Wilson (Catalans Dragons); 4 Sebastien Raguin (Catalans Dragons); 5 Teddy Sadaoui (Carcassonne); 6 Thomas Bosc (Catalans Dragons); 7 Maxime Greseque (Pia); 8 Adel Fellous (Widnes Vikings); 9 Julien Rinaldi (Harlequins); 10 Olivier Elima (Catalans Dragons); 11 Jerome Guisset (Catalans Dragons) (C); 12 Eric Anselme (Leeds Rhinos); 13 Gregory Mounis (Catalans Dragons). Subs (all used): 14 James Wynne (Lezignan); 15 Remi Casty (Catalans Dragons); 16 Jamel Fakir (Catalans Dragons); 17 Christophe Moly (Carcassonne).
Tries: Taylor (16), Guisset (28, 74), Wilson (33), Raguin (54), Moly (80); **Goals:** Bosc 6/6.
SCOTLAND: 1 Michael Robertson (Manly Sea Eagles); 2 Dean Colton (Doncaster); 3 Gavin Cowan (Wests Tigers); 4 Kevin Henderson (Wakefield Trinity Wildcats); 5 Jon Steel (Hull Kingston Rovers); 6 John Duffy (Widnes Vikings); 7 Danny Brough (Wakefield Trinity Wildcats) (C); 8 Scott Logan (Canberra Raiders); 9 Ian Henderson (New Zealand Warriors); 10 Paul Jackson (Huddersfield Giants); 11 Duncan MacGillivray (Wakefield Trinity Wildcats); 12 Iain Morrison (Widnes Vikings); 13 Lee Paterson (Widnes Vikings). Subs (all used): 14 Andrew Henderson (Castleford Tigers); 15 Oliver Wilkes (Wakefield Trinity Wildcats); 16 Chris Armit (Canterbury Bulldogs); 17 Mick Nanyn (Oldham).
Tries: Steel (20), Wilkes (45), Colton (66);
Goals: Brough 3/3.
Rugby Leaguer & League Express
Men of the Match:
France: Jerome Guisset; *Scotland:* Oliver Wilkes.
Penalty count: 6-7; **Half-time:** 18-6; **Referee:** Leon Williamson (New Zealand); **Attendance:** 9,287 *(at Canberra Stadium).*

Saturday 1st November 2008

FIJI 42 FRANCE 6

FIJI: 1 Jarryd Hayne (Parramatta Eels); 5 Akuila Uate (Newcastle Knights) (C); 4 Daryl Millard (Newcastle Knights); 2 Semi Tadulala (Bradford Bulls); 6 Alipate Noilea (Parkes Spacemen); 7 Aaron Groom (Canterbury Bulldogs); 8 Iowane Divavesi (Terrigal Sharks); 10 Ilisoni Vonomateiratu (Lautoka Crushers); 11 Ashton Sims (Brisbane Broncos); 18 Sevania Koroi (West Magpies); 13 Jason Bukuya (Cronulla Sharks). Subs (all used): 12 Osea Sadrau (Fassifern); 14 James Storer (Cronulla Sharks); 15 Nick Bradley-Qalilawa (Manly Sea Eagles); 17 Semisi Tora (Parkes Spacemen).
Tries: Hayne (6, 70), Divavesi (19), Uate (34, 42, 74), Tora (67); **Goals:** Naiqama 7/10.
FRANCE: 1 Jared Taylor (Lezignan); 2 Justin Murphy (Catalans Dragons); 3 John Wilson (Catalans Dragons); 4 Sebastien Raguin (Catalans Dragons); 5 Dimitri Pelo (Catalans Dragons); 6 Thomas Bosc (Catalans Dragons); 7 Christophe Moly (Carcassonne); 8 Jean-Christophe Borlin (St Gaudens); 9 James Wynne (Lezignan); 10 Olivier Elima (Catalans Dragons); 11 Jerome Guisset

(Catalans Dragons) (C); 12 Teddy Sadaoui (Carcassonne); 13 Gregory Mounis (Catalans Dragons). Subs (all used): 14 Laurent Carrasco (Villeneuve); 15 Remi Casty (Catalans Dragons); 16 Jamel Fakir (Catalans Dragons); 17 Maxime Greseque (Pia).
Try: Wilson (30); **Goals:** Bosc 1/1.
Rugby Leaguer & League Express
Men of the Match:
Fiji: Jarryd Hayne; *France:* Jared Taylor.
Penalty count: 10-9; **Half-time:** 18-6;
Referee: Ashley Klein (England);
Attendance: 9,213 *(at WIN Stadium, Wollongong).*

Wednesday 5th November 2008

FIJI 16 SCOTLAND 18

FIJI: 1 Jarryd Hayne (Parramatta Eels); 2 Semi Tadulala (Bradford Bulls); 3 Wes Naiqama (Newcastle Knights) (C); 18 Sevania Koroi (West Magpies); 5 Akuila Uate (Newcastle Knights); 15 Nick Bradley-Qalilawa (Manly Sea Eagles); 7 Aaron Groom (Canterbury Bulldogs); 8 Iowane Divavesi (Terrigal Sharks); 9 Waisale Sukanaveita (Terrigal Sharks); 10 Ilisoni Vonomateiratu (Lautoka Crushers); 11 Ashton Sims (Brisbane Broncos); 17 Semisi Tora (Parkes Spacemen); 13 Jason Bukuya (Cronulla Sharks). Subs (all used): 12 Osea Sadrau (Fassifern); 19 Jone Wesele (Darlington Point); 20 Jone Macilai (Fassifern); 22 Vula Louis Dakuitoga Naqua (Terrigal Sharks).
Tries: Tadulala (26, 73), Bukuya (43);
Goals: Naiqama 2/4.
SCOTLAND: 1 Michael Robertson (Manly Sea Eagles); 2 Wade Liddell (Easts Tigers); 3 Mick Nanyn (Oldham); 4 Kevin Henderson (Wakefield Trinity Wildcats); 5 Jon Steel (Hull Kingston Rovers); 6 John Duffy (Widnes Vikings); 7 Danny Brough (Wakefield Trinity Wildcats) (C); 8 Oliver Wilkes (Wakefield Trinity Wildcats); 9 Ben Fisher (Hull Kingston Rovers); 10 Scott Logan (Canberra Raiders); 11 Iain Morrison (Widnes Vikings); 12 Chris Armit (Canterbury Bulldogs); 13 Ian Henderson (New Zealand Warriors). Subs (all used): 14 Andrew Henderson (Castleford Tigers); 15 Gareth Morton (Widnes Vikings); 16 Paul Jackson (Huddersfield Giants); 17 Neil Lowe (Keighley Cougars).
Tries: Steel (6), Robertson (40), Wilkes (76);
Goals: Brough 3/3.
Rugby Leaguer & League Express
Men of the Match:
Fiji: Jarryd Hayne; *Scotland:* Ian Henderson.
Penalty count: 7-9; **Half-time:** 4-12; **Referee:** Leon Williamson (New Zealand); **Attendance:** 9,720 *(at Bluetongue Stadium, Central Coast).*

POOL 2

	P	W	D	L	F	A	D	Pts
Fiji	2	1	0	1	58	24	34	2
Scotland	2	1	0	1	36	52	-16	2
France	2	1	0	1	42	60	-18	2

POOL 3

Monday 27th October 2008

IRELAND 20 TONGA 22

IRELAND: 1 Michael Platt (Bradford Bulls); 2 Damien Blanch (Wakefield Trinity Wildcats); 3 Sean Gleeson (Wakefield Trinity Wildcats); 4 Stuart Littler (Salford City Reds); 5 Pat Richards (Wigan Warriors); 6 Scott Grix (Wakefield Trinity Wildcats) (C); 7 Karl Fitzpatrick (Salford City Reds); 8 Eamon O'Carroll (Wigan Warriors); 9 Bob Beswick (Widnes Vikings); 10 Ryan Tandy (Wests Tigers); 11 Ben Harrison (Warrington Wolves); 12 Lee Doran (Leigh Centurions); 13 Simon Finnigan (Bradford Bulls). Subs (all used): 14 Michael McIlorum (Wigan Warriors); 15 Liam Finn (Dewsbury Rams); 16 Gareth Haggerty (Harlequins); 17 Mick Cassidy (Barrow Raiders).
Tries: Blanch (28, 51, 66), Platt (30);
Goals: Richards 2/4.
TONGA: 1 Fetuli Talanoa (South Sydney Rabbitohs); 2 Cooper Vuna (Newcastle Knights); 3 Michael Jennings (Penrith Panthers); 4 Etuate Uaisele (Newcastle Knights); 5 Esikeli Tonga (Gold Coast Titans); 6 Feleti Mateo (Parramatta Eels) 7 Joel Taufa'ao (South Sydney Rabbitohs); 8 Antonio Kaufusi (Melbourne Storm); 9 Tevita Leo-Latu (Wakefield Trinity Wildcats); 14 Manase Manuokafoa (South Sydney Rabbitohs); 11 Lopini Paea (Sydney Roosters) (C); 12 Richard Fa'aoso (Newcastle Knights); 13 Willie Manu (Hull FC). Subs (all used): 15 Sam Moa (Cronulla Sharks); 16 Epalahame Lauaki (New Zealand Warriors); 17 Kimi Uasi (Auckland Vulcans); 20 Tony Williams (Parramatta Eels).
Tries: Jennings (10), Vuna (35), Uaisele (58), Tonga (73); **Goals:** Taufa'ao 2/3, Williams 1/1, Mateo 0/1.
Sin bin: Tonga (25) - holding down;
Mateo (48) - dissent.
Rugby Leaguer & League Express
Men of the Match:
Ireland: Scott Grix; *Tonga:* Feleti Mateo.
Penalty count: 16-8; **Half-time:** 10-12;
Referee: Steve Ganson (England).
Attendance: 6,158 *(at Parramatta Stadium).*

Friday 31st October 2008

SAMOA 20 TONGA 12

SAMOA: 1 Smith Samau (Gold Coast Titans); 2 Matt Utai (Canterbury Bulldogs); 3 Willie Talau (St Helens); 4 George Carmont (Wigan Warriors); 5 Francis Meli (St Helens); 6 Nigel Vagana (South Sydney Rabbitohs) (C); 7 Ben Roberts (Canterbury Bulldogs); 8 Kylie Leuluai (Leeds Rhinos); 9 Terrence Seuseu (Cronulla Sharks); 10 Tony Puletua (Penrith Panthers); 11 Lagi Setu (St George-Illawarra Dragons); 12 David Solomona (Bradford Bulls); 13 Harrison Hansen (Wigan Warriors). Subs (all used): 14 Frank Puletua (Penrith Panthers); 15 Ali Lauitiiti (Leeds Rhinos); 16 Joseph Paulo (Penrith Panthers); 17 Albert Talipeau (Souths Logan Magpies).
Tries: Meli (3), Vagana (16), Utai (38), Carmont (53); **Goals:** Roberts 2/4.
On report:
Leuluai (32) - alleged high tackle on Talanoa.
TONGA: 3 Michael Jennings (Penrith Panthers); 2 Cooper Vuna (Newcastle Knights); 4 Etuate Uaisele (Newcastle Knights); 1 Fetuli Talanoa (South Sydney Rabbitohs); 5 Esikeli Tonga (Gold Coast Titans); 6

Feleti Mateo (Parramatta Eels); 13 Willie Manu (Hull FC); 8 Antonio Kaufusi (Melbourne Storm); 9 Tevita Leo-Latu (Wakefield Trinity Wildcats); 10 Awen Guttenbeil (Castleford Tigers); 11 Lopini Paea (Sydney Roosters) (C); 12 Richard Fa'aoso (Newcastle Knights); 20 Tony Williams (Parramatta Eels). Subs (all used): 14 Manase Manuokafoa (South Sydney Rabbitohs); 15 Epalahame Lauaki (New Zealand Warriors); 16 Sam Moa (Cronulla Sharks); 17 Eddie Paea (South Sydney Rabbitohs).
Tries: Jennings (20), Leo-Latu (29);
Goals: Williams 2/2.
On report:
Uaisele (68) - alleged spear tackle on Samau.
Rugby Leaguer & League Express
Men of the Match:
Samoa: Lagi Setu; *Tonga:* Tevita Leo-Latu.
Penalty count: 9-8; **Half-time:** 14-12;
Referee: Shayne Hayne (Australia).
Attendance: 11,787 *(at CUA Stadium, Penrith).*

Wednesday 5th November 2008

IRELAND 34 SAMOA 16

IRELAND: 1 Michael Platt (Bradford Bulls); 2 Damien Blanch (Wakefield Trinity Wildcats); 3 Sean Gleeson (Wakefield Trinity Wildcats); 4 Stuart Littler (Salford City Reds); 5 Pat Richards (Wigan Warriors); 6 Scott Grix (Wakefield Trinity Wildcats) (C); 7 Liam Finn (Dewsbury Rams); 8 Eamon O'Carroll (Wigan Warriors); 9 Bob Beswick (Widnes Vikings); 10 Gareth Haggerty (Harlequins); 11 Ben Harrison (Warrington Wolves); 12 Lee Doran (Leigh Centurions); 13 Simon Finnigan (Bradford Bulls). Subs (all used): 14 Michael McIlorum (Wigan Warriors); 15 Karl Fitzpatrick (Salford City Reds); 16 Wayne Kerr (London Skolars); 17 Ryan Tandy (Wests Tigers).
Tries: Richards (11, 42, 79), Finnigan (13), Gleeson (18), Finn (70); **Goals:** Richards 5/10.
SAMOA: 1 Smith Samau (Gold Coast Titans); 2 Matt Utai (Canterbury Bulldogs); 3 Willie Talau (St Helens); 4 George Carmont (Wigan Warriors); 5 Francis Meli (St Helens); 6 Nigel Vagana (South Sydney Rabbitohs) (C); 7 Ben Roberts (Canterbury Bulldogs); 8 Wayne McDade (Auckland Vulcans); 9 Terrence Seuseu (Cronulla Sharks); 10 Tony Puletua (Penrith Panthers); 11 Lagi Setu (St George-Illawarra Dragons); 12 Ali Lauitiiti (Leeds Rhinos); 13 Harrison Hansen (Wigan Warriors). Subs (all used): 14 Frank Puletua (Penrith Panthers); 15 David Solomona (Bradford Bulls); 16 Joseph Paulo (Penrith Panthers); 17 Misi Taulapapa (Cronulla Sharks).
Tries: Vagana (23), Taulapapa (34), Solomona (74);
Goals: Roberts 2/3.
On report:
Solomona (61) - alleged elbow on Gleeson.
Rugby Leaguer & League Express
Men of the Match:
Ireland: Pat Richards; *Samoa:* Ben Roberts.
Penalty count: 11-10; **Half-time:** 16-12;
Referee: Thierry Alibert (France);
Attendance: 8,602 *(at Parramatta Stadium).*

POOL 3

	P	W	D	L	F	A	D	Pts
Ireland	2	1	0	1	54	38	16	2
Tonga	2	1	0	1	34	40	-6	2
Samoa	2	1	0	1	36	46	-10	2

PLAY-OFFS

Saturday 8th November 2008

SCOTLAND 0 TONGA 48
(2nd, Pool 2 v 2nd, Pool 3)

SCOTLAND: 1 Michael Robertson (Manly Sea Eagles); 2 Wade Liddell (Easts Tigers); 3 Mick Nanyn (Oldham); 4 Kevin Henderson (Wakefield Trinity Wildcats); 5 Gavin Cowan (Wests Tigers); 6 Dave McConnell (Leigh Centurions); 7 John Duffy (Widnes Vikings); 8 Oliver Wilkes (Wakefield Trinity Wildcats); 9 Ben Fisher (Hull Kingston Rovers) (C); 10 Scott Logan (Canberra Raiders); 11 Iain Morrison (Widnes Vikings); 12 Duncan MacGillivray (Wakefield Trinity Wildcats); 13 Ian Henderson (New Zealand Warriors). Subs (all used): 14 Andrew Henderson (Castleford Tigers); 15 Paddy Coupar (Edinburgh Eagles); 16 Chris Armit (Canterbury Bulldogs); 17 Jack Howieson (Sheffield Eagles).
TONGA: 1 Fetuli Talanoa (South Sydney Rabbitohs); 2 Cooper Vuna (Newcastle Knights); 3 Michael Jennings (Penrith Panthers); 4 Toshio Laiseni (Newtown Jets); 5 Etuate Uaisele (Newcastle Knights); 6 Feleti Mateo (Parramatta Eels); 7 Eddie Paea (South Sydney Rabbitohs); 8 Antonio Kaufusi (Melbourne Storm); 9 Tevita Leo-Latu (Wakefield Trinity Wildcats); 10 Lopini Paea (Sydney Roosters) (C); 12 Epalahame Lauaki (New Zealand Warriors); 13 Andrew Emelio (Canterbury Bulldogs); 20 Tony Williams (Parramatta Eels). Subs (all used): 10 Mickey Paea (Sydney Roosters); 15 Sam Moa (Cronulla Sharks); 19 Willie Manu (Hull FC); 17 Kimi Uasi (Auckland Vulcans).
Tries: Mateo (4), E Paea (8), Uaisele (27), Vuna (36, 55), Williams (45), Talanoa (59), Jennings (80); **Goals:** Williams 6/6, E Paea 1/1, Moa 1/1.
Rugby Leaguer & League Express Men of the Match:
Scotland: Scott Logan; *Tonga:* Tony Williams.
Penalty count: 9-7; **Half-time:** 0-24;
Referee: Shayne Hayne (Australia);
Attendance: 5,913 *(at Browne Park, Rockhampton).*

Sunday 9th November 2008

FRANCE 10 SAMOA 42
(3rd, Pool 2 v 3rd, Pool 3)

FRANCE: 1 Jared Taylor (Lezignan); 2 Sebastien Planas (Toulouse Olympique); 3 Teddy Sadaoui (Carcassonne); 4 Sebastien Raguin (Catalans Dragons); 5 Dimitri Pelo (Catalans Dragons); 6 John Wilson (Catalans Dragons); 7 Thomas Bosc (Catalans Dragons); 8 Jerome Guisset (Catalans Dragons) (C); 9 Christophe Moly (Carcassonne); 10 Adel Fellous (Widnes Vikings); 11 Jamel Fakir (Catalans Dragons); 12 Eric Anselme (Leeds Rhinos); 13 Gregory Mounis (Catalans Dragons). Subs (all used): 14 Olivier Elima (Catalans Dragons); 15 Laurent Carrasco (Villeneuve); 16 Mathieu Griffi (Catalans Dragons); 17 Jean-Phillipe Baile (Catalans Dragons).
Tries: Guisset (63), Planas (67); **Goals:** Bosc 1/2.
SAMOA: 1 Tangi Ropati (Easts Tigers); 2 Matt Utai (Canterbury Bulldogs); 3 Francis Meli (St Helens); 4 George Carmont (Wigan Warriors); 5 Misi Taulapapa (Cronulla Sharks); 6 Ben Roberts (Canterbury Bulldogs) (C); 7 Albert Talipeau (Souths Logan Magpies); 8 Kylie Leuluai (Leeds Rhinos); 9 Terrence Seuseu (Cronulla Sharks); 10 Frank

Puletua (Penrith Panthers); 11 Ben Te'o (Wests Tigers); 12 Tony Puletua (Penrith Panthers); 13 Harrison Hansen (Wigan Warriors). Subs (all used): 14 Wayne McDade (Auckland Vulcans); 15 Ali Lauitiiti (Leeds Rhinos); 16 Joseph Paulo (Penrith Panthers); 17 Smith Samau (Gold Coast Titans).
Tries: Utai (5), Meli (11), Te'o (23, 47), Carmont (31), Taulapapa (38), Roberts (60), T Puletua (75); **Goals:** Roberts 3/6, Paulo 2/2.
Rugby Leaguer & League Express Men of the Match:
France: Thomas Bosc; *Samoa:* Francis Meli.
Penalty count: 8-9; **Half-time:** 0-24;
Referee: Thierry Alibert (France);
Attendance: 8,028 *(at CUA Stadium, Penrith).*

SEMI-FINAL QUALIFIER

Monday 10th November 2008

FIJI 30 IRELAND 14
(1st, Pool 2 v 1st, Pool 3)

FIJI: 1 Jarryd Hayne (Parramatta Eels); 2 Semi Tadulala (Bradford Bulls); 3 Wes Naiqama (Newcastle Knights) (C); 4 Daryl Millard (Canterbury Bulldogs); 5 Akuila Uate (Newcastle Knights); 6 Alipate Noilea (Parkes Spacemen); 7 Aaron Groom (Canterbury Bulldogs); 12 Osea Sadrau (Fassifern); 9 Waisale Sukanaveita (Terrigal Sharks); 10 Ilisoni Vonomateiratu (Lautoka Crushers); 11 Ashton Sims (Brisbane Broncos); 18 Sevania Koroi (West Magpies); 13 Jason Bukuya (Cronulla Sharks). Subs (all used): 14 James Storer (Cronulla Sharks); 15 Nick Bradley-Qalilawa (Manly Sea Eagles); 16 Semisi Tora (Parkes Spacemen); 23 Kaliova Nauqe (Fassifern).
Tries: Naiqama (2), Uate (29, 77), Bukuya (55), Hayne (65); **Goals:** Naiqama 5/6.
IRELAND: 1 Michael Platt (Bradford Bulls); 2 Damien Blanch (Wakefield Trinity Wildcats); 3 Sean Gleeson (Wakefield Trinity Wildcats); 4 Stuart Littler (Salford City Reds); 5 Pat Richards (Wigan Warriors); 6 Scott Grix (Wakefield Trinity Wildcats) (C); 7 Liam Finn (Dewsbury Rams); 8 Eamon O'Carroll (Wigan Warriors); 9 Bob Beswick (Widnes Vikings); 10 Gareth Haggerty (Harlequins); 11 Ben Harrison (Warrington Wolves); 12 Lee Doran (Leigh Centurions); 13 Simon Finnigan (Bradford Bulls). Subs (all used): 14 Michael McIlorum (Wigan Warriors); 15 Karl Fitzpatrick (Salford City Reds); 16 Ged Corcoran (Sheffield Eagles); 17 Ryan Tandy (Wests Tigers).
Tries: Blanch (7, 78), Grix (36); **Goals:** Richards 1/4.
Rugby Leaguer & League Express Men of the Match:
Fiji: Wes Naiqama; *Ireland:* Scott Grix.
Penalty count: 10-8; **Half-time:** 12-10;
Referee: Ashley Klein (England);
Attendance: 8,224 *(at Skilled Stadium, Gold Coast).*

SEMI-FINALS

Saturday 15th November 2008

ENGLAND 22 NEW ZEALAND 32

ENGLAND: 1 Paul Wellens (St Helens); 2 Ade Gardner (St Helens); 3 Martin Gleeson (Warrington Wolves); 4 Keith Senior (Leeds Rhinos); 5 Mark Calderwood (Wigan Warriors); 6 Danny McGuire (Leeds Rhinos); 7 Rob Burrow (Leeds Rhinos); 8 James Graham (St Helens); 9 James Roby (St Helens); 10 Jamie Peacock (Leeds Rhinos) (C); 11 Ben Westwood (Warrington Wolves); 12 Gareth Ellis (Leeds Rhinos); 13 Rob Purdham (Harlequins). Subs (all used): 14 Leon Pryce (St Helens); 15 Adrian Morley (Warrington Wolves); 16 Mick Higham (Wigan Warriors); 17 Jon Wilkin (St Helens).
Tries: Peacock (29), McGuire (39, 74), Gleeson (62); **Goals:** Purdham 0/1, Burrow 3/3.
NEW ZEALAND: 1 Lance Hohaia (New Zealand Warriors); 2 Sam Perrett (Sydney Roosters); 3 Simon Mannering (New Zealand Warriors); 4 Jerome Ropati (New Zealand Warriors); 5 Manu Vatuvei (New Zealand Warriors); 6 Benji Marshall (Wests Tigers); 7 Nathan Fien (New Zealand Warriors); 8 Nathan Cayless (Parramatta Eels) (C); 9 Thomas Leuluai (Wigan Warriors); 10 Adam Blair (Melbourne Storm); 17 Bronson Harrison (Wests Tigers); 12 David Fa'alogo (South Sydney Rabbitohs); 13 Jeremy Smith (Melbourne Storm). Subs (all used): 14 Issac Luke (South Sydney Rabbitohs); 15 Greg Eastwood (Brisbane Broncos); 16 Sam Rapira (New Zealand Warriors); 11 Sika Manu (Melbourne Storm).
Tries: Perrett (9), Hohaia (19), Ropati (22, 68), Harrison (56), Marshall (78);
Goals: Smith 3/5, Marshall 1/1.
Rugby Leaguer & League Express
Men of the Match:
England: Jamie Peacock; *New Zealand:* Nathan Fien.
Penalty count: 5-8; **Half-time:** 10-16; **Referee:** Shayne Hayne (Australia); **Attendance:** 26,659 *(at Suncorp Stadium, Brisbane).*

Sunday 16th November 2008

AUSTRALIA 52 FIJI 0

AUSTRALIA: 1 Billy Slater (Melbourne Storm); 2 Joel Monaghan (Canberra Raiders); 3 Greg Inglis (Melbourne Storm); 4 Israel Folau (Melbourne Storm); 5 Brent Tate (New Zealand Warriors); 6 Darren Lockyer (Brisbane Broncos) (C); 7 Johnathan Thurston (North Queensland Cowboys); 8 Steve Price (New Zealand Warriors); 9 Cameron Smith (Melbourne Storm); 10 Petero Civoniceva (Penrith Panthers); 11 Anthony Laffranchi (Gold Coast Titans); 12 Glenn Stewart (Manly Sea Eagles); 13 Paul Gallen (Cronulla Sharks). Subs (all used): 14 Karmichael Hunt (Brisbane Broncos); 15 Brent Kite (Manly Sea Eagles); 16 Anthony Tupou (Sydney Roosters); 17 Craig Fitzgibbon (Sydney Roosters).
Tries: Gallen (2), Tate (5, 15), Slater (8, 37, 49), Thurston (62, 66, 72), Inglis (76);
Goals: Thurston 6/10.
FIJI: 1 Jarryd Hayne (Parramatta Eels); 2 Semi Tadulala (Bradford Bulls); 3 Wes Naiqama (Newcastle Knights) (C); 4 Daryl Millard (Canterbury Bulldogs); 5 Akuila Uate (Newcastle Knights); 6 Alipate Noilea (Parkes Spacemen); 7 Aaron Groom

(Canterbury Bulldogs); 8 Osea Sadrau (Fassifern); 9 Waisale Sukanaveita (Terrigal Sharks); 10 Ilisoni Vonomateiratu (Lautoka Crushers); 11 Ashton Sims (Brisbane Broncos); 12 Sevania Koroi (West Magpies); 13 Jason Bukuya (Cronulla Sharks). Subs (all used): 14 James Storer (Cronulla Sharks); 15 Nick Bradley-Qalilawa (Manly Sea Eagles); 17 Semisi Tora (Parkes Spacemen); 19 Jone Macilai (Fassifern).
On report: Noilea (15) - alleged late tackle.
Rugby Leaguer & League Express
Men of the Match:
Australia: Billy Slater; *Fiji:* Waisale Sukanaveita.
Penalty count: 4-4; **Half-time:** 26-0;
Referee: Ashley Klein (England);
Attendance: 15,855 *(at Sydney Football Stadium).*

FINAL

Saturday 22nd November 2008

AUSTRALIA 20 NEW ZEALAND 34

AUSTRALIA: 1 Billy Slater (Melbourne Storm); 2 Joel Monaghan (Canberra Raiders); 3 Greg Inglis (Melbourne Storm); 4 Israel Folau (Melbourne Storm); 5 David Williams (Manly Sea Eagles); 6 Darren Lockyer (Brisbane Broncos) (C); 7 Johnathan Thurston (North Queensland Cowboys); 10 Petero Civoniceva (Penrith Panthers); 9 Cameron Smith (Melbourne Storm); 15 Brent Kite (Manly Sea Eagles); 11 Glenn Stewart (Manly Sea Eagles); 12 Anthony Laffranchi (Gold Coast Titans); 13 Paul Gallen (Cronulla Sharks). Subs (all used): 14 Karmichael Hunt (Brisbane Broncos); 16 Craig Fitzgibbon (Sydney Roosters); 17 Anthony Tupou (Sydney Roosters); 22 Anthony Watmough (Manly Sea Eagles).
Tries: Lockyer (12, 34), Williams (16), Inglis (65);
Goals: Thurston 2/4.
NEW ZEALAND: 1 Lance Hohaia (New Zealand Warriors); 2 Sam Perrett (Sydney Roosters); 3 Simon Mannering (New Zealand Warriors); 4 Jerome Ropati (New Zealand Warriors); 5 Manu Vatuvei (New Zealand Warriors); 6 Benji Marshall (Wests Tigers); 7 Nathan Fien (New Zealand Warriors); 8 Nathan Cayless (Parramatta Eels) (C); 9 Thomas Leuluai (Wigan Warriors); 10 Adam Blair (Melbourne Storm); 11 David Fa'alogo (South Sydney Rabbitohs); 12 Bronson Harrison (Wests Tigers); 13 Jeremy Smith (Melbourne Storm). Subs (all used): 14 Issac Luke (South Sydney Rabbitohs); 15 Greg Eastwood (Brisbane Broncos); 16 Sam Rapira (New Zealand Warriors); 17 Sika Manu (Melbourne Storm).
Tries: Smith (23), Ropati (27), Hohaia (49, 70 - pen), Marshall (60), Blair (75);
Goals: Luke 3/3, Marshall 2/3.
Rugby Leaguer & League Express
Men of the Match: *Australia:* Darren Lockyer;
New Zealand: Benji Marshall.
Penalty count: 8-5; **Half-time:** 16-12; **Referee:** Ashley Klein (England); **Attendance:** 50,599 *(at Suncorp Stadium, Brisbane).*

KANGAROOS
Since 1908

Australia

PLAYER	CLUB	D.O.B	App(S)	T	G	FG	Pts
Darius Boyd	Brisbane Broncos	17/7/87	1	0	0	0	0
Terry Campese	Canberra Raiders	4/8/84	1	0	0	0	0
Petero Civoniceva	Penrith Panthers	21/4/76	4	0	0	0	0
Craig Fitzgibbon	Sydney Roosters	16/6/77	1(2)	0	0	0	0
Israel Folau	Melbourne Storm	3/4/89	4(1)	2	0	0	8
Paul Gallen	Cronulla Sharks	14/8/81	4(1)	1	0	0	4
Kurt Gidley	Newcastle Knights	7/6/82	(1)	0	0	0	0
Karmichael Hunt	Brisbane Broncos	17/11/86	1(3)	0	0	0	0
Greg Inglis	Melbourne Storm	15/1/87	4	6	0	0	24
Brent Kite	Manly Sea Eagles	7/3/81	2(3)	0	0	0	0
Anthony Laffranchi	Gold Coast Titans	16/11/80	4	2	0	0	8
Darren Lockyer	Brisbane Broncos	24/3/77	4	2	0	0	8
Joel Monaghan	Canberra Raiders	22/4/82	5	4	0	0	16
Josh Perry	Manly Sea Eagles	4/2/81	1(2)	0	0	0	0
Steve Price	New Zealand Warriors	12/3/74	3(1)	0	0	0	0
Scott Prince	Gold Coast Titans	27/2/80	1(1)	2	8	0	24
Billy Slater	Melbourne Storm	18/6/83	4	7	0	0	28
Cameron Smith	Melbourne Storm	18/6/83	5	0	1	0	2
Glenn Stewart	Manly Sea Eagles	11/1/84	4	0	0	0	0
Brent Tate	New Zealand Warriors	3/3/82	4	2	0	0	8
Johnathan Thurston	North Queensland Cowboys	25/4/83	4	3	19	0	50
Anthony Tupou	Sydney Roosters	1/3/83	1(4)	1	0	0	4
Anthony Watmough	Manly Sea Eagles	10/7/83	1(1)	0	0	0	0
David Williams	Manly Sea Eagles	4/8/86	2	4	0	0	16

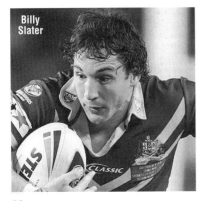

Billy Slater

COACH: Ricky Stuart

England

PLAYER	CLUB	D.O.B	App(S)	T	G	FG	Pts
Rob Burrow	Leeds Rhinos	26/9/82	4	2	3	0	14
Mark Calderwood	Wigan Warriors	25/10/81	3	0	0	0	0
Gareth Ellis	Leeds Rhinos	3/5/81	4	0	0	0	0
Maurie Fa'asavalu	St Helens	12/1/80	(2)	0	0	0	0
Ade Gardner	St Helens	24/6/83	3	2	0	0	8
Martin Gleeson	Warrington Wolves	28/5/80	4	3	0	0	12
James Graham	St Helens	10/9/85	3	0	0	0	0
Mick Higham	Wigan Warriors	18/9/80	1(1)	1	0	0	4
Gareth Hock	Wigan Warriors	5/9/83	1(2)	0	0	0	0
Jamie Jones-Buchanan	Leeds Rhinos	1/8/81	1	0	0	0	0
Jamie Langley	Bradford Bulls	21/12/83	(1)	0	0	0	0
Danny McGuire	Leeds Rhinos	6/12/82	1(2)	2	0	0	8
Adrian Morley	Warrington Wolves	10/5/77	2(2)	0	0	0	0
Jamie Peacock	Leeds Rhinos	14/12/77	4	1	0	0	4
Leon Pryce	St Helens	9/10/81	2(1)	0	0	0	0
Rob Purdham	Harlequins	14/4/80	2	0	4	0	8
James Roby	St Helens	22/11/85	3	1	0	0	4
Keith Senior	Leeds Rhinos	24/4/76	4	0	0	0	0
Kevin Sinfield	Leeds Rhinos	12/9/80	2(1)	0	4	0	8
Lee Smith	Leeds Rhinos	8/8/86	2	3	0	0	12
Paul Sykes	Bradford Bulls	11/8/81	1	0	0	0	0
Paul Wellens	St Helens	27/2/80	4	0	0	0	0
Ben Westwood	Warrington Wolves	25/7/81	1(1)	0	0	0	0
Jon Wilkin	St Helens	11/1/83	(3)	0	0	0	0

COACH: Tony Smith

Martin Gleeson

FIJI
BATI

Fiji

PLAYER	CLUB	D.O.B	App(S)	T	G	FG	Pts
Nick Bradley-Qalilawa	Manly Sea Eagles	28/3/80	1(3)	0	0	0	0
Jason Bukuya	Cronulla Sharks	21/4/89	4	2	0	0	8
Iowane Divavesi	Terrigal Sharks	13/7/80	2	1	0	0	4
Aaron Groom	Canterbury Bulldogs	23/6/87	4	0	0	0	0
Jarryd Hayne	Parramatta Eels	15/2/88	4	3	0	0	12
Sevania Koroi	West Magpies	26/5/80	4	0	0	0	0
Josua Koroibulu	Milton Ulladulla Bulldogs	13/3/82	0	0	0	0	0
Jone Macilai	Fassifern	3/5/83	(2)	0	0	0	0
Daryl Millard	Canterbury Bulldogs	20/2/85	3	0	0	0	0
Wes Naiqama	Newcastle Knights	19/10/82	4	1	14	0	32
Vula Louis Dakuitoga Naqua							
	Terrigal Sharks	16/8/85	(1)	0	0	0	0
Kaliova Nauqe	Fassifern	7/5/85	(1)	0	0	0	0
Alipate Noilea	Parkes Spacemen	21/1/83	3	0	0	0	0
Josateki Ravueta	Sawtell Panthers	28/2/86	0	0	0	0	0
Osea Sadrau	Fassifern	24/4/86	2(2)	0	0	0	0
Ashton Sims	Brisbane Broncos	26/2/85	4	0	0	0	0
James Storer	Cronulla Sharks	16/2/82	(3)	0	0	0	0
Waisale Sukanaveita	Terrigal Sharks	19/7/84	4	0	0	0	0
Semi Tadulala	Bradford Bulls	3/3/78	4	2	0	0	8
Semisi Tora	Parkes Spacemen	28/1/79	1(3)	1	0	0	4
Malakai Yalimaiwai Tuiloa	Milton Ulladulla Bulldogs	29/1/83	0	0	0	0	0
Akuila Uate	Newcastle Knights	6/10/87	4	5	0	0	20
Suguturaga Nemani Valekapa							
	Nabua Broncos	24/9/86	0	0	0	0	0
Ilisoni Vonomateiratu	Lautoka Crushers	5/12/91	4	0	0	0	0
Jone Wesele	Darlington Point	13/4/82	(1)	0	0	0	0

Jarryd Hayne

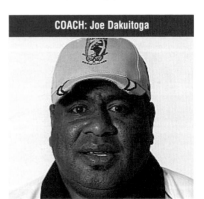

COACH: Joe Dakuitoga

France

PLAYER	CLUB	D.O.B	App(S)	T	G	FG	Pts
Eric Anselme	Leeds Rhinos	20/5/79	2	0	0	0	0
Jean-Phillipe Baile	Catalans Dragons	7/6/87	(1)	0	0	0	0
Jean-Christophe Borlin	St Gaudens	21/12/76	1	0	0	0	0
Thomas Bosc	Catalans Dragons	5/8/83	3	0	8	0	16
Laurent Carrasco	Villeneuve	7/11/76	(2)	0	0	0	0
Remi Casty	Catalans Dragons	5/2/85	(2)	0	0	0	0
Olivier Elima	Catalans Dragons	19/5/83	2(1)	0	0	0	0
Jamel Fakir	Catalans Dragons	30/8/82	1(2)	0	0	0	0
Adel Fellous	Widnes Vikings	16/2/78	2	0	0	0	0
Maxime Greseque	Pia	18/3/81	1(1)	0	0	0	0
Mathieu Griffi	Catalans Dragons	2/3/83	(1)	0	0	0	0
Jerome Guisset	Catalans Dragons	29/8/78	3	3	0	0	12
Christophe Moly	Carcassonne	16/7/82	2(1)	1	0	0	4
Gregory Mounis	Catalans Dragons	18/1/85	3	0	0	0	0
Justin Murphy	Catalans Dragons	14/2/78	2	0	0	0	0
Dimitri Pelo	Catalans Dragons	17/4/85	2	0	0	0	0
Sebastien Planas	Toulouse Olympique	5/5/84	1	1	0	0	4
Sebastien Raguin	Catalans Dragons	14/2/79	3	1	0	0	4
Julien Rinaldi	Harlequins	27/4/79	1	0	0	0	0
Teddy Sadaoui	Carcassonne	18/4/83	3	0	0	0	0
Jared Taylor	Lezignan	21/5/81	3	1	0	0	4
John Wilson	Catalans Dragons	2/7/78	3	2	0	0	8
James Wynne	Lezignan	16/9/76	1(1)	0	0	0	0

COACH: John Monie

Thomas Bosc

Ireland

PLAYER	CLUB	D.O.B	App(S)	T	G	FG	Pts
Ross Barbour	Carlow Crusaders	27/3/81	0	0	0	0	0
Bob Beswick	Widnes Vikings	8/12/84	3	0	0	0	0
Damien Blanch	Wakefield Trinity Wildcats	24/5/83	3	5	0	0	20
Mick Cassidy	Barrow Raiders	8/7/73	(1)	0	0	0	0
Ged Corcoran	Sheffield Eagles	28/3/83	(1)	0	0	0	0
Lee Doran	Leigh Centurions	23/3/81	3	0	0	0	0
Liam Finn	Dewsbury Rams	2/11/83	2(1)	1	0	0	4
Simon Finnigan	Bradford Bulls	8/12/81	3	1	0	0	4
Karl Fitzpatrick	Salford City Reds	13/9/80	1(2)	0	0	0	0
Steve Gibbons	London Skolars	27/9/88	0	0	0	0	0
Sean Gleeson	Wakefield Trinity Wildcats	29/11/87	3	1	0	0	4
Scott Grix	Wakefield Trinity Wildcats	1/5/84	3	1	0	0	4
Brendan Guilfoyle	Treaty City Titans		0	0	0	0	0
Gareth Haggerty	Harlequins	8/9/81	2(1)	0	0	0	0
Ben Harrison	Warrington Wolves	24/2/88	3	0	0	0	0
Graham Holroyd	Halifax	25/10/75	0	0	0	0	0
Wayne Kerr	London Skolars	18/3/84	(1)	0	0	0	0
Stuart Littler	Salford City Reds	19/2/79	3	0	0	0	0
Michael McIlorum	Wigan Warriors	10/1/88	(3)	0	0	0	0
Shayne McMenemy	Unattached	19/7/76	0	0	0	0	0
Eamon O'Carroll	Wigan Warriors	13/6/87	3	0	0	0	0
Michael Platt	Bradford Bulls	23/3/84	3	1	0	0	4
Pat Richards	Wigan Warriors	27/2/82	3	3	8	0	28
Ryan Tandy	Wests Tigers	20/9/81	1(2)	0	0	0	0

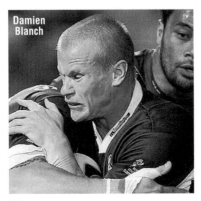

Damien Blanch

COACH: Andy Kelly

NEW ZEALAND
KIWIS

New Zealand

PLAYER	CLUB	D.O.B	App(S)	T	G	FG	Pts
Adam Blair	Melbourne Storm	20/3/86	5	2	0	0	8
Nathan Cayless	Parramatta Eels	28/3/78	4	0	0	0	0
Greg Eastwood	Brisbane Broncos	10/3/87	(5)	1	0	0	4
David Fa'alogo	South Sydney Rabbitohs	9/9/80	3(1)	1	0	0	4
Nathan Fien	New Zealand Warriors	1/8/79	5	1	0	0	4
Dene Halatau	Wests Tigers	27/1/83	(1)	0	0	0	0
Bronson Harrison	Wests Tigers	10/10/85	2(1)	1	0	0	4
Lance Hohaia	New Zealand Warriors	1/4/83	5	4	0	0	16
Krisnan Inu	Parramatta Eels	17/3/87	1	0	6	0	12
David Kidwell	South Sydney Rabbitohs	23/4/77	(1)	0	0	0	0
Thomas Leuluai	Wigan Warriors	22/6/85	5	0	0	0	0
Issac Luke	South Sydney Rabbitohs	29/5/87	(4)	1	6	0	16
Simon Mannering	New Zealand Warriors	28/8/86	5	2	0	0	8
Sika Manu	Melbourne Storm	22/1/87	1(2)	1	0	0	4
Benji Marshall	Wests Tigers	25/2/85	5	2	3	0	14
Steve Matai	Manly Sea Eagles	5/8/84	2	0	1	0	2
Jason Nightingale	St George-Illawarra Dragons	20/9/86	1	1	0	0	4
Sam Perrett	Sydney Roosters	14/5/85	4	3	0	0	12
Sam Rapira	New Zealand Warriors	8/4/87	(4)	0	0	0	0
Jerome Ropati	New Zealand Warriors	23/11/84	5	4	0	0	16
Setaimata Sa	Sydney Roosters	14/9/87	1(1)	0	0	0	0
Jeremy Smith	Melbourne Storm	14/4/80	5	1	4	0	12
Iosia Soliola	Sydney Roosters	4/8/86	0	0	0	0	0
Evarn Tuimavave	New Zealand Warriors	28/6/84	1	0	0	0	0
Manu Vatuvei	New Zealand Warriors	4/3/86	5	4	0	0	16

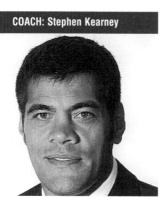

COACH: Stephen Kearney

Issac Luke

Papua New Guinea

PLAYER	CLUB	D.O.B	App(S)	T	G	FG	Pts
Paul Aiton	Penrith Panthers	29/5/85	3	1	0	0	4
Makali Aizue	Hull Kingston Rovers	30/12/77	2	0	0	0	0
Jay Aston	Melbourne Storm	14/2/88	(1)	0	0	0	0
Jason Chan	Windsor Wolves	26/1/84	1(2)	1	0	0	4
Neville Costigan	Canberra Raiders	16/3/85	3	0	0	0	0
Trevor Exton	Ipswich Jets	8/11/81	3	0	0	0	0
Stanley Gene	Hull Kingston Rovers	11/5/74	3	0	0	0	0
Rod Griffin	Northern Pride	5/1/87	3	1	0	0	4
Sam Joe	Melbourne Storm	16/4/89	0	0	0	0	0
George Keppa	Brisbane Norths	29/5/85	2	1	0	0	4
Nickson Kolo	City Rangers		0	0	0	0	0
Anton Kui	Goroka Lahanis	1/1/84	1	0	0	0	0
Tu'u Maori	Sydney Roosters	22/11/88	3	0	0	0	0
Larsen Marabe	Island Guiras	9/6/86	0	0	0	0	0
George Moni	Mendi Muruks	6/12/85	(2)	0	0	0	0
David Moore	Gold Coast Titans	4/11/88	3	1	0	0	4
James Nightingale	Windsor Wolves	25/9/86	3	0	0	0	0
Jessie Joe Parker	City Rangers	22/8/85	2(1)	0	0	0	0
Keith Peters	Penrith Panthers	25/1/86	3	0	0	0	0
Rodney Pora	Mendi Muruks	2/2/80	(2)	0	0	0	0
Kevin Prior	Wentworthville	9/6/80	(1)	0	0	0	0
Nicko Slain	Goroka Lahanis	19/4/83	(1)	0	0	0	0
Charlie Wabo	Mendi Muruks	19/9/83	(2)	0	0	0	0
John Wilshere	Salford City Reds	5/5/78	3	0	5	0	10
Menzie Yere	Agmark Guiras	24/10/83	1	1	0	0	4

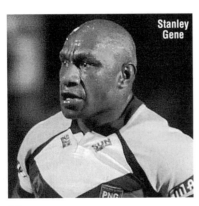

Stanley Gene

COACH: Adrian Lam

Samoa

PLAYER	CLUB	D.O.B	App(S)	T	G	FG	Pts
George Carmont	Wigan Warriors	30/6/78	3	2	0	0	8
David Faiumu	Huddersfield Giants	30/4/83	0	0	0	0	0
Harrison Hansen	Wigan Warriors	26/10/85	3	0	0	0	0
Ali Lauitiiti	Leeds Rhinos	13/7/79	1(2)	0	0	0	0
Tuaalagi Lepupa	Marist Saints	12/11/84	0	0	0	0	0
Kylie Leuluai	Leeds Rhinos	29/3/78	2	0	0	0	0
Wayne McDade	Auckland Vulcans	1/7/81	1(1)	0	0	0	0
Francis Meli	St Helens	20/8/80	3	2	0	0	8
Joseph Paulo	Penrith Panthers	2/1/88	(3)	0	2	0	4
Frank Puletua	Penrith Panthers	8/5/78	1(2)	0	0	0	0
Tony Puletua	Penrith Panthers	25/6/79	3	1	0	0	4
Ben Roberts	Canterbury Bulldogs	8/7/85	3	1	7	0	18
Tangi Ropati	Easts Tigers	15/11/84	1	0	0	0	0
Smith Samau	Gold Coast Titans	15/6/86	2(1)	0	0	0	0
Lagi Setu	St George-Illawarra Dragons	25/2/88	2	0	0	0	0
Terrence Seuseu	Cronulla Sharks	20/11/87	3	0	0	0	0
David Solomona	Bradford Bulls	26/1/78	1(1)	1	0	0	4
Willie Talau	St Helens	25/1/76	2	0	0	0	0
Albert Talipeau	Souths Logan Magpies	5/8/81	1(1)	0	0	0	0
Misi Taulapapa	Cronulla Sharks	25/1/82	1(1)	2	0	0	8
Ben Te'o	Wests Tigers	27/1/87	1	2	0	0	8
Tupu Ulufale	Marist Saints	10/5/87	0	0	0	0	0
Matt Utai	Canterbury Bulldogs	25/5/81	3	2	0	0	8
Nigel Vagana	South Sydney Rabbitohs	7/2/75	2	2	0	0	8

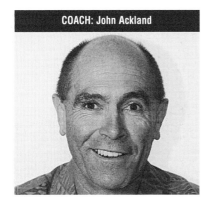

COACH: John Ackland

Nigel Vagana

Scotland

PLAYER	CLUB	D.O.B	App(S)	T	G	FG	Pts
Chris Armit	Canterbury Bulldogs	7/10/83	1(2)	0	0	0	0
Danny Brough	Wakefield Trinity Wildcats	15/1/83	2	0	6	0	12
Dean Colton	Doncaster	18/2/83	1	1	0	0	4
Paddy Coupar	Edinburgh Eagles	26/6/86	(1)	0	0	0	0
Gavin Cowan	Wests Tigers	18/1/87	2	0	0	0	0
John Duffy	Widnes Vikings	2/7/80	3	0	0	0	0
Ben Fisher	Hull Kingston Rovers	4/2/81	2	0	0	0	0
Andrew Henderson	Castleford Tigers	17/6/79	(3)	0	0	0	0
Ian Henderson	New Zealand Warriors	23/4/83	3	0	0	0	0
Kevin Henderson	Wakefield Trinity Wildcats	1/10/81	3	0	0	0	0
Jack Howieson	Sheffield Eagles	28/7/81	(1)	0	0	0	0
Paul Jackson	Huddersfield Giants	29/9/78	1(1)	0	0	0	0
Wade Liddell	Easts Tigers	1/6/79	2	0	0	0	0
Scott Logan	Canberra Raiders	22/6/76	3	0	0	0	0
Neil Lowe	Keighley Cougars	20/12/78	(1)	0	0	0	0
Duncan MacGillivray	Wakefield Trinity Wildcats	25/10/76	2	0	0	0	0
Dave McConnell	Leigh Centurions	25/3/81	1	0	0	0	0
Iain Morrison	Widnes Vikings	6/5/83	3	0	0	0	0
Gareth Morton	Widnes Vikings	21/10/82	(1)	0	0	0	0
Mick Nanyn	Oldham	3/6/82	2(1)	0	0	0	0
Lee Paterson	Widnes Vikings	5/7/81	1	0	0	0	0
Michael Robertson	Manly Sea Eagles	14/4/83	3	1	0	0	4
Jon Steel	Hull Kingston Rovers	14/3/80	2	2	0	0	8
Oliver Wilkes	Wakefield Trinity Wildcats	2/5/80	2(1)	2	0	0	8

Oliver Wilkes

COACH: Steve McCormack

Tonga

PLAYER	CLUB	D.O.B	App(S)	T	G	FG	Pts
Andrew Emelio	Canterbury Bulldogs	18/10/81	1	0	0	0	0
Richard Fa'aoso	Newcastle Knights	8/5/84	2	0	0	0	0
Awen Guttenbeil	Castleford Tigers	14/3/76	1	0	0	0	0
Michael Jennings	Penrith Panthers	20/4/88	3	3	0	0	12
Antonio Kaufusi	Melbourne Storm	27/11/84	3	0	0	0	0
Toshio Laiseni	Newtown Jets	19/6/85	1	0	0	0	0
Taniela Lasalo	Parramatta Eels	2/5/82	0	0	0	0	0
Epalahame Lauaki	New Zealand Warriors	27/1/84	1(2)	0	0	0	0
Tevita Leo-Latu	Wakefield Trinity Wildcats	3/7/81	3	1	0	0	4
Willie Manu	Hull FC	20/3/80	2(1)	0	0	0	0
Manase Manuokafoa	South Sydney Rabbitohs	24/3/85	1(1)	0	0	0	0
Feleti Mateo	Parramatta Eels	2/5/85	3	1	0	0	4
Sam Moa	Cronulla Sharks		(3)	0	1	0	2
Eddie Paea	South Sydney Rabbitohs	8/2/88	1(1)	1	1	0	6
Lopini Paea	Sydney Roosters	19/4/84	3	0	0	0	0
Mickey Paea	Sydney Roosters	25/3/86	(1)	0	0	0	0
Fetuli Talanoa	South Sydney Rabbitohs	23/11/87	3	1	0	0	4
Joel Taufa'ao	South Sydney Rabbitohs	9/1/83	1	0	2	0	4
Esikeli Tonga	Gold Coast Titans	5/2/88	2	1	0	0	4
Etuate Uaisele	Newcastle Knights	12/12/84	3	2	0	0	8
Kimi Uasi	Auckland Vulcans		(2)	0	0	0	0
Cooper Vuna	Newcastle Knights	5/7/87	3	3	0	0	12
Tony Williams	Parramatta Eels	12/12/88	2(1)	1	9	0	22

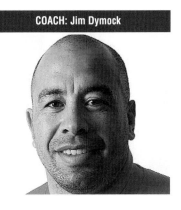

COACH: Jim Dymock

Michael Jennings

WORLD CUP QUALIFIERS

EUROPE - GROUP 1

Sunday 29th October 2006

WALES 14 SCOTLAND 21

WALES: 1 Damian Gibson (Halifax); 2 Bryn Powell (Dewsbury Rams); 3 Adam Hughes (Leigh Centurions); 4 Anthony Blackwood (Halifax); 5 Richard Johnson (Celtic Crusaders); 6 Lee Briers (Warrington Wolves) (C); 7 Mark Lennon (Manly Sea Eagles); 8 David Mills (Harlequins); 9 Ian Watson (Widnes Vikings); 10 Hywel Davies (Celtic Crusaders); 11 Chris Morley (Swinton Lions); 12 Robert Roberts (Leigh Centurions); 13 Phil Joseph (Hull Kingston Rovers). Subs (all used): 14 Gary Hulse (Widnes Vikings); 15 Jordan James (Widnes Vikings); 16 Gareth Price (Celtic Crusaders); 17 Gareth Dean (Celtic Crusaders).
Tries: Johnson (16), Hughes (32), Briers (35);
Goals: Briers 1/3.
SCOTLAND: 1 Wade Liddell (Gateshead Thunder); 2 Jon Steel (Hull Kingston Rovers); 3 Mick Nanyn (Widnes Vikings); 4 Iain Marsh (Batley Bulldogs); 5 Jamie Benn (Featherstone Rovers); 6 Ian Henderson (Bradford Bulls); 7 Danny Brough (Castleford Tigers); 8 Paul Jackson (Huddersfield Giants); 9 Ben Fisher (Hull Kingston Rovers); 10 Neil Lowe (Doncaster Lakers); 11 Spencer Miller (Whitehaven); 12 Gareth Morton (Hull Kingston Rovers); 13 Dave McConnell (Rochdale Hornets) (C). Subs (all used): 14 Ian Sinfield (Swinton Lions); 15 Richard Fletcher (Castleford Tigers); 16 Keir Bell (London Skolars); 17 Dene Miller (St Albans Centurions).
Tries: Liddell (8), Brough (41), Benn (45), Nanyn (67);
Goals: Morton 1/1, Nanyn 1/3; **Field goal:** Brough.
Sin bin: Brough (26) - dissent.
Rugby Leaguer & League Express Men of the Match:
Wales: Lee Briers; *Scotland:* Danny Brough.
Penalty count: 7-4; **Half-time:** 14-6;
Referee: Steve Ganson (England).
Attendance: 2,378 *(at Brewery Field, Bridgend).*

Sunday 4th November 2007

SCOTLAND 16 WALES 18

SCOTLAND: 1 Wade Liddell (Brisbane Easts Tigers); 2 Jamie Benn (Featherstone Rovers); 3 Kevin Henderson (Wakefield Trinity Wildcats); 4 Mick Nanyn (Widnes Vikings); 5 Andy Todd (Edinburgh Eagles); 6 Lee Paterson (Batley Bulldogs); 7 Danny Brough (Castleford Tigers) (C); 8 Paul Jackson (Huddersfield Giants); 9 Ben Fisher (Hull Kingston Rovers); 10 Oliver Wilkes (Widnes Vikings); 11 Iain Morrison (Hull Kingston Rovers); 12 Duncan MacGillivray (Wakefield Trinity Wildcats); 13 Richard Fletcher (Whitehaven). Subs (all used): 14 David Lynn (Edinburgh Eagles); 15 Iain Marsh (Rochdale Hornets); 16 Neil Lowe (York City Knights); 17 Andrew Henderson (Castleford Tigers).
Tries: Fisher (53), Benn (74); **Goals:** Brough 4/4.
WALES: 1 Dave Halley (Bradford Bulls); 2 Anthony Blackwood (Celtic Crusaders); 3 Luke Dyer (Hull Kingston Rovers); 4 Adam Hughes (Oldham); 5 Damian Gibson (Halifax); 6 Iestyn Harris (Warrington Wolves) (C); 7 Lee Briers (Warrington Wolves); 8 Jordan James (Widnes Vikings); 9 Ian Webster (Widnes Vikings); 10 Gareth Dean (Celtic Crusaders); 11 Matt James (Bradford Bulls); 12 Robert Roberts (Oldham); 13 Phil Joseph (Halifax). Subs (all used): 14 Sean Penkywicz (Halifax); 15 Phil Cushion (Celtic Crusaders); 16 Andy Bracek (Warrington Wolves); 17 Craig Kopczak (Bradford Bulls).
Tries: Dyer (7), Hughes (36), Gibson (77);
Goals: Harris 3/4.

Rugby Leaguer & League Express Men of the Match:
Scotland: Mick Nanyn; *Wales:* Dave Halley.
Penalty count: 9-5; **Half-time:** 4-14;
Referee: Phil Bentham (England).
Attendance: 911 *(at Old Anniesland, Glasgow).*

EUROPE - GROUP 1

	P	W	D	L	F	A	D	Pts
Scotland	2	1	0	1	37	32	5	2
Wales	2	1	0	1	32	37	-5	2

* *Georgia withdrew prior to tournament*

EUROPE - GROUP 2

Sunday 22nd October 2006

RUSSIA 12 IRELAND 50

RUSSIA: 1 Joel Rowlins; 2 Sergey Dobrynin; 3 Roman Ovchinnikov; 4 Robert Iliassov; 5 Valentin Baskakov; 6 Blake Muller; 7 Richard Kirian; 8 Jamne Smoll; 9 Mathew Hadojan; 10 Robert Karloff; 11 Yvgeny Bouzhoukof; 12 Din Risko; 13 Joel Rullif. Subs (all used): 14 Denis Koroloev; 15 Oleg Smirnov; 16 Ben Kaminski; 17 Georgy Yinogradov.
Tries: Baskakov (34), Iliassov (69), Ovchinnikov (78);
Goals: Hadojan 0/3.
IRELAND: 1 Gavin Dodd (Widnes Vikings); 2 Steve Gibbons (Carlow Crusaders); 3 Stuart Littler (Salford City Reds); 4 Anthony Stewart (Harlequins); 5 Liam Harrison (Barrow Raiders); 6 Chris Bridge (Warrington Wolves); 7 Bob Beswick (Widnes Vikings); 8 Ryan Tandy (Widnes Vikings); 9 Phil Cantillon (Rochdale Hornets); 10 Barrie McDermott (Widnes Vikings) (C); 11 Mick Cassidy (Widnes Vikings); 12 Ged Corcoran (Oldham); 13 David Allen (Widnes Vikings). Subs (all used): 14 Wayne Kerr (Carlow Crusaders); 15 David Bates (York City Knights); 16 Martin McLoughlin (Batley Bulldogs); 17 Alan Robinson (Coventry Bears).
Tries: Cantillon (16, 58), Littler (24, 39), Dodd (28, 52, 63), Bridge (56, 70); **Goals:** Bridge 7/9.
Rugby Leaguer & League Express Men of the Match:
Russia: Roman Ovchinnikov; *Ireland:* Chris Bridge.
Penalty count: 7-7; **Half time:** 4-20;
Referee: Phil Bentham (England).
(at Sili Stadium, Moscow).

Saturday 28th October 2006

LEBANON 22 RUSSIA 8

LEBANON: 1 Samer El Masri; 2 Adham El Zbaibieh; 3 Daniel Chiha; 4 Frank Samia; 5 Chris Salem; 6 Anthony Farah; 7 Jai Ayoub; 8 Charlie Farah; 9 George Ndaira; 10 Charlie Nohra; 11 John Koborsi; 12 Ali Karouche; 13 Phillip Takchi. Subs (all used): 14 Jad Abinsjsif; 15 Khalid Deeb; 16 Allen Soultan; 17 Mohammed Arrin Kaassalani.
Tries: Samia (7), Deeb (20), El Zbaibieh (28, 75);
Goals: El Masri 3/4.
Sin bin: Soultan (39) - punching;
Chiha (66) - interference.
RUSSIA: 1 Joel Rowlins; 2 Sergey Dobrynin; 3 Denis Koroloev; 4 Robert Iliassov; 5 Valentin Baskakov; 6 Blake Muller; 7 Richard Kirian; 8 Oleg Smirnov; 9 Mathew Hadojan; 10 Jamne Smoll; 11 Roman Ovchinnikov; 12 Din Risko; 13 Joel Rullif. Subs (all used): 14 Yvgeny Bouzhoukof; 15 Andrey Medvedev; 16 Artem Grigorian; 17 Robert Karloff.
Tries: Dobrynin (56), Rullif (78); **Goals:** Hadojan 0/3.
Rugby Leaguer & League Express Men of the Match:
Lebanon: Frank Samia; *Russia:* Richard Kirian.
Penalty count: 16-5; **Half-time:** 16-0;
Referee: Ben Thaler (England).
(at New River Stadium, London).

Sunday 5th November 2006

IRELAND 18 LEBANON 18

IRELAND: 1 Scott Grix (Leigh Centurions); 2 Damien Blanch (Widnes Vikings); 3 Stuart Littler (Salford City Reds); 4 Anthony Stewart (Harlequins); 5 Gavin Dodd (Widnes Vikings); 6 Chris Bridge (Warrington Wolves); 7 Bob Beswick (Widnes Vikings); 8 Ryan Tandy (Widnes Vikings); 9 Phil Cantillon (Rochdale Hornets) (C); 10 Paul McNicholas (Doncaster Lakers); 11 Mick Cassidy (Widnes Vikings); 12 Ged Corcoran (Oldham); 13 David Allen (Widnes Vikings). Subs (all used): 14 Gareth Haggerty (Salford City Reds); 15 Alan Robinson (Coventry Bears); 16 Steve Gibbons (Carlow Crusaders); 17 Steve Nolan (Treaty City Titans).
Tries: Grix (43), Tandy (46), Littler (80);
Goals: Bridge 3/3.
Sin bin: Grix (65) – punching.
LEBANON: 1 Samer El Masri; 2 Adham El Zbaibieh; 3 Daniel Chiha; 4 Frank Samia; 5 Chris Salem; 6 Anthony Farah; 7 Jai Ayoub; 8 Charlie Farah; 9 George Ndaira; 10 Charlie Nohra; 11 John Koborsi; 12 Khalid Deeb; 13 Phillip Takchi. Subs (all used): 14 Allen Soultan; 15 Ali Karouche; 16 Amin Maassarani; 17 Rudi Hachache.
Tries: Chiha (13), Koborsi (31), Salem (56);
Goals: Salem 1/2, El Masri 2/2.
Sin bin: El Zbaibieh (64) – interference.
Rugby Leaguer & League Express Men of the Match:
Ireland: Scott Grix; *Lebanon:* Chris Salem.
Penalty count: 7-7; **Half-time:** 0-10;
Referee: Karl Kirkpatrick (England);
Attendance: 450 (at Tolka Park, Dublin).

Saturday 20th October 2007

IRELAND 58 RUSSIA 18

IRELAND: 1 Scott Grix (Widnes Vikings); 2 Damien Blanch (Widnes Vikings); 3 Stuart Littler (Salford City Reds) (C); 4 Sean Gleeson (Wakefield Trinity Wildcats); 5 Gavin Dodd (Widnes Vikings); 6 Paul Handforth (Featherstone Rovers); 7 Liam Finn (Dewsbury Rams); 8 Eamon O'Carroll (Wigan Warriors); 9 Bob Beswick (Widnes Vikings); 10 Dave Buckley (York City Knights); 11 Lee Doran (Widnes Vikings); 12 Ged Corcoran (Sheffield Eagles); 13 Anthony Stewart (Leigh Centurions). Subs (all used): 14 Steve Gibbons (Carlow Crusaders); 15 Billy Treacy (Treaty City Titans); 16 Wayne Kerr (Carlow Crusaders); 17 Clive Gee (Portlaoise Panthers).
Tries: Blanch (10, 39, 71), Gleeson (16, 24), Littler (31, 57, 63), Beswick (37, 60), Handforth (53);
Goals: Finn 4/6, Handforth 3/5.
RUSSIA: 1 Oleg Logunov; 2 Nikolay Zagoskin; 3 Sergey Dobrynin; 4 Vladimir Vlasiuk; 5 Valentin Baskakov; 6 Victor Nechaev; 7 Artem Grigoryan; 8 Evgeny Bozhukov; 9 Roman Ovchinnikov; 10 Azat Musin; 11 Sergey Matveev; 12 Marat Habibullin; 13 Oleg Smirnov. Subs (all used): 14 Andrey Zdobnikov; 15 Sergey Sidorov; 16 Andrey Medvedev; 17 Georgy Vinogradov.
Tries: Logunov (2), Baskakov (8), Zagoskin (48);
Goals: Grigoryan 2/3, Zdobviikov 1/1.
Rugby Leaguer & League Express Men of the Match:
Ireland: Bob Beswick; *Russia:* Roman Ovchinnikov.
Penalty count: 7-7; **Half-time:** 32-12;
Referee: Phil Bentham (England);
Attendance: 986 (at Carlow).

Saturday 27th October 2007

RUSSIA 0 LEBANON 48

RUSSIA: 1 Oleg Logunov; 2 Sergey Dobrynin; 3 Andrey Zdobnikov; 4 Vladimir Vlasiuk; 5 Valentin Baskakov; 6 Victor Nechaev; 7 Artem Grigoryan; 8 Evgeny Bozhukov; 9 Roman Ovchinnikov; 10 Azat Musin; 11 Sergey Matveev; 12 Marat Habibullin; 13 Oleg Smirnov. Subs (all used): 14 Andre Koltychov; 15 Sergey Sidorov; 16 Andrey Medvedev; 17 Alexandre Lysenkov.
LEBANON: 1 Toufic Nicholas; 2 Adnan Saleh; 3 Frank Samia; 4 Hassan Saleh; 5 Adham El Zbaideh; 6 Anthony Farah; 7 George Ndaira; 8 Charlie Nohra; 9 Jamie Clark; 10 Ray Moujalli; 11 John Korbosi; 12 Chris Saab; 13 Chris Salem. Subs (all used): 14 Allen Soultan; 15 Ali Kourouche; 16 Fred Khoussis; 17 Robin Hachache.
Tries: A Saleh (11, 23), El Zbaideh (29, 65), Nicholas (40), Samia (58, 62), Moujalli (64), Farah (69);
Goals: Farah 2/5, Nicholas 4/4.
Rugby Leaguer & League Express Men of the Match:
Russia: Roman Ovchinnikov; *Lebanon:* George Ndaira.
Penalty count: 7-7; **Half-time:** 0-20;
Referee: Richard Silverwood (England).
Attendance: 1,426 (at Naro Stadium, Narofominsk).

Friday 2nd November 2007

IRELAND 16 LEBANON 16

IRELAND: 1 Scott Grix (Widnes Vikings); 2 Damien Blanch (Widnes Vikings); 3 Stuart Littler (Salford City Reds) (C); 4 Sean Gleeson (Wakefield Trinity Wildcats); 5 Anthony Stewart (Leigh Centurions); 6 Paul Handforth (Featherstone Rovers); 7 Liam Finn (Dewsbury Rams); 8 Mick Cassidy (Widnes Vikings); 9 Bob Beswick (Widnes Vikings); 10 Eamon O'Carroll (Wigan Warriors); 11 Paul Prescott (Wigan Warriors); 12 Ged Corcoran (Sheffield Eagles); 13 Lee Doran (Widnes Vikings). Subs: 14 Chris Bridge (Warrington Wolves); 15 Steve Gibbons (Carlow Crusaders); 16 Billy Treacy (Treaty City Titans) (not used); 17 Wayne Kerr (Carlow Crusaders).
Tries: Finn (2), Handforth (19);
Goals: Finn 2/2, Bridge 2/2.
LEBANON: 1 Toufic Nicholas; 5 Adham El Zbaideh; 3 Frank Samia; 4 Hassan Saleh; 2 Adnan Saleh; 6 Anthony Farah; 7 George Ndaira; 8 Charlie Nohra; 9 Jamie Clark; 10 Ray Moujalli; 11 John Korbosi; 12 Chris Saab; 13 Chris Salem. Subs (all used): 14 Ali Kourouche; 15 Allen Soultan; 16 Robin Hachache; 17 Tom Joseph.
Tries: Ndaira (16), Salem (49), Samia (68);
Goals: Nicholas 2/3.
Sin bin: Nohra (62) - high tackle on Cassidy.
On report: Clark (56) - alleged trip.
Rugby Leaguer & League Express Men of the Match:
Ireland: Damien Blanch; *Lebanon:* George Ndaira.
Penalty count: 16-12; **Half-time:** 12-4;
Referee: Ashley Klein (Australia);
Attendance: 803 (at Tetley's Stadium, Dewsbury).

EUROPE - GROUP 2

	P	W	D	L	F	A	D	Pts
Ireland	4	2	2	0	142	64	78	6
Lebanon	4	2	2	0	104	42	62	6
Russia	4	0	0	4	38	178	-140	0

WORLD CUP QUALIFIERS

OCEANIA

Friday 29th September 2006

SAMOA 30 FIJI 28

SAMOA: 1 Tangi Ropati; 2 Malo Solomona, 3 Peewee Moke, 4 Miguel Start, 5 McConkie Tauasa; 6 George Carmont (C), 7 Chan Ly; 8 Kylie Leuluai, 9 Albert Talipeau, 10 Hutch Maiava, 11 Frank Winterstein, 12 Conrad Ta'amoekiafa, 13 Chris Vaefaga. Subs: 14 Rota Setu, 15 Issak Ah Mau, 16 Chris Afamasaga, 17 Lino Salafai.
Tries: Ta'amoekiafa, Solomona, Winterstein, Tausa, Maiava, Leuluai; **Goals:** Ly 2, Talapeau.
FIJI: 1 Hamilton Hughes; 2 James Lagiloa, 3 Sevanaia Koroi, 4 Daryl Millard, 5 Wes Naiqama; 6 Asaeli Saravaki, 7 Semesa Cadrikilagi (C); 8 Pio Rokomaqisa, 9 Waisale Sukanaveita, 10 Aseri Laing, 11 Iowane Divavesi, 12 Neori Kurumalawai, 13 Netani Suka. Subs: 14 Ilisoni Vonomataivatu, 15 Billy Baleilomaloma, 16 Semisi Tora, 17 Alipate Noilea.
Tries: Lagiloa, Millard, Naiqama, Tara, Divavesi;
Goals: Naiqama 4
Penalty count: 7-5; **Half-time:** 14-10;
Referee: Jared Maxwell

TONGA 56 COOK ISLANDS 14

TONGA: 1 David Pangai; 2 Sosaia Makisini, 3 Andrew Emelio, 4 Fetuli Talanoa, 5 Tyrone Smith; 6 Simione Foliaki, 7 Joel Taufa'ao; 8 Manase Manuakafoa, 9 Kimi Uasi, 10 Joe Falemaka, 11 Solomon Haumono (C), 12 Willie Manu, 13 Willie Tupou. Subs: 14 Makasini Richter, 15 Taufa Fukofuka, 16 John Kite, 17 Sam Moa.
Tries: Richter 2, Falemaka 2, Smith, Makasini, Emelio, Kite, Tupou, Pangai; **Goals:** Taufao 6, Pangai 2
COOK ISLANDS: 1 Turori Matutu; 2 Graeme Jeffries, 3 Rueben Enoka, 4 Ionae Victor, 5 Ben Taia; 6 Mehau Phillips, 7 Marty Mitchell; 8 George Tuakura (C), 9 Damien Takurua, 10 Stacy Katu, 11 Fabien Soutar, 12 Tere Glassie, 13 Brian Thomas. Subs: 14 Dana Wilson, 15 Walter Vaeau, Ali Davys, Henry Turua.
Tries: Taia, Enoka, Victor; **Goal:** Mitchell
Penalty count: 3-7; **Half-time:** 30-4;
Referee: Tony De La Heras

Attendance: 3,013 *(at Campbelltown Stadium).*

Wednesday 4th October 2006

FIJI 30 TONGA 28

FIJI: 1 Hamilton Hughes; 2 James Lagiloa, 3 Sevanaia Koroi, 4 Jone Wesele, 5 Tomujani Koroi; 6 Wes Naiqama, 7 Semesa Cadrikilagi (C); 8 Suliai Koroibuleka, 9 Asaeli Saravaki, 10 Ilisoni Vonomatairatu, 11 Iowane Divavesi, 12 Semisi Tora, 13 Colin Clarke. Subs: 14 Waisale Sukanaveita, 15 Alipate Noilea, 16 Viliame Tukana, 17 Billy Baleilomaloma.
Tries: Hughes, Lagiloa, Naiqama, Tora, Cadrikilagi;
Goals: Naiqama 5
TONGA: 1 John Sinisa; 2 Makasini Richter, 3 Andrew Emelio, 4 Fetuli Talanoa, 5 Tyrone Smith; 6 Simione Foliaki, 7 Joel Taufa'ao; 8 Manase Manuakafoa, 9 Kimi Uasi, 10 Fuifui Moimoi, 11 Solomon Haumono (C), 12 Willie Manu, 13 Willie Tupou. Subs: 14 Lopini Paea, 15 Mickey Paea, 16 Richard Fa'aoso, 17 Saia Makisi.
Tries: Talanoa, Sinisa, Manukafoa, Tupou, Emelio;
Goals: Taufa'ao 4
Penalty count: 8-7; **Half-time:** 8-10;
Referee: Gavin Badger

SAMOA 46 COOK ISLANDS 6

SAMOA: 1 Tangi Ropati; 2 Malo Solomona, 3 Miguel Start, 4 George Carmont (C), 5 Smith Samau; 6 Rota Setu, 7 Chan Ly; 8 Kylie Leuluai, 9 Albert Talipeau, 10 Hutch Maiava, 11 Frank Winterstein, 12 Gray Viane, 13 Peewee Moke. Subs: 14 Jeff Lima, 15 Chris Vaefaga, 16 McConkie Tauasa, 17 Lino Salafai.
Tries: Carmont 3, Ly 2, Solomona 2, Lima, Moke;
Goals: Setu 3, Ly 2
COOK ISLANDS: 1 Turori Matutu; 2 Graeme Jeffries, 3 Nathan Ford, 4 Ionae Victor, 5 Rueben Enoka; 6 Mehau Phillips, 7 Marty Mitchell; 8 Adam Cook, 9 Damien Takurua, 10 Adam Watene (C), 11 Dana Wilson, 11 Fabien Soutar, 12 Stacy Katu, 13 Tere Glassie. Subs: 14 Fred Charlie, 15 Nathan Robinson, 16 Tinirau Arona, 17 Brian Thomas.
Try: Arona; **Goal:** Mitchell
Penalty count: 4-3; **Half-time:** 26-6;
Referee: Jason Robinson

Attendance: 3,813
(at Western Weekender Stadium, St Mary's).

Sunday 7th October 2006

FIJI 40 COOK ISLANDS 4

FIJI: 1 Hamilton Hughes; 2 James Lagiloa, 3 Akuila Uate, 4 Jone Wesele, 5 Tomujani Koroi; 6 Wes Naiqama, 7 Semesa Cadrikilagi (C); 8 Billy Baleilomaloma, 9 Asaeli Saravaki, 10 Suliai Koroibuleka, 11 Iowane Divavesi, 12 Neori Kurumalawai, 13 Waisale Sukanaveita. Subs: 14 Alipati Tani, 15 Semisi Tora, 16 Viliame Tukana, 17 Sevirio Matairakula.
Tries: Saravaki 2, Naiqama, Uate, Cadrikilagi, Koroi, Suka; **Goals:** Naiqama 6
COOK ISLANDS: 1 Nathan Robinson; 2 Graeme Jeffries, 3 Nathan Ford, 4 Ionae Victor, 5 Junior Lupena; 6 Mehau Phillips, 7 Marty Mitchell; 8 Tere Glassie (C), 9 Damien Takurua, 10 Stacy Katu, 11 Henry Turua, 12 Fabien Soutar, 13 Brian Thomas. Subs: 14 Kevin Iro, 15 Walter Vaeau, 16 Terry Taia, 17 Tinirau Arona.
Try: Jeffries
Penalty count: 7-6; **Half-time:** 28-0;
Referee: Tony Archer
Attendance: 1,713 *(at CUA Stadium, Penrith).*

Sunday 22nd October 2006

SAMOA 10 TONGA 18

SAMOA: 1 Tangi Ropati (Wynnum); 2 Malofou Solomona (Auckland Lions); 3 Miguel Start (New Zealand Warriors); 4 George Carmont (Newcastle Knights) (C); 5 Smith Samau (Brisbane Norths); 6 Rota Setu (St George-Illawarra Dragons); 7 Chan Ly (Windsor Wolves); 8 Hutch Maiava (Cronulla Sharks); 9 Albert Talipeau (Wynnum); 10 Shannon Stowers (Hibiscus Coast); 11 Frank Winterstein (Sydney Roosters); 12 Gray Viane (Castleford Tigers); 13 McConkie Tausa (Central Comets). Subs (all used): 14 Chris Vaefaga (Bulldogs); 15 Peewee Moke (Cronulla Sharks); 16 Junior Tiakilifu (Hibiscus Coast); 17 Conrad Ta'akimoeaka (Manly Sea Eagles).
Tries: Ta'akimoeaka (36), Solomona (45);
Goals: Ropati 1/2.
TONGA: 1 Fetuli Talanoa (South Sydney Rabbitohs); 2 Tonga Etuate Uisele (Parramatta Eels); 3 Andrew Emelio (Bulldogs); 4 Lelea Paea (Sydney Roosters); 5 Tyrone Smith (Harlequins); 6 Feleti Mateo (Parramatta Eels); 7 Joel Taufa'ao (South Sydney Rabbitohs); 8 Fuifui Moimoi (Parramatta Eels); 9 Kimi Uasi (Counties Manukau); 10 Solomon Haumono (Harlequins) (C); 11 Lopini Paea (Sydney Roosters); 12 Richard Fa'aoso (Castleford Tigers); 13 Willie Tupou (St George-Illawarra

Dragons). Subs (all used): 14 Mickey Paea (Newtown); 15 Taniela Tuiaki (Wests Tigers); 16 Sam Moa (Balmain); 17 Makasini Richter (Western Suburbs). **Tries:** Tuiaki (22), Haumono (39), Richter (58); **Goals:** Taufa'ao 3/3.
Rugby Leaguer & League Express Men of the Match: *Samoa:* Tangi Ropati, *Tonga:* Solomon Haumono. **Penalty count:** 7-5; **Half-time:** 6-12; **Referee:** Steve Ganson (England). **Attendance:** 5,547 *(at Headingley Carnegie Stadium, Leeds).*

OCEANIA

	P	W	D	L	F	A	D	Pts
Tonga	3	2	0	1	102	54	48	4
Fiji	3	2	0	1	98	62	36	4
Samoa	3	2	0	1	86	52	34	4
Cook Islands	3	0	0	3	24	142	-118	0

ATLANTIC PLAY-OFF

Saturday 28th October 2006

USA 54 JAPAN 18

USA: 1 Eric Hollingsworth; 2 Ric Dortone, 3 Jeff Preston (C), 4 Corey Sheridan, 5 Louis Tulio; 6 Conway Maraki, 7 David Nui; 8 Justin Zadnick, 9 Marcus Vassilakopoulos, 10 Ed Woodbridge, 11 Chris Craig, 12 Kevin Deal, 13 Shayne Mains. Subs: 14 Mike Edwards, 15 Fred Backhaus, 16 Ryan Coleman, 17 Phil Shipos. **Tries:** Tulio 3, Vassilakopoulos 2, Maraki 2, Sheridan, Zadnik, Shipos, Dortone; **Goals:** Vassilakopoulos 5
JAPAN: 1 Kazunori Ijuin; 2 Hirofumi Kita, 3 Kazunobu Nakai, 4 Narihisa Ushida, 5 Mitsutaka Inoue; 6 Hiroshi Miyazaki, 7 Jin Iguchi; 8 Mitsuo Takashino, 9 Noriyuki Tainaka (C), 10 Mansanori Kazoaka, 11 Ryo Kondo, 12 Norihiro Oriyama, 13 Amane Konishi. Subs: 14 Masamichi Itagaki, 15 Yasunori Oshima, 16 Benedict Pender, 17 Shunsuke Tamura.
Tries: Amane, Noriyuki, Mansanori; **Goals:** Norihiro 3 **Half-time:** 32-6; **Referee:** Robert Irvin **Attendance:** 1,200
(at Ashton Community Center Field, Philadelphia).

QUALIFYING SEMI-FINALS

Friday 9th November 2007

SAMOA 42 USA 10

SAMOA: 1 Tangi Ropati (Wynnum Manly); 2 Smith Samau (Gold Coast Titans); 3 Andreas Bauer (Hull Kingston Rovers); 4 George Carmont (Newcastle Knights); 5 Afa Lesa (Marist); 6 Nigel Vagana (South Sydney Rabbitohs) (C); 7 Joseph Paulo (Penrith Panthers); 8 Hutch Maiava (Hull FC); 9 Chris Vaefaga (Bulldogs); 10 Frank Puletua (Penrith Panthers); 11 Tony Puletua (Penrith Panthers); 12 Ali Lauitiiti (Leeds Rhinos); 13 Harrison Hansen (Wigan Warriors). Subs (all used): 14 Chris Leisham (Chanelle); 15 Ponofasio Vasa (Marist); 16 Manulua Lafi (Nagenae); 17 Phil Leuluai (Salford City Reds).
Tries: Vagana (2), Maiava (5), T Puletua (30), Leisham (40), Samau (48), Hansen (64, 70), Ropati (79); **Goals:** Paulo 5/8.
USA: 1 Matt Petersen; 2 Tyrone Coppedge; 3 Ben Kelly; 4 Mark O'Halloran; 5 Eric Dortone; 6 Ryan McGoldrick; 7 David Myles; 8 Edward Woodbridge; 9 Dave Marando; 10 Ashley Laffranchi; 11 Mark Cantoni; 12 Curtis Kunz; 13 Marcus Vassilakopoulos. Subs (all used): 14 Louis Tulio; 15 Greg Stelutti; 16 Nick Isbrandtsen; 17 Bryan Confer. **Tries:** McGoldrick (45), Myles (59); **Goals:** Vassilakopoulos 0/1, Marando 1/1.
Rugby Leaguer & League Express Men of the Match: *Samoa:* Tony Puletua; *USA:* Matt Petersen. **Penalty count:** 8-6; **Half-time:** 22-0; **Referee:** Ashley Klein (Australia).

LEBANON 50 WALES 26

LEBANON: 1 Toufic Nicholas; 2 Adham El Zbaideh; 3 Frank Samia; 4 Adnan Saleh; 5 Tom Joseph; 6 Anthony Farah; 7 George Ndaira; 8 Ray Moujalli; 9 Jamie Clark; 10 Khalid Deeb; 11 Phillip Tatchi; 12 Chris Saab; 13 Chris Salem. Subs (all used): 14 Ali Kourouche; 15 Robin Hachache; 16 Danny Chiha; 17 John Korbosi. **Tries:** Samia (20), Salem (39, 46, 68), Ndaira (52), Moujalli (55), Kourouche (61), Saab (75), El Zbaideh (79); **Goals:** Nicholas 7/9.
WALES: 1 Dave Halley (Bradford Bulls); 2 Damian Gibson (Halifax); 3 Luke Dyer (Hull Kingston Rovers); 4 Adam Hughes (Oldham); 5 Anthony Blackwood (Celtic Crusaders); 6 Iestyn Harris (Bradford Bulls) (C); 7 Lee Briers (Warrington Wolves); 8 Craig Kopczak (Bradford Bulls); 9 Ian Webster (Widnes Vikings); 10 Jordan James (Widnes Vikings); 11 Matt James (Bradford Bulls); 17 Andy Bracek (Warrington Wolves); 13 Phil Joseph (Halifax). Subs (all used): 14 Sean Penkywicz (Halifax); 15 Mark Roberts (Halifax); 16 Gareth Dean (Celtic Crusaders); 12 Rob Roberts (Oldham). **Tries:** Gibson (4, 24, 43), Bracek (9), Blackwood (72); **Goals:** Harris 2/4, Briers 1/1.
Rugby Leaguer & League Express Men of the Match: *Lebanon:* George Ndaira; *Wales:* Lee Briers. **Penalty count:** 7-10; **Half-time:** 10-16; **Referee:** Thierry Alibert (France).

Attendance: 753 *(at Halton Stadium, Widnes).*

QUALIFYING FINAL

Wednesday 14th November 2007

LEBANON 16 SAMOA 38

LEBANON: 1 Adnan Saleh (Sydney Bulls); 2 Adham El Zbaideh (Cessnock); 3 Frank Samia (St George-Illawarra Dragons); 4 Danny Chiha (Windsor); 5 Tom Joseph (Manly Sea Eagles); 6 Toufic Nicholas (Sydney Bulls); 7 George Ndaira (Newtown); 8 Ray Moujalli (Cronulla Sharks); 9 Jamie Clark (Bulldogs); 10 Khalid Deeb (Newtown); 11 Phillip Tatchi (Sydney Bulls); 12 Chris Saab (Cessnock); 13 Chris Salem (Sydney Bulls) (C). Subs (all used): 14 Ali Kourouche (LAU); 15 John Korbosi (Bulldogs); 16 Daniel Sayegh (LAU); 17 Robin Hachache (LAU).
Tries: Tatchi (18), El Zbaideh (35), Chiha (50), Joseph (61); **Goals:** Nicholas 0/3, Clark 0/1.
SAMOA: 1 Tangi Ropati (Wynnum Manly); 2 Smith Samau (Gold Coast Titans); 3 Willie Talau (St Helens); 4 George Carmont (Newcastle Knights); 5 Andreas Bauer (Hull Kingston Rovers); 6 Nigel Vagana (South Sydney Rabbitohs) (C); 7 Joseph Paulo (Penrith Panthers); 8 Hutch Maiava (Hull FC); 9 Chris Vaefaga (Bulldogs); 10 Frank Puletua (Penrith Panthers); 11 Tony Puletua (Penrith Panthers); 12 Ali Lauitiiti (Leeds Rhinos); 13 Harrison Hansen (Wigan Warriors). Subs (all used): 14 Taualagi Lupupa (Marist); 15 Ponofasio Vasa (Marist); 16 Chris Leisham (Chanelle); 17 Phil Leuluai (Salford City Reds).
Tries: Vaefaga (7), Ropati (11), Vagana (26), F Puletua (30), Bauer (45), Maiava (74); **Goals:** Paulo 7/8.
Rugby Leaguer & League Express Men of the Match: *Lebanon:* George Ndaira; *Samoa:* Joseph Paulo. **Penalty count:** 6-7; **Half-time:** 8-28; **Referee:** Ashley Klein (Australia); **Attendance:** 1,323 *(at Chris Moyles Stadium, Featherstone).*

71

EUROPEAN PRELIMINARY QUALIFIERS

Friday 28th April 2006

HOLLAND 14 RUSSIA 40

HOLLAND: 1 Joel Barrett (Sheffield Hallam), 2 Kees Foxon (Nottingham Outlaws), 3 Duncan Taylor (unattached), 4 Ronald Van Der Broek (Haagsche), 5 Roeland Haar (Leeuwarden), 6 Jorik Moree (Rotterdam), 7 Aaron De Jager (Huddersfield Underbank), 8 Bevan Williamson (Rotterdam), 9 Chris Hodgetts (Hemel Stags), 10 Phil Parkinson (Nottingham Outlaws), 11 James Howitt (Coventry Bears), 12 Raymond Den Engelsman (Hoek van Holland) 13 Jason Bruygoms (Rotterdam). Subs: 14 Benjamin Blom (Sassenheim)15 Johnny Qua (Rotterdam) 16 Soerd Niebor (WC Haaglanden) 17 Jonathan McKenzie (Sassenheim)
Tries: Howitt (6, 38), De Jager (79); **Goal:** De Jager
RUSSIA: 1 Oleg Sokolov (Strela Kazan), 2 Nikolay Zagoskin (Lokomotiv Moscow), 3 Sergey Dobrynin (Lokomotiv Moscow), 18 Denis Korolev (Lokomotiv Moscow), 5 Sergey Bychkov (Vereya Bears), 6 Victor Nechaev (Lokomotiv Moscow), 7 Artem Grigoryan (Lokomotiv Moscow), 8 Andrey Dumalkin (Lokomotiv Moscow), 9 Roman Ovchinnikov (Lokomotiv Moscow), 10 Robert Illiasov (Lokomotiv Moscow), 12 Oleg Smirnov (Vereya Bears), 13 Vladimir Vlasyuk (Vereya Bears). Subs: 14 Andrey Koltykhov (Lokomotiv Moscow), 11 Yan Gvozdev (Lokomotiv Moscow), 16 Sergey Konstantinov (Vereya Bears), 22 Georgy Vinogradov (Lokomotiv Moscow)
Tries: Korolev (10, 22, 30, 50), Dobrynin (12), Bychkov (25), Koltykhov (43, 61); **Goals:** Grigoryan 4
Half time: 10-26 *(at Hoekse Boys FC)*

Saturday 13th May 2006

SERBIA 10 GEORGIA 45

SERBIA: 1 Dalibor Vukanovic (Warrington Wizards); 2 Dimitris Daly (Dorcol Spiders); 3 Nenad Tomic (Dorcol Spiders); 4 Milan Dordevic (Dorcol Spiders); 5 Zoran Pesic (Warrington Wizards); 6 Luke Simeunovic (Halifax); 7 Mate Granvic (Dorcol Spiders); 8 Radoslav Novakovic (C) (Dorcol Spiders); 9 Jovan Vujosevic (Dorcol Spiders); 10 Mario Milosavljevic (Vodjvodina Rams); 11 Marko Jankovic (Dorcol Spiders); 12 David Milovanovic (Blacktown St Pats, Penrith); 13 Marko Zebeljan (Vodjvodina Rams); Subs (all used): 14 Valcic Radovan (Dorcol Spiders) 15 Milos Milinkovic (Dorcol Spiders); 16 Soni Radvanovic (Warrington Wizards); 17 Darko Nerandzic (Pancevo Warriors)
Tries: Tomic (27), Pesic (71); **Goal:** Vukanovic
GEORGIA: 1 George Asatiani; 2 Lexo Gugava; 3 Manughar Namchevadze; 4 Alexandre Gilauri; 5 Zviadi Koberidze; 6 Merab Kuirikashvili; 7 George Sordia; 8 Tornike Ashvetia; 9 Beqa Kurashvili; 10 George Khositashvili; 11 Nikoloz Mkheidze; 12 Shalva Sutiashvili; 13 Kakhaber Kobakhidze; Subs (all used): 14 Pridon Udesiani; 15 Vakhtang Akhvlediani; 16 Roin Chikvaidze; 17 George Nemsadze
Tries: Kuirikashvili (2, 30, 78), Nemsadze (37), Asatiani (48), Udesiani (60), Gugava (62, 67); **Goals:** Kuirikashvili 6; **Field goal:** Kuirikashvili
Half-time: 6-19; **Referee:** Matthew Kidd (England)
(at FK Radnicki Stadium, Belgrade)

Friday 26th May 2006

GEORGIA 57 HOLLAND 16

GEORGIA: 1 George Asatiani; 2 Lexo Gugava; 3 Revaz Gigauri; 4 Alexander Gilauri; 5 Zviad Koberidze; 6 Merab Kvirikashvili; 7 George Sordia; 8 Tornike Ashvetia; 9 Beqa Kurashvili; 10 Davis Gasviani; 11 Nika

Mkheideidze; 12 Shalva Sutiashvili; 13 Kakhaber Kobakhidze (C); Subs (all used); 14 Grigol Nishnianidze; 15 George Nemsadze; 16 Irakli Natriashvili; 17 Manuchar Namchevadze
Tries: Asatiani (13), Gigauri (23) Gugava (31) Kvirikashvili (37), Ashvetia (50), Mkheideidze (58), Koberidze (60, 78), Kurashvili (64), Sutiashvili (79); **Goals:** Kvirikashvili 8; **Field goal:** Kvirikashvili
HOLLAND: 1 Kees Foxton; 2 Roelof Haar; 3 Duncan Taylor; 4 Ronald Van Der Broek; 5 Jamie Groeneweg; 6 Aaron De Jager (C); 7 Benjamin Blom; 8 Phil Parkinson; 9 Chris Hodgetts; 10 Bevan Williamson; 11 Raymond Den Engelsam; 12 Bernard Van Holstein; 13 Alex Hoogezand; Subs (all used); 14 Vincent Grimbergen; 15 Johnny Qua; 16 Sjoerd Nieboer; 17 Jason Bruygoms
Tries: Duncan (39, 58); **Goals:** De Jager 4
Half-time: 23-10; **Referee:** Andrew Smith (England);
Attendance: 10,935 *(at Locomotiv Stadium, Tbilisi)*

Sunday 4th June 2006

SERBIA 6 RUSSIA 44

SERBIA: 1 Dalibor Vukanovic; 2 Dimitris Dajc; 3 Milan Radojevic; 4 Milan Djordjevic; 5 Nenad Grbic; 6 Mate Granic; 7 Jovan Vujosevic; 8 Radoslav Novakovic (C); 9 Zoran Pesic; 10 Soni Radovanovic; 11 Darko Nerandzic; 12 Nemanja Popsogorovic; 13 Luka Simeunovic; Subs (all used); 14 Ivan Susnjara; 15 Nenad Tomic; 16 David Milovanovic; 17 Milos Milinkovic
Goals: Vukanovic 3
RUSSIA: 1 Oleg Zukov; 2 Nikolay Zagoskin; 3 Sergey Dobrynin; 4 Denis Korolev; 5 Valentin Baskakov; 6 Victor Nechaev; 7 Artem Grigoryn; 8 Ian Gvozdev; 9 Roman Ochinnikov; 10 Robert Illiassov; 11 Andrey Medvedev; 12 Sergey Konstantinov; 13 Vladimir Vlasyk; Subs (all used); 14 Georgy Vinogradov; 15 Sergey Bychkov; 16 Sergey Konstantinov; 17 Vadim Fedchlic
Tries: Grigoryn 2, Dobrynin 2, Zukov 2, Zagoskin, Vinogradov, Smirnov; **Goals:** Grigoryn 4
Half-time: 6-16; **Referee:** Matthew Thomasson (England)
(at FK Radnicki Stadium, Belgrade)

Saturday 17th June 2006

HOLLAND 38 SERBIA 26

HOLLAND: 1 Rudy Stanford-Smyth; 2 Jamie Groeneweg; 3 Dayne Neirinckx; 4 Ronald Van Der Broek; 5 Cyril Breinburg; 6 Benjamin Blom; 7 Aaron De Jager; 8 Bernard Van Holsteijn; 9 Chris Hodgetts; 10 Bevan Williamson; 11 Vincent Grimbergen; 12 Raijmond Den Engelsman; 13 Duncan Taylor; Subs (all used); 14 Johnny Qua; 15 Alex Hoogezound; 16 Jason Bruygoms; 17 Justin De Hey
Tries: Den Engelsman (2, 58), Grimbergen (21), Stanford-Smyth (27, 79), Neirinckx (30), Taylor (34); **Goals:** De Jager 5
Sin bin: Neirinckx (10) - fighting
SERBIA: 1 Dalibor Vukanovic; 2 Dimitris Dajc; 3 Milan Radojevic; 4 Milan Dordevic; 5 Nenad Grbic; 6 Luke Simeunovic; 7 Mate Granic; 8 Radoslav Novakovic; 9 Jovan Vujosevic; 10 Soni Radovanovic; 11 Darko Nerandzic; 12 Nemanja Popsogorovic; 13 James Simeunovic; Subs (all used); 14 Zoran Pesic; 15 Vukasin Popovic; 16 Marko Zebeljan; 17 David Milovanovic
Tries: Grbic (18, 77), J Simeunovic (43), Pesic (49, 55); **Goals:** Vukanovic 3
Sin bin: Vujosevic (10) - fighting; Popsogorovic (50) - professional foul
Half-time: 26-6; **Referee:** Peter Brook (England)
(at Rotterdamse RC Beekweg, Rotterdam)

OTHER WORLD CUPS

STUDENT WORLD CUP *(held at Langlands Park & Griffith University, Brisbane, 5th - 19th July 2008)*

FINAL: England 18 Australia 26
SEMI-FINALS: England 30 New Zealand 22; Australia 26 Wales 10; Scotland 4 France 34 *(Plate)*; Greece 28 Ireland 10 *(Plate)*
RANKING GAMES: New Zealand 24 Wales 18 *(3rd/4th)*; France 12 Greece 14 *(Plate Final)*; Scotland 18 Ireland 22 *(7th/8th)*
POOL GAMES: France 42 Wales 6 *(at Burleigh)*; New Zealand 32 Ireland 10; Australia 54 Greece 0; Scotland 0 England 32; France 11 Ireland 2; New Zealand 28 Wales 10; England 12 Greece 20; Australia 58 Scotland 0; New Zealand 22 France 10; Ireland 12 Wales 32; Scotland 0 Greece 14; Australia 24 England 0

POLICE WORLD CUP

FINAL: Fiji 20 New Zealand 12
RANKING GAME: Great Britain 2 Australia 22
POOL GAMES: New Zealand 26 Fiji 20; Australia 34 Papua New Guinea 6; Great Britain 18 Papua New Guinea 16; Fiji 40 Australia 4; New Zealand 40 Papua New Guinea 6; Australia 32 Great Britain 16; Fiji 72 Papua New Guinea 12; New Zealand 40 Great Britain 0; Fiji 38 Great Britain 8; New Zealand 14 Australia 10

ARMED FORCES WORLD CUP

FINAL *(Sunday 16th November 2008)*
Great Britain 26 Australia 16 *(at Sydney Football Stadium)*
RANKING GAME: New Zealand 32 Cook Islands 10

POOL GAMES: Great Britain 36 New Zealand 26; Australia 38 Papua New Guinea 0; Australia 38 Cook Islands 14; Great Britain 84 Papua New Guinea 6; Australia 18 New Zealand 13; Cook Islands 50 Papua New Guinea 12; Great Britain 36 Australia 16; New Zealand 38 Cook Islands 22; Great Britain 40 Cook Islands 20; New Zealand 76 Papua New Guinea 4

WOMENS WORLD CUP

FINAL *(Saturday 15th November 2008)*
Australia 0 New Zealand 34 *(at Suncorp Stadium, Brisbane)*
SEMI-FINALS: England 4 New Zealand 16; Australia 32 Pacific Islands 6
MINOR SEMI-FINALS: Samoa 32 France 0; Russia 24 Tonga 12
RANKING GAMES: England 24 Pacific Islands 0 *(3rd/4th)*; Samoa 52 Russia 8 *(5th/6th)*; Tonga 34 France 4 *(7th/8th)*
POOL GAMES: England 72 Russia 0; Australia 60 France 0; New Zealand 72 Pacific Islands 0; Tonga 0 Samoa 40; Australia 72 Russia 0; England 54 France 4; New Zealand 42 Tonga 4; Pacific Islands 26 Samoa 22; New Zealand 26 Samoa 4; Pacific Islands 44 Tonga 14; Russia 18 France 12; Australia 22 England 4

WHEELCHAIR WORLD CUP

FINAL: England 44 Australia 12
SEMI-FINALS: England 66 Pacific Island Barbarians 0; Australia 22 France 20
RANKING GAME: Pacific Island Barbarians 0 France 52
POOL GAMES: England 78 Pacific Island Barbarians 4; England 34 Australia 26; England 26 France 18; France 100 Pacific Island Barbarians 0; Australia 82 Pacific Island Barbarians 0; France 44 Australia 18

POOL 1

ENGLAND 32 PAPUA NEW GUINEA 22

ABOVE: Ade Gardner and David Moore contest a high ball

LEFT: Jason Chan (centre) jumps for joy following his try

BELOW: Martin Gleeson goes past George Moni to score

AUSTRALIA 30 NEW ZEALAND 6

ABOVE: Josh Perry brought down by Adam Blair and Nathan Fien

RIGHT: Greg Inglis flicks out a pass under pressure from Thomas Leuluai

NEW ZEALAND 48 PAPUA NEW GUINEA 6

BELOW: Adam Blair crashes over for a try

AUSTRALIA 52 ENGLAND 4

ABOVE: A dejected England side reflect on a heavy defeat

RIGHT: Billy Slater holds off Leon Pryce on the way to a try

BELOW: Rob Burrow upends Israel Folau

POOL 1

ENGLAND 24 NEW ZEALAND 36

ABOVE: England turn their backs as New Zealand perform the Haka

BELOW: Jamie Jones-Buchanan can't stop Nathan Fien from scoring

AUSTRALIA 46
PAPUA NEW GUINEA 6

ABOVE: Darius Boyd gets to grips with Keith Peters

FRANCE 36 SCOTLAND 18

LEFT: Andrew Henderson feels the force of Jamel Fakir's challenge

POOL 2

FIJI 42 FRANCE 6

ABOVE: Semisi Tora goes airborne to score

FIJI 16 SCOTLAND 18

RIGHT: Oliver Wilkes celebrates a crucial try

ABOVE: Joy for Scotland following their first ever World Cup win

ABOVE RIGHT: Vula Naqua dumped by Danny Brough

POOL 3

IRELAND 20 TONGA 22

ABOVE: Michael Jennings beats Scott Grix on the way to scoring the opening try of the game

IRELAND 34 SAMOA 16

RIGHT: Harrison Hansen and Tony Puletua block the path of Gareth Haggerty

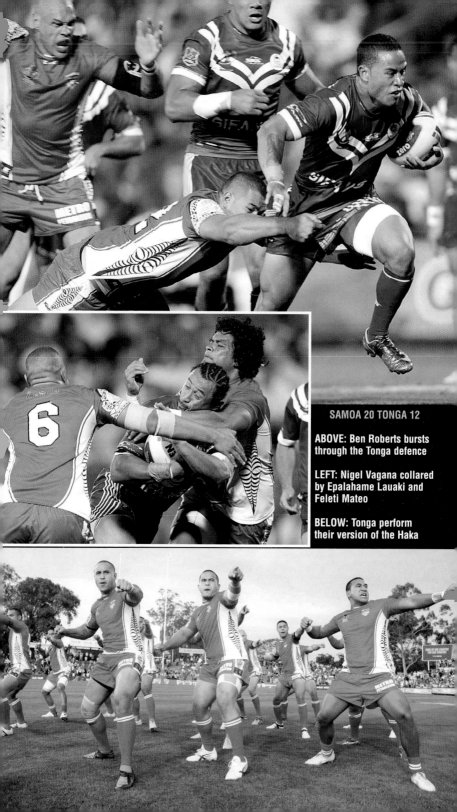

SAMOA 20 TONGA 12

ABOVE: Ben Roberts bursts through the Tonga defence

LEFT: Nigel Vagana collared by Epalahame Lauaki and Feleti Mateo

BELOW: Tonga perform their version of the Haka

PLAY-OFFS

SCOTLAND 0 TONGA 48

ABOVE: Sam Moa pushes off Oliver Wilkes, as Andrew Henderson is grounded

FRANCE 10 SAMOA 42

LEFT: Francis Meli races in for a try

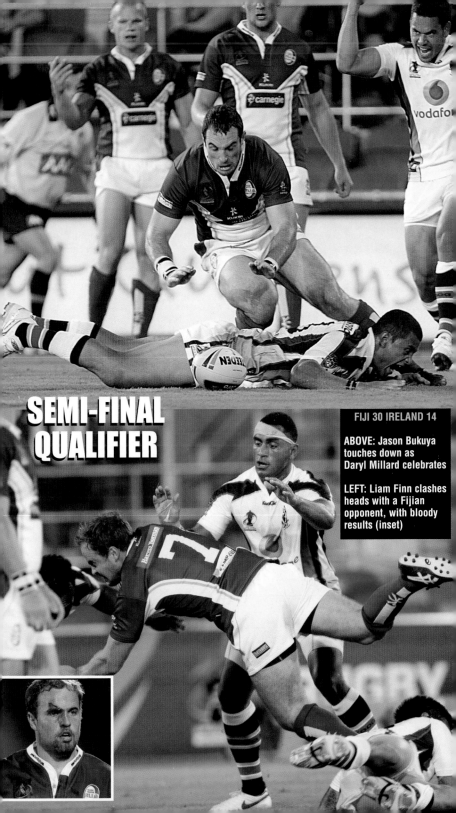

SEMI-FINAL QUALIFIER

FIJI 30 IRELAND 14

ABOVE: Jason Bukuya touches down as Daryl Millard celebrates

LEFT: Liam Finn clashes heads with a Fijian opponent, with bloody results (inset)

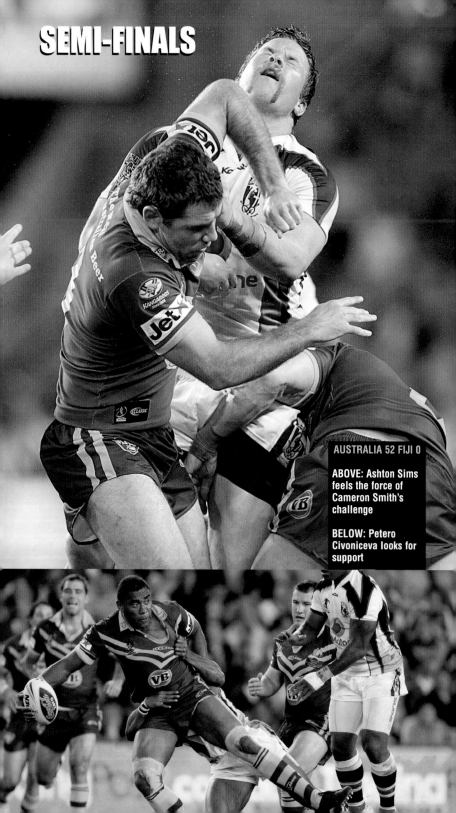

AUSTRALIA 52 FIJI 0

ABOVE: Ashton Sims feels the force of Cameron Smith's challenge

BELOW: Petero Civoniceva looks for support

ENGLAND 22 NEW ZEALAND 32

LEFT: Jamie Peacock crashes over for a try

BELOW LEFT: Jon Wilkin and James Roby get to grips with Lance Hohaia

BELOW: A despondent Adrian Morley thanks the England fans for their support

AUSTRALIA 20 NEW ZEALAND 34

ABOVE: Anthony Tupou hit by Sam Rapira

BELOW: Benji Marshall and the Kiwis face up to the Australian side during the Haka

FINAL

ABOVE: New Zealand
- 2008 World Cup Winners

BELOW: Nathan Cayless,
flanked by Wayne Bennett
(left) and Stephen Kearney
(right) lift the World Cup

ELOW and RIGHT: Fans of the competing
ations enjoy the 2008 World Cup

TWO THAT MISSED OUT ON 2008.

ABOVE: Wales' Ian Webster in
action against Scotland

LEFT: Lebanon line up before the
Qualifying Final with Samoa,
at Featherstone

2

A HISTORY OF THE RUGBY LEAGUE WORLD CUP

1954

The credit for getting the World Cup off the ground must go to the French. Almost as soon as France began playing League in the 1930s they had urged their British neighbours to recognise the value of an international World Championship.

By early 1952, on the back of their sensationally successful first tour of Australia the summer before, when France returned triumphant from a three-match series, the dynamic young president of the French League, Paul Barriere, was more eager than ever to grasp the opportunities offered by a World Cup.

Air travel to and from the southern hemisphere was becoming a reality for Rugby League teams, and with only four Test-playing nations - France, Great Britain, Australia and New Zealand - the logistics of bringing them all together for a World Cup appeared to be fairly straightforward.

Barriere's idea was backed by RFL secretary Bill Fallowfield but the Australians were opposed to having a World Cup. It was only after the French offered to stage the first tournament in the autumn of 1954, with a financial guarantee of £25,000 to cover the travel costs of the visiting teams, that the Aussies were persuaded to go ahead.

The World Cup story was born. And a lot of the best known Rugby League players were left to rue the fact that they turned down the opportunity to go down in history as a member of the first British team, in any sport, to be crowned World Cup winners.

The story of Great Britain's

Paul Barriere arranged for the Federation Francaise de Jeu a Treize (the game was still at this stage denied use of the word 'rugby' by the French authorities) to donate the original World Cup - a magnificent trophy, standing two-and-a-half feet high and weighing over half a hundredweight. The magnificent cup was lost sometime after the World Cup of 1968, when a new trophy was cast in honour of the sponsors of the 1970 competition and turned up in the mid-1990s in a builder's skip in Bradford. The trophy was restored and presented to Australia, winners of the 2000 competition.

triumph in the very first Rugby League World Cup is a true sporting legend. Inspired by their captain Dave Valentine, the British boys defied all the pre-tournament predictions. Described by critics back home as 'no hopers', they crossed the Channel and returned as conquering heroes.

The triumph of Scotsman Valentine and his men put the icing on the cake of what, with hindsight, has come to be recognised as a wonderfully successful inaugural World Cup tournament.

It's part of the game's folklore now that, coming so soon after a long and particularly gruelling tour to Australia and New Zealand in the summer of 1954, most of Great Britain's recognised international players declared themselves unavailable to travel to France for the first World Cup. Only three of the returned tourists - Dave Valentine, Phil Jackson and Gerry Helme - took part in what turned out to be an amazing triumph.

Legend has it that twenty-three players, including seven from the tour squad made themselves unavailable and two, Billy Boston and Geoff Gunney had to withdraw because of injury, although Halifax prop John Thorley claimed in an interview in Rugby League World magazine in 2004, on the 50th anniversary of the first World Cup final, that Boston and Gunney were the only two withdrawals. 'The money was incidental - we played for honour and for Great Britain,' said Thorley. The pay for three weeks away from home was £25, though the Rugby Football League promised to pay a £10 bonus if the cup was won, subsequently raised to £25.

The cost-cutting extended to taking a coach round France - which the team shared with accompanying British journalists, who Thorley says became almost part of the team, and where they usually sang a Scottish anthem, led by David Rose and Valentine. In the days before coaches became so important, Great Britain's rugby coach, Wigan's Joe Egan, was left at home.

'We had two training sessions - one at Rochdale and one at Huddersfield, but Joe wasn't allowed to come,' said Thorley. 'So what we did instead when we went out training was we all did a different exercise ourselves, and Dave Valentine used to oversee training.'

The British players even overcame arriving at one training session in Paris without a ball - so Thorley remembers Jack Bentley and his fellow reporters parcelling up their coats into makeshift replacements.

The Australians, having just won back the Ashes from Great Britain, went to France as favourites for the World Cup. But both the Aussies and the New Zealanders would be handicapped by a lack of match fitness, their domestic seasons having finished some two months before the tournament started, and neither having played any warm-up games.

The Kiwis had the honour of playing in the very first World Cup game against the host nation as the competition kicked off on Saturday,

Great Britain captain Dave Valentine holds aloft the World Cup after the Lions had triumphed in the first tournament

October 30th, 1954 in Paris. A crowd of 13,240 paying spectators were at the Parc des Princes to see the World Cup open in an atmosphere of uncertainty. The relative form of the teams was unknown, and the success of the tournament as a whole could have been made or marred by that first game.

There was no need to worry. Right from the kick-off, a high standard of play was set, which was maintained throughout the series, rising to a dramatic crescendo in the final (unscheduled) deciding match - also at the Parc des Princes.

For maximum impact the French organisers had chosen to stage the six matches of the first Rugby League World Cup in big cities the length and breadth of France – Paris, Lyon, Bordeaux, Marseille, Toulouse and Nantes. The major municipal stadiums, including the capital's Parc des

Great Britain's John Thorley halted by the Australian defence

Princes, would host the matches, which were to be played over a three-week period.

France, captained by their famous fullback Puig Aubert, got off to the winning start they and the tournament needed, beating the gallant Kiwis 22-13. Kiwi winger Jim Edwards had the honour of scoring the competition's first try, but it wasn't long before the French took control. Livewire hooker Jean Audoubert and big second-rower Guy Delaye proved unstoppable from close range and, despite a rallying try from Kiwi captain Cyril Eastlake, the French were worthy winners.

That left the spotlight to fall on Great Britain's opening match against Australia the following day at the huge Stade Gerland in Lyon.

Britain's 28-13 victory was greeted with great enthusiasm, the new look young team, superbly led by captain Valentine, upsetting all the odds with a courageous display to be ranked alongside many of their finest moments in the history of Test football.

'Salute the new Britain,' commented one national newspaper report. 'Forty years later the spirit of Rorke's Drift can still confound the Aussies.'

It was a game that marked the Great Britain debut of 20-year-old Mick Sullivan, then of Huddersfield, who went on to become the most capped British player in the history of the game.

Sullivan exemplified the British attitude in what the Daily Express called 'the bulldog courage, the driving enthusiasm that whipped Australia in this duel in the sun'. Flattened by Harry Wells in a head-on tackle, the young Huddersfield star staggered off the field with a gash over his eye, but returned patched up to put in a huge defensive effort that helped the British to a surprise win.

Helme dictated play from the scrum-base, while young Leeds stand-off Gordon Brown and Jackson both touched down twice. Leigh winger Frank Kitchen scored the try of the match following a 60-metre run, Huddersfield's Rose ran in another from the opposite wing and fullback Jimmy Ledgard, who had pulled off two try-saving tackles, kicked five goals.

'No complaints,' said Australia's coach Vic Hey. 'Great Britain were the better team. They opened at a killing pace and ran us out of it.' Great Britain captain Dave Valentine reflected: 'I wouldn't have missed this for anything, particularly after all these withdrawals. I wonder how some of the chaps back home are feeling now.'

The Great Britain team left Lyon on a 13-hour coach trip to Toulouse, breaking their journey at Avignon, before facing the other unbeaten side, France, the following Sunday. The match decisively showed the French appetite for spectacular rugby as a record crowd of 37,471 spectators turned up to watch this first full international to be played in Toulouse. With eight of the 1951 touring side in their ranks, France had an established side that would prove a severe test for the improvised British team.

It was a thrilling, combative game. Britain thought they had the match won when Helme dummied his way over, following tries by Rose and Brown. Fine handling by the French backs, though, ended with winger Raymond Contrastin plunging over in the corner. But Puig Aubert, apparently tired out from having been given the run-around by the British kicking game, later claimed he didn't have the energy to add the goal which would have won the match for the French, and it ended in a 13-all draw.

That proved to be a crucial stroke of good fortune for the inaugural World Cup tournament because, as events unfolded, the draw meant France and Great Britain finished the scheduled fixtures level on points, and a play-off became necessary to decide the title.

Remarkably, the Rugby League authorities didn't take the hint and recognise the dramatic impact of having a final as the climax of each World Cup. The game had to wait another 14 years, until the 1968 tournament, before an 'official' World Cup final would be played.

Whilst Great Britain and France were involved in that epic draw in Toulouse, Australia and New Zealand met in Marseille, before another 20,000 spectators, and it was the Aussies, inspired by their captain Clive Churchill, who came out on top 34-15, centre Alex Watson scoring three tries.

That left the two European nations both needing to win their remaining match to finish level. And both did, on Thursday, Armistice Day, November 11th, with Great Britain comfortably overcoming New Zealand in Bordeaux 26-6, and France killing off Australia's hopes of salvaging something from the tournament by winning 15-5 in front of over 13,000 people in the city of Nantes.

And so the stage was set for the first ever Rugby League World Cup final, remarkably arranged at just two days' notice. A crowd of over 30,000 filled the Parc des Princes in Paris almost to capacity to see France, skippered by Puig Aubert, and Great Britain, led by Dave Valentine, produce a match full of passion, colour and excitement.

It was a tense affair, full of cut and thrust. France took an early lead from a fine Puig Aubert penalty goal, kicked with typical nonchalance, but it was Great Britain who controlled the first period. Rose and Brown both posted first-half tries to maintain their record of having scored in every round, Ledgard converting the second before Puig Aubert added another penalty to give an 8-4 half-time score. But when Vincent Cantoni's strong running brought a converted try, France took a one-point lead, to which the British, with Valentine again giving the lead, responded by increasing their efforts.

Helme jinked his way under the posts for Ledgard to convert and Britain were back in front. Brown's second try stretched their lead but the French came back at them, Contrastin cutting the deficit with a well-taken try. The pressure was intense, but Britain held on and, against all predictions, became the first-ever world champions.

THE FIRST WORLD CUP FINAL

GREAT BRITAIN beat FRANCE 16-12.
November 13, 1954
at Parc des Princes, Paris.

GREAT BRITAIN: Ledgard, Rose, Jackson, Naughton, Sullivan, Brown, Helme, Thorley, Smith, Coverdale, Watts, Robinson, Valentine.
Tries: Brown 2, Rose, Helme.
Goals: Ledgard 2

FRANCE: Puig Aubert, Contrastin, Merquey, Tesseire, Cantoni, Jiminez, Crespo, Rinaldi, Audobert, Krawzyk, Save, Pambrun, Verdier.
Tries: Cantoni, Contrastin.
Goals: Puig Aubert 3

Referee: Charlie Appleton
(Warrington, England)
Attendance: 30,368

1954 WORLD CUP RESULTS

FRANCE beat NEW ZEALAND 22-13
At Parc de Princes, Paris. Crowd: 13,240

GREAT BRITAIN beat AUSTRALIA 28-13
At Lyon. Crowd: 10,250

AUSTRALIA beat NEW ZEALAND 34-15
At Marseille. Crowd: 20,000

FRANCE drew with GREAT BRITAIN 13-13
At Toulouse. Crowd: 37,471

FRANCE beat AUSTRALIA 15-5
At Nantes. Crowd: 13,000

GREAT BRITAIN beat NEW ZEALAND 26-6
At Bordeaux. Crowd: 14,000

FINAL TABLE

	P	W	D	L	F	A	Pts
Great Britain	3	2	1	0	67	32	5
France	3	2	1	0	50	31	5
Australia	3	1	0	2	52	58	2
New Zealand	3	0	0	3	34	82	0

Valentine and Gerry Helme were carried shoulder-high at the end by delighted teammates to the cheers of the small band of British pressmen and supporters who were privileged enough to be in Paris on that famous day - Saturday, November 13th, 1954.

The team, with so little international experience, had been given no chance before the tournament, but Valentine and his men became British sporting heroes that day.

The enormity of what the Great Britain team achieved can never be overstated. But for the game as a whole, the spoils were even greater. As well as seeing over 30,000 people in Paris, and other stadiums packed in the major cities of the country as Rugby League fever swept the French nation, the final was televised live in the United Kingdom.

The impact of that was enormous, as one of the very first sporting events to be beamed back live from the continent, and most certainly the very first occasion, in any sport, that a British team had been seen in action on foreign soil in a World Cup final. Millions of television viewers throughout the country saw a marvellous exhibition of Rugby League, and a wonderful British victory.

It was a glorious response to all that early dithering back home. Alfred Drewry, in the Yorkshire Post, wrote: 'The glory of their achievement lies in the fact that the playing standard reached as a combination greatly exceeded the sum of the talents of the 13 members of it. There is no spectacle in sport more stirring than that of a team accomplishing more than theoretically it should be capable of doing'.

The tournament itself was judged a triumph of initiative and forward-thinking and the £40,000 outlay had been more than recouped. Drewry reported on the eve of the final that it had been shown that 'a tournament embracing all the Rugby League playing countries can be made into a success, which must rank as one of the most important milestones in the history of the game.'

The World Cup's architect, Paul Barrière, however, refused to his dying day in 2008 to allow his name to be given to the trophy, saying that it should be associated with all of French Rugby League, its players and officials.

On their way home after the inaugural World Cup in France, Australia and New Zealand played two exhibition games in California.

The ballyhoo before the games at Long Beach Memorial Stadium and the Los Angeles Coliseum was typically American. Australian captain, Clive Churchill, was given the Key to the City and escorted to the arena by police with their car sirens blaring.

Australia won both matches - 30-13 (before 1,000 spectators) and 28-18 (4,554 attendance).

The second encounter was called off early after a pea-soup fog descended on the ground and the players couldn't find the ball after it had been kicked into touch.

About 10 minutes after the players had left the field, it was realised that Australian winger Des Flannery was nowhere to be seen. He was found still in the fog, calling out for his mates. Or so the story goes!

1957

What a difference three years made. The Australians had been lukewarm about taking part in the inaugural World Cup. After all, their major competitions had finished a month before kick-off in the first game. Some of their players hadn't had a hit-out in more than two months. And unlike the modern era, no warm-up games were considered. The Aussies reckoned they had been lured into that tournament as nothing more than cannon-fodder for Great Britain and France who were battle-hardened after a couple of months of their respective seasons.

It was a different kettle of fish when it was suggested that Australia host the second World Cup. The Australian administrators under chairman 'Jersey' Flegg, one of the pioneers of the game Down Under, saw the financial success of the first tournament. The players in the Australian squad would be match-fit. And, more importantly, it would be a great way of celebrating the Silver Jubilee of the game in Australasia. In the official yearbook Flegg described the tournament as 'the most ambitious step yet undertaken by the code'. And he was spot on when adding 'it is bound to be a winner'.

However the Great Britain players were supremely confident. They had won back the Ashes only months earlier after beating the

Australia's 1957 World Cup hero Brian Carlson was unique. Carlson was chosen as a winger in the Australian squad, but switched to fullback after the regular custodian, Keith Barnes, was injured in the first game. Carlson's play in the remaining matches was a decisive factor in Australia's first Cup success.

Despite all this, as far as the club with which he had been playing was concerned, he was persona non grata. Carlson was captain-coach of the Blackall side in the Queensland country when he was selected for the Cup. The Blackall officials asked him to pull out of the squad and concentrate on club football. When he refused, the club dismissed him.

Unconcerned, Carlson went ahead to become the top-scorer in the World Cup with two tries and 15 goals. And North Sydney was only too pleased to snap up his services once the tournament was over.

touring Kangaroos in a series that saw the end of the illustrious Test career of Clive Churchill. The man Australians dubbed 'The Little Master' had been dropped after the First Test and been replaced by Newtown fullback Gordon 'Punchy' Clifford. The third and deciding encounter, at Swinton's Station Road ground had been a 19-0 walkover for the home side. No wonder the British were convinced of their impending success when they landed in the Western Australian capital of Perth after a flight halfway across the world that had taken three days.

Co-manager Hector Rawson summed up the mood in the British camp: 'This is the best English team to visit Australia. The side is strong in every department. We can't pick a weakness anywhere.' His comments were backed up by the famous English journalist and broadcaster Eddie Waring who later explained: 'I incurred the wrath of Australian fans by suggesting it was hardly worth paying the cost of taking the big trophy to Sydney. I reckoned that Great Britain could give Australia five points' start and France and New Zealand 10. Sadly, I was wrong.'

It all began to go pear-shaped in a warm-up game in Perth. Ray Price, who had played such an important role at pivot during the Ashes series, was injured. The Warrington stand-off missed all the World Cup games. Without Price Britain's prospects went downhill. Australia, under captain-coach Dick Poole, the fine centre from Newtown, had problems, too. Poole's clubmate Clifford was ruled out injured after being selected at No 1. His replacement was Welsh-born Balmain star Keith Barnes. As history would have it Barnes was destined to captain the Kangaroos on their next tour of Britain and France in two years' time. Also a late withdrawal was Australia's first-choice stand-off Bob Banks. He was replaced by Ken McCaffery.

In their opening match, against New Zealand at the Brisbane Cricket Ground ('The Gabba'), the Australians suffered further disruption. Veteran scrum-half Keith Holman twisted his left knee. Barnes, in his international debut, fractured his right cheekbone when courageously diving to tackle the rampaging Maori prop Henry Maxwell. And Holman's halfback partner Greg Hawick fell victim to a stiff-arm tackle that loosened two teeth that eventually had to be extracted. Neither Holman nor Barnes played again in the Cup series, although Hawick did turn out in what was basically a promotional match to conclude the Cup – Australia v the Rest of the World

Despite the setbacks, the Australians were untroubled to beat New Zealand 25-5, scoring five tries to one. Their first touchdown was a sensational effort from deep in their own territory. Poole scooped up a dropped ball and sent winger Brian Carlson on a long run. He in turn offloaded to a trailing Greg Hawick and then positioned himself for a return pass and the chance to score near the posts. It was the start of a great World Cup for Carlson (see accompanying story).

Poole, Holman and Hawick then combined to send South Sydney speedster Ian Moir in for a try and a 10-2 lead for Australia at the break. The Kiwis' lone try came early in the second half. A New Zealand kick saw the ball roll over behind Australia's tryline. Carlson and New Zealand captain Cliff Johnson raced to ground the ball. Johnson had a metre or so start and Carlson, realising he could not make up the distance, tugged at the Kiwi's shirt. The ball beat them over the dead-ball line, but New Zealand referee Vic Belsham awarded a penalty try.

It made no difference. The great second-row combination of Norm Provan and Kel O'Shea triumphed, each with a try before the ever-reliable Western Suburbs centre Harry Wells rubbed salt into the wound with a late touchdown.

On the same day at the Sydney Cricket Ground, the British made their expected good start to the tournament, overwhelming France 23-5 on a water-logged pitch in front of a huge crowd of 50,077, the most ever to watch an international match not involving Australia. The attendance would have been even greater but for the torrential overnight and morning rain that broke a long drought and kept at least 10,000 fans at home.

It was a very different French side than that which had mesmerised the Australian fans when France toured two years earlier. Only the legendary backs Jacques Merquey and Gilbert Benausse and the evergreen second-rower Gilbert Berthomieu remained from that winning combination.

Wigan centre Eric Ashton, who passed away in 2008, went on to captain what is generally regarded as the finest Great Britain team ever to tour Australia, when he would lead the famous 1962 Ashes-winning Great Britain tourists. But five years earlier, Ashton was a young player making his way in the game, and later spoke of the adventure the World Cup trip turned out to be.

'The plane took three days to get there. We had to come down and re-fuel frequently in those days, because the maximum flying time was just four or five hours.

'But when we arrived in Sydney it was amazing. I'd never experienced a city like it that was Rugby League mad. The game was so popular, and everybody wanted to see the tourists. We started with a function in Sydney Town Hall, and we were feted everywhere we went. I thought all my birthdays had come at once. They couldn't do enough for us.'

The friendship ended once the games began, however, although Ashton would only play against New Zealand in the tournament proper, before his selection for the Rest of the World side that took on the Aussies after the tournament had been completed.

Great Britain had an impressive line-up. Could there have been a better international threequarter line-up in the world than Billy Boston (Wigan), Phil Jackson (Barrow), Alan Davies (Oldham) and Mick

Sullivan (Huddersfield)? One would doubt it. The Welsh great Lewis Jones (Leeds) was at stand-off. The young Derek 'Rocky' Turner (Oldham) was about to show his superiority at loose forward and up front was the future 'Captain Courageous' Alan Prescott (St Helens) and arguably the greatest hooker in the world, Tommy Harris (Hull).

Again it was a case of five tries to one. Turner was the star of the match, standing wide in the rucks and confusing the French defenders. But it was the outside backs that helped themselves to the spoils, Sullivan scoring a brace. Merquey did not disappoint, but he didn't have the classy players around him as he did on the tour two years earlier.

Just two days later, on the Monday of the Queen's Birthday holiday weekend, the World Cup was decided. Ironically, the injuries Australia suffered in their opening match proved to be a bonus. And Great Britain suffered because of injuries sustained during the match.

Carlson had been switched to fullback for Australia. The hard-tackling Brian 'Poppa' Clay, who was equally at home at either loose forward or stand-off moved to No 6. Contemporaries were adamant that Clay was the most devastating tackler of his era. And it showed as he continually crunched Jones. The unfashionable McCaffery took over the scrum-half role. Britain's Turner was to always rate McCaffery as one of the greatest Australians – if not the greatest Australian – with whom he locked horns during his career.

The fans were ready for a traditionally tough encounter between the old enemies and 57,955 packed the Sydney Cricket Ground on a fine Monday afternoon. But Great Britain's hopes went out the window just 16 minutes after kick-off with Australia ahead 5-4. In a heavy tackle Davies ripped a thigh muscle and was forced to quit. In those days there were no substitutes, so the British were forced to play the remaining 64 minutes one man down. Midway through the second half Boston also sprained ligaments in his left knee. But by that stage the Australians were well and truly on top. Provan and O'Shea starred once again, driving through the rucks to give the backs space out wide in which to move.

Jones scored all of Great Britain's points. But he had a nightmare afternoon as Clay continuously crash-tackled him to the ground, sweeping his legs from under him. The Welsh wizard never graced the international arena again after the World Cup tournament – and later moved to Australia to finish his great career in Sydney's second-string competition.

On the same day at Brisbane's Exhibition Ground, some 22,142 fans watched France hold off a late New Zealand surge for a 14-10 victory. The Kiwis should have won, but their fullback Pat Creedy missed four easy attempts at goal from inside the 25-yard line. They had one of the greatest goalkickers in history Bill Sorensen as a back-up but never used him. To add to their torment, second-rower John Yates dropped the ball close to France's tryline with just two minutes left on the clock. In an unusual procedure, Benausse used a drop-kick to boot a penalty goal from 40 yards out during the match.

Australia only needed to beat France the following Saturday to claim the World Cup. Once again torrential rain kept the attendance down – this time to just 35,158. Gale-force winds didn't help either.

Carlson was in great form for Australia. He set up the only try of the first half. A towering kick was fumbled by Benausse and O'Shea was on the spot to gather the loose ball and score. Carlson also booted four goals, one from almost the halfway line for Australia to lead 11-4 at the interval. The French did not give up – especially centre Jean Foussat, who had scored two tries against the British. He was the best in the French line-up. He finished the game limping from an ankle injury. But his courage was evident when it was revealed later that he had played most of the match with a fractured cheekbone, too.

Seventeen minutes from full-time New Zealand referee Belsham sent off French loose forward Francis Levy for dissent. It was unfair. Levy had been pointing out that while Belsham's back was turned, Carlson had moved the ball five metres nearer the posts for the attempt of a conversion of a try by Poole.

Australia went on to beat the French 26-9 and claim the World Cup.

This left Great Britain and New Zealand to battle over second place. What an anti-climax it was

Auckland's Vic and Sel Belsham are two of the select few brothers to have played for New Zealand. But that's not why they are best remembered in the annals of Rugby League history.

Vic's international career was short-lived, touring Australia with the 1948 Kiwis, missing out on selection in the two Tests but playing in four of the six minor games. He achieved much more in later years by becoming one of only three New Zealand international players to referee Tests and the only one to control a World Cup game. He and Australia's Darcy Lawler were in charge during the 1957 World Cup.

Scrum-half Sel Belsham made his Test debut at the age of 24 on the 1955-56 tour of Great Britain and France, toured Australia in 1956 and returned a year later for the World Cup, his last international appearance.

Twice during the World Cup, Vic Belsham refereed matches in which his brother played - New Zealand v Australia and the Rest-of-the-World v Australia.

This feat is unique in international Rugby League.

with only 14,263 fans turning up at the Sydney Cricket Ground on the following Tuesday. For Alan Prescott's British team it was the final humiliation, losing 29-21 to the Kiwis. Each side scored five tries. The difference was Sorensen's seven goals to the three kicked by Jones.

The tournament wound up with Australia beating the Rest of the

World, captained by Merquey, 20-11. But the world side was a man short for most of the second half after Benausse was injured in a heavy tackle by Hawick. Carlson, who was named Man of the Tournament, had another great day. But the British showed just what might have been with an ounce of luck as winger Eric Ashton and loose forward Johnny Whiteley were stand-outs for Rest of the World.

The tournament was a great experience for international debutant Ashton, who had only been in the senior ranks with Wigan, for two years. Five years later he was to lead the Lions on their tour of Australasia. To this day Australian critics regarded Ashton's 1962 combination as the finest British side ever to tour. And only Puig Aubert's 1951 Frenchman are talked about with the same awe.

After the World Cup the British and French visited South Africa, where they played three games against each other in Johannesburg, Durban and East London.

1957 WORLD CUP RESULTS

GREAT BRITAIN beat FRANCE 23-5
At Sydney. Crowd: 50,007

AUSTRALIA beat NEW ZEALAND 25-5
At Brisbane. Crowd: 29,636

AUSTRALIA beat GREAT BRITAIN 31-6
At Sydney. Crowd: 57,955

FRANCE beat NEW ZEALAND 14-10
At Brisbane. Crowd: 28,000

AUSTRALIA beat FRANCE 26-9
At Sydney. Crowd: 35,158

NEW ZEALAND beat GREAT BRITAIN 29-21
At Sydney. Crowd: 14,263

FINAL TABLE

	P	W	D	L	F	A	Pts
Australia	3	3	0	0	82	20	6
Great Britain	3	1	0	2	50	65	2
New Zealand	3	1	0	2	44	60	2
France	3	1	0	2	28	59	2

1960

After seeing France and Australia stage the first two very successful tournaments in 1954 and 1957, the British got their turn to host the World Cup in 1960. And Great Britain won back the famous trophy first held aloft by Dave Valentine on that memorable day in Paris six years before.

However, victory in the 1960 World Cup, whilst it might have tasted just as sweet for the players, carried none of the romance that saw their first victory in 1954 generate such an impact.

On the contrary, the match that decided the destiny of the 1960 Word Cup - a rugged and spiteful slog between Britain and Australia in the mud of Odsal - did little to help the image of international Rugby League in the eyes of a national television audience.

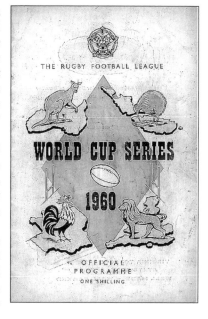

As in the first two tournaments, no final was scheduled, with the winners of the World Cup being declared as the team which finished top of the table after the round-robin of matches had been completed. With Great Britain and Australia viewed as the pre-tournament favourites, most predictions were that the deciding match would be when these two locked horns, so - with a keen sense of drama by the fixture planner, RFL secretary Bill Fallowfield - this key encounter was left to the final weekend of the competition.

In 1960, all six matches in the tournament were staged in the Rugby League heartlands of Lancashire and Yorkshire. There was no thought of taking a game to London, although when the Yorkshire Post announced the original itinerary on 16th February, 1960, New Zealand's game with France and the Great Britain-Australia tie were scheduled for midweek at Hull City's Boothferry Park and Leeds United's Elland Road respectively. The soccer authorities turned the plan down, so instead, only the established Test match venues of Wigan, Bradford, Leeds and Swinton were allocated games in the 1960 World Cup, with both Central Park and Odsal Stadium staging two matches each.

Another point, which fans of today might find hard to believe, but on each of the three Saturdays (no midweek games like in the 1954 and 1957 tournaments) on which World Cup games were played, the normal full programme of Rugby League club fixtures was also staged.

And only two referees were employed to take control of the six games - Eric 'Sergeant Major' Clay, from Castleford, and Frenchman Edouard Martung, a Police Inspector from Bordeaux, who in his warm-up club match failed to impress Salford and Halifax supporters by awarding 40 penalties amid 83 scrums.

Each of the four competing nations was allowed a squad of 18 players for the duration of the 1960 World Cup tournament, with Great Britain captained by Wigan centre Eric Ashton.

Britain were top dog over the Australians going into the competition, having retained the Ashes so dramatically on the sensational 1958 Lions tour (Alan Prescott's tour) and successfully retained them on home soil against the Kangaroos in 1959. That 1959 Ashes series had left the Aussies feeling badly done to, and less than happy about referee Clay.

The British team was able to recall a couple of the heroes (who, with the passing of time have become legends) of the 1958 Lions tour - Alex Murphy and Vince Karalius. Both had missed the 1959 Ashes series and, as events were to unfold, the 1960 World Cup triumph - and beating the Australians to achieve it - was to be the only really big moment for them both in international football in their own country.

Karalius's selection had not been a foregone conclusion, especially as he missed the World Cup trial at St Helens after turning up only 25 minutes before kick-off. And then when he was named he hinted he might not be able to make the first training session (two days before the opening game) because of work commitments. Widnes stand-off Frank Myler, who went on to captain the 1970 Ashes-winning Lions, scored three tries in the trial to force himself into the squad.

The recall of Karalius, along with forwards like Derek Turner, Jack Wilkinson and Hunslet's Brian Shaw, allied to the fact that the Aussies had virtually the same pack who felt so aggrieved at losing in the Ashes Tests just 12 months before (a pack including less than delicate flowers like Noel Kelly, Dud Beattie, Rex Mossop, Elton Rasmussen and Brian Hambly) was a recipe for explosive confrontation. 'The next few weeks are pregnant with uncertainty', the Times reported in one of its infrequent mentions of the World Cup.

The tournament got off to a great start, with 20,000-plus crowds at both the opening fixtures. Great Britain defeated New Zealand fairly comfortably, 23-8, at Odsal Stadium, although the biggest talking point surrounded Billy Boston. The Wigan winger was declared not fit enough to play at the start of the World Cup, so in Britain's first two games, against New Zealand and France, the Warrington pair of Bobbie Greenhalgh, a stand-off, and Jim Challinor wore the number two jersey. But, Billy - all 15 stones of him - was to return for the decider against Australia with devastating effect.

Whilst Eric Ashton was leading his men to that first-up win against the Kiwis, back at his home ground, Central Park, Australia and France were locked in a titanic battle. The Aussies got home by just one point, 13-12, thanks largely to the touches of individual brilliance provided by Reg Gasnier and Johnny Raper. France were considered unlucky not to have won the game, with drop-goal (worth two points) attempts by Claude Mantoulan, Georges Fages, Jackie Merquey and Louis Poletti all missing the target, while Andre Lacaze missed a penalty.

At the time, Bernard Ingham, who went on to gain notoriety as chief press secretary to British Prime Minister Margaret Thatcher, was a reporter at the Yorkshire Post and he described the tussle as 'a rousing opening', describing Australian tour manager Pat Duggan as having an 'unpractised hiker's glad to be home look' after the game.

> *Welshman Billy Boston is a true legend of Rugby League and at the time of the third World Cup in 1960 he was in his prime, selected in Great Britain's squad despite being injured on the Saturday before it was named in a league game for Wigan against Whitehaven. He only recovered in time for the decider against Australia at Bradford, scoring the first of Britain's two tries in typical fashion, handing off his opposite number, Brian Carlson, with his left hand and then powering to the corner.*
>
> *In all he won 31 caps for Great Britain, initially being selected for the 1954 Lions tour after a mere handful of games for Wigan, scoring a record 36 tries. He scored 571 career tries in total.*
>
> *Boston missed the 1954 World Cup through injury, but played in two games in the second tournament down under in 1957. On the way home, Great Britain's 1957 World Cup squad went to South Africa without him when the apartheid laws prevented him from travelling with them.*

France were captained in the 1960 World Cup by big second-rower Jean Barthe, a famous rugby union international who was equally successful after changing codes. Amongst a new breed of player, the French still had one survivor from their famous 1951 touring team - Jackie Merquey, who played stand-off in all three of their 1960 World

France's Henri Lacaze on the charge against Australia

Cup games.

The French had put everything into their monumental effort against the Australians in their opening game, and found they couldn't raise their game to similar heights in the following weeks against Great Britain and New Zealand. But while Great Britain always seemed to have the measure of the French on home soil - and duly beat them 33-7, a record World Cup score up to that point, before a near 23,000 crowd at Station Road, Swinton - the Australians always found France to be much tougher opponents, and the green and golds were mighty relieved to get that one-point victory over the Tricolours at Wigan.

Incidentally, Britain's big win at Swinton was not without incident, with the Times reporting that Barthe and Karalius were sent off 'after the third and frankest fist fight of the match'.

The Aussies had another close encounter before they managed to beat New Zealand, 21-15, at Headingley, thus setting up their match against Great Britain as the World Cup decider - a World Cup Final in everything but name - and 33,026 paid receipts of £9,113, to see it on a wet and murky afternoon at Bradford's Odsal Stadium.

But if those fans came to see the flowing, exciting football for which Rugby League was famous, they went home disappointed after what the Times described as '…this gloomy, muscular battle in the black bowl of Odsal'. Another newspaper report commented: 'Great Britain, with this win against the Aussies, lifted the World Cup, but the real winner in the

Things get heated between Great Britain and France at Station Road, Swinton

disappointing forward slog was the mud. It beat all attempts to make this match worthy of the meeting of the two best teams in the world.

'It reduced movement to a slow tempo - fitfully the football came to the surface with three excellent tries - two for the British and one for the Aussies. But most times tempers were fretfully near the boil; almost every tackle for 20 minutes in the second half had a neat slug packed into it.

'Three times the game boiled over into a brawling, milling mass of men. These Aussies do not stand on ceremony and are not the men for half measures, but I thought they would have had enough common sense to know that the British would not duck a battle. Certainly not with such men as Jack Wilkinson, Vincent Karalius and Derek Turner in the pack. These are men of raw courage and rare stamina. In the second half when the Aussies looked like they would get on top, it was this trio that kept the forward battle going Britain's way.'

Skipper Eric Ashton had won the toss for Great Britain, and he knew it was a good toss to win, because he was able to make the Australians play the first half with driving rain and a stiff wind blowing into their faces.

As well as bringing Billy Boston in on the right wing, Great Britain also had Saints' Austin Rhodes replacing Eric Fraser at fullback. And as a measure of Britain's first-half territorial superiority, with the wind and rain at their backs, Rhodes had no less than seven shots at goal, of which he successfully landed two.

The fireworks started after Australia's young star centre Reg Gasnier just managed to duck and avoid a vicious stiff-arm attempt. Soon after, British winger Mick Sullivan was flattened on the touchline and several forwards had a flare-up.

But Great Britain could still play some football, and Boston proved that the risk in playing him would pay dividends as he pushed off Brian Carlson and shot into the corner. Rhodes kicked a gem of a conversion from the touchline.

Soon after, Mick Sullivan came back to the fray to finish off a break by Murphy, created by Karalius's cleverly delayed inside pass.

With a 10-nil interval lead, and the mud beginning to take its toll, Great Britain looked in control, as the second half deteriorated in the Odsal gloom. Tempers did not improve as flare-ups continued, with referee Martung having a hard job to keep control amid the intermittent brawling.

Ten minutes from the end, Australia scored a consolation try by winger Carlson after a long run by Tony Brown.

The legendary Eddie Waring commented: 'The mud was the winner in a match where the best players, like Gasnier for instance, were never seen.'

Another famous British journalist of the time, Phil King of 'The People', was more stinging in his criticism. He reported: 'The World Cup came deservedly back to Great Britain. But if Rugby League folk think the televising of the fantastic second-half niggle was a good advert for the game, they must surely be the most optimistic salesmen in the world.'

1960 WORLD CUP RESULTS

GREAT BRITAIN beat NEW ZEALAND 23-8
At Odsal Stadium, Bradford.
Crowd: 20,577

AUSTRALIA beat FRANCE 13-12
At Central Park, Wigan. Crowd: 20,278

GREAT BRITAIN beat FRANCE 33-7
At Station Road, Swinton. Crowd: 22,923

AUSTRALIA beat NEW ZEALAND 21-15
At Headingley, Leeds. Crowd: 10,773

GREAT BRITAIN beat AUSTRALIA 10-3
At Odsal Stadium, Bradford.
Crowd: 32,773

NEW ZEALAND beat FRANCE 9-0
At Central Park, Wigan. Crowd: 2,876

FINAL TABLE	P	W	D	L	F	A	Pts
Great Britain	3	3	0	0	66	18	6
Australia	3	2	0	1	37	37	4
New Zealand	3	1	0	2	32	44	2
France	3	0	0	3	19	55	0

Alfred Drewry wrote in the Yorkshire Post: 'Some of the players all the time, and most of them some of the time, behaved more like hooligans than international footballers.'

Meanwhile, on the same afternoon as Odsal's war of attrition, over at Central Park, New Zealand and France fought out their own battle to avoid the wooden spoon. The Kiwis won, 9-nil, in front of only 2,876 spectators. Everyone else was at home watching Eric Ashton and his men lift the World Cup.

On Tuesday 11th October the Times reported that the RLIB met in Leeds to discuss the standard of play in the recently ended World Cup, particularly rough play. 'Tom Mitchell, vice chairman of the English Council promised concerted action'.

Despite some patchy attendances and foul British autumn weather, the 1960 World Cup showed a modest profit, the BBC's rights for the tournament netting £5,500. In his report, RFL secretary Bill Fallowfield wrote: 'Public attention has been focussed on low attendances, on rough play which was seen in one or two of the games, on the possible effect on League attendances, and on anything else which would assist the practice of criticising destructively, which seems to prevail in this day and age. Overlooked by many are the following points, that it was England's duty to promote the

The 1960 World Cup decider was one of the less glamorous encounters in the history of the tournament, spoiled by the Odsal wind and rain, as well as some brutality from both sides.

On the Monday morning after, the Yorkshire Post's Rugby League writer Alfred Drewry led his report: 'The receipts of £9,133 from this championship bout at Odsal enabled the promoters of the Rugby League World Cup just about to make ends meet. If it had produced a profit of £100,000 this game would still have been better not played...If the World Cup is going to foster this sort of savage rivalry, a lot of people who supported the idea wholeheartedly must regretfully have second thoughts.'

third World Cup series, that in spite of the drawbacks it paid its way, that in one game at least this country can take on all comers.'

1968

A World Cup had been scheduled in 1965, but when the 1964 French tour of Australia proved a financial disaster, the ARL unilaterally abandoned the idea. The touring Frenchmen had been outclassed even by moderate country sides. Embarrassed French players were subjected to the humiliation of wandering around venues selling autographed photographs to make ends meet. And to attract an even moderate attendance at the Third Test in Sydney, the ARL scheduled a curtain-raiser between NSW Colts and Other Nationalities, the latter side containing many former British and Kiwi Test stars playing in the local Premiership.

The World Cup was rescheduled for 1968. But it was only when France caused an upset series victory over the 1967-68 Kangaroos led by Johnny Raper that the Australians finally agreed to go ahead with the tournament. And the French were to ultimately prove to be the surprise packets of the competition.

After the anticlimax of the 1957 and 1960 World Cups where the winner was decided in the round-robin and the winners took on a Rest of the World combination, this time it was decided that the top two sides would play-off for the trophy in a final. It had really been New Zealand's turn to stage the tournament. But they realised not enough fans could be drawn through the turnstiles to make it a financial success. Just two matches were played in New Zealand – both in Auckland.

New rules would also play a significant role. In 1966 Britain had introduced the four-tackle rule and the southern hemisphere nations followed suit at the start of their season the following year. There is no doubt that the rule, to be amended in 1971 to six tackles, was a major factor in arguably some of the worst international displays of the post-World War II era.

And the spectacle as a whole was hardly helped by pedantic refereeing from New Zealander John Percival. It was the first time in the international arena that a referee had continually penalised players for back-chat. So often did Percival add another 10 yards to a penalty that the Australian media dubbed him 'Ten Yard Jack'. Most of the penalties for dissent were against the British, particularly hooker Kevin Ashcroft.

Even though they had been beaten in the Ashes series the previous year, the British had flown to Australia full of hope. Gone was Ashes captain, Hull Kingston Rovers' Bill Holliday. The great centre Neil Fox had been pencilled in as his replacement as skipper, but he had fallen victim to injury. So Leeds fullback Bev Risman, the son of the legendary Welshman Gus Risman, led the British with just two Rugby League Tests under his belt (against France earlier in the year) after eight internationals for England and four for the Lions in rugby union. The British had several new forwards including John Warlow (St Helens), Mick Clark (Leeds), Ray French (Widnes) and Charlie Renilson (Halifax). Renilson's form in the tournament so impressed officials of the Newtown club that he was back in Australia the following year playing for the Bluebags in the Premiership. And he was to eventually become an Australian Test selector.

Nearly the entire Australian squad was chosen from the Sydney Premiership ranks. There was no country representative on the selection panel which probably accounted for the fact that no player from 'The Bush' was in the 19-man side. And there were only three Queenslanders, prop Denis Manteit, hooker Brian Fitzgibbon and winger (and shock selection) Lionel Williamson.

Among the international debutants were two who were to carve a place in history. South Sydney fullback Eric Simms, who was later to be the catalyst for field goals to be reduced in value from two points to one, was an obvious choice after Kangaroo Les Johns was ruled out injured.

Bob Fulton, considered unlucky not to have toured with the 1967-68 Kangaroos, was to go on to become a legend in the game and one of the seven so-called 'Immortals' of the Australian game. Indeed five of Australia's 'Team of the Century' named in 2008 were in the squad – Fulton, fellow 'Immortals' Johnny Raper, Graeme Langlands and Arthur Beetson and a future World Cup-winning captain Ron Coote.

Australia got off to the perfect start when 62,256 fans packed the Sydney Cricket Ground to see the home side beat the British 25-10 in an uninspiring spectacle ruined by the haphazard panic football created by the four-tackle rule. And it would have been only the most xenophobic Australian who did not realise how much the refereeing of Percival contributed to the final result. He caned the British in the penalties 15-8. And Simms used those penalties to Australia's advantage, booting eight goals from nine attempts.

Hooker Ashcroft was dumfounded: 'I gave up with the referee. I didn't even strike for the ball when the scrums were near our posts. He was right impossible. I mean, he broke a man's heart.' RFL secretary and Great Britain manager Bill Fallowfield was asked by journalists what he had thought about Percival's effort. A wry smile spread over his face. 'In England it is an offence to criticise a referee,' he noted. 'Mind you, I'm

12,000 miles from home. But it's an ingrown habit with me not to criticise refs.'

The great Reg Gasnier, watching from the Members Stand, was not shackled by ARL rules: 'He was technically correct in his rulings, but there were too many stoppages. I would rather see the English system adopted where referees let matches run along as much as possible. At least, we would see some football that way. I hate to see play pulled up and a penalty awarded for a minor technicality.'

On the same day, across the Tasman Sea in Auckland, some 18,000 spectators packed the famous Carlaw Park arena to see the Frenchmen triumph over the Kiwis 15-10, more convincingly than the scoreline suggested, only five penalties by big winger Ernie Wiggs keeping the Kiwis in the game. New Zealand never had any real chance after second-rower Brian Lee was given his marching orders after just 12 minutes by Australian referee Col Pearce. The clever French stand-off Jean Capdouze, less than a year into his illustrious career that would see him capped 26 times, scored the only try of the game and added five goals for a personal tally of 13. The match also created history with World Cup substitutes being allowed for the first time – Adolphe Alésina (France) and Henry Tatana (New Zealand).

The Kiwis looked to have been back on track at Brisbane's Lang Park the following Saturday when they led Australia 7-4 at half-time. An upset seemed to be looming. The normally quiet-spoken Australian coach Harry Bath adopted a change of character as he talked to the Aussies as they licked their wounds.

'No, I didn't give them any needles in the dressing room,' the former champion Balmain, Warrington and St George player noted. 'I told them to get in and back up the man with the ball. The New Zealand forwards went to water. They didn't come back in the second half.'

But the master stroke was to pull Fulton off the bench to replace the pedestrian stand-off Tony Branson. It was Fulton's first international appearance – and it changed the whole equation.

'He livened up the attack,' said Bath. 'I was very pleased with him.' Pleased with him? The Australians ran in five second-half tries, while the Kiwis managed just one. Such was the confidence of the Australians that at one stage man of the match Ron Coote was across the tryline but instead of scoring a try himself he handed the ball to winger Johnny King to touch down.

'Johnny's been out of luck,' said Coote. 'I reckoned he deserved a try.' It wasn't a case of contempt for the Kiwis – but Coote was stating the obvious. The St George winger was really back in luck because later Fulton could also have scored but flung the ball to King because he was in a better position.

The final score of 31-12 had Kiwis coach Des Barchard shouting Australia's praises. 'No other side in the world has the speed or power of this Australian side,' he said. 'As far as I am concerned the World Cup is over.'

The British still believed it wasn't. But France, having suffered the indignity of being told they weren't up to standard for a World Cup in 1965, were determined to show the passion for Rugby League that still burned in their country.

Carlaw Park was always muddy. And by the time the British took on France the next day, rain during the week had turned it into a quagmire. It shouldn't have worried the Great Britain players. The conditions were so much like they would experience back home in the middle of winter. But somehow they were caught short. And they came up against some superb French defence.

How did the game attract 15,760 enthusiasts to watch a clash that didn't involve the Kiwis – and in the most appalling weather that normally would keep most people rugged up at home? Perhaps they were starved of international rugby. France accounted for Great Britain 7-2. The British ignored the conditions and threw the ball around. But all to no avail. Winger Jean-René Ledru scored the only try of the match to help the Frenchmen into the final. With their eyes on the decider the French then seemed to be too lackadaisical in their preliminary match against Australia at Brisbane's Lang Park and the host nation had no trouble in posting a 37-4 victory. Williamson and Fulton each grabbed a brace of tries for the Australians.

Britain and New Zealand fought to avoid the wooden spoon in their clash at the Sydney Cricket Ground. It drew one of the smallest attendances in the history of international matches in Australia – just 14,105. And most of them left well before full-time by which time the British had asserted their superiority to the tune of 38-14.

The Sydney Sunday Telegraph was scathing in its report of the encounter, suggesting those who had stayed until referee Col Pearce

THE 1968 WORLD CUP FINAL

AUSTRALIA beat FRANCE 20-2.
Monday 10 June, 1968
at Sydney Cricket Ground

AUSTRALIA: Simms, Williamson, Langlands, Greaves, Rhodes, Fulton, Smith, Wittenberg, Jones, Beetson, Thornett, Raper (C), Coote. Sub used: Rasmussen
Tries: Williamson (2), Greaves, Coote.
Goals: Simms 4

FRANCE: Cros, Pelerin, J Gruppi, Lecompte, Ledru, Capdouze, Garrigues, Sabatie, Begou, Ailleres (C), De Nadai, Marracq, Clar
Goal: Capdouze

Referee: John Percival (New Zealand)
Attendance: 54,290

1968 WORLD CUP RESULTS

AUSTRALIA beat GREAT BRITAIN 25-10
At Sydney. Crowd: 62,256

FRANCE beat NEW ZEALAND 15-10
At Auckland. Crowd: 18,000

AUSTRALIA beat NEW ZEALAND 31-12
At Brisbane. Crowd: 23,608

FRANCE beat GREAT BRITAIN 7-2
At Auckland. Crowd: 15,760

AUSTRALIA beat FRANCE 37-4
At Brisbane. Crowd: 32,662

GREAT BRITAIN beat NEW ZEALAND 38-14
At Sydney. Crowd: 14,105

FINAL TABLE						
	P	W	D	L	F	A	Pts
Australia	3	3	0	0	93	26	6
France	3	2	0	1	26	49	4
Great Britain	3	1	0	2	50	46	2
New Zealand	3	0	0	0	36	84	0

blew his whistle to register full-time deserved a medal: 'In a season of miserable representative matches, yesterday's had the dubious distinction of being by far the worst. It was dreadful. Nobody wants to watch a game of football in which players from both sides are quite obviously just going through the motions.'

Five of Australia's 'Team of the Century' named in 2008 were in the World Cup-winning squad of 1968 – Bobby Fulton, fellow 'Immortals' Johnny Raper, Graeme Langlands and Arthur Beetson and a future World Cup-winning captain Ron Coote.

The Great Britain players realised from the start that the Kiwis were going to offer little opposition and played accordingly. The British led 10-nil after 17 minutes, 20-4 at the interval and finished with eight tries, three of them to Welsh winger Clive Sullivan. Casual British defence gifted Kiwi centre Paul Schultz two second-half tries.

Despite the fact that Australia had flogged the Frenchmen only two days earlier, 54,290 fans still turned up at the SCG for the repeat clash in the World Cup final. The tournament organisers had expected it to have been an Australia-Britain encounter, otherwise the draw would have been arranged differently. The French showed a small improvement, but not enough to make a real match of it, Australia winning 20-2. Two of Australia's four tries came in the final nine minutes as the French tired. Once again referee Percival earned the ire of both sides. French captain Georges Ailleres fumed when Percival penalised France twice in successive play-the-balls to give Eric Simms a simple attempt at a penalty goal right in front of the posts.

The Sunday Telegraph noted: 'The Frenchmen tried valiantly. They tackled tenaciously, but did not have the class of this Australian side. There were no players of the class of [Elie] Brousse, [Edouard] Ponsinet, [Jacky] Merquey, Puig Aubert or Jean Dop to lift the team to a dangerous attacking force. In defence the players delighted the amazingly big crowd with some copybook low tackling. But [the Australians'] size told in the end.'

The Frenchmen stormed off at full-time while the Australian players were carrying captain Johnny Raper and coach Harry Bath shoulder high around the pitch. And they refused to return for the presentation ceremony despite pleas from their management.

Simms finished the tournament with a World Cup record 50 points (from 25 goals), topping the 36 scored by fellow-Australian Brian Carlson in 1957. Raper was inspirational, leading by example. And that other great back-rower Ron Coote was also prominent, achieving the remarkable feat for a forward of scoring a try in each of Australia's four games.

Prop Arthur Beetson, destined to become a legend of the game, continued his journey to greatness, two years after making his Test debut against the touring British Lions. Fulton, too, showed more than a glimpse of the talent that was to plague opposition sides for the next decade. Another Australian youngster, Canterbury threequarter Johnny Rhodes was voted Man of the Tournament. Sadly his career was plagued by chronic leg and shoulder injuries and his only other appearances in the green and gold were in the 1975 World Championship.

There was much soul-searching in the Great Britain ranks after losing their world title without even having made the final. But there were some bright spots, especially the displays by halfbacks Roger Millward and Tommy Bishop. As well as tormenting Australian Test sides, both were destined to make their marks in the Aussie Premiership with the Sydney club Cronulla.

Just as it had done in the first World Cup in 1954 when an unscheduled play-off had to be hastily arranged, the large crowd at the Final ensured a financial profit was made.

Buoyed by the financial success of the tournament the members of the International Board immediately announced that the next World Cup would be staged in England and France the following year.

It didn't surprise anyone when it wasn't!

1970

The fifth Rugby League World Cup tournament, which began with such a sense of optimism for Great Britain, ended in bitter disappointment for them.

It also ended amid unsavoury scenes in a Headingley final which did little to promote the image of the game.

The Headingley final would be the last time that the great Malcolm Reilly would ever wear a Great Britain shirt. Reilly would soon emigrate to Australia to play with Manly, and was an absentee from future Test series and World Cups played against Australia.

The 1970 competition, coming some 16 years after the first World Cup, saw three significant innovations for Rugby League.

First was the introduction of a tournament sponsor, and as a result the introduction of a new trophy. And the 1970 tournament also gave us the first World Cup games to be played under floodlights, and the first full internationals to be staged on Sundays in England.

The world of sponsorship, which rapidly became such an integral part of all major sports, was only beginning to open up back in 1970, when it was announced that the teams in the World Cup Series would be playing to win the 'V & G Trophy'.

Those initials stood for the Vehicle & General group of

During the 2008 World Cup, Ron Coote, one of Rugby League's all-time greats, remembered the 1970 World Cup Final played in Leeds as one of the hardest games of all time.

'The 1970 World Cup final was the toughest game of football I have ever played in,' said Coote. 'The final itself was brutal but nothing compared to the action after the full-time whistle involving every player on the Australian and Great Britain side.

'Great Britain winger John Atkinson went up to our fullback Eric Simms and gave him a whack across the shoulder. It was no love bite. From there the field erupted into an all-out brawl.

'Earlier Great Britain's Syd Hynes and our Billy Smith had been sent off and there was spite in every tackle.'

The Australian squad for the 1970 World Cup featured the only clergyman to have played international Rugby League for any country.

Father John Cootes was a Roman Catholic priest from Newcastle who was one of a select few of his profession who had been ordained by the Pope at the Vatican.

The World Cup was the highlight of a brief stay in the international limelight. Father Cootes had made his Test debut on the 1969 tour of New Zealand and retained his international jersey when the British Lions visited Australia the following year before he was named in Australia's 19-man squad for the Cup.

He was the focus of British media attention, especially when starting each day by saying mass at St Mary's Parish Church in Bradford.

'I'm a priest, that's what I do,' he explained to an interviewer from the BBC. Father Cootes even rated a full-page story in the Daily Sketch newspaper.

He was no slouch on the field, topping the World Cup tryscoring lists with five touchdowns - two each against New Zealand and France and another in Australia's 12-7 victory over Great Britain in the final at Headingley. And he scored Australia's only try when the tourists beat France 7-2 in an international at Perpignan on the way home.

This was his international farewell.

He later quit the priesthood and worked for a time as a television sports reporter before setting up a furniture business.

insurance companies. Sadly, becoming one of Rugby League's first major sponsors didn't appear to do them too much good because, just a few years later, the company went bust.

In a significant pointer of things to come in British Rugby League, respect for tradition was quickly pushed out of the window. The original World Cup trophy, borne with pride by the winning captains in the first four World Cup tournaments, was replaced by a rather puny little cup bearing the sponsor's name. The new trophy was to be won outright by the winning team, never to be seen again.

In the meantime it took fully 30 years for the magic of the original World Cup to be restored, when it was presented to the winning captain in the 2000 competition for the first time since Australia's Johnny Raper proudly carried it around the Sydney Cricket Ground in 1968.

There was an excuse for not using the original trophy for a large part of those 30 years, because it was stolen from the Aussies' hotel during the 1970 tournament and did not resurface for a quarter of a century, when it was found, by chance, on a rubbish tip in Bradford. Such was the lack of regard for the great original trophy in 1970 that The Times reported RFL secretary Bill Fallowfield as saying: 'Whoever has stolen the trophy has stolen the wrong one'.

As a precursor to the introduction of a sponsor,

television had definitely arrived in Rugby League, and the BBC covered all the Saturday and Sunday games live, plus highlights of the two Wednesday night matches.

It was ten years since the north of England had previously staged the World Cup - and the 1970 tournament was not finally confirmed until February that year. Nevertheless Great Britain were very confident they could repeat the feat of the victorious 1960 team.

Although the Australians were the Cup holders, having won it on home soil in 1968, just three months before the 1970 World Cup the British had won the Ashes back from the Aussies on the last successful Lions tour.

Great Britain's superiority in the two deciding Tests in Sydney suggested Australia had little hope of turning the tables in the World Cup. But the one enforced change to Britain's first-choice team proved to be highly significant. Roger Millward, so important in the Ashes win, was injured. His place at stand-off was taken by Mick Shoebottom, moving up from fullback, where the goal-kicking Ray Dutton came in.

How Great Britain were to miss Millward's attacking flair as they struggled unsuccessfully to break the Australian defence in the 1970 World Cup Final.

Quite the most remarkable thing about the 1970 competition was that Australia went home crowned as World Champions, having won only one of their three qualifying games. The Aussies finished level on points with both France and New Zealand, who also won one match apiece, whilst Great Britain stood unbeaten at the top of the table. Only a better points scoring difference, achieved by virtue of their big win over the Kiwis at Wigan in the opening game, gave the Australians a place in the Final.

How Great Britain must have wished the old World Cup format of first past the post and no Final, which was used in the first three tournaments, had been in operation in 1970.

The key match, inevitably, was seen as the Great Britain versus Australia encounter. This was Britain's opening game in the competition, whilst the Aussies were backing up three days after beating New Zealand.

In a tight and intense game, Great Britain won 11-4 at Headingley, with just one try, from Britain's centre Syd Hynes, breaking the defensive deadlock.

That win boosted everybody's confidence that Great Britain, again captained by Frank Myler, would carry on from where they left off on the Lions tour and add the World Cup to their achievements.

And the British duly completed a 100 per cent record by beating France 6-0, in a very tight encounter under floodlights in the rain at Castleford, the first full international to be played at Wheldon Road, and New Zealand, more easily, in a much more open and entertaining match

Mick Shoebottom jumps for joy as Syd Hynes crosses to score against Australia

at Swinton.

It was the French, more than anybody, who had cause to count themselves unfortunate not to reach the World Cup Final in 1970. Only by incurring the wrath of English referees Billy Thompson and Fred Lindop, who were the only two officials involved in the tournament, did France manage to lose by conceding penalty goals against both New Zealand and Great Britain.

Against the Kiwis at Hull, France had only themselves to blame, as they missed numerous chances, as well as seeing New Zealand fullback Don Ladner kick five goals, before going down by one point, 16-15. This was the game in which the little French winger Serge Marsolan thrilled the Boulevard crowd by scoring a 100-yard try that started behind his own goal-line.

And the French showed that their reaching the 1968 World Cup Final was no fluke when they

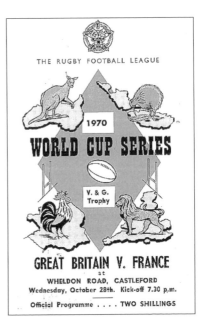

THE RUGBY FOOTBALL LEAGUE

1970

WORLD CUP SERIES

V. & G.
Trophy

GREAT BRITAIN V. FRANCE
at
WHELDON ROAD, CASTLEFORD
Wednesday, October 28th. Kick-off 7.30 p.m.

Official Programme . . . . TWO SHILLINGS

pushed Great Britain - featuring almost the same team that had just won the Ashes - all the way at Castleford. In a try-less game, it took three penalties from fullback Ray Dutton to give Britain their 6-nil win.

Four days later, France shocked Australia, and most observers, when they beat the Aussies 17-15 at Odsal, with the brilliant Marsolan registering another two tries and Jean Capdouze in fine form with the boot. And this after Bobby Fulton scored a try from the first play-the-ball of the match - after only 15 seconds of play.

John Cootes scored both second-half Australia tries, but Eric Simms missed three goals against the wind, and Capdouze's 42-yard drop goal 12 minutes from the end of a terrific match proved the gamebreaker.

The Australians had plenty of humble-pie to eat after the defeat to France, and there were some embarrassed faces around as it was learned that, because of a better points difference, the green and golds would still get a place in the World Cup Final, and not France. How the French must have been kicking themselves for that one point loss against New Zealand.

It meant that, after all, we got the World Cup Final everyone expected, with Great Britain lining up against Australia at Headingley on November 7, 1970.

All form suggested it would be Britain's Cup, but not everyone had been impressed by Britain's performances, as Alfred Drewry in the Yorkshire Post commented after the comfortable win over New Zealand: 'The scoring of five tries did not entirely allay suspicions that this side might not be good enough to beat Australia a second time. The weak spot in all three games has been scrum half. Hepworth again played like a man who has had either too much or too little football in the last year.'

Drewry's comments proved to be perceptive. Instead of glory for Great Britain, the final turned out to be one of Australia's finest hours.

The game turned into a cross between chess and trench-warfare, as Great Britain's pack of hard men, including Tony Fisher (who recovered from a shoulder injury and replaced Kevin Ashcroft, and whose signing by Leeds from Bradford was announced on the morning of the final), Cliff Watson and Malcolm Reilly put too much emphasis on the tough stuff instead of playing the football they had shown in previous games.

Great Britain dominated the play, but the try that would have turned the game for them in the second half continued to elude them.

'Our form was a great disappointment,' said British coach Johnny Whiteley. We had our best chance just after the interval, but we let Australia off the hook three times. We lost all our composure. We even started niggling and that's something we have never gone in for.'

Reilly was a magnificent hard-working loose forward. But it was a rare error by him that gave Australia the initiative just before half-time. In possession, Reilly had the ball snatched from his grasp in a tackle by his opposite number, Aussie skipper Ron Coote, who swooped rapidly

Malcolm Reilly and Mick Shoebottom put a stop to this Australian attack during the 1970 World Cup Final

to put centre John Cootes over for a try.

Father John Cootes was actually a Catholic priest, a rarity which provoked plenty of media interest from people who were amazed that a man of the cloth could be involved at such a high level in such a tough, physical contact sport. The amazement grew several notches as the second half of the 1970 World Cup Final erupted into a niggling, spiteful clash, with plenty of fists and boots flying.

Australia, with Bobby Fulton in commanding form at stand-off, and a pack of forwards who wrote their names into the folklore of Aussie Rugby League that day - among them Ron Coote, John 'Lurch' O'Neill, Bob 'Bear' O'Reilly and Bobby McCarthy - held on to win 12-7.

As Britain's frustration grew, the niggle increased, erupting into fisticuffs several times. Eventually, referee Fred Lindop decided enough was enough, and centre Syd Hynes and Aussie scrum-half Billy Smith were sent-off. They walked off arm in arm, moments after being caught slugging punches at each other.

Not so amusing, however, were the incidents which came at the end of the game, which were sparked when Australian fullback Eric Simms,

Billy Smith of Australia and Great Britain's Syd Hynes leave the field after being sent off for fighting during the 1970 World Cup Final

elated at the victory, went to shake hands with Great Britain winger John Atkinson - later to become a member of the RFL Disciplinary Committee - and was greeted with a punch.

The brawling scenes shown on television brought a torrent of bad publicity for Rugby League, the most vitriolic being the 'Daily Mail', which howled that the innocent youth of our country should be protected from seeing such loutish behaviour, and provided a banner headline saying 'Get these thugs off our TV screens.'

There were even some individuals out to make a name for themselves on the back of the Headingley brawl. Ronald Teeman, then a Leeds councillor, who went on to become President of the Rugby Football League, threatened to table the following question at the Council meeting of 2nd December 1970: 'in view of the display of crude violence and lack of sporting content in the Great Britain-Australia match last Saturday, which indicates conclusively that Rugby League football is degenerating into street corner brawls, will the chairman of the Education Committee consider the active discouragement of the playing of Rugby League football in Leeds schools'. Nothing came of it, as a procession of teachers came forward to rubbish the idea.

Australian reaction was less dramatic, although a Sydney Daily Telegraph editorial read: 'Does anyone expect Australia to rejoice in a victory that leaves that sort of taste in the victors' mouths?'

It seemed at the time a grossly over-the-top reaction if one was to look closely at some of things happening elsewhere in the world of sport. But, as ever, Rugby League was an easy target, and a dog every chinless-wonder liked to kick.

The Yorkshire Post was more composed as Drewry wrote: 'Rugby League matches between Great Britain and Australia have so often degenerated into brawls that to assume a posture of righteous indignation over the squalid goings-on which disfigured Saturday's World Cup final at Headingley is little more than an academic exercise.'

Smith and Hynes were both reprimanded and a profit was made. The BBC's £25,000 fee led to gross receipts of £55,624 and a shareout of 7,130 for each of the four nations.

The Yorkshire Post's Drewry's comment on the after match put the Anglo-Australian antipathy into context when he wrote: 'another soothing note: while a doctor was stitching away at deep cuts as busily as a cobbler on piece work, players with swollen faces and black eyes were exchanging quips and bottles of beer as readily as they had been trading punches only a few minutes earlier – yes, even into overtime at the final whistle. It's a baffling world.'

THE 1970 WORLD CUP FINAL

AUSTRALIA beat GREAT BRITAIN 12-7.
Saturday November 7, 1970
at Headingley, Leeds

AUSTRALIA: Eric Simms, Lionel Williamson, John Cootes, Paul Sait, Mark Harris, Bob Fulton, Billy Smith, John O'Neill, Ron Turner, Bob O'Reilly, Bob McCarthy, Ron Costello, Ron Coote. Subs: Ray Branighan, Elwyn Walters.
Tries: Williamson, Cootes.
Goals: Simms 3

GREAT BRITAIN: Ray Dutton, Alan Smith, Syd Hynes, Frank Myler, John Atkinson, Mick Shoebottom, Keith Hepworth, Dennis Hartley, Tony Fisher, Cliff Watson, Jimmy Thompson, Doug Laughton, Malcolm Reilly. Subs: Chris Hesketh, Bob Haigh.
Try: Atkinson
Goals: Dutton, Hynes

Referee: Fred Lindop (England)
Attendance: 18,776

1970 WORLD CUP RESULTS

AUSTRALIA beat NEW ZEALAND 47-11
At Wigan. Crowd: 9,586

GREAT BRITAIN beat AUSTRALIA 11-4
At Headingley, Leeds. Crowd: 15,084

NEW ZEALAND beat FRANCE 16-15
At the Boulevard, Hull. Crowd: 3,824

GREAT BRITAIN beat FRANCE 6-0
At Castleford. Crowd: 8,958

GREAT BRITAIN beat NEW ZEALAND 27-17
At Swinton. Crowd: 5,609

FRANCE beat AUSTRALIA 17-15
At Bradford. Crowd: 6,215

FINAL TABLE

	P	W	D	L	F	A	Pts
Great Britain	3	3	0	0	44	21	6
Australia	3	1	0	2	66	39	2
France	3	1	0	0	32	37	2
New Zealand	3	1	0	0	44	89	2

1972

It was 1954 all over again as Great Britain scored a memorable triumph to win the sixth World Cup tournament in 1972. And, fittingly, the inspirational captain of the first British World Cup winners in France 18 years before, Dave Valentine, was present among the small band of Great Britain supporters to see them do it in an epic final at Lyon.

The similarities between 1954 and 1972 were uncanny, not just for the fact that the tournament was again staged in France and played at many of the same stadiums - stadiums which also went on to host numerous games in the 1998 soccer world cup - but also because Great Britain once again crossed the channel with the 'no hoper' tag around their necks.

Australia were defending the world crown they had won two years earlier in that infamous battle of Headingley, whilst Great Britain - just as in 1954 - had a new crop of players eager to rebuild an international reputation which had taken a battering soon after the memorable Ashes triumph by the 1970 Lions.

The omens had not looked good for Britain as the famous 1970 team broke up after its disappointment in the World Cup final of that year. Twelve months later, against New Zealand, a new look British team flopped embarrassingly, enabling the Kiwis to win a Test series on British soil for the first time since Albert Baskiville's original pioneers, the 'All Golds', way back in 1908.

It was going to require a remarkable up-turn in the level of performance by the Great Britain team for them to win the 1972 World Cup, and there's little doubt the Australians - who had little knowledge of the quality of the new breed of players in the British team - went into the tournament over-confident and believing they couldn't lose.

But Britain got the up-turn they needed, thanks to the introduction of virtually a whole new team of players who rapidly established their reputations as internationals of the highest quality.

So much so that the Aussies, who had never heard of them before, were falling over themselves to sign the British stars to follow in the footsteps of Malcolm Reilly, who had already departed for Manly.

Among the men the Australian clubs were to get were Phil Lowe, Mick Stephenson and Brian Lockwood.

The victorious team of 1972 retained only one player from the 1970 World Cup Final, Leeds winger John Atkinson. Roger Millward, who would have been a first choice, was again absent through injury, leaving Dennis O'Neill and David Topliss seemingly to battle for the number six jersey - although, as things turned out, it was the 18-year-old John Holmes who emerged at stand-off to become one of Great Britain's 1972 World Cup heroes.

The British clinched the World Cup after a tension-packed Final against Australia at the Stade de Gerland in Lyon. It was the very same stadium in which Valentine's men had shocked the Aussies in their opening game of the first World Cup in 1954.

Skipper Clive Sullivan lifted the cup for Great Britain after a 10-all draw, after extra-time, saw the British declared winners on a countback because they had most league points from the qualifying matches.

Effectively, the 1972 World Cup was won by Britain at Perpignan in their opening match against the Aussies.

It was widely quoted how the British boys had arrived in the Catalan city to see the super-fit, super-confident Aussies strolling around, looking awesomely invincible.

But reputations counted for nothing as a Great Britain pack, anchored by the veteran Terry Clawson - who also proved to be a valuable goal-kicker throughout the tournament - marshalled by clever hooker Stephenson from Dewsbury, and featuring a mighty back-three of Lowe, Lockwood and George Nicholls, outsmarted Arthur Beetson and his men.

The British won a superb nine-try thriller at the Stade Gilbert Brutus, 27-21, much to the joy of the Catalan crowd who got behind the underdogs as they knocked the confident Aussies off their stride.

'Even our own press said we had no chance, but hoped we gave them a decent game and didn't lose by too big a margin' recalled Stephenson on the eve of the 2000 World Cup.

It was a great start to the tournament. I remember going to breakfast on the morning of the game, and Jim Challinor, our coach, said: 'Look boys, just think about what this means to you, to your country.' He gave this speech and it was like Churchill, we'll fight them on the beaches.

We knew that if we could hold them in the forwards, we had the class and the speed in the backs in players like John Atkinson and Clive Sullivan.

'Before the game, there was a great moment.

'The French like their music, and if the band was playing you couldn't go out onto the field. So we had to wait in the tunnel for about five minutes, nervously standing side-by-side with the Australians just inches away.

The refereeing interpretations in the 1972 World Cup cause some confusion, as Great Britain hooker Mike Stephenson, who went on to become a popular TV presenter with SkySports, recalled an incident in Great Britain's pool game with Australia.

'The referee was French, a fella called Jameau, and he created the first ever seven-point try. John Atkinson scored in the corner, and jumped up to celebrate. As he did, a bloke called Elford, a tough second-rower, hit Atko and sent him flying over the fence.

'It was all on, one big massive brawl.

'When it eventually settled down, Claw stepped up and converted the try with a great kick from the touchline, a fantastic effort that gave us a great lift.

'So Graeme Langlands, the Aussie fullback and skipper, went to re-start the game - but every time he went to run up and kick it, the referee would stand over the ball, wave him back and shout "Non".

'I should explain that, for a penalty, the French referees point not to the team that has won the penalty, but in the direction the ball should be kicked, like in rugby union.

'So he was pointing back towards the Australian posts.

'Well, there was total confusion - no-one knew what was happening. We hadn't a clue, the Aussies hadn't, and so both teams congregated around the ball in the middle of the pitch. You can imagine the language from Langlands, who was trying to say he had to kick off but the ref kept saying, "Non, Non".

'Eventually, an interpreter was called for and he came running onto the pitch. Then he started arguing with the referee, then Langlands joins in, then Clive Sullivan went to ask what on earth was going on.

'In the end, it was Clawson who clicked first. He tapped the ref on the shoulder, and said in a silly French accent: "Me kicko ballo over posto."

'And to our amazement, the referee said, "Oui".

'Langlands then blew up again, but eventually it dawned on everyone that we had got a penalty for the late tackle on Atkinson.

'The Aussies went crazy, Claw put the ball on the spot, turned round, winked at me, and kicked the goal.'

'Eventually, Clive Sullivan led us out, with the rest of the team following in number order. So I had Terry Clawson, the number eight in front of me.

'As we're walking out, Terry turned round to me and said: "Bloody hell, they're big aren't they - who's that?"

'He points towards this six foot six giant of a bloke, big broad shoulders and a nose that looked like a baseball bat had smashed it 48 times.

'Well, this bloke turned round, and he had a number three on his back. It was Mark Harris, a centre. The Claw turned to me and said: 'Bloody hell, what's the forwards gonna be like'?'

The World Cup tournament had kicked off the night before Britain's crucial triumph over Australia, as the hosts, France, emerged 20-9 winners over New Zealand in the famous Velodrome Stadium in Marseille. Both teams scored three tries, but the French got home on goal kicks leaving the Kiwis feeling badly done to and most observers fairly confident that neither of these two would be contesting the Final a couple of weeks later.

From Perpignan, Great Britain's road to the final took them first to Grenoble, in the shadow of the Alps, where they comfortably beat France 13-4. Second-rower Phil Lowe was the man of the match, scoring two 30-metre tries and setting up another for Clive Sullivan in the dying seconds of the game. But it was a performance that largely left coach Jim Challinor unimpressed, and he was anxious to see his team smarten up for their third game, against New Zealand.

The British travelled back to the south west, to the picturesque town of Pau, for the game with the Kiwis. Challinor got his wish. Great Britain played sensational attacking rugby, breaking all kinds of records, as they swept New Zealand aside 53-19. It had a local crowd of over 7,000 in raptures.

Widnes stand-off O'Neill had played in the opening two wins over Australia and France, but coach Challinor decided to give the Leeds teenager Holmes a run against the Kiwis. And with big prop Clawson also rested, Holmes was handed the goal-kicking role to go with the number six jersey. The result was a piece of history, as Holmes scored two tries and ten goals to set a then international world record of 26 points. It also meant that he could not be left out of the team for the World Cup Final.

The Australians, meanwhile, had been locked in a tense battle with New Zealand, before edging home 9-5. The match was played under lights in Paris, at the newly renovated Parc des Princes (venue of the first World Cup Final in 1954) and a crowd reported at 8,000 turned out in the French capital.

That left the Aussies having to beat France to qualify for the Final, which they did easily, running up a 31-9 win over the hosts in Toulouse, setting up the Great Britain versus Australia Final that was to etch its way in Rugby League folklore.

Sadly, in a poor piece of planning, the Final was played in the city of Lyon, a long way from the rugby heartlands of the south of France. And, with the French not involved, public interest was minimal with the result that one of the most epic games in international Rugby League history was played out in front of a vast almost empty stadium, containing little more than 4,000 spectators.

Any lack of atmosphere in the stands did not dampen the electricity on the pitch as both teams ripped into each other.

Powerful Aussie backs like Bob Fulton and big Mark Harris were met head-on by Britain's centre pairing of Chris Hesketh and John

Great Britain's Clive Sullivan receives the 1972 World Cup

Walsh, and in the forwards Aussie giants like Beetson, O'Neill and O'Reilly found Clawson, Nicholls and company standing firm like granite. Behind them was the brilliant little halfback Steve Nash, controlling the rucks and tackling everything that moved.

Prop 'Lurch' O'Neill galloped 30 yards to score at the corner and Australia looked in control as half-time approached. Then came one of the most famous incidents in Rugby League folklore, as loose forward Nicholls hit the huge centre Harris with a massive tackle as he headed for the line. The ball jolted loose, and British skipper Clive Sullivan swooped to pick it up and sprint 80 yards down the touchline to score and put his team level. It was a wonderful moment.

And, in the second half, Britain came back again after the Aussies had gone ahead 10-5. Just seven minutes from full-time, Sullivan found a gap and passed to Lockwood, who wrong-footed the defence to send hooker Stephenson over. Finger-nails were being bitten, but Clawson showed nerves of steel to slot over the equalising conversion.

The game was not without controversy, and the Aussies still swear to this day they had a perfectly good try disallowed by the French referee Georges Jameau, after Dennis Ward had put a kick up for captain-coach Langlands to run on to. Langlands dived, caught the ball on the full with spectacular ability, and touched down - only to be ruled offside by Monsieur Jameau. 'The referee came in afterwards and apologised,' Langlands later claimed. 'He said he was wrong and was sorry.'

With the scores locked at 10-all, 20 minutes of extra-time was played. In pouring rain, in front of near deserted terraces, the tension was almost unbearable for those in the respective camps. After looking like a fighter on the ropes as the Aussies pounded them earlier in the game, the British boys rose to the challenge and grew stronger and more confident with every minute of the extra-time period.

At the end of it, the scores were still tied-up at 10-10, and that meant the World Cup belonged to Clive Sullivan and his brave British team. Australian coach Harry Bath and his team had no complaints. 'We knew the rules,' said Bath. 'We had our chances but we didn't take them. We lost the series at Perpignan.'

On Langlands' disallowed try, Mike Stephenson recalled: 'The referee couldn't believe anyone could get to a ball that quickly from so far back, so he ruled offside. Now today, with a video referee, it would have been awarded. I've looked at the film since, and Langlands was well on-side.

'The Aussies were upset, and they responded with the first try. Then Sullivan scored that famous 80-yard try. As soon as he got the ball in clear space, I thought that's it, no-one will catch him.

'But of all people, the Aussie prop John O'Neill chased him down and forced Sully into the corner. It was incredible, an 18-stone prop almost catching a winger, our fastest man.

'We weren't playing well, it was coming up to half-time and we needed a converted try. We'd done well to keep players like Bobby Fulton quiet, and our centre Chris Hesketh had done a great job on Harris.

'But the Aussies still led 5-0, and we needed that Sully try. Then up stepped the Claw and he banged the goal over to level it for half-time.

THE 1972 WORLD CUP FINAL

GREAT BRITAIN 10 AUSTRALIA 10
(After extra-time)
Saturday 11 November, 1972 *at Lyon*

GREAT BRITAIN: Charlton, Sullivan, Hesketh, Walsh, Atkinson, Holmes, Nash, Clawson, Stephenson, Jeanes, Lowe, Lockwood, Nicholls. Sub who came on: Irving.
Tries: Sullivan, Stephenson
Goals: Clawson 2

AUSTRALIA: Langlands, Grant, Harris, Starling, Branighan, Fulton, Ward, O'Neill, Walters, O'Reilly, Beetson, Stevens, Sullivan.
Tries: O'Neill, Beetson
Goals: Branighan 2

Referee: G Jameau (France)
Attendance: 4,231

1972 WORLD CUP RESULTS

FRANCE beat NEW ZEALAND 20-9
At Marseille. Crowd: 20,748

GREAT BRITAIN beat AUSTRALIA 27-21
At Perpignan. Crowd: 6,324

AUSTRALIA beat NEW ZEALAND 9-5
At Parc des Princes, Paris. Crowd: 8,000

GREAT BRITAIN beat FRANCE 13-4
At Grenoble. Crowd: 5,321

GREAT BRITAIN beat NEW ZEALAND 53-19
At Pau. Crowd: 7,500

AUSTRALIA beat FRANCE 31-9
At Toulouse. Crowd: 10,332

FINAL TABLE

	P	W	D	L	F	A	Pts
Great Britain	3	3	0	0	93	44	6
Australia	3	2	0	1	61	41	4
France	3	1	0	2	33	53	2
New Zealand	3	0	0	0	33	82	0

Great Britain's George Nicholls on the attack against Australia

'Beetson scored next, but it was a fluke try. On one of the few occasions they breached us, he threw a dummy out wide, sailed over, and tried to run behind the posts.

'I was chasing him, and I knew I couldn't stop him because he was such a big man. So I came from behind and tried to knock the ball from his grasp. Up popped the ball, and it could have gone anywhere - but it fell straight back down into his arms and he put it down for a try.

'They kicked the goal, and it was 10-5. We were trying everything we knew, but they had the speed and the strength.

'Then, seven minutes from the end, Brian Lockwood threw a

wonderful dummy, made a step, and suddenly a huge gap opened up. I came back on the inside, shouted for it, and got a clear 25-yard run to the line.

'We were playing on a soccer pitch, and they hadn't properly painted out the lines. So as I'm heading for the line, I saw this other line looming that I wasn't sure about and I just got the ball down as quick as I could, midway between the posts and the touchline. I was so relieved to have scored, but Sullivan came up to me and went crazy, saying I should have gone under the posts.

'I thought, oh no, what have I done...

'But Clawson came up and said, " don't worry mate, this is no problem, I can kick these with me eyes shut."

'Talk about pressure - if he misses, Australia have won the World Cup.

'But sure enough, he added the goal, and we were level at 10-10.

'That was such a sweet feeling. We knew we'd have to play extra time, but know we were in the driving seat and they had to score. So we changed our tactics, and bottled everything up.

'It must have been awful to watch, but we knew the cup was ours.'

Two of the lightest players ever to pull on the green and gold for Australia have featured in World Cup finals.

Scrum-half Dennis Ward was 8st 10lb (55.2kg) when he was called into Canterbury-Bankstown's lower-grade ranks in 1962. By the time he reached first-grade he weighed 9st 10lb (61.6kg) and when he played for Australia in the 1972 World Cup in France he was still only 10st 4lb (65.2kg).

Only fractionally heavier was John Kolc, the Parramatta halfback who played in the 1977 World Championship final. Kolc was only 5ft 3ins (1.6m) tall and weighed 10st 8lb (67kg).

1975

There was a complete change of format for the 1975 tournament. The sport's hierarchy decided to vary from the previous set-up where the four nations played each other once in a particular part of the world to decide who ruled the world. Instead they opted for a home-and-away league with games spread over a period from March to November. There would be no final and no Great Britain side. Instead England and Wales would compete as single entities. And the authorities decided to call the competition the World Championship, rather than the World Cup.

The inclusion of the Welsh team followed an emotional return of the international game to Wales earlier in the year. When Wales beat France 21-8 in the European Championship on February 16th at Swansea, it was the first time the Welsh had played a match on their own soil in 24 years.

As history would show, the inclusion of Wales was to have a vital bearing on the destiny of the World Championship. A Welsh victory over England in Wales' so-called home game, played halfway across the world in Brisbane, cost the English success. The Australians were crowned World Champions after finishing top of the table. But they never beat the English – playing a 10-all draw in Sydney and losing 16-13 at Wigan. The loss to Wales and a draw with the Kiwis meant England fell one point short on the league ladder.

The Championship kicked off at Toulouse in early March with France accounting for Wales 14-7 in what was to prove the only victory for the Frenchmen. A fortnight later England had no trouble against the Frenchmen at Headingley, posting a 20-2 victory.

After a break of almost two months, the championship resumed in Australasia. That the tournament would prove to be a financial disaster was evident from the first match Down Under. There was an attendance of only 10,000 at Lang Park to see Australia thrash the Kiwis 36-8. Not even enough to cover costs. Captain-coach Graeme Langlands defied the critics who reckoned he was too old, scoring two tries himself (in a period of just six minutes) and providing the inspiration for his teammates.

Although no one realised it at the time, nine days later at the same

135

venue the game that was to decide the world title was staged – England v Wales. In a vicious, brutal encounter the Welsh won both the game (12-7) and they also came out on top in the succession of all-in brawls. It seemed like each side had been saving everything for this grudge match against the traditional enemy. Referee Don Lancashire said after the game that he would have been completely justified in sending off every single player in the 'boots and all' clash.

The Welsh hardly used their skilful backs such as David Watkins, Bill Francis and Clive Sullivan. Instead it was left to their rugged pack, with Jim Mills, Tony Fisher, Bobby Wanbon and John Mantle to the fore. They ran out into the pouring rain, fired up by coach Les Pearce, and turned on the rough stuff. They succeeded in knocking the England players off their stride. And when the English fell into the trap of getting into the fisticuffs, Wales turned on some fine rugby. It was Sullivan, Great Britain's World Cup hero just three years earlier, who scored the winning try.

Four days later it was a very different story when Wales backed up against Australia at the Sydney Cricket Ground. The match against England had obviously physically taken its toll – and while the likes of Mills, Wanbon and Kel Coslett matched the Aussies in the first half, after the interval the Welsh wilted. Australia's halves Tom Raudonikis and Tim Pickup led the Welshmen a merry dance. The Australians claimed a 30-13 victory, with Fisher scoring the visitors' only try as a consolation two minutes from full-time.

Meanwhile across the Tasman Sea on a Carlaw Park mudheap, New Zealand had no trouble in disposing of France 27-nil. The difference was even more pronounced when it is considered that the Kiwis had two tries disallowed. Loose forward Murray Eade and scrum-half Ken Stirling were the best for the Kiwis.

In the words of the well-worn cliché the Lang Park clash between Australia and France was a match of two halves. In the first stanza the Aussies looked sensational, scoring 18 points as big Arthur Beetson ran riot through the rucks. But after the break, with the game in their keeping, the Australians just went through their paces with no enthusiasm at all to finish 26-6 before New Zealand referee Jack Percival blew the full-time whistle and put the 9,000 spectators out of their misery.

The English have good reason never to forget Kiwi centre Dennis Williams. Four years earlier, a day after his 18th birthday, he made his Test debut against Great Britain at Salford and scored the first time he touched the ball. By 2008 he still remains the youngest player to score a try in international Rugby League. At Carlaw Park in June 1975, he made the English sit up and take notice again. He was a stand-out man of the match as England and New Zealand fought out a 17-all draw. Williams scored two tries himself, spearheading the Kiwis' attack as well as thwarting many a promising attacking movement by England with crunching defence. The New Zealanders were on top for much of the match, until the second try to England fullback George Fairbairn leveled the scores.

A week later, at the Sydney Cricket Ground, the world's two best teams drew 10-all, in front of the championship's biggest crowd, 33,858. The draw breathed new life into the tournament just when it appeared the matches in the northern hemisphere autumn would be just an anti-climax.

The English were lucky not to lose scrum-half Steve Nash 12 minutes into the action after he hit Mark Harris with a high tackle that smashed the nose of the powerhouse centre. As the xenophobic crowd bayed for blood, New Zealand referee Jack Percival decided against a send-off. But with his nose a bloody, pulped mess, Harris was finished for the afternoon. It was a body blow for the Australians as much of the home side's tactics were planned around the big man.

However, England lost much of their creativity when Roger Millward later went off injured. Without Harris, the likes of Beetson, Ron Coote and Raudonikis lifted their game. But such was the strength of England's defence that gaps were rare, despite Beetson's bullocking charges and the scheming of 'Tom Terrific'. It was ironic that it was a lapse by Beetson early in the proceedings that had handed the English their first try. Millward

> *Only a select few individuals have captained their country in a World Cup and later returned to the fray as coach.*
>
> *The legendary French fullback Puig Aubert was skipper of the side that went down to Great Britain in the final of the inaugural tournament in 1954. And he was coach of the French side that played in the 1975 World Championships.*
>
> *David Watkins was captain of Wales in the 1975 tournament and two years later was back as coach of the Great Britain side led by Roger Millward, who had also captained England in 1975.*
>
> *That great Australian centre-cum-fullback Graeme Langlands was skipper of his country in the 1972 tournament. Langlands started the 1975 World Series as captain-coach of Australia. But after suffering injury, he held the coaching reins from the sideline while Arthur Beetson led the Australians on the field.*

snapped up his loose pass, and flung the ball to winger Keith Fielding who zipped past stand-off Tim Pickup to touch down.

Beetson made amends by setting up the equaliser for his Eastern Suburbs clubmate Ron Coote. The Australians' other try was a controversial one. The British media were convinced that winger Chris Anderson had scored off a forward pass. And they reported that Percival agreed with their opinion after he had seen a television replay the next morning. Australian journalists told a different story.

The best try of the afternoon came with just four minutes left on the clock when Nash bamboozled the Australians to send Ken Gill, Millward's replacement, over the stripe. One Australian match report described it as 'a masterpiece in deception'. George Fairbairn kicked two goals for England but he missed another four, any one of which could have won the game for England.

On the same day at Carlaw Park, New Zealand played a man short for most of the second half after Eade was sent off by Australian referee Laurie Bruyeres for a stiff-arm tackle on Welsh fullback Bill Francis. But the Kiwis still managed to account for Wales to the tune of 13-8. Winger Phil Orchard equalled Roger Bailey's record for the number of tries scored in matches for New Zealand, 37 in 39 appearances.

It was a very different Australian side that headed to Britain for the return matches in the championship. But first they had to overcome New Zealand in Auckland. Eastern Suburbs, the side that had won the Premiership under the tutelage of Jack Gibson, who 33 years later was to be named Australia's Coach of the Century, had a lion's share of spots in the squad – Beetson, centre John Brass, prop Ian Mackay, half Johnny Mayes, stand-off John Peard and exciting 19-year-old winger Ian Schubert. Coote and Harris would have been there, too, but for injuries.

The Kiwis were no match for their Trans-Tasman neighbours, falling 24-8. This despite the fact that that the Australians were caned 16-6 in the penalties by English referee Fred Lindop. The home side's only points came from four penalty goals to Warren Collicoat. A 17-6 victory over Auckland was followed by a 44-6 drubbing of Salford once the Australians reached Britain. The Salford humiliation would have been more dramatic had not Mick Cronin missed with seven attempts at goal. Schubert at fullback and winger Johnny Rhodes, back in the international arena after a seven-year absence, were in top form.

England gave a depleted French side no hope in their World Championship clash at Bordeaux. England manager Bill Oxley noted after the 48-2 victory: "I don't remember a worse French team." Millward's elusive running kept his backs moving. Salford winger Keith Fielding scored four tries and Leeds centre John Holmes and Hull KR's Ged Dunn each touched down twice. The French improved to manage a 12-all draw with New Zealand at Marseille

Australia warmed up for their clash with Wales at Swansea with a solid 32-7 victory over a St Helens side that was debuting guest Balmain stand-off Les Mara. The Swansea encounter was another brutal encounter, a feature of so many of Wales' matches during the championships. Three major brawls broke out as referee Percival failed to dampen the players' fire. One melee rolled off the pitch and into the grandstand at Vetch Field where several officials including Australia's coach Graeme Langlands joined in. But the fans on hand (officially 11,112

A familiar sight in the 1975 World Cup -
Ian Schubert touches down for an Australian try

but looking more like around 16,000) were also treated to a wonderful display by man of the match Schubert, who nabbed a hat-trick.

The following weekend England easily accounted for New Zealand 27-12 at Bradford's Odsal Stadium. Despite his side running in seven tries, with a hat-trick to Gill, England coach Alex Murphy was unimpressed. 'We should have had another nine,' he stormed. 'Once we had the Kiwis down, we should have kept them there and piled on the points.' The following day, with Schubert rested, Australia thumped France 41-2 at Perpignan in what was little more than a training-run.

England could not knock Australia off the top of the championship ladder when they locked horns at Wigan's Central Park at the start of November. But you would never have guessed it – such was the enthusiasm shown by both sides in what was probably the best game of the whole series, if not all of the previous World Cups. It was a shame that only 9,393 fans were there to see it.

Schubert was again in superb form, with yet another hat-trick of tries. But even his great individual effort was not enough to deny England a 16-13 victory. Millward was again the brains behind England's success. As ARL supremo Kevin Humphreys admitted after the match: 'Millward is a great match-winning halfback, the sort we don't seem to produce. It was a game that could have gone either way until the final seconds. But England held on and the game was a triumph for Rugby League at its best.'

The Australians were unhappy with a try awarded to John Holmes three minutes before half-time. Steve Norton had kicked a loose ball over the Australian tryline. Schubert and England centres Holmes and Les Dyl dived for it. And referee Percival ruled Holmes had touched down for the three-pointer. Later television replays and a graphic still photograph seemed to show Dyl obstructing Schubert instead of going

1975 WORLD CUP RESULTS

FRANCE beat WALES 14-7
At Toulouse. Crowd 7,563

ENGLAND beat FRANCE 20-2
At Headingley, Leeds. Crowd 10,842

AUSTRALIA beat NEW ZEALAND 36-8
At Brisbane. Crowd: 10,000

WALES beat ENGLAND 12-7
At Brisbane. Crowd 6,000

AUSTRALIA beat WALES 30-13
At Sydney. Crowd 25,386

NEW ZEALAND beat FRANCE 27-0
At Christchurch. Crowd 2,500

NEW ZEALAND and ENGLAND drew 17-17
At Auckland. Crowd 12,000

AUSTRALIA beat FRANCE 26-6
At Brisbane. Crowd 9,000

AUSTRALIA and ENGLAND drew 10-10
At Sydney. Crowd 33,858

NEW ZEALAND beat WALES 13-8
At Auckland. Crowd 9,368

ENGLAND beat WALES 22-16
At Warrington. Crowd 5,034

AUSTRALIA beat NEW ZEALAND 24-8
At Auckland. Crowd 20,000

ENGLAND beat FRANCE 48-2
At Bordeaux. Crowd 1,581

FRANCE and NEW ZEALAND drew 12-12
At Marseille. Crowd 18,000

AUSTRALIA beat WALES 18-6
At Swansea. Crowd 11,112

ENGLAND beat NEW ZEALAND 27-12
At Bradford. Crowd 5,937

AUSTRALIA beat FRANCE 41-2
At Perpignan. Crowd 10,440

ENGLAND beat AUSTRALIA 16-13
At Wigan. Crowd 9,393

WALES beat NEW ZEALAND 25-24
At Swansea. Crowd 2,645

WALES beat FRANCE 23-2
At Salford. Crowd 2,247

FINAL TABLE

	P	W	D	L	F	A	Pts
Australia	8	6	1	1	198	69	13
England	8	5	2	1	167	84	12
Wales	8	3	0	5	110	130	6
New Zealand	8	2	2	4	121	149	6
France	8	1	1	6	40	204	3

for the ball. It mattered not. The Australians had won the World Championship.

There were two meaningless games remaining. Wales beat New Zealand 25-24 at Swansea and followed that up with a 23-2 success over France at Salford. The former game was yet another vicious affair. Welsh prop Jim Mills stood on the face of Kiwi front-rower John Greengrass in the last minute of the match. Angry officials of the New Zealand Rugby League decided that the Kiwis would never play another game in which Mills was chosen, and had to withdraw from the 1977 tournament, to be played in Australia and New Zealand.

England's coach Murphy singled out two Australians for special praise at the end of the tournament, his one and only stint at the helm of an international side. 'Arthur Beetson is one of the best forwards we've ever had in the game. But the lad I would like to have playing for me is Ian Schubert. He staggered me with his performances and potential. I wish we had a few wingers like him.'

Sadly, the new format had been a financial disaster, and Wales didn't enter a World Cup as a standalone team again until 1995.

After England beat Australia at Wigan the Aussies received the World Championship Trophy. It didn't sit well with the English who immediately issued a challenge for the two sides to meet again in just under a fortnight's time, at Headingley. Australia readily agreed and warmed up with wins over Oldham (20-10) and York (45-4). A considerably-changed England team was no match for the Australians, motivated by what they saw as a slur on their world title claims.

Tempers flared from the start. England's skipper Millward insisted on playing despite having an important Cup-tie three days later. When the ball emerged from the first scrum of the match, Millward went down under a suspect tackle from Australia's half Tom Raudonikis. When Raudonikis hit him again a few minutes later and the pair traded blows referee sent the fiery Australian from the pitch. Then, showing no bias, he dismissed Millward, too.

The England side never recovered and was outplayed 25-nil.

1977

The Rugby League world's hierarchy decided that in 1977 the game would have its fifth tournament in just nine years to decide the best nation in the world. And no one was quite sure what to call the event. Some of the media called it the World Cup. A few decided on the World Championship. But, at least in the host nations of Australia and New Zealand, World Series seemed to be the most popular moniker.

Two years earlier the 1975 World Championship, spread across southern and northern hemispheres over a period of nine months of home-and-away games, had been a financial flop. And with good reason when you consider the Welsh home game against England was played at Brisbane's Lang Park. At least the 1977 tournament returned to the formula that had been such a fiscal success in 1968, with Australia and New Zealand sharing the role of hosts, and England and Wales reunited under the Great Britain banner.

Nevertheless, there were several instances of officialdom shooting itself in the foot. The first came when it was decided on the make-up of the British squad. Because England had performed so dismally in the European Championship earlier in the year, beaten by both Wales and France, the man who was expected to coach the British side, Peter Fox, was shown the door. And the coach of Wales, David Watkins was given the job, even though at one stage he was quoted as saying: "How can I tell people like [Great Britain's captain] Roger Millward how to play the game?"

Coaches don't usually make such comments.

There were plenty more statements made by the British that in hindsight they wished they hadn't. Senior officials of the RFL kept threatening to boycott the tournament. First they said they wouldn't come if they weren't paid money they claimed was owed from the 1975 competition. Agreement was eventually reached. Then they again threatened to stay away if both England and Wales weren't invited as separate entities. Again the matter was resolved.

There was also a furore over the renowned British forward Phil Lowe. The International Board had agreed he was a disqualified player because he was playing in England for Hull Kingston Rovers while still under contract to Manly in Australia. Then the New Zealanders objected to Welshman Jim Mills being chosen in the British side. They had banned him from ever playing in New Zealand after an on-pitch incident at Swansea during the 1975 tournament. Mills had been sent off and subsequently suspended for allegedly walking on the face of Kiwi prop John Greengrass.

Lowe decided to withdraw from the Great Britain team to avoid throwing the whole tournament into jeopardy. He was replaced by 23-year-old Barrow loose forward Phil Hogan. Mills also withdrew 'for personal reasons' and was replaced by Featherstone's Peter Smith. The British squad was further weakened by the withdrawal through injury of St Helens centre Eddie Cunningham and Warrington's clever second-rower Tommy Martyn. Ironically, Martyn's replacement, the rotund Leeds prop Steve Pitchford proved to be one of the heroes of the British squad during the World Series.

Hopes for a promotional success for the tournament nosedived when the French side played a pre-tournament game in Port Moresby and, in front of 14,500 wildly-enthusiastic local fans, were humbled 37-6 by the Papua New Guinea Kumuls, who hadn't even been invited to the Australasian sportsfest.

It was then Australia's turn to be embarrassed. The legendary Arthur Beetson was named as captain for the opening match, against New Zealand. Then he learned that he hadn't even been chosen in the Australian side when the selectors first sat down to chose the squad. When ARL supremo Kevin Humphreys saw Beetson had been omitted, he stormed into the selectors' meeting and demanded that his name be included. Realising this, the humble Aboriginal star had no hesitation in quitting.

'I feel I've probably kept someone else out of the team,' Beetson explained. 'The other person, originally chosen, should go. I wouldn't feel right going to New Zealand in these circumstances. But I will be available for Australia's games against England [sic] and France if they want me.' Parramatta's Graham Olling was drafted into Australia's squad as Beetson's replacement and Queenslander Greg Veivers was handed the captaincy. Of course, once the furore was over Beetson was back as Australia's captain.

Without Beetson, Australia warmed up for the World Series with a 68-5 humiliation of New Zealand's South Island, in driving rain at Christchurch. Of 14 tries, centre Steve Rogers scored four.

Before kick-off in the tournament, respected Manchester-based expatriate Aussie journalist Jack McNamara revealed the British hopes to fans in his former country: 'Britain's hopes may prove to be in the inside backs. Roger Millward is playing magnificently at either halfback or five-eighth [stand-off]. There is pace to spare on the wings. Keith

Fielding is the fastest man in England and Stuart Wright is a glorious runner in the classic mould. At fullback George Fairbairn is probably the safest in the land. While there are doubts about the squad's all-round lack of pace and queries over the strength of the pack, Britain will still take some beating.'

The bookmakers framed their odds: Australia favourites at 9-10, Britain 2-1, France 3-1 and New Zealand 10-1. They were almost correct.

The series got underway with a convincing 27-12 victory by the Australians over the Kiwis at Auckland's Carlaw Park. Despite the final score Australia had to fight hard. Debutant centre Mark Thomas of Brisbane Brothers club scored the first try after just five minutes and from then on the Aussies never looked like being caught. English referee Billy Thompson made a great impression with a clear five metres that let the backs show their skills.

Meanwhile the preparations continued. Auckland, with plenty of the New Zealand hopefuls involved, beat the Australians 19-15 in a match the latter side didn't really want to play. And the Aussies' nemesis, referee John Percival, didn't endear himself to the visitors by caning them 15-6 in the penalties. The French morale slipped further as they were beaten 14-12 by Brisbane's representative side. Several times the referee Stan Scamp had to call an interpreter onto the pitch to explain his decisions.

For their first match of the series, against France and also at Carlaw Park, Britain switched Millward to stand-off to accommodate the solid scrum-half Steve Nash, who the British were convinced could tame the rough-tough Australian No 7, Tom Raudonikis. And Barrow loose forward Phil Hogan was included at the expense of the more experienced Len Casey. It was a master stroke, with Hogan turning in a man of the match effort as the British cruised to a 23-4 victory. Hogan's strong runs through the mud were a highlight of the game and helped inspire his fellow forwards to completely dominate the French pack. But he did retire early with a shoulder injury.

The French had no luck. They went into the encounter without their major strike-weapon, centre Jean-Marc Bourret. And they were annoyed when late in the game New Zealand referee Bob Cooper disallowed a try to second-rower Jean-Pierre Sauret. The French and the media watching from the stands were sure he had crossed the line, but Cooper ordered Sauret to play the ball half-a-metre short of the stripe. To compound the hurt, Cooper then penalised Sauret for an incorrect play-the-ball.

Daily Mail journalist Brian Batty was circumspect about the victory: 'There was little flag-waving or popping of champagne corks. The structure of the championship now seems that France can be rated no higher than third-class, New Zealand possibly second, and Australia first. Where Great Britain's newly-constructed side comes in this rating will be decided when they tackle the Kiwis at Christchurch.'

145

In the lead-up, the British struggled to beat a makeshift Northern Maori side 18-14 at Huntly after leading 13-4 at half-time. On the same day the Frenchmen posted their first victory on their visit to the southern hemisphere with an unimpressive 8-0 success over the Wellington provincial side.

The farcical nature of local rules was highlighted when Cronulla captain Greg Pierce was ruled out of Australia's side to play France after being suspended for striking in a club game. But New Zealand's Test centre Fred Ah Kuoi was allowed to play against Great Britain despite his similar suspension for an almost identical offence. Ah Kuoi was allowed to serve his ban in club matches after the World Series.

Arthur Beetson was back as Australia's captain for the encounter with France at the Sydney Cricket Ground. Torrential rain in the lead-up not only cruelled the Frenchmen's hopes of playing a free-flowing style of rugby but kept the attendance down to a meagre 13,231. And those hardy fans were subjected to a very forgettable experience.

Respected Australian journalist Ian Heads wished he hadn't been there: 'Australia's slow-motion win over the French visitors, 21-9, turned out to be Rugby League's bore of the year. Fans went along hoping for a little champagne but had to settle instead for the vin ordinaire of an extremely poor match which never once hit top gear and provided barely a single thrill. Spectators would be hard put to remember a match of such stupefying dullness.'

Australia scored five tries to one, including a brace to fullback Graham Eadie. But after leading 13-0 at the break they seemed to coast in the second half. In his first appearance in Australia the much-vaunted French centre Bourret limped off after 37 minutes with the recurrence of an ankle injury. It cost him a chance of playing in the NSWRL Premiership. Balmain and Newtown had been interested in signing him, even after he demanded a package deal with World Cup scrum-half Guy Alard, but the two clubs' interest quickly cooled.

The Christchurch confrontation the following day between Britain and New Zealand was vital to the whole tournament. The winner would almost certainly line up against Australia in the final. The below-par display by the British against the Northern Maori had buoyed the Kiwis hopes. And Watkins was well aware of this. 'The Huntly match brought us down to earth,' he explained. 'It was a warning to us.'

Great Britain heeded the warning with a stunning 30-12 victory. Man of the match Millward was inspirational. His performance was capped by a sensational 70-yard solo try. But the platform for victory was laid by some wonderful forward displays by George Nicholls, Eddie Bowman and Hogan. Each was rewarded with a try.

It was off to Brisbane for Great Britain and Australia, where a sensational fullback display by Manly's 23-year-old custodian Graham Eadie helped set up a 19-5 victory. Australia had looked vulnerable in the first half with Great Britain's skill around the rucks catching them unawares. And the barrel-chested Pitchford regularly ripped open the Aussie defence in the middle of the pitch. Workington Town back-rower Bowman cleverly set up a try for Millward six minutes before half-time, giving Great Britain a real chance of causing an upset.

In the second half the British wilted in the hot and humid Brisbane conditions. But the biggest blow was the loss of hooker David Ward with an ankle injury. He tried to continue but, eventually a couple of minutes into the second half, he limped off. He had an 8-3 lead in the scrums at the time, but after his departure Great Britain struggled to gain any scrum possession.

Eadie was devastating. He scored two tries and set up the third, to his Manly clubmate Terry Randall. Eadie also tackled ferociously and was safe under the high kicks. It was an engrossing battle, with the only flaw being some strange decisions by French referee Marcel Caillol. This led to the unusual move by Australia to ask that England's Billy Thompson control the final at the Sydney Cricket Ground the following Saturday.

France stumbled from disaster to disaster. They were beaten 19-12 by Newcastle and 14-10 by Toowoomba before cancelling a third tour game against Wide Bay at Gympie because they had only eight fit players. They were then penalised out of their game against New Zealand by Australian referee Don Lancashire. Each side scored four tries, but New Zealand's stand-off Chris Jordan booted eight goals to France's winger Jose Moya's four as the Kiwis triumphed 28-20.

Australia's fans believed the final would be a one-sided affair – so much so that a paltry 24,457 turned up at the Sydney Cricket Ground. Those who stayed away must have kicked themselves for missing one of the most thrilling Anglo-Australian encounters in many years.

The gripping see-sawing match will also be remembered for arguably the greatest hard-luck story in Britain's Rugby League history. Some 21 minutes into the encounter and with Great Britain trailing 8-5, Thompson was too quick to signal a penalty when he ruled obstruction against Australia. As his whistle blew British winger Stuart Wright had just intercepted a wayward pass from Australian loose forward Greg Pierce. Wright was away, with no defender in sight, and would have scored between the posts. Most critics believed Thompson should have played the advantage. But the referee defended his actions: "I had already blown the penalty to Great Britain before the Australian player passed the ball," he explained. It was just one of those things that happen."

As history shows, Australia went on to win the final by just one point – 13-12. The Australians had another slice of luck before the Wright incident. Britain's fullback George Fairbairn had missed the simplest of penalty goal attempts from in front of the uprights. Fairbairn had a match he would rather forget. Early in the first half he dropped a pass that was scooped up by debutant centre Russel Gartner, who cleared away for a simple try. In the second half, Fairbairn fumbled a kick from Mick Cronin. Aussie winger Allan McMahon kicked ahead and regathered. From the ensuing play-the-ball tiny scrum-half Johnny Kolc scampered across the line to score. They were Australia's only two tries of the series finale. As coach Watkins noted: "Both our tries came from our own ball skills. The two by Australia were from our mistakes." In the dying moments of the final, Fairbairn had a penalty shot to win the game. But his attempt fell short.

As for the match itself, Cronin and Randall were stand-outs for Australia. But once again the Australians had their work cut out trying to control Pitchford. His barnstorming bursts continually broke the Aussie defence. He was responsible for both British tries, scoring the first himself and setting up the other for substitute Ken Gill. Halves Millward and Nash caused plenty of problems, too. Nash had been a revelation. The little dynamo played every minute of every match on the tour – the World Cup encounters as well as seven minor games.

Among the latter, future Australian Test winger Larry Corowa, then just 19, scored five tries as Monaro beat the tourists 33-12. Corowa was promptly signed by Balmain and at the end of the 1978 season toured Britain and France with the Kangaroos. Great Britain beat Queensland 18-13 in a fiery clash at Lang Park. There were more brawls at Townsville when North Queensland overcame Britain 17-14. An injury to Fairbairn resulted in coach Watkins turning out at fullback against New South Wales. There were more fireworks as the Blues won easily 35-5, with Hull KR loose forward Len Casey sent off and fined $200. The tour

THE 1977 WORLD CUP FINAL

AUSTRALIA beat GREAT BRITAIN 13-12
Saturday, 25 June
at Sydney Cricket Ground

AUSTRALIA: Graham Eadie, Alan McMahon, Mick Cronin, Russell Gartner, Mark Harris, John Peard, John Kolc, Greg Veivers, Nick Geiger, Terry Randall, Arthur Beetson (Capt.), Ray Higgs, Greg Pierce. Sub (used): Dennis Fitzgerald.
Tries: McMahon, Gartner, Kolc.
Goals: Cronin 2

GREAT BRITAIN: George Fairbairn, Stuart Wright, John Holmes, Les Dyl, Bill Francis, Roger Millward (Capt.), Steve Nash, Jimmy Thompson, Keith Elwell, Steve Pitchford, Len Casey, Eddie Bowman, Phil Hogan. Subs: Ken Gill, Peter Smith.
Tries: Pitchford, Gill
Goals: Fairbairn 3

Referee: Billy Thompson (England);
Attendance: 24,457

1977 WORLD CUP RESULTS

AUSTRALIA beat NEW ZEALAND 27-12
At Auckland. Crowd: 18,000

GREAT BRITAIN beat FRANCE 23-4
At Auckland. Crowd: 10,000

AUSTRALIA beat FRANCE 21-9
At Sydney. Crowd: 13,321

GREAT BRITAIN beat NEW ZEALAND 30-12
At Christchurch. Crowd: 9,000

AUSTRALIA beat GREAT BRITAIN 19-5
At Brisbane. Crowd: 27,000

NEW ZEALAND beat FRANCE 28-20
At Auckland. Crowd: 8,000

FINAL TABLE

	P	W	D	L	F	A	Pts
Australia	3	3	0	0	67	26	6
Great Britain	3	2	0	1	58	35	4
New Zealand	3	1	0	2	52	77	2
France	3	0	0	3	33	72	0

concluded with a 54-6 thrashing of Southern Division at Gosford, Salford winger Keith Fielding scoring four tries.

Several of the British tourists had received offers from Sydney clubs. But their hopes of a financial bonanza were shattered when, in the week leading up to the final, the International Board imposed a four-year ban on transfers of players between Britain, Australia and New Zealand. That meant that only three of the eight British Test stars playing in the Premiership in 1977 would be able to remain in Sydney the following year – Mike Stephenson (Penrith), John Gray (North Sydney) and Brian Lockwood (Balmain). The other five – David Topliss (Penrith), Gary Stephens and Steve 'Knocker' Norton (both Manly) and Jeff Grayshon and David Eckersley (Cronulla) were officially 'on loan' from their British clubs

The 1977 Great Britain World Cup coach David Watkins was one man delighted and excited by the prospect of seeing all the best British players turning out for their country again.

'I doubt whether Australia will beat Great Britain for the next six years,' said Watkins in 1977. 'They may never beat them again.'

How wrong could someone be?

1985-88

After 1977 the Rugby League World Cup went into hibernation, as the game's international administrators returned to staging full Lions, Kangaroos and Kiwi tours.

Rather than do the obvious thing of slotting a high-profile World Cup tournament into each four-yearly cycle, after a gap of eight years Rugby League's international brainstrust came up with the novel idea of re-introducing the World Cup, but spreading it over a three-year period.

The plan was for each of the now five Test playing nations (by this time Papua New Guinea had been accepted into the fold) to play each other both home and away, with one chosen Test match of an already existing series designated as a World Cup qualifying game.

Points would be awarded for these games, and a league table would be compiled over the three-year period. At that point the top two countries in the league would play off in a World Cup Final.

The logic behind this scheme was to give additional meaning to the final Test of a series, designating it as a World Cup qualifier, and giving additional impetus to what could otherwise be a dead rubber.

The long drawn out tournament had plenty of critics, for obvious reasons. But it still managed to produce some memorable moments, and culminated in a spectacular climax.

Of course, it could just as easily have done that over a period of three weeks, rather than three years.

This ninth World Cup both began and ended in the city of Auckland, providing New Zealand Rugby League with one its most famous, and then its most infamous, occasions.

The Kiwis kicked off the tournament by beating Australia 18-0 at Carlaw Park, in the third Test of their 1985 series.

New Zealand had lost the previous two Tests very narrowly, and controversially, both to last-minute tries by John Ribot.

But when the same two teams lined up three years later in the same city for the final of the same competition, things were very, very different.

The personnel of both Australian and New Zealand teams had

changed a lot. Their respective coaches, and even the way the game was played, had moved on considerably too, and the venue was vastly different, as public interest in the League code in New Zealand was building dramatically to the high that would culminate with the birth of the Auckland Warriors.

An awful lot of football had to be played in various countries before the Kiwis and the Aussies were to emerge at Auckland's Eden Park for the 1988 World Cup Final.

Great Britain got their first taste of the tournament with a hard-fought draw against New Zealand at Elland Road, Leeds in November 1985.

It was an emotional moment, as a late penalty goal by Lee Crooks levelled the scores at six apiece, and enabled Britain to share the series, as well as the World Cup points, with the Kiwis.

Maurice Bamford was Great Britain's coach then, as he steadily rebuilt the prestige of the national team following the disasters of the 1982 Ashes series and 1984 Lions tour.

But the British got a shock when they travelled to Avignon to play France in their first away game in the World Cup. The Kiwis had won 22-0 in France, and Great Britain expected to triumph just as comfortably, but ended up being grateful to get a point from another draw against a young French side coached by Tas Baitieri.

Emerging youngsters Patrick Entat and Gilles Dumas made their Test debuts in that 10-all draw.

> *Lee Crooks kicked well over 1,000 goals in a wonderful 17-year career and the greatest of them all was the one he kicked for Great Britain to square the Test series against New Zealand in 1985 - Britain's first game of the protracted ninth World Cup. The old Rothmans RL Yearbook rated it the place-kick goal of the decade and it could well be Britain's Test goal of the century.*
>
> *It was a real pressure cooker of a kick. There was just one minute left of a torrid third Test with New Zealand leading 6-4 and looking set to clinch the series. Then the Kiwis were penalised for yet another foul, 30 yards out and close to the touchline. The tension was unbearable, but the coolest person in the Elland Road ground was Crooks, who was still only 21. After coming on as a 23rd minute substitute he had taken over the kicking duties from Mick Burke, who had missed two penalties, and duly banged over his third penalty goal.*

Dumas, playing at fullback, scored all his team's points, and if he had kicked a pretty straight-forward penalty shot in the dying minutes France would have been celebrating a victory.

But that achievement at Avignon in February 1986 was as good as it got for France in this World Cup. Twelve months later their game was thrust into crisis with serious financial problems, and their League's president was thrown out of office.

Great Britain's Tony Myler (6) congratulates Joe Lydon on a successful conversion against Australia at Wigan in 1986. The celebrations proved to be in vain as the Aussies went on to win 24-15

The financial crisis meant France could not afford to tour Down Under, and thus were unable to fulfil their away fixtures in Australia, New Zealand and Papua New Guinea.

Instead, those three nations were all automatically awarded two points in lieu towards the World Cup table. Great Britain had already played and beaten France at Leeds before the French crisis blew up.

Papua New Guinea made its World Cup debut in the 1985-88 tournament and, remarkably, achieved a momentous victory in their opening game against New Zealand. Just 12 months earlier the Kiwis had been on a high, thrashing the Aussies, and the defeat in Port Moresby marked the end of Graham Lowe's reign as New Zealand's coach.

Despite putting up a much improved performance in the third Test of the 1986 Ashes series, Great Britain still lost their home World Cup qualifier with Australia, in an exciting match played at Wigan, which was only decided late in the game, with a controversial obstruction try being awarded to Dale Shearer, and a piece of Wally Lewis magic.

That meant Britain's hopes of qualifying for the World Cup Final rested on the results of their southern hemisphere Lions tour of 1988.

Everybody knew that Australia would make the Final, and Great Britain were given the huge incentive of knowing that the Aussies, despite being first past the post, were prepared to give up home advantage to play the Final at Wembley Stadium if Britain qualified to be their opposition.

Papua New Guinea was safely negotiated in Port Moresby, and then Great Britain gave their World Cup Final hopes a massive, if unexpected, boost by beating Australia 26-12 in the third Test of the 1988 series.

The Ashes had already been lost again in disappointing fashion, but the British boys won a famous victory against the Aussies in that final Test. It was Britain's first Test win over Australia in 10 years, and it just happened to be the World Cup-designated match. It was a tremendous result for new Great Britain coach Malcolm Reilly, with two-try hero Henderson Gill being just one player to cement his reputation in front of the sceptical Australians.

And so, despite the drawn out process of a qualifying tournament spread over three years, everything bubbled up into a sudden death, winner takes all, shoot out between New Zealand and Great Britain, just one week after the Lions' famous victory in Sydney.

Conditions in the cold and wet of Christchurch on New Zealand's South Island could hardly have contrasted more with the pleasant Sydney sunshine, as the Lions and Kiwis slugged out a titanic battle in the mud.

In the end, New Zealand won, controversially, by just two points, after two key tries by Gary Freeman, who came off the substitutes' bench to win the game for the Kiwis. Their 12-10 win left the Great Britain team bitterly disappointed, and the British game as a whole deflated, as they saw what would have been a huge occasion at Wembley slither away in the Christchurch mud.

Instead, it was Rugby League in New Zealand that was destined to have its place in the sun as, for the first time, the Kiwis took part in a World Cup Final.

Public interest in the Final, scheduled after the end of the domestic Australian season in early October, was immense in New Zealand. The country had never been so crazy about Rugby League, and the decision to stage the game at Auckland's Eden Park, the city's traditional rugby union venue, was a measure of League's growing status.

The attendance of 47,363 at Eden Park was the biggest crowd ever to watch a Rugby League match in New Zealand. And the game made history by having a neutral referee - Graham Ainui - from Papua New Guinea.

Sadly for the home nation, amid all the hype and hysteria, so foreign to the League code in New Zealand, everybody forgot about the football, and the 1988 World Cup Final turned into a huge anti-climax for the Kiwis' new audience. The New Zealand team was totally overawed by the occasion, too many of them seemed to want to fight rather than play football, and a superb Australian team blitzed them with early points. The Aussies had the game won well before half-time, leaving the huge crowd stunned.

This was a very different Australian team to the one which had lost so embarrassingly (for them) against Great Britain in Sydney a couple of months earlier.

With the Aussies now out of season, gone were the political selections based on State of Origin results, and in their place was an Australian team based very much on the power of the Sydney clubs, in particular the Grand Finalists Canterbury and Balmain.

Apart from skipper Wally Lewis, only two Queenslanders were in the World Cup Final team. New scrum-half Alfie Langer replaced the injured Peter Sterling, and winger Dale Shearer retained his place. In contrast, the Australian team beaten by Great Britain in July 1988 had contained no less than nine Queenslanders.

Captain Wally had mixed feelings on the 1988 World Cup Final, as he saw his team win an emphatic victory, but in the process he suffered a broken arm.

Lewis sustained the injury midway through the first half as he tackled winger Tony Iro, and whilst he continued for almost the rest of the half despite his obvious discomfort, he didn't do an Alan Prescott and stay on the field for the full 80 minutes. He didn't need to.

With Gavin Miller giving a man-of-the-match display, Ben Elias and Wayne Pearce inspirational, and the brilliant Terry Lamb slotting effortlessly

Andrew Farrar made just one appearance in Australia's colours - in the 1988 World Cup final. The big centre won his spot in the international line-up after a blockbusting display as Canterbury scored a 24-12 win over Balmain in the ARL Premiership grand final a fortnight earlier.

Although he played a dominant role in Australia's World Cup success at Auckland's Eden Park, Farrar never played for Australia again. He is remembered by British fans for a season with Wigan in 1992-93.

into Wally 's stand-off role, Australia cruised home 25-12. After the game, New Zealand coach Tony Gordon called Lewis 'the greatest footballer to ever pull on a boot.'

The World Cup was Australia's once again, for the sixth time in nine competitions.

The new format may not have been what Rugby League really needed, but it had eventually provided the game in New Zealand with the biggest day in its history, and the Aussies with one of their most satisfying and deserved victories.

THE 1988 WORLD CUP FINAL

AUSTRALIA beat NEW ZEALAND 25-12
9 October, 1988 *at Eden Park, Auckland*

AUSTRALIA: Garry Jack, Dale Shearer, Andrew Farrar, Mark McGaw, Michael O'Connor, Wally Lewis, Allan Langer, Paul Dunn, Benny Elias, Steve Roach, Paul Sironen, Gavin Miller, Wayne Pearce. Subs: Terry Lamb, David Gillespie.
Tries: Langer 2, Shearer, Miller.
Goals: O'Connor 4. Field goal: Elias

NEW ZEALAND: Gary Mercer, Tony Iro, Kevin Iro, Dean Bell, Mark Elia, Gary Freeman, Clayton Friend, Peter Brown, Wayne Wallace, Adrian Shelford, Mark Graham, Kurt Sorensen, Mark Horo. Subs: Shane Cooper, Sam Stewart.
Tries: T Iro, K Iro
Goals: Brown 2

Referee: Graham Ainui
(Papua New Guinea)
Attendance: 47,363

1985-88 WORLD CUP RESULTS

NEW ZEALAND beat AUSTRALIA 18-0
At Auckland. Crowd: 19,000

GREAT BRITAIN drew with NEW ZEALAND 6-6
At Elland Road, Leeds. Crowd: 22,209

NEW ZEALAND beat FRANCE 22-0
At Perpignan. Crowd: 5,000

FRANCE drew with GREAT BRITAIN 10-10
At Avignon. Crowd: 5,000

AUSTRALIA beat NEW ZEALAND 32-12
At Sydney. Crowd: 22,811

PAPUA NEW GUINEA beat NEW ZEALAND 24-22
At Port Moresby. Crowd: 15,000

AUSTRALIA beat PAPUA NEW GUINEA 62-12
At Port Moresby. Crowd: 17,000

AUSTRALIA beat GREAT BRITAIN 24-15
At Wigan. Crowd: 20,169

AUSTRALIA beat FRANCE 52-0
At Carcassonne. Crowd: 3,000

GREAT BRITAIN beat FRANCE 52-4
At Headingley, Leeds. Crowd: 6,567

GREAT BRITAIN beat PAPUA NEW GUINEA 42-0
At Wigan. Crowd: 9,121

FRANCE beat PAPUA NEW GUINEA 21-4
At Carcassonne. Crowd: 5,000

GREAT BRITAIN beat PAPUA NEW GUINEA 42-22
At Port Moresby. Crowd: 12,077

GREAT BRITAIN beat AUSTRALIA 26-12
At Sydney. Crowd: 15,994

NEW ZEALAND beat PAPUA NEW GUINEA 66-14
At Auckland. Crowd: 8,392

NEW ZEALAND beat GREAT BRITAIN 12-10
At Christchurch. Crowd: 8,525

AUSTRALIA beat PAPUA NEW GUINEA 70-8
At Wagga Wagga. Crowd: 11,685

FINAL TABLE

	P	W	D	L	F	A	Pts
Australia *	7	5	0	2	252	91	12
New Zealand *	7	4	1	2	158	86	11
Great Britain	8	4	2	2	203	90	10
PNG *	7	1	0	6	84	325	4
France	5	1	1	3	35	140	3

* Awarded two points in lieu of France's non-fulfilment of fixtures in the southern hemisphere.

1989-92

The tenth Rugby League World Cup was, like the previous tournament, spread across three years and both hemispheres. Like its predecessor, it produced a magnificent event as its climax.

When Great Britain and Australia marched out at Wembley for the World Cup Final on October 24th, 1992, international Rugby League in the northern hemisphere reached its peak, as the biggest crowd ever to watch an international match in Britain - 73,631 - packed into the nation's most famous stadium. The Rugby League boys were playing in a World Cup Final in the very same place as Bobby Moore, Geoff Hurst and company had lifted that other World Cup in 1966.

The very fact that the game was played at Wembley was the key. Rugby League had finally broken the ice and staged a major international occasion in the national stadium two years earlier, when Great Britain had scored a famous victory over the Australians in the first Test of the 1990 Ashes series.

Contrary to the negative thinking of the doubters, that match had been a huge success at the gate, proving that Rugby League could present itself on a national stage, and no longer had to hide its considerable wares in the north of England.

A World Cup Final was a one-off big event that everybody could relate to, far more than a three-match Ashes series, which was more for the traditionalists, something the instant-fix mentality created by the tabloids couldn't really concentrate on long enough to appreciate.

In addition, of course, another very important factor was the air of expectancy surrounding Great Britain's team. There was very real confidence that Britain were going to beat the Australians this time, and win the World Cup. They'd proved in the recent past that they could beat the Aussies in a one-off match, but couldn't quite sustain it over a three-match series. And the Wembley World Cup Final was to be a one-off.

Great Britain's confidence, and public expectancy, had grown because of the two most recent Ashes series.

The first, played at home in 1990, included that famous win at Wembley, and then the epic Manchester Test in which only Ricky

Stuart's injury-time break and Mal Meninga's shoulder charge on Carl Gibson saved the Aussies.

Britain's new, very real competitiveness was confirmed two years later on the Lions tour to Australia, in which a tough first Test defeat in Sydney was followed by a sensational victory in Melbourne, setting up a decider in Brisbane. A very intense battle was fought out under the Lang Park floodlights, before Mal Meninga's Aussie team emerged victors by just six points, two tries to one.

Not since Chris Hesketh led his 1974 Lions to Australia had Great Britain gone so close to regaining the Ashes as they had in both 1990 and 1992. It was the pinnacle of the rebirth of the British national team, supervised and inspired by coach Malcolm Reilly, and, if Britain couldn't get the Ashes, the World Cup title in 1992 would be a very nice consolation prize.

Thousands of British fans had followed the team in Australia in the summer of 1992, and as autumn came around they couldn't wait to get another crack at the Aussies at Wembley.

The Australians themselves, despite having capacity crowds at all three Ashes Tests in 1992 - the first time since 1974 a series against Great Britain had provoked the same kind of feverish public interest down-under as it always did in the old days - were more than happy to give up the home advantage they could have claimed for the chance to stage the final at Wembley.

Australia's right to home advantage came because they finished top of the league table, following the completion of the three year home-and-away series of World Cup qualifiers.

The Aussies had a 100 per cent record, with eight wins out of eight. Great Britain finished level on points with New Zealand, and only got into the World Cup Final on a better points for-and-against record. It was tough luck on the Kiwis, but sweet revenge for the British, who had themselves been edged out of the previous World Cup Final in 1988 so narrowly by New Zealand.

As the World Cup qualifying period of 1989-1992 evolved, once again the clashes between Great Britain and New Zealand proved to be crucial. Both were very closely contested by two very evenly matched teams, and both were won narrowly by the respective home teams.

Great Britain beat the Kiwis at Wigan in 1989 by 10-6, after an epic battle. The victory brought much joy for Malcolm Reilly's men, not only because two World Cup points had been won, but more so because it clinched their first major series win over either Australia or New Zealand since the 1979 Lions had beaten the Kiwis on their own soil.

Great Britain managed to retain their whip-hand over the Kiwis by winning the 1990 series in New Zealand, a victory against all expectations after so many front-line international players had declined the tour.

Great Britain's David Hulme and referee Greg McCallum stand over a prone Martin Offiah during the Lions' 10-6 victory over the Kiwis at Wigan in 1989

Inspired by captain Garry Schofield, the British had wrapped up the series in the first two Tests, before they travelled to the South Island for the third, which was the World Cup qualifier.

New Zealand scraped home to a 21-18 win, thanks largely to six goals by Matthew Ridge and a boob by Martin Offiah, when he dropped the ball over the line in the act of touching down for what would, as things turned out, have been a decisive try. Offiah's mistake did not go down well with coach Reilly, who recognised that it could, in the final wash-up, cost Great Britain a place in the World Cup Final. Thankfully, it didn't.

With Australia reigning supreme in all their games against Great Britain and New Zealand, despite having to negotiate some pretty competitive opposition, there was no doubt that the British and the Kiwis were very much on an even keel together on the second rung of the world Rugby League ladder.

Further down it lay France and Papua New Guinea. The French had a much better record in the 1989-1992 World Cup compared to the previous tournament. At least this time they were able to complete all their fixtures in the southern hemisphere, and they performed relatively well against both Australia and New Zealand, avoiding the hammerings most people had predicted.

France's spirited display against the Australians, on a freezing cold night in the New South Wales country town of Parkes, came on the back of their famous victory over Great Britain at Headingley in April 1990.

The French had the consolation of winning their World Cup game in Papua New Guinea a year later, despite their 1991 squad being nowhere near as good as the 1990 team. As both Great Britain and New Zealand knew only too well, it wasn't always easy to win in the heat and humidity of Papua New Guinea.

But despite taking the Frenchmen to the hostile environment of Goroka, the Kumuls could not beat a 'Tricolours' team superbly led by prop Thierry Buttignol and guided by halfbacks Patrick Entat and Pascal Fages.

France managed a double over Papua New Guinea, leaving the Kumuls without a single point in the World Cup table. They did, however, enjoy one of their finest moments in international Rugby League by giving Australia a real run for their money in a Test play in North Queensland, at Townsville, in the aftermath of the Lions tour to Australia in 1992.

The Aussies won 36-14, rather than by the predicted massacre, and the game was best remembered for a superb display and solo try by Kumuls scrum-half Aquila Emil. Big winger Graham Mackay scored two tries for Australia that night.

Things were very different for Australia as they stepped into the cauldron of Wembley for the World Cup Final on October 24th. The exhibition match attitude, and sunshine and hard ground of Townsville, had been replaced by a dull, damp English autumn day, and a lush turf made slippery by the drizzle. In addition, they faced a Great Britain team pumped up by their own self-belief, and the urgings of the massive 73,000-plus crowd.

For the first time, Wembley was a virtual sell-out for an international

Phil Clarke swamped by the Australian defence

Australian skipper Mal Meninga celebrates his side's 1992 success

Rugby League match, and the atmosphere was much more like the Challenge Cup Final in which the winner was going to take all.

In the event, it all proved to be a disappointment for the British. The letdown was intensified because they went so very close to victory, and were left to rue chances missed and mistakes made.

Australia retained the World Cup with a 10-6 win, after a close - many critics described it as dour - encounter of the toughest kind. There was little flowing football, as both teams had their defences planned to perfection. Instead, it became like a game of chess, thought out in an environment of intense physical contact in which only the toughest could survive.

Great Britain's pack was magnificent, superbly prompted by scrum-half Deryck Fox, who also kept his team ahead on the scoreboard with three penalty goals. But there was little creative attack from the British, and coach Malcolm Reilly later admitted it had been a mistake to play Shaun Edwards at stand-off, with Garry Schofield moved out to centre.

There was a controversial incident early in the game, when hooker Martin Dermott hit Australia's key man, Brad Fittler, with a high shot. It was later discovered that Fittler had sustained a broken jaw, but he bravely played on. Aussie critics were livid that referee Dennis Hale had allowed Dermott to stay on the field.

The deciding moment of the 1992 World Cup Final came late in the second half, when a mistake by ex-rugby union man John Devereux, on the field as a substitute, allowed Aussie centre Steve Renouf - playing his first match in the green and gold - to get around him on the outside and score the only try of the game. It was the only time in the match Britain's defence had been found wanting, and that one mistake proved crucial.

That meant it was Mal Meninga who lifted the 1992 World Cup, leaving Great Britain so frustrated that they had gone so, so close to glory. Coach Reilly was desperately disappointed with the outcome. 'We live in anticipation,' he said. 'I'm sick of losing. We're getting so close.'

But it had been a wonderful occasion for Rugby League, at last on show on the biggest stage of all.

THE 1992 WORLD CUP FINAL

AUSTRALIA beat GREAT BRITAIN 10-6
24 October, 1992 *at Wembley Stadium*

AUSTRALIA: Tim Brasher, Willie Carne, Steve Renouf, Mal Meninga, Michael Hancock, Brad Fittler, Allan Langer, Glenn Lazarus, Steve Walters, Mark Sargent, Paul Sironen, Bob Lindner, Brad Clyde. Subs: David Gillespie, Kevin Walters, John Cartwright.
Try: Renouf.
Goals: Meninga 3

GREAT BRITAIN: Joe Lydon, Alan Hunte, Gary Connolly, Garry Schofield, Martin Offiah, Shaun Edwards, Deryck Fox, Kevin Ward, Martin Dermott, Andy Platt, Denis Betts, Phil Clarke, Ellery Hanley. Subs: John Devereux, Alan Tait, Kelvin Skerrett, Richie Eyres.
Goals: Fox 3

Referee: Dennis Hale (New Zealand)
Attendance: 73,631

1989-92 WORLD CUP RESULTS

AUSTRALIA beat NEW ZEALAND 22-14
At Auckland. Crowd: 15,000

GREAT BRITAIN beat NEW ZEALAND 10-6
At Wigan. Crowd: 20,346

NEW ZEALAND beat FRANCE 34-0
At Carcassonne. Crowd: 4,208

GREAT BRITAIN beat PAPUA NEW GUINEA 40-8
At Port Moresby. Crowd: 5,969

AUSTRALIA beat FRANCE 34-2
At Parkes, NSW. Crowd: 12,384

NEW ZEALAND beat GREAT BRITAIN 21-18
At Christchurch. Crowd: 3,133

NEW ZEALAND beat PAPUA NEW GUINEA 18-10
At Port Moresby. Crowd: 10,000

AUSTRALIA beat GREAT BRITAIN 14-0
At Elland Road, Leeds. Crowd: 32,500

AUSTRALIA beat FRANCE 34-10
At Perpignan. Crowd: 3,428

GREAT BRITAIN beat FRANCE 45-10
At Perpignan. Crowd: 3,965

NEW ZEALAND beat FRANCE 32-10
At Christchurch. Crowd: 2,000

FRANCE beat PAPUA NEW GUINEA 20-18
At Goroka. Crowd: 11,485

AUSTRALIA beat NEW ZEALAND 40-12
At Brisbane. Crowd: 29,139

AUSTRALIA beat PAPUA NEW GUINEA 40-6
At Port Moresby. Crowd: 14,500

GREAT BRITAIN beat PAPUA NEW GUINEA 56-4
At Wigan. Crowd: 4,193

FRANCE beat PAPUA NEW GUINEA 28-14
At Carcassonne. Crowd: 1,440

GREAT BRITAIN beat FRANCE 36-0
At Hull. Crowd: 5,250

AUSTRALIA beat GREAT BRITAIN 16-10
At Brisbane. Crowd: 32,313

NEW ZEALAND beat PAPUA NEW GUINEA 66-10
At Auckland. Crowd: 3,000

AUSTRALIA beat PAPUA NEW GUINEA 36-14
At Townsville. Crowd: 12,470

FINAL TABLE

	P	W	D	L	F	A	Pts
Australia	8	8	0	0	236	68	16
Great Britain	8	5	0	3	215	79	10
New Zealand	8	5	0	3	203	120	10
France	8	2	0	6	80	247	4
PNG	8	0	0	8	84	304	0

Gary Connolly and a determined Deryck Fox stop Brad Fittler in his tracks

Steve Walters evades the challenge of Shaun Edwards

1995

The 1995 Rugby League World Cup, the eleventh in the eventful history of the competition, was staged in Britain as the focal point of the game's Centenary celebrations. It was the first World Cup tournament for 18 years in which all the nations would come together in one place at one time for a festival of Rugby League. And it was the biggest gathering of nations in the game's 100-year history.

For a sport that for so long had seen its World Cup contested by just four established countries, the prospect of ten nations taking part was dreamlike. Adding icing to the cake for internationalists was a secondary tournament for Emerging Nations, in which a further seven countries took part.

The 1995 World Cup had a major sponsor, the Halifax Building Society, and another new trophy, despite the fact that the original World Cup, which went missing in 1970, had by this time been recovered.

The Halifax Centenary World Cup was a silver trophy manufactured by the famous London jewellers Tiffany's, and was reported to have cost some £10,000.

The tournament, once the players got to work on the field, turned out to be a huge success. Staged throughout an unusually warm and sunny October, bigger than expected crowds flocked to see the variety of nations in action, creating a wonderfully uplifting atmosphere of celebration.

Sadly, that was more than the Rugby League's own Centenary efforts had managed to achieve, resulting in the build-up to the 1995 World Cup being plagued by controversies and months of public pessimism.

It seemed that Rugby League fans, so used to seeing their game kicked around and mismanaged, had developed their own self-doubts about the game's ability to attract public interest in such an ambitious international event.

Most of the public criticism was aimed at the RFL's chief executive Maurice Lindsay, who had also taken on the role as World Cup tournament director at a time when he had quite enough on his plate in the aftermath of the announcement of Rupert Murdoch's attempted take-over of the game, causing the Super League war to rage in Australia.

Lindsay managed to fend off the criticisms by insisting that the players would make the World Cup a success by their performances on the field. And, as ever, the players didn't let anybody down.

The tournament was played out against the background of the game's civil war in Australia, and effectively was the last throw of the dice for the old Australian Rugby League as they saw the rest of the world submerged by Super League.

It was a cruel irony that, as all the other nations deserted the ARL and opted to take the money from Murdoch instead, it was almost exclusively thanks to the efforts of the ARL (notably their creation of the World Sevens and their work in the South Pacific islands) that the 1995 World Cup was able to include, for the first time, fully fledged teams from Tonga, Fiji, Western Samoa and South Africa.

The biggest casualty of the 'war' was the Australian team itself.

The ARL stuck rigidly to a policy of not choosing any players who had aligned themselves with Super League, meaning almost a whole team of the biggest stars in the Australian game were left at home.

The one star who stayed loyal to the ARL, Brad Fittler, captained a team of players who knew they

The 1995 and 2000 World Cups featured a pointscoring frenzy that saw several Australasians earn a place in the record books.

When Australia beat South Africa 86-6 at Gateshead in 1995, Newcastle Knights' scrum-half Andrew Johns made an incredible international debut, scoring two tries and booting 11 goals for a personal tally of 30 points.

This equalled the world's best in an international clash set by Michael O'Connor, who scored four tries and kicked seven goals in Australia's 70-8 Test victory over Papua New Guinea in 1988.

Johns' 11 goals equalled the previous world record shared by New Zealand's Des White (in a 1952 Test against Australia) and Kangaroo Rod Wishart (against France in 1994).

Australia's 86 points was also a record score for Test or World Cup encounters.

Five years later, also at Gateshead, Australia's Mat Rogers topped Johns' pointscoring with 34 (four tries and nine goals) as Fiji went down 66-8.

A day later, as New Zealand crushed the Cook Islands 84-10, stand-off Tasesa Lavea booted 12 goals for a new world best. He also scored two tries, but his 32 points couldn't quite match Rogers' record.

But both records lasted only a few days. Australia inflicted a world record 110-4 defeat on Russia. And Ryan Girdler scored 46 of the points (three tries and 17 goals).

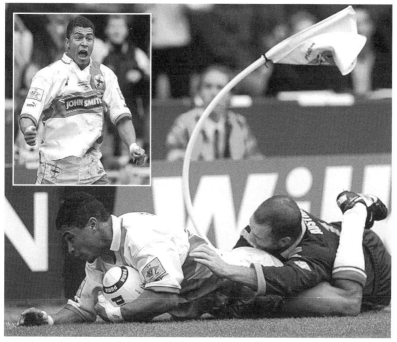

England winger Jason Robinson crashes past the challenge of Australian fullback
Tim Brasher and the corner flag to score in the 1995 opening game at Wembley,
and *(inset)* shows his delight

were perceived as second-stringers.

But, with coach Bob Fulton at the helm, these Aussies developed a real siege mentality that increased as the tournament progressed and the pressure mounted. Fulton didn't win himself many friends in England, but he could certainly put this Australian team's eventual victory in the 1995 World Cup down as his greatest coaching achievement against all the odds.

England, coached by Phil Larder and with Shaun Edwards as captain (until he was injured), knew they would never get a better chance to beat Australia and win the World Cup.

It didn't matter to the English players or fans that these weren't Australia's first-choice men. They were still Aussies, and they were still wearing the famous green and gold uniforms.

And England got off to the flying start they wanted by beating the Aussies 20-16 in a rain-soaked opening game at Wembley.

Despite all the negative vibes about lack of public interest, slavishly whipped up by the media, a crowd of over 41,000 were at Wembley to see ex-Supreme Diana Ross provide the pre-match entertainment (as she had done at the launch of the soccer World Cup in Chicago the previous year).

The Fijian squad perfom their version of the Haka, before the game with
South Africa at Keighley

The crucial try came in the 68th minute when, with the scores level, a double tackle from Barrie Jon Mather and Lee Jackson on John Hopoate caused the Tongan winger to spill the ball. Jason Robinson reacted like a flash and was over in the corner despite a desperate cover tackle from Tim Brasher. Paul Newlove's interception try six minutes later settled the issue.

England's victory in the opener, one of the few games that was televised by the BBC, had a galvanising and positive effect which set up the rest of the World Cup tournament.

Any lingering doubts were joyously swept away the following day by two wonderful exhibitions of Rugby League in matches involving some of the junior nations.

At a packed Cougar Park in Keighley, the sensational attacking skills of the Fijians - coached by Australian Graham Murray - had the crowd in raptures as they swept past the South Africans, scoring 52 exhilarating points.

And at Warrington, Tonga and New Zealand fought out a match that will live in the memory as one of the best games of Rugby League ever seen. Nobody quite knew what to expect from the Tongans up against the mighty Kiwis, but they soon found out. Tonga were outstanding in their debut full international, and led New Zealand 24-12 with just ten minutes to go. It took a last minute equaliser, followed by an injury-time field goal by skipper Matthew Ridge, to save the Kiwis' blushes, as Tonga lost so cruelly, 25-24.

From then on, nobody had any doubts that the 1995 World Cup was going to be a great tournament, as the football flowed and the excitement mounted.

There was another superb game at Hull the following Tuesday night as Papua New Guinea played their first game of the tournament, at the Boulevard. Tonga, unlucky to be beaten by the Kiwis, raced into a 20-nil half-time lead, with two of the four tries being scored by Awen Guttenbeil.

But incredibly, inspired by captain Adrian Lam and a then unknown stand-off called Stanley Gene, the Kumuls fought back and a last-minute try to Lucas Solbat earned them a 28-all draw, and a chance to qualify for the semi-finals if they could beat New Zealand three days later at St Helens.

They gave the Kiwis one heck of a game before exiting the World Cup after a 22-6 defeat. A poor start cost the Kumuls again as Frank Endacott's side raced into a 12-0 lead in nine minutes through tries to captain Matthew Ridge and centre Richie Blackmore. But PNG came back and early in the second half were held up over the line three times. It wasn't until ten minutes from time that the Kiwi defence succumbed when Marcus Bai tore over from 40 metres. It was too late and a late try from Sean Hoppe took New Zealand into a semi-final with Australia.

The competition was split into three pools. The one staged in South Wales involving the Welsh, Western Samoa and France, was christened the 'group of death', and it did prove to be the toughest of the lot.

The Welsh, skippered by Jonathan Davies, having his last fling in Rugby League, knew they faced an epic against the mighty Samoans, coached by Graham Lowe and another nation making their debut on the big stage in Rugby League.

Wales, coached by Clive Griffiths, had to get past France first, and they did so with some difficulty in a tough game in front of over 10,000 Welsh fans at Ninian Park - with a teenage Iestyn Harris starring from fullback, and winger Anthony Sullivan registering a hat-trick.

The poor French really drew the short straw and, after taking a physical battering from the big Welsh pack, had to back up just three days later against the even more awesome looking Samoans. Va'aiga Tuigamala, Vila Matautia and Tony Tatupu each scored braces in Samoa's monster 56-10 win at Ninian Park in Cardiff.

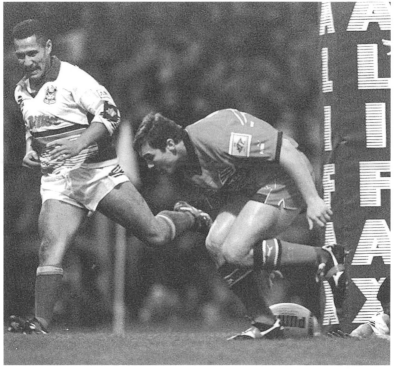

Wales' Iestyn Harris touches down against Western Samoa at Swansea

That midweek game set up a Sunday night showdown between Wales and Western Samoa at Swansea. Over 15,000 Welshmen in the capacity crowd at the Vetch Field looked on as one of the fiercest battles in recent times was fought out in an incredible atmosphere.

Wales won 22-10 in one of the most memorable matches in the history of Welsh Rugby League. The Samoans stood accused of forgetting about the football to concentrate on physical domination and it was a night of heroics from all 17 Welsh players. Scrum-half Kevin Ellis scored a try in injury time to take the Welsh into the first semi-final of the World Cup, in which they would meet England at Manchester's Old Trafford.

1995 WORLD CUP RESULTS

GROUP ONE

ENGLAND beat AUSTRALIA 20-16
At Wembley; Crowd: 41,271

FIJI beat SOUTH AFRICA 52-6
At Keighley; Crowd: 4,845

AUSTRALIA beat SOUTH AFRICA 86-6
At Gateshead; Crowd: 9,191

ENGLAND beat FIJI 46-0
At Wigan; Crowd: 26,263

AUSTRALIA beat FIJI 66-0
At Huddersfield; Crowd: 7,127

ENGLAND beat SOUTH AFRICA 46-0
At Leeds; Crowd: 14,014

GROUP ONE TABLE

	P	W	D	L	F	A	Pts
England	3	3	0	0	112	16	6
Australia	3	2	0	1	168	26	4
Fiji	3	1	0	2	52	118	2
South Africa	3	0	0	0	12	184	0

GROUP TWO

NEW ZEALAND beat TONGA 25-14
At Warrington; Crowd: 8,083

PAPUA NEW GUINEA and TONGA drew 28-28
At Hull; Crowd: 5,121

NEW ZEALAND beat PAPUA NEW GUINEA 22-6
At St Helens; Crowd: 8,679

GROUP TWO TABLE

	P	W	D	L	F	A	Pts
New Zealand	2	2	0	0	47	30	4
Tonga	2	0	1	1	52	53	1
PNG	2	0	1	1	34	50	1

GROUP THREE

WALES beat FRANCE 28-6
At Cardiff; Crowd: 10,250

WESTERN SAMOA beat FRANCE 56-10
At Cardiff; Crowd: 2,173

WALES beat WESTERN SAMOA 22-10
At Swansea; Crowd: 15,385

GROUP THREE TABLE

	P	W	D	L	F	A	Pts
Wales	2	2	0	0	50	16	4
Western Samoa	2	1	0	1	66	32	2
France	2	0	0	2	16	84	0

England had won their group, with over 26,000 people flocking to Wigan's Central Park to see them beat Fiji 46-0, with Bobbie Goulding having a blinder at scrum-half to put pressure on the incumbent Shaun Edwards.

Goulding retained his place for the 46-0 win over South Africa at Headingley. The Rhinos, coached by former Great Britain Test hooker Tony Fisher, tackled heroically, despite their lack of top level experience, in front of a 14,000-plus Saturday-night crowd.

The televised England-Wales semi-final captured the imagination of the sporting public. With one side of the Old Trafford stadium closed due to building works, the 30,000 crowd for the England Wales semi-final was a capacity figure as, at last, British Rugby League had its own domestic international rivalry presented on the big stage.

England, carefully guided by Bobbie Goulding - Shaun Edwards still absent with a knee infection - and man of the match Lee Jackson - won comfortably enough by 25-10 to progress to the final at Wembley, running in five tries against one, two of them to Martin Offiah.

This Old Trafford semi-final proved to be Jonathan Davies' last game in Rugby League before he went back to Welsh rugby union. And the excitement that Wales' high profile campaign had created - it was estimated that over 10,000 had made the trip from South Wales to support the national side - subsided.

Twenty-four hours after England's win, Australia and New Zealand fought out another epic in the second semi-final at Huddersfield's new McAlpine Stadium.

Australia had enjoyed big victories over Fiji and South Africa - a crowd of over 9,000 at Gateshead watching their 86-6 hammering of the Rhinos - and having whitewashed New Zealand in a Test series earlier in the year were expected to have little trouble.

It looked like that indeed would be the case as Australia led 20-6 after three-quarter time, after shooting into an early 10-0 lead through Tim Brasher and Steve

SEMI-FINALS

ENGLAND beat WALES 25-10
At Old Trafford, Manchester. Crowd: 30,042

AUSTRALIA beat NEW ZEALAND 30-20
(After extra-time. 80 mins score: 20-20)
At McAlpine Stadium, Huddersfield.
Crowd: 16,608

New Zealand's Matthew Ridge attempts the famous last-minute drop goal to try and break the 20-20 semi-final deadlock between the Kiwis and the Aussies

Menzies tries. After a try by Mark Coyne, Menzies got his second to seemingly ensure Australia's place in the final.

What followed was amazing. Not only did the Kiwis, on the back of eight penalties awarded by English referee Russell Smith, level the scores at 20-all with tries to Richie Barnett and one each to the Iro brothers Kevin and Tony, they could have stolen the game in the dying seconds. When Richie Blackmore put Kevin over in the corner in the 78th minute, Matthew Ridge had the chance to win the game with a touchline conversion, which he failed to take. Ridge thought he had won the game seconds later when his long-range field goal attempt sailed for the posts, only to miss by millimetres and set up extra time for the first time in a World Cup match since the GB-Australia final of 1972.

In extra-time, Barnett and Andrew Johns both missed with field-goal attempts, but on 87 minutes Australia scored a try worthy of winning a memorable match. Jason Smith, Terry Hill, Jim Dymock and Matthew Johns were all involved in a thrilling build-up that saw Hill race 30 metres for the crucial score. Brad Fittler's try on 92 minutes sealed a 30-20 win.

How English supporters would have cheered had Ridge's goal gone over! But they still travelled to Wembley with plenty of confidence that this battling Aussie team was there for the taking.

But missed chances, some straight down the line refereeing decisions by Stuart Cummings, and the remarkable resilience of the Australians, superbly prompted by Andrew Johns in the unaccustomed role of hooker, led to another World Cup disappointment for England.

Gary Connolly was making his first appearance in the tournament, following a bout of pneumonia, and he replaced Nick Pinkney in the centre, with Pinkney dropping to the bench. Chris Joynt also came into the squad on the bench, while Dean Sampson and Simon Haughton dropped out of the squad that had beaten Wales. The Australians made no changes from the squad that had seen off New Zealand in the semi-final.

The game was tense and tight. The Aussies took a sixth-minute lead, after Andrew Johns kicked through to the line for Rod Wishart to touch down, and from then on they never looked like losing in a game that didn't feature too many exciting incidents.

Down 10-4 at the break, England threatened to come back when Paul Newlove scored after making a powerful charge from the play-the-ball on 44 minutes, bringing the score back to 10-8. But it was Australia who would complete the scoring, with a try to Tim Brasher on 67 minutes, goaled again by Johns. Brad Fittler received the Halifax World Cup from HRH Prince Edward.

The Aussies had held out to win 16-8 in front of a 66,540 crowd - not bad for a tournament that much of the media had claimed nobody was interested in.

The whole tournament had been a triumph for Rugby League, destroying the millstone of the game's old parochial image, if only temporarily, as nations from all around the world gathered to play the game with such obvious enjoyment. Such was the spirit of the competition that not a single player was sent off for the duration of the whole tournament.

And crowds of over 26,000 at Wigan and 14,000 at Leeds for England's night games against Fiji and South Africa respectively could never have been predicted beforehand by even the most optimistic pundits.

Andrew Johns was named the outstanding player of the 1995 World Cup. Yet, remarkably, he couldn't find a place in the official World XIII named after the tournament, losing out to Papua New Guinea captain Adrian Lam for the scrum-half slot, and England's Lee Jackson for the hooking role.

Cook Islands won the Emerging Nations competition, beating Ireland 22-6 in the final at Gigg Lane, Bury. Both countries, along with fellow emerging nations Russia and Scotland, were to compete in the World Cup proper, five years later.

THE 1995 WORLD CUP FINAL

AUSTRALIA beat ENGLAND 16-8
28 October, 1995 *at Wembley Stadium*

AUSTRALIA: Tim Brasher, Rod Wishart, Mark Coyne, Terry Hill, Brett Dallas, Brad Fittler, Geoff Toovey, Dean Pay, Andrew Johns, Mark Carroll, Steve Menzies, Gary Larson, Jim Dymock. Subs. Jason Smith, Robbie O'Davis, Matthew Johns, Nik Kosef.
Tries: Wishart, Brasher.
Goals: A Johns 4

ENGLAND: Kris Radlinski, Jason Robinson, Gary Connolly, Paul Newlove, Martin Offiah, Tony Smith, Bobbie Goulding, Karl Harrison, Lee Jackson, Andy Platt, Denis Betts, Phil Clarke, Andy Farrell. Subs. Nick Pinkney, Barrie-Jon Mather, Mick Cassidy, Chris Joynt.

Try: Newlove. **Goals:** Goulding 2

Referee: Stuart Cummings (England)
Attendance: 66,540

A rampaging Andy Farrell tries to break free from the clutches of Gary Larson

Brett Dallas, Jim Dymock, Dean Pay and Jason Smith enjoy the moment

Jubilant Australian captain Brad Fittler lifts the World Cup at Wembley in 1995

Andy Farrell grounded by Australian duo Geoff Toovey and Steve Menzies

2000

Australia's dominance of world Rugby League was irrefutable after they secured their sixth successive World Cup title with a record-breaking seven-try 40-12 victory over the Kiwis in the final at Old Trafford, Manchester. They had held the World Cup since 1975 and had now won the trophy nine times out of a possible twelve since it was inaugurated in 1954.

After the great success of the 1995 tournament held in England and Wales, there was a further expansion of the number of teams in the 2000 World Cup, with no less than 16 teams competing in four groups of four, with matches scheduled for England, Wales, Scotland, Northern Ireland, Eire and France. The tournament was sponsored by a US financial investment company and was known as the Lincoln Financial Group World Cup.

There was also a second Emerging Nations competition, won by the British Amateur Rugby League Association, who beat Italy in the final.

For the first time there had been a qualifying tournament involving a Pacific Group and a Mediterranean Group, the winners of which played off for the 16th World Cup spot. Lebanon were the qualifier, beating the USA 62-8 in the play-off held at Disney's Wide World of Sports in Orlando, Florida.

Sadly, the weather did not treat the 2000 World Cup as kindly as it had done five years earlier. Britain was hit with freezing cold, windy, wet weather that caused widespread flooding and disrupted transport systems right from the very first game at Windsor Park in Belfast, televised on a Saturday afternoon, with Ireland playing Samoa in front of what looked like a virtually empty stadium. From that point onwards the 2000 World Cup was struggling to shake off the perception it was a failure.

A tournament that was budgeted to make a profit of more than 2.5 million pounds, ended up making a loss of almost 600,000, although this after the Australian RL netted 350,000 pounds for winning the tournament, and 50,000 as a participating nation. Over-optimistic financial projections, coupled with appalling autumn weather combined to hit the World Cup hard.

The biggest deficit was the income from gate receipts, which was budgeted at over four million pounds. The actual income was just over 2.5 million pounds from a series of disappointing attendances.

It took another eight years before the Rugby League International Federation plucked up the courage to stage the next World Cup.

GROUP ONE

The winner of Group One was decided on the opening day of the 2000 World Cup when, hours after Ireland and Samoa had opened the tournament in Belfast, Australia beat England 22-2 at rain-soaked Twickenham - Wembley Stadium had been demolished to make way for a new stadium.

2000 WORLD CUP

GROUP ONE

England 2 ....Australia 22
Fiji 38 ....Russia 12
Australia 66 ....Fiji 8
England 76 ....Russia 4
Australia 110 ....Russia 4
England 66 ....Fiji 10

GROUP ONE TABLE

	P	W	D	L	F	A	D	Pts
Australia	3	3	0	0	198	14	184	6
England	3	2	0	1	144	36	108	4
Fiji	3	1	0	2	56	144	-88	2
Russia	3	0	0	3	20	224	-204	0

England, coached by John Kear, were well beaten, but it was not the massacre many feared. Australia's Dream Team was held in check for most of the game, before scoring two tries towards the end of this historic first ever Rugby League match at rugby union headquarters.

Lacking match fitness after playing just a couple of easy matches – against PNG (82-0) and New Zealand Residents (108-0) - in the previous two months, Australia showed only flashes of the form that made them red-hot favourites. The slippery conditions also slowed them down, and their flat attacking formation suited England, who were very much in their faces.

Australia's biggest threat came from their smallest player, scrum-half Brett Kimmorley, who ruled midfield all night. It was Kimmorley's keen eye and perfectly-placed kick that led to Australia's first try after only four minutes. Spotting acres of space on England's left wing he plopped a kick over near the flag to leave Wendell Sailor with plenty of time to pick up the ball and stroll round for the touchdown. Later in the half Kimmorley linked with Brad Fittler to send Matthew Gidley sliding over.

It was still only 10-2, after Australia had opted for a pressure-easing penalty well into the second half, when a break by Kimmorley set up the position from which Adam MacDougall scored the try that really finished off England. Mat Rogers' goal made it 16-2, and England did well not to concede another try until the last minute, when Australia flashed the ball out for Sailor to grab his second.

Australia's winning margin would have been greater but for two first-half video rulings going against them. Ryan Girdler was penalised

Adrian Morley receives some close attention from Scott Hill at Twickenham as England go down to Australia in the opening game

for a double movement, and Fittler was adjudged to have knocked on when following up another neat kick by Kimmorley.

The nearest England went to scoring a try was when Sean Long made a break and was obstructed. The referee allowed play to go on, however, and Paul Rowley hacked towards the corner, where Leon Pryce gathered before being bundled into touch as his inside pass went to ground.

Stuart Spruce was a late English withdrawal because of illness, 18 year old Chev Walker making a confident full international debut, along with other youngsters Pryce, Kevin Sinfield and Paul Wellens.

The day after at Craven Park, Barrow, Russia, in the tournament for the first time, gave Fiji a run for their money before going down 38-12. But the Bears - captained by Eastern Suburbs front-rower Ian Rubin - were bedevilled by handling errors throughout and completed only one set of six in the entire first half.

The Fijians, coached by former Kangaroos coach Don Furner - were much steadier and found enough possession to show their full range of running and handling skills, with Tabua Cakacaka at prop and Sam Marayawa in the second row starring up front.

Rubin was outstanding for Russia and others to impress were scrum-half Ivor Gavriline, fullback Robert Iliassov and wingmen Mikhail Mitrofanov and Maxim Romanov. But Fiji captain, Brisbane winger Lote Tuqiri was the star of the show at fullback.

Tuqiri was once again outstanding but there was no stopping Australia at Gateshead the following Wednesday. Mat Rogers broke Andrew Johns' Australian Test record when he scored 34 points, through four tries and nine goals.

As it turned out, it was a mark which would last only until the following Saturday night, when the records tumbled again at The Boulevard as the world champions ruthlessly piled up 110 points against Russia's four at the Boulevard. Ryan Girdler scored three tries and kicked 17 goals from 19 attempts.

The 28 year old Penrith centre set a new world record for goals in an international match but fell two short of Hazem El Masri's 48-point record for Lebanon against Morocco in 1999 when the previous record international score, 104-0, was established.

The ink was hardly dry in the record books after Tasesa Lavea's 12 goals for the Kiwis against the Cook Islands on the previous Thursday, but Girdler surpassed that with ease and his 46-point tally was also a record for a World Cup game.

Girdler's two misses at goal came in succession as he failed to add conversions to the Australians' sixth and seventh tries of the evening, the first attempt hitting a post, but he then went on to kick 12 goals in succession. Winger Wendell Sailor also equalled the Australian and World Cup record with four tries.

The Russians earned the admiration of the small crowd with some brave tackling and adventurous attacking moves and they got their reward with a try made in Australia. After Western Suburbs winger Matthew Donovan, who qualified for Russia through his grandparents, went close with a darting inside run, prop Robert Campbell took Igor Gavriline's pass and drilled a low kick to the left corner. Donovan gleefully pounced for the score that was allowed after referee Stuart Cummings went to the screen.

England also had little trouble getting through their other two group games. At St Helens they ran up a record 76-4 win against Russia, beating their previous best of 73-6 against France in 1996

England, without six players who played against Australia, struggled early in the game despite taking a 30-2 interval lead, and looked a lot sharper when Sean Long replaced Andy Farrell at stand-off. England hooker Paul Rowley deservedly took the man of the match award with an all-action two-try display. The game attracted a meagre attendance of 5,736.

On the Saturday, England beat Fiji 66-10 at Headingley. Andy Farrell equalled two England records with nine goals and 22 points, including a clever solo try when he dummied through in classic style.

The spectators were thrilled with the exciting running of Lote Tuqiri. From his first brilliant kick and run raid in the opening minutes to his breakaway 75th minute try, the tall fullback looked one of the most outstanding players of the competition.

The crowd showed their appreciation as the Fijians took a lap of honour, their World Cup at an end.

GROUP TWO

2000 WORLD CUP

GROUP TWO

Lebanon 0	New Zealand 64
Wales 38	Cook Islands 6
Cook Islands 10	New Zealand 84
Wales 24	Lebanon 22
Cook Islands 22	Lebanon 22
Wales 18	New Zealand 58

GROUP TWO TABLE

	P	W	D	L	F	A	D	Pts
New Zealand	3	3	0	0	206	28	178	6
Wales	3	2	0	1	80	86	-6	4
Lebanon	3	0	1	2	44	110	-66	1
Cook Islands	3	0	1	2	38	144	-106	1

Wales began their World Cup campaign with a six-try 38-6 defeat of the Cook Islands at the Racecourse Ground, Wrexham, dominating after the break to score 32-unopposed points in the second half, on the back of an outstanding hat-trick from Kris Tassell. The Salford centre, who was born in Mount Isa in Queensland but whose grandfather was born in Pontypridd, sparked the Welsh revival with a superb finish just after the interval. Due to a late change in numbers, he heard the PA announcer credit all three of his tries to Jason Critchley.

The Welsh had three survivors from the side that played at Old Trafford in the semi-final five years before in skipper Iestyn Harris, Anthony Sullivan and Keiron Cunningham. The Cooks had two remaining players, Craig Bowen and Jason Temu, from the side that won the Emerging Nations World Cup in 1995.

On another rain-swept, bitterly cold night, Wales struggled for fluency against some committed tackling from the Cooks in a scrappy first half and were disappointed to go in at the interval on level terms, 6-6. But when Harris's superb pass created room for Tassell down the left channel just after the break and the Australian finished incisively from 25 metres, and Harris landed the touchline conversion for a 12-6 lead. On the back of an 8-0 penalty count in the second half, Wales were in control of the game and Tassell completed a successful evening with two late tries to complete his hat-trick.

A virtuoso performance by the brilliant Iestyn Harris in a 24-22 win over Lebanon at Stradey Park, Llanelli, the following Thursday ensured Wales' qualification for the last eight.

Harris beat Lebanon virtually off his own bat, scoring two tries and having a decisive hand in the other three while adding two goals, rising above the vile, cold and wet conditions and the lack of sense of occasion - a crowd of just under 1500 was recorded.

The Cedars looked out of sorts in the opening half-hour, giving Harris far too much respect as the Welsh set the platform for a seemingly comfortable win as they built an 18-0 lead. But in the end Wales were thankful for Wes Davies's converted try midway through the second half that just gave them enough breathing space in the face of a stirring Lebanese revival.

The final standings in group two were decided conclusively on the Sunday when New Zealand hammered Wales 58-18 in Cardiff. Making their debut at the Millennium Stadium, the Welsh were enthusiastically

Justin Morgan (11) congratulates Lee Briers on scoring against the Cook Islands

roared on by a 17,000-plus crowd, and the majority went home happy in the knowledge that their League Dragons had fallen to one of the strongest Kiwi sides of recent times. Given the amount of withdrawals and injuries that led to pre-tournament predictions that they wouldn't win a game, Wales' rag, tag and bob-tail side had done remarkably well.

The inspirational Keiron Cunningham and leading try-scorer Kris Tassell were missing, there was a hooker (Mick Jenkins) in the back row and a centre pairing of a current rugby union player – Jason Critchley - and a young former union player with just three months of reserve-grade Rugby League experience behind him, in Hefin O'Hare.

Lesley Vainikolo, Willie Talau and Henry Paul all crossed before the first of Wales' three tries, and it was 30-6 at half-time. Tonie Carroll was amongst the Kiwi try-scorers.

New Zealand had already easily accounted for Lebanon by 64-0 at Kingsholm, Gloucester in incessant heavy rain and a howling wind. Several Lebanon players were suffering from mild hypothermia by the end of the game.

Inspiring Kiwi captain Richie Barnett – playing his first game since an horrific facial injury suffered in the Anzac Test the previous April was outstanding.

On the Thursday the Kiwis beat Cook Islands 84-10 at Madejski Stadium, Reading. The Kiwis ran in 15 tries in total as the Cook Islands defence burst its banks quicker than some of England's rain-swollen rivers. Frank Endacott's team came close to breaking every record in the book. Tasesa Lavea personally grabbed 32 points on his debut to establish a new Kiwi Test record.

The Melbourne Storm stand-off kicked twelve goals, beating the previous mark of Henry Paul, the man he was replacing, and scored two tries to take the man of the match award. For the 20-year-old Lavea, it was a new goals-in-a-World Cup match record that was to stand for only two days.

There was no separating Cook Islands and Lebanon as they fought out a 22-all draw in a game played as part of the double header at Millennium Stadium, Cardiff.

The game made history as the first international to be played 'indoors', the sliding roof being closed before kick-off to keep out the torrential rain.

A superb fightback by the gallant Lebanese, 22-10 down with four minutes to go, having been 18-4 behind at the break, ensured the honours were deservedly shared.

It was a fine end to the tournament for the two nations, who went back to their countries to spread the League gospel.

GROUP THREE

Group Three was played solely in France, which meant British fans didn't get the opportunity to see a teenage Willie Mason first make his mark on the international game with Tonga.

The group was launched with a double header at Charlety Stadium, which had been the home of Paris Saint Germain for the two years of their Super League existence in 1996 and 1997.

2000 WORLD CUP

GROUP THREE

France 20 ....Papua New Guinea 23
South Africa 18..................................Tonga 66
France 28 ....Tonga 8
Papua New Guinea 16 ....South Africa 0
France 56 ....South Africa 6
Papua New Guinea 30.........................Tonga 22

GROUP THREE TABLE

	P	W	D	L	F	A	D	Pts
PNG	3	3	0	0	69	42	27	6
France	3	2	0	1	104	37	67	4
Tonga	3	1	0	2	96	76	20	2
South Africa	3	0	0	3	24	138	-114	0

Papua New Guinea overturned a 16-0 deficit to spoil France's party and claim a valuable 23-20 win in the opening match. PNG captain and scrum-half Adrian Lam produced a superb performance to take his side to victory, against the run of play, scoring a solo try out of the top drawer and dropping a goal that dented French hopes.

France were well organised and were growing in confidence as they led 12-0 at half-time and went further ahead after the break. PNG, by contrast, had relied on their talented individuals, in particular Lam, Stanley Gene and Marcus Bai.

Melbourne's Bai signalled PNG's comeback, first being held five metres short of the line and then going over for the Kumuls' first try after 53 minutes of play. Three minutes later, Gene's break, followed by Lam's kick over the top, caught the French defence napping and substitute Alex Krewanty dived in to score PNG's second.

At 16-10 France were under siege. Their big lead had gone to their heads. Yacine Dekkiche and Laurent Frayssinous, within seconds of each other, threw out extravagant passes when something much simpler might have brought results. Then Banquet failed with a drop-goal attempt.

PNG were putting their game together. Lam's pass sent Gene on a 30-metre run, before the stand-off delayed his pass for David Buko to score under the posts. With ten minutes left, Wilshere converted to equalise at 16-all. Then Lam sold two dummies to cross the line without a hand laid on him to give his side the lead for the first time three minutes from time. Two minutes later he was there again to drop the goal from which there would be no return for the French.

Tonga trampled all over South Africa's Rhinos in a 66-18 win to set up a do-or-die encounter in Carcassonne the following Wednesday afternoon. Three-try Bradford Bulls hero Tevita Vaikona led the rout in the second match of the double header as Tonga looked hot favourites to win the group

A huge crowd of 10,288 packed into Stade Albert Domec on a gloriously sunny Wednesday afternoon in Carcassonne to see France keep their qualification hopes alive after a 28-8 win over Tonga. Few gave France a chance against a Tonga side still bristling with confidence after their 66-18 annihilation of South Africa.

France great Puig Aubert's statue was unveiled that morning before an audience of VIPs and both sets of players produced a display which did the Gallic spirit of "Pipette" great justice.

Where France had buckled in the face of an opposition comeback at the Charlety Stadium, this time they held on and pulled away from a highly competent Tonga side with two breathtaking late tries from Jean-Marc Garcia and Pascal Jampy.

A noisy, musical crowd, sky-divers, packed terraces, Olympic champions symbolically kicking the game off, all combined to create the sort of atmosphere that World Cups were made for.

From the moment that Freddie Banquet crossed for France's first try after 26 minutes - to wipe out an eleventh minute 4-0 lead to the Tongans established by centre David Fisi'iahi - Gilles Dumas' men had made a start on re-establishing the national credibility of rugby a treize.

Banquet converted both his own effort and St Gaudens winger Claude Sirvent's four-pointer four minutes before the break, from a long Fabien Devecchi pass, to give France a deserved 12-4 lead while Tongan sub Nelson Lomi was in the sin bin for a flop.

The alarm bells began ringing again when Fisi'iahi's brother Paul opened the second-half scoring for Tonga after 51 minutes. But this time the French side was made of sterner stuff. With 14 minutes left, Sirvent's club-mate Arnaud Dulac skipped through a rare defensive hole to make it 16-8.

And - after Sirvent had a try disallowed and Lomi found himself on

Jubilant Papua New Guinea skipper Adrian Lam celebrates his side's win over France

report for a late tackle - Garcia and Jampy's sensational last-minute double put France in great heart for their Sunday afternoon clash with South Africa.

Tonga coach Murray Hurst, the North Queensland Cowboys assistant now had to prepare his shell-shocked side for a huge showdown against Papua New Guinea in Saint-Esteve the following Monday.

The Kumuls made hard work of beating South Africa by 16-0 on a rainy night in Toulouse. PNG had to wait until the 25th minute to register their first points when Brisbane Souths centre Eddie Aila darted through from 20 metres, with John Wilshere converting. Aila's try and a 31st minute Wilshere effort - together with the winger's second conversion - were the only first-half points PNG could muster.

Had substitute Justin Jennings made the most of a gift chance instead of knocking on with the line at his mercy two minutes into the second half, the outcome could have been very different. The Rhinos held PNG to a mere four points - a 52nd minute Elias Paiyo try.

France made certain of a quarter-final place with a comprehensive 56-6 success against 12-man South Africa in Albi.

France's final home match - watched by another bumper crowd in the treiziste heartland - was predictable even before the kick-off but South African skipper Jamie Bloem gave France a little assistance by getting sent off on the half-hour, after giving Australian referee Steve Clark an unwanted opinion as he was sin-binned for interference at the play-the-ball.

And Stanley Gene-inspired Papa New Guinea finished top of the group with a Monday night 30-22 win over Tonga in St Esteve, to set up a quarter-final clash with Wales.

GROUP FOUR

It was a damp and grey World-Cup opening in Belfast, as Ireland justified their pre-tournament billing as Group Four winners with a professional 30-16 win over ring-rusty Samoa.

Sub-gale-force winds and ice-cold rain lashed Ulster all afternoon, deterring all of the floating voters who World Cup organisers were banking on rolling up to the home of the Linfield soccer club.

2000 WORLD CUP

GROUP FOUR

Ireland 30	Samoa 16
Scotland 16	Aotearoa Maori 17
Aotearoa Maori 16	Samoa 21
Ireland 18	Scotland 6
Ireland 30	Aotearoa Maori 16
Scotland 12	Samoa 20

GROUP FOUR TABLE

	P	W	D	L	F	A	D	Pts
Ireland	3	3	0	0	78	38	40	6
Samoa	3	2	0	1	57	58	-1	4
Aotearoa Maori	3	1	0	2	49	67	-18	2
Scotland	3	0	0	3	34	55	-21	0

The wide empty spaces around the ground didn't provide the type of backdrop that the tournament needed for its launch. But the 3,000-plus locals, as well as a handful of Samoan supporters, were absorbed as Ireland's game came together in the last 40 minutes, after a first half of bruising defence from both sides.

There was no panic in the Ireland camp, even after ten minutes of relentless Samoan pressure just before the break had put the game in the balance. Ireland had a shaky looking 12-10 lead at that point. Barrie McDermott had given them a wonder start when he stepped opposite number Jerry Seuseu 20 metres out and bumped off Laloa Milford, before offloading to Chris Joynt for the try. Steve Prescott added a fine conversion. But within five minutes Samoa winger Bryan Leauma somehow got a hand to Anthony Swann's kick into the right corner. Willie Poching mis-cued the conversion badly, and it wasn't until the 24th minute that Ireland were able to breach the Samoa defence again. A delayed pass from Ryan Sheridan sent Michael Withers through on the angle, and his pass found Luke Ricketson on the inside for the try.

But fullback Milford pulled back a try just before the half hour on the back of a mounting penalty count, and stand-off Simon Geros's conversion – Poching was excused from the job after missing a kickable penalty – finished the first-half scoring.

The Samoans were very physical, much in the mould of the 1995 team, with many unknown names from the competitions down under. And they had a genuine class player in David Solomona, a giant in the Sydney Roosters pack in 2000.

But the first seven minutes after the turnaround secured Ireland's winning start. On 43 minutes Tommy Martyn gave Michael Eagar a metre to work in down the left, and the Tigers' centre beat three men on a storming run down the wing. Four minutes Withers put Brian Carney in at the right corner.

Prescott kicked a straight penalty, and then scored a try, when Sheridan's kick against the post protector fooled Milford – who thought

Ireland celebrate after they had defeated the Maori to reach the quarter-finals

he had got a hand to it first - to put Ireland out of sight.

Hooker Monty Betham got a consolation score for Samoa, but they had little hope by then.

Ireland won their other two games to top the group, beating Scotland 18-6 in a midweek game, and the Maori 30-16, both in Dublin.

With Ireland leading 12-6 against the Scots, the game turned in a five-minute spell around the hour mark. First Lee Gilmour failed to cling onto a peach of a scoring pass from Vowles before the Castleford stalwart was sin-binned, a result of cumulative offsides by the Bravehearts.

In his absence the Irish conjured up the best move of the game to ensure victory. Terry O'Connor started the rumble and magnificent passes out of the tackle as they fell by Prescott and Carney saw Michael Withers power into the corner for a spectacular try. The only other score was a fifth Prescott goal late on.

Ireland out-muscled the physical Maori in the battle up front, with props Terry O'Connor and Barrie McDermott providing them with tremendous go-forward and back-rowers David Barnhill and Kevin Campion tireless workers throughout.

Samoa finished second in Group Four. After their defeat to Ireland they travelled to Derwent Park, Workington for a midweek clash with the Maori that lit up the World Cup. The two sides played out a wonderful drama before an enthralled Cumbrian crowd as the rain gods relented to provide a fine, calm evening. The crowd was already enthused by the pre-match hakas, with the Maori performing their pre-match ritual twice. The Samoans, though, outdid them after a tremendous 21-16 win by repeating their's twice for a crowd that was reluctant to go home.

Maori coach Cameron Bell's squad rotation back-fired as the rested Gene Ngamu wasn't on hand to decide the tie, replacement stand-off Luke Goodwin fluffing two field goal attempts when the game was poised at 16-16 late on. (A late field goal from Gene Ngamu had given the Maori a 17-16 win over Scotland in their opening game in Glasgow).

On the other hand, Darrell Williams was delighted with the changes he had wrung, especially bringing in Auckland Warrior Henry Aau Fa'afili at stand-off, as he was outstanding.

Willie Swann landed a good field goal to steal the game and Milford's last-second try was just the full-stop at the end of a superb night.

Samoa earned the dubious privilege of a quarter-final meeting with Australia with a 20-12 win over Scotland in Edinburgh.

Scotland, despite having lost both their previous game, needed to win by two or more points to make the quarter-finals but Samoa won a deserved victory inspired by their brilliant fullback Milford and two-try winger Bryan Leauma.

QUARTER-FINALS

AUSTRALIA 66 SAMOA 10

Australia's 12-try romp over the brave but eventually outclassed Samoans at Watford brought the world champions' points-tally to 264 in four games.

Second row forward Bryan Fletcher led the way with his first senior hat-trick as Andrew Johns, the official man of the match, and Brett Kimmorley bossed the midfield, allowing Scott Hill and skipper Brad Fittler to make hay in the teeming rain.

The wet weather again followed the World Cup roadshow but the Australians adapted impressively to the conditions.

At 40-10, with ten minutes to go, Samoa coach Darrell Williams could have been well pleased with his side's efforts. But Australia ran in 26 points, including five tries, in the closing ten minutes as the mighty effort of the first half took its toll on the Samoan defence.

FRANCE 6 NEW ZEALAND 54

The Kiwis made smooth progress through to the semi-finals with a ten-try demolition of the French at Castleford.

They were too big, fast and powerful for a gallant France side with Robbie Paul - standing in for the rested Stacey Jones - leading the way with three tries and brother Henry adding seven goals.

History was against a French side that had improved steadily as the tournament had progressed as their last win over the Kiwis had been 20 years before, by a 6-5 margin in Perpignan.

But the big defeat wasn't enough to disperse the new tide of optimism that had permeated French Rugby League on the back of a successful World Cup in 2000.

England's Andy Farrell collides with Ireland's David Barnhill

ENGLAND 26 IRELAND 16

The first meeting between the two home nations at Headingley was all that had been predicted with Ireland forcing England to battle all the way for their place in the semi-finals.

England needed to re-group when Ireland led 10-4 midway through the first half. Having fought back, they spread the ball wide to run in three excellent tries.

Stuart Fielden battered the Irish front line, and also stood out in defence, overhauling Kevin Campion to end the second-rower's 60-metre break just short of the England line. It was a crucial tackle as a try and goal would have pulled Ireland back to only 20-16 down with 15 minutes left.

England took full advantage of the try-saver to scramble possession from Ireland's next play and power back with a match-clinching try from Chev Walker.

Ireland had done their country proud throughout the World Cup.

Wales' Dean Busby is halted by Papua New Guinea's Elias Paiyo

WALES 22 PAPUA NEW GUINEA 8

Wales progressed to the semi-finals with unexpected ease against a Papua New Guinea side that played with plenty of passion, courage and no little flair, but paid the price for a five-minute spell midway through the first half when they conceded two vital tries.

Having won more games than ever before on an overseas tour, the Kumuls returned home to bask in a heroes' welcome despite never really hitting their straps against a determined Welsh side.

A five-minute spell in the middle of the half saw Wales score two vital tries.

First Adrian Lam, attempting to offload in a tackle, sent the ball straight into the hands of Jason Critchley who romped away from 40 metres for the game's opening try.

From the re-start, superb Welsh defence forced John Wilshere to concede a drop-out, and after Keiron Cunningham had gone close, the ball was spread wide to the left where Iestyn Harris and Lee Briers combined for the Warrington scrum-half to dummy through and stretch over near the corner.

New Zealand's Stacey Jones collared by England captain Andy Farrell

SEMI-FINALS

ENGLAND 6 NEW ZEALAND 49

Red-hot New Zealand shattered England's World Cup dream at the Reebok Stadium with a near-perfect display.

Every Kiwi looked top class, none more so than Bradford Bulls' stand-off Henry Paul, who gave one of the outstanding performances of the tournament.

From the second minute, when he sent in Stephen Kearney for the first try to when he put Logan Swann through for the last, Paul was in total command. He was involved in five tries altogether and kicked nine goals including a field goal, with his first two-pointer giving him a century of points for New Zealand in Test and World Cup matches.

191

Jason Cayless is halted by Andy Farrell and Paul Anderson

England raised faint hopes of a rally when they scored their only try early in the second half with Tony Smith touching down Sean Long's neat kick and Andy Farrell adding the goal.

But New Zealand's response was to deliver another shattering blow as a typical hefty tackle caused Paul Sculthorpe to cough up the ball and a few swift passes brought Willie Talau his first try.

It became a procession after that as Nigel Vagana, Lesley Vainikolo, Talau and Logan Swann swept in for tries to rack up a record defeat for England, beating the 42-13 loss against France back in 1951.

AUSTRALIA 46 WALES 22

Australia made their predicted progress through to the World Cup Final but not before Clive Griffiths' gallant Welsh side had lifted the spirits of a nation.

The Welsh produced an outstanding display of enterprise and commitment to the cause, holding a 22-14 lead early in the second half before the Kangaroos dominated the latter stages of a truly memorable encounter.

Lee Briers, Keiron Cunningham, Paul Highton and skipper Iestyn Harris all played superbly in a wonderful team effort as the mighty Kangaroos were rocked by the sheer pride of a Wales side written off as no-hopers before the tournament.

But second-half tries by Bryan Fletcher, Darren Lockyer (two), Brad Fittler, Craig Gower and Ben Kennedy - the culmination of one of the most glorious passages of football ever seen in a World Cup - ended the impossible dream.

Wales' Iestyn Harris is all wrapped up against Australia

2000 WORLD CUP FINAL

AUSTRALIA 40 NEW ZEALAND 12

Man of the match Wendell Sailor equalled the record for tries in a final with a decisive brace in four minutes, after the Kiwis had fought back to trail only 12-18 midway through the second half at Old Trafford.

Mat Rogers, with six goals and twelve points, set new records for a final and Australia's winning margin surpassed their previous record 25-12 score-line against New Zealand in 1988, the Kiwis' only previous final appearance.

Sailor, with ten tries, and Rogers, with 27 goals and 70 points, also topped the World Cup 2000 scoring charts between them.

The Kangaroos had held the World Cup since 1975 and had won the trophy nine times out of a possible twelve since it was inaugurated in 1954.

The unstoppable Kangaroos - hot favourites at the start of the competition - dominated the final quarter, amassing 22 points in the last

14 minutes.

But it was the monster defensive effort demanded from the Kiwis in the first half that won the game for the Kangaroos.

Australian coach Chris Anderson dubbed the win: 'as good a team performance as you could ask for under pressure.'

Skipper Brad Fittler, Brett Kimmorley, Andrew Johns and Scott Hill all rivalled the magnificent Sailor for the man-of-the-match accolade.

Kimmorley's kicking game was superb and his ability to take the ball to the line and release his runners was never better demonstrated. Fittler, too, capped a memorable day with a fine try while Johns justified his switch to hooker with astute distribution. Hill's ability to join the line and combine with Fittler and Kimmorley was crucial.

Of the younger players, centre Matthew Gidley capped a magnificent personal tournament, while Trent Barrett looked another superstar in the making.

The world champions dominated right from the opening stages, with Kimmorley dictating their attacks and soon demonstrating his vast repertoire of attacking kicks.

The Kiwis' first attack took eleven minutes to mount but Sailor calmly knocked away Jones' kick with a foot in the dead-ball area to set up a 20-metre tap.

The forward battle was as tough and unrelenting as forecast but the Kangaroos looked to have made the breakthrough when Sailor blasted over in the right corner but the video referee ruled that Stephen Kearney's despairing tackle had succeeded in preventing Sailor from grounding the ball.

But the Kangaroos were not to be denied three minutes later when Sailor drilled the ball through and Gidley just got a hand to it before it went dead. The video referee gave his assent and Rogers converted from the touch-line.

It was the only score of the first half, but Kimmorley began the second in the same dominant form and, after another testing kick, Nigel Vagana was trapped behind his own line by a magnificent Rogers tackle from dummy-half. From the resulting drop-out the Kangaroos engineered their second converted try as Johns and Fittler combined to send Nathan Hindmarsh stretching over on the left for a converted try.

But the big crowd came to life as the Kiwis mounted their revival, Vainikolo grabbing his ninth try of the World Cup after Matt Rua had challenged Lockyer to Jones' high, angled kick to the left, Henry Paul adding the conversion after the video referee had again been called upon.

Within three minutes the Kangaroos restored their 12-point advantage when Kimmorley dummied to the right before cutting through to unselfishly provide the supporting Darren Lockyer with a run-in on the inside.

But the Kiwis were back in the game when centre Tonie Carroll received from Henry Paul and twice eluded Adam MacDougall - in for Ryan Girdler, injured the previous week - on a blockbusting 30-metre run for a try that Henry Paul converted.

With Bradford's Robbie Paul brought off the bench, the Kiwis spied their chance and Sailor, rescuing his side after Jones and Kearney combined to almost send Vainikolo in, knocked-on ten metres from his own line.

But the Kiwis were unable to take advantage of the opportunity and the Kangaroos took over after, first, Henry Paul had knocked on at dummy-half and then Carroll couldn't hold a pass, both in attacking positions.

The decisive try came in the 66th minute when Gidley took out three defenders with an exquisite inside pass and Sailor twisted over in Robbie Paul's last ditch tackle, Rogers again negotiating the tricky goal attempt.

Henry Paul compounded the Kiwis' misery by kicking-off directly into touch and, three minutes later, the Australians were home and dry as Johns, Lockyer and Gidley laid on Sailor's second.

Fittler, stepping inside the cover from Lockyer's pass in his own inimitable way, and Barrett, with a magnificent 60-metre effort from Fittler's pass, added further converted tries in the dying minutes.

The weather gods had relented for the game but, after the presentations by Britain's Olympic legend Steve Redgrave had been completed, the rain returned.

The crowds were sent on their way home with a drenching to remind them of the horrific weather that had plagued the 2000 World Cup.

THE 2000 WORLD CUP FINAL

AUSTRALIA 40 ....**NEW ZEALAND 12**
At Old Trafford, Manchester,
Saturday 25 November 2000
Australia: T - Gidley (26), N Hindmarsh (46), Lockyer (53), Sailor (66, 69), Fittler (74), Barrett (76); G - Rogers 6
New Zealand: T - Vainikolo (50), Carroll (57); G - H Paul 2

Australia: 1 Darren Lockyer (Brisbane Broncos); 5 Wendell Sailor (Brisbane Broncos); 4 Matthew Gidley (Newcastle Knights); 3 Adam MacDougall (Newcastle Knights); 2 Mat Rogers (Cronulla Sharks); 6 Brad Fittler (C) (Sydney Roosters); 7 Brett Kimmorley (Melbourne Storm); 8 Shane Webcke (Brisbane Broncos); 9 Andrew Johns (Newcastle Knights); 10 Robbie Kearns (Melbourne Storm); 11 Gorden Tallis (Brisbane Broncos); 12 Bryan Fletcher (Sydney Roosters); 13 Scott Hill (Melbourne Storm). Subs (all used): 17 Jason Stevens (Cronulla Sharks) for Webcke (13); 16 Darren Britt (Sydney Bulldogs) for Kearns (20); 15 Nathan Hindmarsh (Parramatta Eels) for Fletcher (20); Fletcher for Tallis (27); Webcke for Stevens (57); Tallis for Fletcher (62); 14 Trent Barrett (St George-Illawarra Dragons) for MacDougall (64); Kearns for Hindmarsh (78)
New Zealand: 1 Richie Barnett (C) (Sydney City Roosters); 2 Nigel Vagana (Auckland Warriors); 3 Tonie Carroll (Brisbane Broncos); 4 Willie Talau (Canterbury Bulldogs); 5 Lesley Vainikolo (Canberra Raiders); 6 Henry Paul (Bradford Bulls); 7 Stacey Jones (Auckland Warriors); 8 Craig Smith (St George-Illawarra Dragons); 9 Richard Swain (Melbourne Storm); 10 Quentin Pongia (Sydney City Roosters); 11 Matt Rua (Melbourne Storm); 12 Stephen Kearney (Melbourne Storm); 13 Ruben Wiki (Canberra Raiders). Subs (all played): 16 Nathan Cayless (Parramatta Eels) for Smith (14); 15 Joe Vagana (Auckland Warriors) for Pongia (14); 17 Logan Swann (Auckland Warriors) for Rua (20); Pongia for J Vagana (31); Smith for Cayless (31); Rua for Wiki (41); 14 Robbie Paul (Bradford Bulls) for Swain (58); J Vagana for Smith (58); Cayless for Pongia (58); Wiki for Kearney (70); Smith for J Vagana (75); Pongia for Cayless (75).

Attendance: 44,329
Referee: Stuart Cummings (England)
Half-time: 6-0

Joe Vagana upended during the World Cup Final

Brad Fittler lifts the 2000 World Cup

Tonie Carroll tries to break free

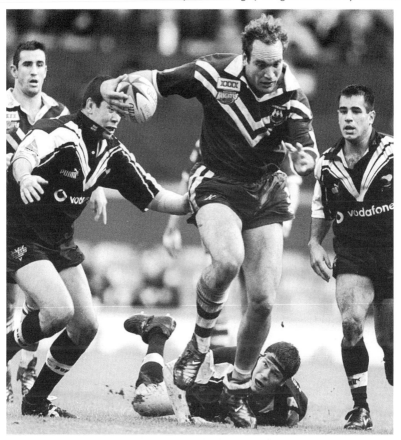

Gorden Tallis rampages through the New Zealand defensive ranks

Australia celebrate victory over New Zealand in the World Cup Final

3
RUGBY LEAGUE WORLD CUP STATISTICS

Rugby League World Cup Statistics

1954

FRANCE 22 ....**NEW ZEALAND 13**
At Parc de Princes, Paris, Saturday, October 30, 1954
Attendance: 13,240; **Referee:** Cyril Appleton (England)
France: T - Contrastin, Delaye, Crespo, Audobert;
G - Puig Aubert 5
New Zealand: T - Edwards, Eastlake, McKay; G - Bond 2
France: Puig Aubert (c), Vincent Cantoni, Jackie
Merquey, Antoine Jiminez, Raymond Contrastin, Claude
Teisseire, Gilbert Benausse, Francois Rinaldi, Jean
Audoubert, Joseph Krawzyk, Guy Delaye, Jean
Pambrun, Joseph Crespo.
New Zealand: Doug Anderson, Jim Edwards, Cyril
Eastlake (c), George Menzies, Ron McKay, Bill
Sorensen, Bill McLennan, Lory Blanchard, Cliff
Johnson, John Bond, John Yates, Lenny Eriksen,
Alistair Atkinson.

GREAT BRITAIN 28.........................**AUSTRALIA 13**
At Stade de Gerland, Lyon, Sunday, October 31, 1954
Attendance: 10,250; **Referee:** Rene Guidicelli (France)
Great Britain: T - Brown 2, Jackson 2, Kitchen, Rose;
G - Ledgard 5
Australia: T- Wells 2, Kearney; G - Pidding 2
Great Britain: Jim Ledgard, David Rose, Phil Jackson,
Mick Sullivan, Frank Kitchen, Gordon Brown, Gerry
Helme, Bob Coverdale, Sam Smith, John Thorley, Don
Robinson, Basil Watts, Dave Valentine (c).
Australia: Clive Churchill (c), Noel Pidding, Alex
Watson, Harry Wells, Ian Moir, Ken McCaffery, Keith
Holman, Roy Bull, Ken Kearney, Duncan Hall, Brian
Davies, Norm Provan, Peter Diversi.

AUSTRALIA 34 ....**NEW ZEALAND 15**
At Marseilles, Sunday, November 7, 1954
Attendance: 20,000; **Referee:** Rene Guidicelli (France)
Australia: T - Watson 3, Hawick, Bull, Kearney, O'Shea,
Diversi; G - Pidding 5
New Zealand: T - Eriksen; G - McKay 6
Australia: Clive Churchill (c), Noel Pidding, Alex
Watson, Harry Wells, Denis Flannery, Bob Banks, Greg
Hawick, Roy Bull, Ken Kearney, Brian Davies, Kel
O'Shea, Mick Crocker, Peter Diversi.
New Zealand: Nev Denton, Jim Edwards, Cyril Eastlake
(c), Ron McKay, George Menzies, Bill Sorensen, Lenny
Eriksen, Bill McLennan, Lory Blanchard, Cliff Johnson,
Jock Butterfield, John Yates, Alistair Atkinson.

FRANCE 13.............................**GREAT BRITAIN 13**
At Toulouse, Sunday, November 7, 1954
Attendance: 37,471 *(French record)*
Referee: Cyril Appleton (England)
France: T - Contrastin 2, Krawzyk; G - Puig Aubert 2
Great Britain: T - Rose, Brown, Helme; G - Ledgard 2
France: Puig Aubert (c), Vincent Cantoni, Jackie
Merquey, Antoine Jiminez, Raymond Contrastin, Gilbert
Benausse, Joseph Crespo, Francois Rinaldi, Jean
Audoubert, Joseph Krawzyk, Guy Delaye, Jean
Pambrun, Roger Guilhem.
Great Britain: Jim Ledgard, David Rose, Phil Jackson,
Albert Naughton, Mick Sullivan, Gordon Brown, Gerry
Helme, Bob Coverdale, Sam Smith, John Thorley, Don
Robinson, Basil Watts, Dave Valentine (c).

FRANCE 15 ....**AUSTRALIA 5**
At Nantes, Thursday, November 11, 1954
Attendance: 13,000; **Referee:** Cyril Appleton (England)
France: T - Merquey, Contrastin, Cantoni;
G - Puig Aubert 3
Australia: T - O'Shea: G - Pidding
France: Puig Aubert (c), Vincent Cantoni, Jackie
Merquey, Claude Teisseire, Raymond Contrastin,
Antoine Jiminez, Joseph Crespo, Francois Rinaldi, Jean
Audoubert, Joseph Krawzyk, Armand Save, Jean
Pambrun, Gilbert Verdie
Australia: Clive Churchill (c), Noel Pidding, Alex
Watson, Greg Hawick, Denis Flannery, Bob Banks, Keith
Holman, Roy Bull, Ken Kearney, Brian Davies, Kel
O'Shea, Mick Crocker, Peter Diversi.

GREAT BRITAIN 26 ....**NEW ZEALAND 6**
At Bordeaux, Thursday, November 11, 1954
Attendance: 14,000; **Referee:** Rene Guidicelli (France)
Great Britain: T - Kitchen 2, Brown, Rose, Jackson,
Ledgard; G - Ledgard 4
New Zealand: G - McKay 3
Great Britain: Jim Ledgard, David Rose, Phil Jackson,
Mick Sullivan, Frank Kitchen, Gordon Brown, Gerry
Helme, Bob Coverdale, Sam Smith, John Thorley, Don
Robinson, Basil Watts, Dave Valentine (c).
New Zealand: Ian Grey, Jim Edwards, Cyril Eastlake (c),
Ron McKay, Jim Austin, Bill Sorensen, Lenny Eriksen,
Bill McLennan, Lory Blanchard, John Bond, Jock
Butterfield, George McDonald, Alistair Atkinson.

FINAL TABLE

	P	W	D	L	F	A	Pts
Great Britain	3	2	1	0	67	32	5
France	3	2	1	0	50	31	5
Australia	3	1	0	2	52	58	2
New Zealand	3	0	0	3	34	82	0

FINAL

FRANCE 12.............................**GREAT BRITAIN 16**
At Parc de Princes, Paris, Saturday, November 13, 1954
Attendance: 30,368; **Referee:** Cyril Appleton (England)
France: T - Cantoni, Contrastin; G - Puig Aubert 3
Great Britain: T - Brown 2, Rose, Helme; G - Ledgard 2
France: Puig Aubert (c), Vincent Cantoni, Jackie
Merquey, Claude Teisseire, Raymond Contrastin,
Antoine Jiminez, Joseph Crespo, Francois Rinaldi, Jean
Audoubert, Joseph Krawzyk, Armand Save, Jean
Pambrun, Gilbert Verdie.
Great Britain: Jim Ledgard, David Rose, Phil Jackson,
Albert Naughton, Mick Sullivan, Gordon Brown, Gerry
Helme, Bob Coverdale, Sam Smith, John Thorley, Don
Robinson, Basil Watts, Dave Valentine (c).

THE 1954 SQUADS

AUSTRALIA *(Coach: Vic Hey)*

	M	T	G	Pts
Bob Banks (Toowoomba)	2	-	-	-
Roy Bull (Manly-Warringah)	3	1	-	3
Clive Churchill (South Sydney) (c)	3	-	-	-
Mick Crocker (Parramatta)	2	-	-	-
Brian Davies (Brisbane Brothers)	3	-	-	-
Peter Diversi (North Sydney)	3	1	-	3
Denis Flannery (Ipswich)	2	-	-	-
Duncan Hall (Brisbane Wests)	1	-	-	-
Greg Hawick (South Sydney)	2	1	-	3
Keith Holman (Western Suburbs)	2	-	-	-
Ken Kearney (St George)	3	2	-	6
Ken McCaffery (Toowoomba)	1	-	-	-
Ian Moir (South Sydney)	1	-	-	-
Kel O'Shea (Ayr)	2	2	-	6
Noel Pidding (Maitland)	3	-	8	16
Norm Provan (St George)	1	-	-	-
Alex Watson (Brisbane Wests)	3	3	-	9
Harry Wells (Wollongong)	2	2	-	6

FRANCE *(Coaches: Jean Duhau & Rene Duffort)*

	M	T	G	Pts
Jean Audobert (Lyon)	4	1	-	3
Gilbert Benausse (Carcassonne)	2	-	-	-
Vincent Cantoni (Toulouse)	4	2	-	6
Andre Carrere (Villeneuve)a	-	-	-	-
Raymond Contrastin (Bordeaux)	4	5	-	15
Joseph Crespo (Lyon)	4	1	-	3
Guy Delaye (Avignon)	2	1	-	3
Roger Guilhem (Carcassonne)	1	-	-	-
Antoine Jiminez (Villeneuve)	4	-	-	-
Joseph Krawzyck (Lyon)	4	1	-	3
Jackie Merquey (Avignon)	4	1	-	3
Jean Pambrun (Marseille)	4	-	-	-
Francois Rinaldi (Marseille)	4	-	-	-
Puig Aubert (XIII Catalan) (c)	4	-	13	26
Armand Save (Bordeaux)	2	-	-	-
Claude Teissiere (Carcassonne)	3	-	-	-
Gilbert Verdie (Albi)	2	-	-	-
Maurice Voron (Lyon)	-	-	-	-

GREAT BRITAIN *(Coach: Joe Egan ∗)*

	M	T	G	Pts
Billy Banks (Huddersfield)	-	-	-	-
Harry Bradshaw (Huddersfield)	-	-	-	-
Gordon Brown (Leeds)	4	6	-	18
Bob Coverdale (Hull)	4	-	-	-
Gerry Helme (Warrington)	4	2	-	6
Phil Jackson (Barrow)	4	3	-	9
Frank Kitchen (Leigh)	2	3	-	9
Jim Ledgard (Leigh)	4	1	13	29
Albert Naughton (Warrington)	2	-	-	-
Don Robinson (Wakefield Trinity)	4	-	-	-
David Rose (Leeds)	4	4	-	12
Ron Rylance (Huddersfield)	-	-	-	-
Sam Smith (Hunslet)	4	-	-	-
Mick Sullivan (Huddersfield)	4	-	-	-
John Thorley (Halifax)	4	-	-	-
Dave Valentine (Huddersfield) (c)	4	-	-	-
Basil Watts (York)	4	-	-	-
Johnny Whiteley (Hull)	-	-	-	-

∗ pre-tournament only - no coach in France

NEW ZEALAND *(Coach: Jim Amos)*

	M	T	G	Pts
Doug Anderson (Auckland)	1	-	-	-
Alistair Atkinson (Canterbury)	3	-	-	-
Jim Austin (Auckland)	1	-	-	-
Lory Blanchard (Canterbury)	3	-	-	-
John Bond (Canterbury)	2	-	2	4
Jock Butterfield (Canterbury)	2	-	-	-
Nev Denton (Auckland)	1	-	-	-
Cyril Eastlake (Auckland) (c)	3	1	-	3
Jim Edwards (Auckland)	3	1	-	3
Lenny Eriksen (Auckland)	3	1	-	3
Ian Grey (Auckland)	1	-	-	-
Cliff Johnson (Auckland)	2	-	-	-
George McDonald (Waikato)	1	-	-	-
Ron McKay (Taranaki)	3	1	9	21
Bill McLennan (West Coast)	3	-	-	-
George Menzies (West Coast)	2	-	-	-
Bill Sorensen (Auckland)	3	-	-	-
John Yates (Auckland)	2	-	-	-

1957

AUSTRALIA 25 .... NEW ZEALAND 5
At Brisbane Cricket Ground, Saturday, June 15, 1957
Attendance: 29,636; **Referee:** Vic Belsham
(New Zealand)
Australia: T - Provan, Carlson, O'Shea, Moir, Wells;
G - Barnes 5
New Zealand: T - Johnson; G - Sorensen
Australia: Keith Barnes, Ian Moir, Harry Wells, Dick
Poole (c), Brian Carlson, Greg Hawick, Keith Holman,
Brian Davies, Ken Kearney, Bill Marsh, Norm Provan,
Kel O'Shea, Brian Clay.
New Zealand: Pat Creedy, Vern Bakalich, Bill Sorensen,
Ron Ackland, Tom Hadfield, George Menzies, Sel
Belsham, Henry Maxwell, Jock Butterfield, Bill
McLennan, John Yates, Cliff Johnson (c), Rex Percy.

GREAT BRITAIN 23 .... FRANCE 5
At Sydney Cricket Ground, Saturday, June 15, 1957
Attendance: 50,007; **Referee:** Darcy Lawler (Australia)
Great Britain: T - Sullivan 2, Boston, Stevenson,
Jackson; G - Jones 4
France: T - Merquey; G - Benausse
Great Britain: Glyn Moses, Billy Boston, Phil Jackson,
Alan Davies, Mick Sullivan, Lewis Jones, Jeff
Stevenson, Alan Prescott (c), Tommy Harris, Syd Little,
Jack Grundy, Geoff Gunney, Derek Turner.
France: Andre Rives, Guy Husson, Antoine Jiminez,
Jackie Merquey (c), Maurice Voron, Gilbert Benausse,
Rene Jean, Rene Ferrero, Nick Appelian, Gabriel
Berthomieu, Armand Save, Augustin Parent, Jean
Rouqueirol.

AUSTRALIA 31 .... GREAT BRITAIN 6
At Sydney Cricket Ground, Monday, June 17, 1957
Attendance: 57,955; **Referee:** Vic Belsham
(New Zealand)
Australia: T - McCaffery 2, Moir 2, O'Shea, Wells, Clay;
G - Carlson 4, Davies
Great Britain: G - Jones 3
Australia: Brian Carlson, Ian Moir, Harry Wells, Dick
Poole (c), Alex Watson, Brian Clay, Ken McCaffery,
Brian Davies, Ken Kearney, Bill Marsh, Norm Provan,
Kel O'Shea, Don Schofield.
Great Britain: Glyn Moses, Billy Boston, Eric Ashton,
Alan Davies, Mick Sullivan, Lewis Jones, Jeff
Stevenson, Alan Prescott (c), Tommy Harris, Syd Little,
Jack Grundy, Johnny Whiteley, Derek Turner.

NEW ZEALAND 10 .... FRANCE 14
At Brisbane Exhibition Ground, Monday, June 17, 1957
Attendance: 22,142; **Referee:** Darcy Lawler (Australia)
New Zealand: T - Sorensen, Hadfield;
G - Creedy, Sorensen
France: T - Foussat 2; G - Benausse 4
New Zealand: Pat Creedy, Vern Bakalich, Bill Sorensen,
Ron Ackland, Tom Hadfield, George Menzies, Sel
Belsham, Henry Maxwell, Jock Butterfield, Bill
McLennan, John Yates, Cliff Johnson (c), Rex Percy.
France: Andre Rives, Guy Husson, Jackie Merquey (c),
Maurice Voron, Jean Foussat, Gilbert Benausse, Rene
Jean, Henri Delhoste, Nick Appelian, Robert Medus,
Gabriel Berthomieu, Augustin Parent, Jean Rouqueirol.

AUSTRALIA 26 .... FRANCE 9
At Sydney Cricket Ground, Saturday, June 22, 1957
Attendance: 35,158; **Referee:** Vic Belsham
(New Zealand)
Australia: T - Carlson, Poole, O'Shea, Marsh;
G - Carlson 7
France: T - Benausse; G - Benausse 3
Australia: Brian Carlson, Ian Moir, Harry Wells, Dick
Poole (c), Alex Watson, Brian Clay, Ken McCaffery,
Brian Davies, Ken Kearney, Bill Marsh, Norm Provan,
Kel O'Shea, Don Schofield.
France: Andre Rives, Guy Husson, Antoine Jiminez (c),
Jean Foussat, Maurice Voron, Gilbert Benausse, Rene
Jean, Henri Delhoste, Nick Appelian, Rene Ferrero,
Robert Medus, Augustin Parent, Francis Levy.

NEW ZEALAND 29 .... GREAT BRITAIN 21
At Sydney Cricket Ground, Tuesday, June 25, 1957
Attendance: 14,263; **Referee:** Darcy Lawler (Australia)
New Zealand: T - Hadfield, Turner, Menzies, McLennan,
Riddell; G - Sorensen 7
Great Britain: T - Jackson, Jones, Sullivan, Little,
Grundy; G - Jones 3
New Zealand: Pat Creedy, Reece Griffiths, George
Turner, Bill Sorensen, Tom Hadfield, George Menzies,
Sel Belsham, Henry Maxwell, Jock Butterfield, Bill
McLennan, John Yates, Cliff Johnson (c), Jim Riddell.
Great Britain: Glyn Moses, Eric Ashton, Phil Jackson,
Lewis Jones, Mick Sullivan, Austin Rhodes, Jeff
Stevenson, Alan Prescott (c), Tom McKinney, Syd Little,
Jack Grundy, Geoff Gunney, Derek Turner.

FINAL TABLE

	P	W	D	L	F	A	Pts
Australia	3	3	0	0	82	20	6
Great Britain	3	1	0	2	50	65	2
New Zealand	3	1	0	2	44	60	2
France	3	1	0	2	28	59	2

No Final required. Australia won the Cup.

AUSTRALIA 20 .... REST OF THE WORLD 11
At Sydney Cricket Ground, Saturday, June 22, 1954
Attendance: 30,675; **Referee:** Vic Belsham
(New Zealand)
Australia: T - Provan, Moir, Poole, Ritchie; G - Carlson 3;
FG - Carlson
World: T - Benausse, Ashton, Merquey; G - Sorensen
Australia: Brian Carlson, Ian Moir, Harry Wells, Dick
Poole (c), Ray Ritchie, Greg Hawick, Ken McCaffery,
Brian Davies, Ken Kearney, Bill Marsh, Norm Provan,
Kel O'Shea, Brian Clay.

Rugby League World Cup Statistics

World: Lewis Jones (GB), Maurice Voron (France), Jackie Merquey (France) (c), Bill Sorensen (NZ), Eric Ashton (GB), Gilbert Benausse (France), Sel Belsham (NZ), Cliff Johnson (NZ), Nick Appelian (France), Henry Maxwell (GB), Geoff Gunney (GB), Jim Riddell (NZ), Johnny Whiteley (GB).

THE 1957 SQUADS

AUSTRALIA *(Captain-coach: Dick Poole)*

	M	T	G	Pts
Keith Barnes (Balmain)	1	-	5	10
Brian Carlson (Blackall) *	4	2	15	36
Brian Clay (St George)	4	1	-	3
Brian Davies (Brisbane Brothers)	4	-	1	2
Greg Hawick (Wagga Wagga)	2	-	-	-
Keith Holman (Western Suburbs)	1	-	-	-
Ken Kearney (St George)	4	-	-	-
Ken McCaffery (North Sydney)	3	2	-	6
Bill Marsh (Balmain)	4	1	-	3
Ian Moir (South Sydney)	4	4	-	12
Kel O'Shea (Western Suburbs)	4	3	-	9
Dick Poole (Newtown) (c)	4	2	-	6
Norm Provan (St George)	4	2	-	6
Ray Ritchie (Manly-Warringah)	1	1	-	3
Don Schofield (Cessnock)	2	-	-	-
Tom Tyquin (Brisbane Souths)	-	-	-	-
Alex Watson (Brisbane Wests)	2	-	-	-
Harry Wells (Western Suburbs)	4	2	-	6

* sacked by club at start of World Cup

GREAT BRITAIN *(Captain-coach: Alan Prescott)*

	M	T	G	Pts
Eric Ashton (Wigan)	3*	1	-	3
Billy Boston (Wigan)	2	1	-	3
Alan Davies (Oldham)	2	-	-	-
Phil Jackson (Barrow)	2	2	-	6
Jack Grundy (Barrow)	3	1	-	3
Geoff Gunney (Hunslet)	3*	-	-	-
Tommy Harris (Hull)	2	-	-	-
Lewis Jones (Leeds)	4*	1	10	23
Syd Little (Oldham)	3	1	-	3
Tom McKinney (St Helens)	1	-	-	-
Glyn Moses (St Helens)	3	-	-	-
Alan Prescott (St Helens) (c)	3	-	-	-
Ray Price (Warrington)	-	-	-	-
Austin Rhodes (St Helens)	1	-	-	-
Jeff Stevenson (Leeds)	3	1	-	3
Mick Sullivan (Huddersfield)	3	3	-	9
Derek Turner (Oldham)	3	-	-	-
Johnny Whiteley (Hull)	2*	-	-	-

* one match for Rest of the World

FRANCE *(Coach: Jean Duhau)*

	M	T	G	Pts
Nick Appelian (Marseille)	4*	-	-	-
Gilbert Benausse (Carcassonne)	4*	2	8	22
Gabriel Berthomieu (Albi)	2	-	-	-
Henri Delhoste (XIII Catalan)	2	-	-	-
Rene Ferrero (Marseille)	2	-	-	-
Jean Foussat (Villeneuve)	2	2	-	6
Guy Husson (Albi)	3	-	-	-
Rene Jean (Avignon)	3	-	-	-
Antoine Jiminez (Villeneuve)	2	-	-	-
Francis Levy (XIII Catalan)	1	-	-	-
Robert Medus (XIII Catalan)	2	-	-	-
Jackie Merquey (c) (Avignon)	3*	2	-	6
Augustin Parent (Avignon)	3	-	-	-
Andre Rives (Albi)	3	-	-	-
Jean Rouqueirol (Avignon)	2	-	-	-
Arnaud Save (Bordeaux)	1	-	-	-
Gilbert Verdier (Albi)	-	-	-	-
Maurice Voron (Lyon)	4*	-	-	-

* one match for Rest of the World

NEW ZEALAND *(Coach: Bill Telford)*

	M	T	G	Pts
Ron Ackland (Auckland)	2	-	-	-
Vern Bakalich (Auckland)	2	-	-	-
Keith Bell (Auckland)	-	-	-	-
Sel Belsham (Auckland)	4*	-	-	-
Jock Butterfield (Canterbury)	3	-	-	-
Pat Creedy (Canterbury)	3	-	1	2
Tom Hadfield (Auckland)	3	2	-	6
Reece Griffiths (West Coast)	1	-	-	-
Cliff Johnson (Auckland) (c)	4*	1	-	3
Bill McLennan (West Coast)	3	1	-	3
Henry Maxwell (Auckland)	4*	-	-	-
George Menzies (West Coast)	3	1	-	3
Kevin Pearce (Canterbury)	-	-	-	-
Rex Percy (Auckland)	1	-	-	-
Jim Riddell (Auckland)	2*	1	-	3
Bill Sorensen (Auckland)	4*	1	10	23
George Turner (Auckland)	1	1	-	3
John Yates (Auckland)	3	-	-	-

* one match for Rest of the World

1960

GREAT BRITAIN 23 .... **NEW ZEALAND 8**
At Odsal Stadium, Bradford, Saturday, September 24, 1960
Attendance: 20,577; **Referee:** Edouard Martung (France)
Great Britain: T - Ashton, Davies, Myler, Murphy, McTigue; G - Fraser 4
New Zealand: T - Hadfield, Cooke; G - Sorensen
Great Britain: Eric Fraser, Bobby Greenhough, Eric Ashton (c), Alan Davies, Mike Sullivan, Frank Myler, Alex Murphy, Jack Wilkinson, Tommy Harris, Brian McTigue, Johnny Whiteley, Vince Karalius, Derek Turner.
New Zealand: Cyril Eastlake, Tom Hadfield, George Turner, Bill Sorensen, Neville Denton, George Menzies, Keith Roberts, Cliff Johnson (c), Jock Butterfield, Henry Maxwell, Ron Ackland, Trevor Kilkelly, Mel Cooke.

AUSTRALIA 13 .... **FRANCE 12**
At Central Park, Wigan, Saturday, September 24, 1960
Attendance: 20,278; **Referee:** Eric Clay (Great Britain)
Australia: T - Raper, Kelly, Gasnier; G - Carlson 2
France: T - Gruppi 2; G - Lacaze 3
Australia: Brian Carlson, Ken Irvine, Reg Gasnier, Harry Wells, Lionel Morgan, Tony Brown, Barry Muir (c), Dud Beattie, Noel Kelly, Rex Mossop, Elton Rasmussen, Brian Hambly, Johnny Raper.
France: Louis Poletti, Jacques Dubon, Claude Mantoulan, Roger Rey, Raymond Gruppi, Jackie Merquey, Georges Fages, Aldo Quaglio, Andre Casas, Angelo Boldini, Robert Eramouspe, Jean Barthe (c), Andre Lacaze.

GREAT BRITAIN 33 .... **FRANCE 7**
At Station Road, Swinton, Saturday, October 1, 1960
Attendance: 22,923; **Referee:** Edouard Martung (France)
Great Britain: T - Rhodes 2, Davies 2, Wilkinson, Sullivan, Myler; G - Fraser 6
France: T - Dubon; G - Lacaze 2
Great Britain: Eric Fraser, Jim Challinor, Austin Rhodes, Alan Davies, Mike Sullivan, Frank Myler, Alex Murphy, Jack Wilkinson, John Shaw, Brian McTigue, Brian Shaw, Vince Karalius, Johnny Whiteley (c).
France: Louis Poletti, Jacques Dubon, Claude Mantoulan, Roger Rey, Raymond Gruppi, Jackie Merquey, Joseph Guiraud, Aldo Quaglio, Andre Casas, Robert Eramouspe, Jean Barthe (c), Yves Mezard, Andre Lacaze.

AUSTRALIA 21 ....NEW ZEALAND 15
At Headingley, Leeds, Saturday, October 1, 1960
Attendance: 10,773; **Referee:** Eric Clay (Great Britain)
Australia: T - Carlson 3, Gasnier, Wells; G - Carlson 3
New Zealand: T - Hadfield, Turner, Menzies;
G - Eastlake 3
Australia: Keith Barnes (c), Ken Irvine, Reg Gasnier, Harry Wells, Brian Carlson, Tony Brown, Barry Muir, Dud Beattie, Noel Kelly, Gary Parcell, Rex Mossop, Brian Hambly, Johnny Raper.
New Zealand: Gary Phillips, Tom Hadfield, George Turner, Cyril Eastlake, Neville Denton, George Menzies, Keith Roberts, Cliff Johnson (c), Jock Butterfield, Henry Maxwell, Ron Ackland, Laurie Oliff, Mel Cooke.

GREAT BRITAIN 10 ....AUSTRALIA 3
At Odsal Stadium, Bradford, Saturday, October 8, 1960
Attendance: 32,773; **Referee:** Edouard Martung (France)
Great Britain: T - Boston, Sullivan; G - Rhodes 2
Australia: T - Carlson
Great Britain: Austin Rhodes, Billy Boston, Eric Ashton (c), Alan Davies, Mike Sullivan, Frank Myler, Alex Murphy, Jack Wilkinson, John Shaw, Brian McTigue, Brian Shaw, Derek Turner, Vince Karalius.
Australia: Keith Barnes (c), Ron Boden, Reg Gasnier, Harry Wells, Brian Carlson, Tony Brown, Barry Muir, Dud Beattie, Noel Kelly, Gary Parcell, Rex Mossop, Elton Rasmussen, Brian Hambly.

FRANCE 0 ....NEW ZEALAND 9
At Central Park, Wigan, Saturday, October 8, 1960
Attendance: 2,876; **Referee:** Eric Clay (Great Britain)
New Zealand: T - Reid; G - Eastlake 3
France: Louis Poletti, Jacques Dubon, Claude Mantoulan, Roger Rey, Raymond Gruppi, Jackie Merquey, Georges Fages, Aldo Quaglio, Andre Vadon, Aldo Boldini, Robert Eramouspe, Jean Barthe (c), Andre Lacaze.
New Zealand: Gary Phillips, Tom Hadfield, George Turner, Cyril Eastlake, Reece Griffiths, George Menzies, Keith Roberts, Cliff Johnson (c), Jock Butterfield, Tom Reid, Ron Ackland, Laurie Oliff, Mel Cooke.

FINAL TABLE

	P	W	D	L	F	A	Pts
Great Britain	3	3	0	0	66	18	6
Australia	3	2	0	1	37	37	4
New Zealand	3	1	0	2	32	44	2
France	3	0	0	3	19	55	0

GREAT BRITAIN 33 ....REST OF THE WORLD 27
At Odsal Stadium, Bradford, Monday, October 10, 1960
Attendance: 3,908; **Referee:** Edouard Martung (France)
Great Britain: T - Murphy 2, Myler 2, Ashton 2, Sullivan, Davies, B Shaw; G - Rhodes 3
World: T - Menzies 3, Gruppi 2, Hadfield, Gourbal; G - Mantoulan 2, Eastlake
Great Britain: Austin Rhodes, Jim Challinor, Eric Ashton (c), Alan Davies, Mike Sullivan, Frank Myler, Alex Murphy, Jack Wilkinson, John Shaw, Brian McTigue, Brian Shaw, Derek Turner, Vince Karalius.
World: Cyril Eastlake (NZ), Tom Hadfield (NZ), Ron Boden (Aust), Claude Mantoulan (France), Raymond Gruppi (France), George Menzies (NZ), Barry Muir (Aust), Cliff Johnson (NZ) (c), Bill Rayner (Aust), Dud Beattie (Aust), Robert Eramouspe (France), Yvon Gourbal (France), Brian Hambly (Aust).

THE 1960 SQUADS

AUSTRALIA *(Captain-coach: Keith Barnes)*

	M	T	G	Pts
Keith Barnes (Balmain) (c)	2	-	-	-
Dud Beattie (Ipswich)	4*	-	-	-
Tony Brown (Newtown)	3	-	-	-
Bob Bugden (St George)	-	-	-	-
Bill Rayner (Parramatta)	1*	-	-	-
Ron Boden (Parramatta)	2*	-	-	-
Brian Carlson (North Sydney)	3	4	5	22
Reg Gasnier (St George)	3	2	-	6
Brian Hambly (Parramatta)	4*	-	-	-
Ken Irvine (North Sydney)	2	-	-	-
Noel Kelly (Ipswich)	3	1	-	3
Lionel Morgan (Wynnum-Manly)	1	-	-	-
Rex Mossop (Manly-Warringah)	3	-	-	-
Barry Muir (Brisbane Wests)	4*	-	-	-
Gary Parcell (Ipswich)	3	-	-	-
Johnny Raper (St George)	2	1	-	3
Elton Rasmussen (Toowoomba)	1	-	-	-
Harry Wells (Western Suburbs)	3	1	-	3

* one match for Rest of the World

FRANCE *(Coaches: Rene Duffort & Jean Duhau)*

	M	T	G	Pts
Jean Barthe (Roanne) (c)	3	-	-	-
Angelo Boldini (Villeneuve)	2	-	-	-
Andre Casas (XIII Catalan)	2	-	-	-
Jacques Dubon (Villeneuve)	3	1	-	3
Robert Eramouspe (Roanne)	4*	-	-	-
George Fages (Albi)	2	-	-	-
Yvon Gourbal (XIII Catalan)	1*	1	-	3
Raymond Gruppi (Villeneuve)	4*	4	-	12
Joseph Guiraud (Limoux)	1	-	-	-
Andre Lacaze (Villeneuve)	3	-	5	10
Claude Mantoulan (Roanne)	4*	-	2	4
Andre Marty (Carcassonne)	-	-	-	-
Jackie Merquey (Villeneuve)	3	-	-	-
Yves Mezard (Avignon)	1	-	-	-
Louis Poletti (Carcassonne)	3	-	-	-
Aldo Quaglio (Roanne)	3	-	-	-
Roger Rey (Avignon)	3	-	-	-
Andre Vadon (Albi)	1	-	-	-

* one match for Rest of the World

GREAT BRITAIN *(Captain-coach: Eric Ashton)*

	M	T	G	Pts
Eric Ashton (Wigan) (c)	3*	3	-	9
Billy Boston (Wigan)	1	1	-	3
Jim Challinor (Warrington)	2*	-	-	-
Alan Davies (Oldham)	4*	3	-	9
Eric Fraser (Warrington)	2	1	10	23
Bobby Greenhough (Warrington)	1	-	-	-
Tommy Harris (Hull)	1	-	-	-
Vince Karalius (St Helens)	4*	-	-	-
Brian McTigue (Wigan)	4*	1	-	3
Alex Murphy (St Helens)	4*	3	-	9
Frank Myler (Widnes)	4*	4	-	12
Austin Rhodes (St Helens)	3*	2	5	16
Brian Shaw (Hunslet)	3*	1	-	3
John Shaw (Halifax)	3*	-	-	-
Mick Sullivan (Wigan)	4*	3	-	9
Derek Turner (Wakefield Trinity)	3*	-	-	-
Johnny Whiteley (Hull)	2	-	-	-
Jack Wilkinson (Wakefield Trinity)	4*	1	-	3

* one match against Rest of the World

NEW ZEALAND *(Coach: Travers Hardwick)*

	M	T	G	Pts
Ron Ackland (Auckland)	3	-	-	-
Jock Butterfield (Canterbury)	3	-	-	-
Mel Cooke (Canterbury)	3	1	-	3
Ron Cooke (Auckland)	-	-	-	-
Neville Denton (Auckland)	2	-	-	-
Cyril Eastlake (Auckland)	4*	-	7	14
Reece Griffiths (West Coast)	1	-	-	-
Tom Hadfield (Auckland)	4*	3	-	9
Cliff Johnson (Auckland) (c)	4*	-	-	-
Trevor Kilkelly (West Coast)	3	-	-	-
Henry Maxwell (Auckland)	2	-	-	-
George Menzies (West Coast)	4*	4	-	12
Laurie Oliff (Auckland)	2	-	-	-
Gary Phillips (Auckland)	2	-	-	-
Tom Reid (West Coast)	1	1	-	3
Keith Roberts (Canterbury)	3	-	-	-
Bill Sorensen (Auckland)	1	-	1	2
George Turner (Auckland)	3	1	-	3

* one match for Rest of the World

Rugby League World Cup Statistics

1968

AUSTRALIA 25 ....**GREAT BRITAIN 10**
At Sydney Cricket Ground, Saturday, May 25, 1968
Attendance: 62,256; **Referee:** John Percival
(New Zealand)
Australia: T - Coote, Smith, Raper; G - Simms 8
Great Britain: T - Brooke, Sullivan; G - Risman 2
Australia: Eric Simms, John Rhodes, Johnny Greaves, Graeme Langlands, Johnny King, Tony Branson, Billy Smith, John Wittenberg, Fred Jones, Arthur Beetson, Dick Thornett, Ron Coote, Johnny Raper (c).
Great Britain: Bev Risman (c), Ian Brooke, Mick Shoebottom, Alan Burwell, Clive Sullivan, Roger Millward, Tommy Bishop, Cliff Watson, Kevin Ashcroft, Mick Clark, Bob Haigh, Ray French, Charlie Renilson.

NEW ZEALAND 10 ....**FRANCE 15**
At Carlaw Park, Auckland, Saturday, May 25, 1968
Attendance: 18,000; **Referee:** Col Pearce (Australia)
New Zealand: G - Wiggs 5
France: T - Capdouze; G - Capdouze 5, Garrigue
New Zealand: Roger Tait, Bob Mincham, Ray Sinel, Paul Schultz, Ernie Wiggs, James Bond (c), Gary Clarke, Oscar Danielson, Colin O'Neil, Gary Smith, Brian Lee, Kevin Dixon, Tony Kriletich. Replacement: Henry Tatana.
France: Jean-Pierre Cros, Daniel Pellerin, Jean-Pierre Lecompte, Michel Molinier, Andre Ferren, Jean Capdouze, Roger Garrigue, Christian Sabatie, Yves Begou, Georges Ailleres (c), Francis De Nadai, Henri Marracq, Jean-Pierre Clar.

AUSTRALIA 31 ....**NEW ZEALAND 12**
At Lang Park, Brisbane, Saturday, June 1, 1968
Attendance: 23,608; **Referee:** John Percival
(New Zealand)
Australia: T - King 2, Rhodes, Coote, Jones;
G - Simms 6; FG - Simms 2
New Zealand: T - Dunn, Schultz; G - Wiggs 3
Australia: Eric Simms, John Rhodes, Johnny Greaves, Graeme Langlands, Johnny King, Tony Branson, Billy Smith, John Wittenberg, Fred Jones, Elton Rasmussen, Dick Thornett, Ron Coote, Johnny Raper (c). Replacement: Bob Fulton (for Branson).
New Zealand: Doug Ellwood, Bob Mincham, Spencer Dunn, Paul Schultz, Ernie Wiggs, James Bond (c), Gary Clarke, Henry Tatana, Colin O'Neil, Gary Smith, Kevin Dixon, Brian Lee, Tony Kriletich. Replacement: Roger Tait (for Bond)

GREAT BRITAIN 2 ....**FRANCE 7**
At Carlaw Park, Auckland, Sunday, June 2, 1968
Attendance: 15,760; **Referee:** Col Pearce (Australia)
Great Britain: G - Risman
France: T - Ledru; G - Garrigue, Capdouze
Great Britain: Bev Risman (c), John Atkinson, Ian Brooke, Alan Burwell, Clive Sullivan, Roger Millward, Tommy Bishop, Cliff Watson, Peter Flanagan, Mick Clark, Bob Haigh, Arnold Morgan, Charlie Renilson. Replacement: John Warlow.
France: Jean-Pierre Cros, Daniel Pellerin, Jean-Pierre Lecompte, Michel Molinier, Jean-Rene Ledru, Jean Capdouze, Roger Garrigue, Christian Sabatie, Yves Begou, Georges Ailleres (c), Herve Mazard, Henri Marracq, Jean-Pierre Clar.

AUSTRALIA 37 ....**FRANCE 4**
At Lang Park, Brisbane, Saturday, June 8, 1968
Attendance: 32,662; **Referee:** John Percival
(New Zealand)
Australia: T - Williamson 2, Fulton 2, Greaves, Smith, Coote; G - Simms 5; FG - Smith 3
France: G - Capdouze 2
Australia: Eric Simms, Brian James, John Rhodes, Johnny Greaves, Lionel Williamson, Bob Fulton, Billy Smith, John Wittenberg, Brian Fitzsimmons, Arthur Beetson, Dennis Manteit, Ron Coote, Johnny Raper (c).
France: Jean-Pierre Cros, Andre Ferren, Michel Molinier, Jacques Gruppi, Jean-Rene Ledru, Jean Capdouze, Marius Frattini, Christian Sabatie, Yves Begou, Nestor Serrano, Adolphe Alesina, Herve Mazard, Jean-Pierre Clar. Replacement: Francis De Nadai (for Sabatie).

GREAT BRITAIN 38 ....**NEW ZEALAND 14**
At Sydney Cricket Ground, Saturday, June 8, 1968
Attendance: 14,105; **Referee:** Col Pearce (Australia)
Great Britain: T - Sullivan 3, Brooke, Burwell 2, Shoebottom, Morgan; G - Risman 7
New Zealand: Schultz 2; G - Wiggs 4
Great Britain: Bev Risman (c), John Atkinson, Ian Brooke, Alan Burwell, Clive Sullivan, Roger Millward, Tommy Bishop, John Warlow, Peter Flanagan, Mick Clark, Ray French, Arnold Morgan, Charlie Renilson. Replacements: Mick Shoebottom and Cliff Watson.
New Zealand: Doug Ellwood, Bob Mincham, Spencer Dunn, Paul Schultz, Ernie Wiggs, Roger Tait, Eric Carson, Colin McMaster, Colin O'Neil, Gary Smith, Ray Sinel, Brian Lee, Tony Kriletich. Replacement: Kevin Dixon.

FINAL TABLE
	P	W	D	L	F	A	Pts
Australia	3	3	0	0	93	26	6
France	3	2	0	1	26	49	4
Great Britain	3	1	0	2	50	46	2
New Zealand	3	0	0	3	36	84	0

FINAL
AUSTRALIA 20....................................**FRANCE 2**
At Sydney Cricket Ground, Monday, June 10, 1968
Attendance: 54,290; **Referee:** John Percival
(New Zealand)
Australia: T - Williamson 2, Greaves, Coote; G - Simms 4
France: G - Capdouze
Australia: Eric Simms, John Rhodes, Johnny Greaves, Graeme Langlands, Lionel Williamson, Bob Fulton, Billy Smith, John Wittenberg, Fred Jones, Arthur Beetson, Dick Thornett, Ron Coote, Johnny Raper (c). Replacement: Elton Rasmussen.
France: Jean-Pierre Cros, Daniel Pellerin, Jacques Gruppi, Jean-Pierre Lecompte, Jean-Rene Ledru, Jean Capdouze, Roger Garrigue, Christian Sabatie, Yves Begou, Georges Ailleres (c), Francis De Nadai, Henri Marracq, Jean-Pierre Clar.

THE 1968 SQUADS

AUSTRALIA *(Coach: Harry Bath)*
	M	T	G	Pts
Arthur Beetson (Balmain)	3	-	-	-
Tony Branson (St George)	2	-	-	-
Ron Coote (South Sydney)	4	4	-	12
Brian Fitzsimmons (Townsville)	1	-	-	-
Bob Fulton (Manly-Warringah)	3	2	-	6
Johnny Greaves (Canterbury-Bankstown)	4	2	-	6
Brian James (South Sydney)	1	-	-	-
Fred Jones (Manly-Warringah)	3	1	-	3
Johnny King (St George)	2	2	-	6
Graeme Langlands (St George)	3	-	-	-
Dennis Manteit (Brisbane Brothers)	1	-	-	-
Johnny Raper (St George) (c)	4	1	-	3
Elton Rasmussen (St George)	2	-	-	-
John Rhodes (Canterbury-Bankstown)	4	1	-	3
Eric Simms (South Sydney)	4	-	25	50
Billy Smith (St George)	4	2	3	12
Dick Thornett (Parramatta)	3	-	-	-
Lionel Williamson (Innisfail)	2	4	-	12
John Wittenberg (St George)	4	-	-	-

FRANCE *(Coach: Rene Lacoste)*
	M	T	G	Pts
Georges Ailleres (c) (Toulouse)	3	-	-	-
Adolphe Alesina (Carcassonne)	1	-	-	-
Yves Begou (Toulouse)	4	-	-	-
Jean Capdouze (XIII Catalan)	4	1	9	21
Jean-Pierre Clar (Villeneuve)	4	-	-	-
Jean-Pierre Cros (Albi)	4	-	-	-
Francis De Nadai (Limoux)	3	-	-	-
Andre Ferren (Toulouse)	2	-	-	-
Marius Frattini (Avignon)	1	-	-	-
Roger Garrigue (Saint-Gaudens)	3	-	2	4
Jacques Gruppi (Villeneuve)	2	-	-	-
Jean-Pierre Lecompte (Saint-Gaudens)	3	-	-	-

Jean-Rene Ledru (Marseille)	3	1	-	3
Henri Marracq (Saint-Gaudens)	3	-	-	-
Herve Mazard (Lezignan)	2	-	-	-
Michel Molinier (Saint-Gaudens)	3	-	-	-
Daniel Pellerin (Villeneuve)	3	-	-	-
Christian Sabatie (Villeneuve)	4	-	-	-
Nestor Serrano (Saint-Gaudens)	1	-	-	-

GREAT BRITAIN (Coach: Colin Hutton)
	M	T	G	Pts
Kevin Ashcroft (Leigh)	1	-	-	-
John Atkinson (Leeds)	2	-	-	-
Tommy Bishop (St Helens)	2	-	-	-
Ian Brooke (Wakefield Trinity)	3	2	-	6
Alan Burwell (Hull Kingston Rovers)	3	2	-	6
Mick Clark (Leeds)	3	-	-	-
Derek Edwards (Castleford)	-	-	-	-
Peter Flanagan (Hull Kingston Rovers)	2	-	-	-
Ray French (Widnes)	2	-	-	-
Bob Haigh (Wakefield Trinity)	2	-	-	-
Roger Millward (Hull Kingston Rovers)	3	-	-	-
Arnold Morgan (Featherstone Rovers)	3	1	-	3
Charlie Renilson (Halifax)	3	-	-	-
Bev Risman (Leeds) (c)	3	-	10	20
Mick Shoebottom (Leeds)	2	1	-	3
Clive Sullivan (Hull)	3	4	-	12
John Warlow (St Helens)	2	-	-	-
Cliff Watson (St Helens)	3	-	-	-
Chris Young (Hull Kingston Rovers)	-	-	-	-

NEW ZEALAND (Coach: Des Barchard)
	M	T	G	Pts
James Bond (Canterbury) (c)	2	-	-	-
Eric Carson (Auckland)	1	-	-	-
Gary Clarke (Canterbury)	2	-	-	-
Oscar Danielson (Auckland)	1	-	-	-
Kevin Dixon (West Coast)	3	-	-	-
Spencer Dunn (Canterbury)	2	1	-	3
Doug Ellwood (Auckland)	2	-	-	-
Tony Kriletich (Auckland)	3	-	-	-
Brian Lee (Auckland)	3	-	-	-
Colin McMaster (West Coast)	1	-	-	-
Bob Mincham (Auckland)	3	-	-	-
Colin O'Neil (Wellington)	3	-	-	-
Dave Parkinson (Waikato)	-	-	-	-
Paul Schultz (Auckland)	3	3	-	9
Ray Sinel (Auckland)	2	-	-	-
Gary Smith (Wellington)	3	-	-	-
Roger Tait (Auckland)	3	-	-	-
Henry Tatana (Auckland)	2	-	-	-
Ernie Wiggs (Auckland)	3	-	12	24

1970

AUSTRALIA 47 ....NEW ZEALAND 11
At Central Park, Wigan, Wednesday, October 21, 1970
Attendance: 9,805; **Referee:** Billy Thompson (Great Britain)
Australia: T - Cootes 2, Branighan, Fulton, Smith, McCarthy, Coote, Turner, Simms; G - Simms 9; FG - Simms
New Zealand: T - Smith; G - Ladner; FG - Ladner 3
Australia: Eric Simms, Ray Branighan, John Cootes, Bob Fulton, Lionel Williamson, Denis Pittard, Billy Smith, Bob O'Reilly, Elwyn Walters, John O'Neill, Pail Sait, Bob McCarthy, Ron Coote (c). Replacement: Ron Turner (for Coote).
New Zealand: Don Ladner, Bob McGuinn, Roy Christian (c), Bernie Lowther, Mocky Brereton, Gary Woollard, Graham Cooksley, Doug Gailey, Colin O'Neil, Eddie Heatley, Bill Deacon, Gary Smith, Tony Kriletich. Replacements: John Greengrass and Lummy Graham.

GREAT BRITAIN 11 ....AUSTRALIA 4
At Headingley, Leeds, Saturday, October 24, 1970
Attendance: 15,084; **Referee:** Fred Lindop (Great Britain)
Great Britain: T - Hynes: G - Dutton 3; FG - Hynes
Australia: FG - Simms, Fulton

Great Britain: Ray Dutton, Alan Smith, Frank Myler (c), Syd Hynes, John Atkinson, Mick Shoebottom, Keith Hepworth, Cliff Watson, Tony Fisher, Dennis Hartley, Jim Thompson, Doug Laughton, Mal Reilly.
Australia: Eric Simms, Mark Harris, Ray Branighan, Bob Fulton, Lionel Williamson, Denis Pittard, Billy Smith, Bob O'Reilly, Elwyn Walters, John O'Neill. Pail Sait, Bob McCarthy, Gary Sullivan. Replacement: Ron Turner.

FRANCE 15 ....NEW ZEALAND 16
At The Boulevard, Hull, Sunday, October 25, 1970
Attendance: 3,824; **Referee:** Billy Thompson (Great Britain)
France: T - Marsolan 2, Bonal; G - Capdouze 3
New Zealand: T - Brereton, Cooksley; G - Ladner 5
France: Jean-Pierre Cros, Serge Marsolan, Michel Molinier, Andre Ruiz, Elie Bonal, Jean Capdouze, Roger Garrigue, Floreal Bonet, Jacques Cabero, Christian Sabatie, Roger Biffi, Herve Mazard, Jean-Pierre Clar (c). Replacement: Francis De Nadai.
New Zealand: Don Ladner, John Whittaker, Roy Christian (c), Bernie Lowther, Mocky Brereton, Gary Woollard, Graham Cooksley, Doug Gailey, Colin O'Neil, John Greengrass, Elliot Kereopa, Gary Smith, Tony Kriletich. Replacements: Lummy Graham and Bill Deacon.

GREAT BRITAIN 6 ....FRANCE 0
At Wheldon Road, Castleford, Wednesday, October 28, 1970
Attendance: 8,958; **Referee:** Fred Lindop (Great Britain)
Great Britain: G - Dutton 3
Great Britain: Ray Dutton, Keri Jones, Frank Myler (c), Syd Hynes, John Atkinson, Mick Shoebottom, Keith Hepworth, Cliff Watson, Kevin Ashcroft, Dennis Hartley, Jim Thompson, Doug Laughton, Mal Reilly.
France: Jean-Pierre Cros, Serge Marsolan, Michel Molinier, Andre Ruiz, Elie Bonal, Jean Capdouze, Germain Guiraud, Francis De Nadai, Jacques Cabero, Christian Sabatie, Gerard Cremoux, Herve Mazard, Jean-Pierre Clar (c). Replacements: Daniel Pellerin and Floreal Bonet.

GREAT BRITAIN 27 ....NEW ZEALAND 17
At Station Road, Swinton, Saturday, October 31, 1970
Attendance: 5,609; **Referee:** Fred Lindop (Great Britain)
Great Britain: T - Hesketh, Watson, Hynes, Laughton, Atkinson; G - Dutton 6
New Zealand: T - Kriletich, Christian, Smith; G - Ladner 4
Great Britain: Ray Dutton, Keri Jones, Chris Hesketh, Syd Hynes, John Atkinson, Mick Shoebottom, Keith Hepworth, Cliff Watson, Kevin Ashcroft, Dave Chisnall, Jim Thompson, Bob Haigh, Doug Laughton. Replacement: Paul Charlton.
New Zealand: Don Ladner, John Whittaker, Roy Christian (c), Bernie Lowther, Mocky Brereton, Gary Woollard, Graham Cooksley, Elliot Kereopa, Colin O'Neil, John Greengrass, Gary Smith, Eddie Heatley, Tony Kriletich. Replacement: Lummy Graham.

FRANCE 17 ....AUSTRALIA 15
At Odsal Stadium, Bradford, Sunday, November 1, 1970
Attendance: 6,215; **Referee:** Billy Thompson (Great Britain)
France: T - Marsolan 2, Capdouze; G - Capdouze 2; FG - Garrigue, Capdouze
Australia: T - Cootes 2, Fulton; G - Simms 3
France: Jean-Pierre Cros, Serge Marsolan, Michel Molinier, Jacques Gruppi, Daniel Pellerin, Jean Capdouze, Roger Garrigue, Floreal Bonet, Jacques Cabero, Christian Sabatie, Roger Biffi, Francis De Nadai, Jean-Pierre Clar (c).
Australia: Eric Simms, Ray Branighan, John Cootes, Bob Fulton, Lionel Williamson, Denis Pittard, Billy Smith, Bob O'Reilly, Elwyn Walters, Barry McTaggart. Pail Sait, Bob McCarthy, Ron Coote (c). Replacements: Ron Turner (for McTaggart), Gary Sullivan (for Pittard).

Rugby League World Cup Statistics

FINAL TABLE

	P	W	D	L	F	A	Pts
Great Britain	3	3	0	0	44	21	6
Australia	3	1	0	2	66	39	2
France	3	1	0	2	32	37	2
New Zealand	3	1	0	2	44	89	2

FINAL

GREAT BRITAIN 7 ....**AUSTRALIA 12**
At Headingley, Leeds, Saturday, November 7, 1970
Attendance: 18,776; **Referee:** Fred Lindop (Great Britain)
Great Britain: T - Atkinson; G - Dutton; FG - Hynes
Australia: T - Cootes, Williamson; G - Simms 2;
FG - Simms
Great Britain: Ray Dutton, Alan Smith, Frank Myler (c),
Syd Hynes, John Atkinson, Mick Shoebottom, Keith
Hepworth, Cliff Watson, Tony Fisher, Dennis Hartley.
Jim Thompson, Doug Laughton, Mal Reilly.
Replacements: Bob Haigh, Chris Hesketh.
Australia: Eric Simms, Mark Harris, John Cootes, Paul
Sait, Lionel Williamson, Bob Fulton, Billy Smith, Bob
O'Reilly, Ron Turner, John O'Neill, Bob McCarthy, Ron
Costello, Ron Coote (c). Replacements: Ray Branighan,
Elwyn Walters.

THE 1970 SQUADS

AUSTRALIA *(Coach: Harry Bath)*

	M	T	G	Pts
Ray Branighan (South Sydney)	4	1	-	3
Johnny Brown (Brisbane Norths)	-	-	-	-
Ron Coote (South Sydney) (c)	3	1	-	3
John Cootes (Newcastle)	3	5	-	15
Ron Costello (Canterbury-Bankstown)	1	-	-	-
Bob Fulton (Manly-Warringah)	4	2	1	8
Mark Harris (Eastern Suburbs)	2	-	-	-
Bob McCarthy (South Sydney)	4	1	-	3
Barry McTaggart (Balmain)	1	-	-	-
John O'Neill (South Sydney)	3	-	-	-
Bob O'Reilly (Parramatta)	4	-	-	-
Dennis Pittard (South Sydney)	3	-	-	-
Paul Sait (South Sydney)	4	-	-	-
Eric Simms (South Sydney)	4	1	17	37
Billy Smith (St George)	4	1	-	3
Gary Sullivan (Newtown)	2	-	-	-
Ron Turner (Cronulla-Sutherland)	4	1	-	3
Elwyn Walters (South Sydney)	4	-	-	-
Lionel Williamson (Newtown)	4	1	-	3

FRANCE *(Coach: Jep Lacoste)*

	M	T	G	Pts
Roger Biffi (Saint-Gaudens)	2	-	-	-
Jean-Marie Bonal (Carcassonne)	2	1	-	3
Floreal Bonet (Saint-Esteve)	3	-	-	-
Jacques Cabero (XIII Catalan)	3	-	-	-
Jean Capdouze (XIII Catalan)	3	1	6	15
Jean-Pierre Clar (Villeneuve) (c)	3	-	-	-
Gerard Cremoux (Villeneuve)	1	-	-	-
Jean-Pierre Cros (Albi)	3	-	-	-
Francis De Nadai (Limoux)	3	-	-	-
Roger Garrigue (Saint-Gaudens)	2	1	-	2
Jacques Gruppi (Villeneuve)	1	-	-	-
Germain Guiraud (Limoux)	1	-	-	-
Serge Marsolan (Saint-Gaudens)	3	4	-	12
Herve Mazard (Lezignan)	2	-	-	-
Michel Molinier (Saint-Gaudens)	3	-	-	-
Daniel Pellerin (Villeneuve)	2	-	-	-
Andre Ruiz (Carcassonne)	2	-	-	-
Christian Sabatie (Villeneuve)	3	-	-	-

GREAT BRITAIN *(Coach: Johnny Whiteley)*

	M	T	G	Pts
Kevin Ashcroft (Leigh)	2	-	-	-
John Atkinson (Leeds)	4	2	-	6
Paul Charlton (Salford)	1	-	-	-
Dave Chisnall (Leigh)	1	-	-	-
Ray Dutton (Widnes)	4	-	13	26
Tony Fisher (Leeds)	2	-	-	-
Bob Haigh (Leeds)	2	-	-	-
Dennis Hartley (Castleford)	3	-	-	-

	M	T	G	Pts
Keith Hepworth (Castleford)	4	-	-	-
Chris Hesketh (Salford)	2	1	-	3
Syd Hynes (Leeds)	4	2	2	10
Keri Jones (Wigan)	2	-	-	-
Doug Laughton (Wigan)	4	1	-	3
Frank Myler (St Helens) (c)	3	-	-	-
Mal Reilly (Castleford)	3	-	-	-
Mick Shoebottom (Leeds)	4	-	-	-
Alan Smith (Leeds)	2	-	-	-
Jim Thompson (Featherstone Rovers)	4	-	-	-
Cliff Watson (St Helens)	4	1	-	3

NEW ZEALAND *(Coach: Lory Blanchard)*

	M	T	G	Pts
Mocky Brereton (West Coast)	3	1	-	3
Bill Burgoyne (Auckland)	-	-	-	-
Eric Carson (Auckland)	-	-	-	-
Roy Christian (Auckland) (c)	3	1	-	3
Graham Cooksley (Canterbury)	3	1	-	3
Bill Deacon (Waikato)	2	-	-	-
Doug Gailey (Auckland)	2	-	-	-
Lummy Graham (Auckland)	3	-	-	-
John Greengrass (Canterbury)	3	-	-	-
Eddie Heatley (Auckland)	2	-	-	-
Elliott Kereopa (Midlands)	2	-	-	-
Tony Kriletich (Auckland)	3	1	-	3
Don Ladner (West Coast)	3	-	13	26
Bernie Lowther (Auckland)	3	-	-	-
Bob McGuinn (Auckland)	1	-	-	-
Colin O'Neil (Wellington)	3	-	-	-
Gary Smith (Wellington)	3	2	-	6
John Whittaker (Wellington)	2	-	-	-
Gary Woollard (Auckland)	3	-	-	-

FRIENDLIES BY WORLD CUP SQUADS

AUSTRALIA

ST HELENS 37 ....**AUSTRALIA 10**

FRANCE 4 ....**AUSTRALIA 7**
France: G - J Capdouze
Australia: T - J Cootes; G - E Simms 2

FRANCE B 8 ....**AUSTRALIA 36**
France B: T - J Managnin; G - J Saurat; FG - Pere
Australia: T - M Harris 2, W Smith 2, E Simms, E
Walters, R Branighan, R McCarthy; G - E Simms 6

NEW ZEALAND

BARROW 10 ....**NEW ZEALAND 14**

BRADFORD NORTHERN 17 ....**NEW ZEALAND 28**

SALFORD 7 ....**NEW ZEALAND 8**

FRANCE 16 ....**NEW ZEALAND 2**
France: T - M Molinier, F De Nadai, J Gruppi, S
Marsolan; G - J Capdouze 2
New Zealand: G - G Smith

FRANCE B 8 ....**NEW ZEALAND 28**
France B: T - J Calle, V Serrano; G - V Serrano
New Zealand: T - C O'Neil, R Christian, G Cooksley, B
Deacon, J Whittaker, B Lowther; G - B Deacon 5

1972

FRANCE 20 ....**NEW ZEALAND 9**
*At Stade Municipal, Marseille, Saturday, October 28,
1972*
Attendance: 20,748; **Referee:** George Jameau (France)
France: T - Bonal 2, Ruiz; G - Guilhem 4, Bonal;
FG - Frattini
New Zealand: T - Orchard 2, Brereton
France: Raymond Toujas, Serge Marsolan, Michel
Molinier, Andre Ruiz, Jean-Marie Bonal, Bernard Guilhem,
Marius Frattini, Francis De Nadai (c), Jacques Franc,
Jacques Garzino, Nestor Serrano, Serge Gleyzes, Michel
Anglade. Replacement: Charles Zalduendo (for Garzino).

New Zealand: John Whittaker, Phil Orchard, John O'Sullivan, Roy Christian (c), Mocky Brereton, Dennis Williams, Brian Tracey, Mita Mohi, Bill Burgoyne, Bob Paul, Doug Gailey, Peter Gurnick, Murray Eade. Replacements: Graeme Cooksley (for Tracey), Tony Coll (for Paul).

GREAT BRITAIN 27 ....**AUSTRALIA 21**
At Stade Gilbert Brutus, Perpignan, Sunday, October 29, 1972
Attendance: 6,324; **Referee:** Claude Tissiere (France)
Great Britain: T - Sullivan, Lowe, Atkinson, O'Neill, Stephenson; G - Clawson 6
Australia: T - Fulton 3, Raudonikis; G - Langlands 4; FG - McCarthy
Great Britain: Paul Charlton, Clive Sullivan (c), Chris Hesketh, John Walsh, John Atkinson, Dennis O'Neill, Steve Nash, David Jeanes, Mike Stephenson, Terry Clawson, Brian Lockwood, Phil Lowe, George Nicholls. Replacement: John Holmes (for Walsh).
Australia: Graeme Langlands (c), Stephen Knight, Geoff Starling, Ray Branighan, Mark Harris, Bob Fulton, Tom Raudonikis, Arthur Beetson, Elwyn Walters, John O'Neill, John Elford, Bob McCarthy, Gary Sullivan. Replacements: Dennis Ward (for Beetson), Paul Sait (for Branighan).

AUSTRALIA 9 ....**NEW ZEALAND 5**
At Parc de Princes, Paris, Wednesday, November 1, 1972
Attendance: 8,000; **Referee:** Mick Naughton (Great Britain)
Australia: T - Ward, Fulton; G - Branighan; FG - Fulton
New Zealand: T - Whittaker; G - Wilson
Australia: Graeme Langlands (c), Stephen Knight, Geoff Starling, Ray Branighan, John Grant, Bob Fulton, Dennis Ward, Bob O'Reilly, Elwyn Walters, John O'Neill, John Elford, Gary Sullivan, Paul Sait. Replacement: Gary Stevens (for Sait).
New Zealand: John Wilson, Phil Orchard, Mocky Brereton, Roy Christian (c), John Whittaker, Dennis Williams, Brian Tracey, Doug Gailey, Bill Burgoyne, Don Mann, Bob Paul, Murray Eade, Peter Gurnick. Replacement: Rodney Walker (for Paul).

FRANCE 4 ....**GREAT BRITAIN 13**
At Stade Municipal, Grenoble, Wednesday, November 1, 1972
Attendance: 5,321; **Referee:** Francois Gril (France)
France: G - Bonal, Serrano
Great Britain: T - Lowe 2, Sullivan; G - Clawson 2
France: Raymond Toujas, Serge Marsolan, Michel Molinier, Andre Ruiz, Jean-Marie Bonal, Bernard Guilhem, Jean-Marie Imbert, Francis De Nadai (c), Jacques Franc, Jean-Pierre Sauret, Nestor Serrano, Serge Gleyzes, Guy Rodriguez. Replacement: Charles Zalduendo (for Sauret).
Great Britain: Paul Charlton, Clive Sullivan (c), Chris Hesketh, John Walsh, John Atkinson, Dennis O'Neill, Steve Nash, Terry Clawson, Mike Stephenson, Brian Lockwood, Phil Lowe, Colin Dixon, George Nicholls.

GREAT BRITAIN 53 ....**NEW ZEALAND 19**
At Stade du Hameau, Pau, Saturday, November 4, 1972
Attendance: 7,500; **Referee:** Georges Jameau (France)
Great Britain: T - Holmes 2, Atkinson 2, Nicholls, Sullivan, Charlton, Hesketh, Stephenson, Jeanes, Nash; G - Holmes 10
New Zealand: T - Whittaker, Coll, Williams, Burgoyne, Eade; G - Wilson 2
Great Britain: Paul Charlton, Clive Sullivan (c), Chris Hesketh, John Walsh, John Atkinson, John Holmes, Steve Nash, David Jeanes, Mike Stephenson, Brian Lockwood, Phil Lowe, Bob Irving, George Nicholls. Replacements: David Redfearn (for Sullivan), Tony Karalius (for Stephenson).
New Zealand: John Wilson, Phil Orchard, Mocky Brereton, Roy Christian (c), John Whittaker, Dennis Williams, Brian Tracey, Doug Gailey, Bill Burgoyne, Don Mann, Murray Eade, Tony Coll, Peter Gurnick. Replacements: Rodney Walker (for Gurnick), Warren Collicoat (for Wilson).

FRANCE 9 ....**AUSTRALIA 31**
At Stade de Minimes, Toulouse, Sunday, November 5, 1972
Attendance: 10,332; **Referee:** Mick Naughton (Great Britain)
France: T - Ruiz; G - Bonal 3
Australia: T - Harris 2, Sait 2, Fulton, O'Neill, Walters; G - Branighan 5
France: Raymond Toujas, Serge Marsolan, Michel Molinier, Andre Ruiz, Jean-Marie Bonal, Michel Mazare, Marius Frattini, Serge Gleyzes, Francis De Nadai (c), Nestor Serrano, Jacques Garzino, Jacques Franc, Charles Zalduendo. Replacements: Bernard Guilhem (for Toujas) Michel Anglade (for Zalduendo).
Australia: Graeme Langlands (c), Ray Branighan, Mark Harris, Geoff Starling, John Grant, Bob Fulton, Dennis Ward, Bob O'Reilly, Elwyn Walters, John O'Neill, Arthur Beetson, Gary Stevens, Paul Sait.

FINAL TABLE

	P	W	D	L	F	A	Pts
Great Britain	3	3	0	0	93	44	6
Australia	3	2	0	1	61	41	4
France	3	1	0	2	33	53	2
New Zealand	3	0	0	3	33	83	0

FINAL

GREAT BRITAIN 10 ....**AUSTRALIA 10**
At Stade de Gerland, Lyon, Saturday, November 11, 1972
Attendance: 4,500; **Referee:** Georges Jameau (France)
Great Britain: T - Sullivan, Stephenson; G - Clawson 2
Australia: T - O'Neill, Beetson; G - Branighan 2
Great Britain: Paul Charlton, Clive Sullivan (c), Chris Hesketh, John Walsh, John Atkinson, John Holmes, Steve Nash, David Jeanes, Mike Stephenson, Terry Clawson, Brian Lockwood, Phil Lowe, George Nicholls. Replacement: Bob Irving (for Jeanes).
Australia: Graeme Langlands (c), Ray Branighan, Geoff Starling, Mark Harris, John Grant, Bob Fulton, Dennis Ward, Bob O'Reilly, Elwyn Walters, John O'Neill, Gary Stevens, Arthur Beetson, Gary Sullivan.

(There was no further score after extra time - 10 minutes each way - was played. Britain was awarded the World Cup because of its better record in preliminary matches.)

THE 1972 SQUADS

AUSTRALIA *(Coach: Harry Bath)*

	M	T	G	FG	Pts
Arthur Beetson (Eastern Suburbs)	3	1	-	-	3
Ray Branighan (Manly-Warringah)	4	-	8	-	16
John Elford (Western Suburbs)	2	-	-	-	-
Bob Fulton (Manly-Warringah)	4	5	-	1	16
John Grant (Brisbane Souths)	3	-	-	-	-
Mark Harris (Eastern Suburbs)	3	2	-	-	6
Fred Jones (Manly-Warringah)	-	-	-	-	-
Stephen Knight (Western Suburbs)	2	-	-	-	-
Graeme Langlands (St George) (c)	4	-	4	-	8
Bob McCarthy (South Sydney)	1	-	-	1	1
John O'Neill (Manly-Warringah)	4	2	-	-	6
Bob O'Reilly (Parramatta)	3	-	-	-	-
Tom Raudonikis (Western Suburbs)	1	1	-	-	3
Paul Sait (South Sydney)	3	2	-	-	6
Geoff Starling (Balmain)	4	-	-	-	-
Gary Stevens (South Sydney)	3	-	-	-	-
Gary Sullivan (Newtown)	3	-	-	-	-
Elwyn Walters (South Sydney)	4	1	-	-	3
Dennis Ward (Manly-Warringah)	4	1	-	-	3

FRANCE *(Coach: Antoine Jiminez)*

	M	T	G	FG	Pts
Michel Anglade (Saint-Gaudens)	2	-	-	-	-
Elie Bonal (Carcassonne)	-	-	-	-	-
Jean-Marie Bonal (Carcassonne)	3	2	5	-	16
Francis De Nadai (Limoux)	3	-	-	-	-
Jacques Franc (Carcassonne)	3	-	-	-	-
Marius Frattini (Avignon)	2	-	-	1	1
Jacques Garzino (Avignon)	2	-	-	-	-

Rugby League World Cup Statistics

	M	T	G	FG	Pts
Serge Gleyzes (Carcassonne)	3	-	-	-	-
Bernard Guilhem (Carcassonne)	3	-	4	-	8
Jean-Marie Imbert (Avignon)	1	-	-	-	-
Serge Marsolan (Saint-Gaudens)	3	-	-	-	-
Michael Mazare (Villeneuve)	1	-	-	-	-
Michel Molinier (Saint-Gaudens)	3	-	-	-	-
Guy Rodriguez (Toulouse)	1	-	-	-	-
Andre Ruiz (Carcassonne)	3	2	-	-	6
Jean-Pierre Sauret (XIII Catalan)	1	-	-	-	-
Nestor Serrano (Saint-Gaudens)	3	-	1	-	2
Raymond Toujas (Carcassonne)	3	-	-	-	-
Charles Zalduendo (Toulouse)	3	-	-	-	-

GREAT BRITAIN *(Coach: Jim Challinor)*

	M	T	G	FG	Pts
John Atkinson (Leeds)	4	3	-	-	9
Paul Charlton (Salford)	4	1	-	-	3
Terry Clawson (Leeds)	3	-	10	-	20
Colin Dixon (Salford)	1	-	-	-	-
Chris Hesketh (Salford)	4	1	-	-	3
John Holmes (Leeds)	3	2	10	-	26
David Jeanes (Leeds)	3	1	-	-	3
Bob Irving (Oldham)	2	-	-	-	-
Tony Karalius (St Helens)	1	-	-	-	-
Brian Lockwood (Castleford)	4	-	-	-	-
Phil Lowe (Hull Kingston Rovers)	4	3	-	-	9
Steve Nash (Featherstone Rovers)	4	1	-	-	3
George Nicholls (Widnes)	4	1	-	-	3
Dennis O'Neill (Widnes)	2	1	-	-	3
David Redfearn (Bradford Northern)	1	-	-	-	-
Mike Stephenson (Dewsbury)	4	3	-	-	9
Clive Sullivan (Hull)	4	4	-	-	12
David Topliss (Wakefield Trinity)	-	-	-	-	-
John Walsh (St Helens)	4	-	-	-	-

NEW ZEALAND *(Coach: Des Barchard)*

	M	T	G	FG	Pts
Mocky Brereton (Canterbury)	3	1	-	-	3
Bill Burgoyne (Auckland)	3	1	-	-	3
Roy Christian (Auckland) (c)	3	-	-	-	-
Tony Coll (West Coast)	2	1	-	-	3
Warren Collicoat (Auckland)	1	-	-	-	-
Graeme Cooksley (Canterbury)	1	-	-	-	-
Murray Eade (Auckland)	3	1	-	-	3
Doug Gailey (Auckland)	3	-	-	-	-
Peter Gurnick (Auckland)	3	-	-	-	-
Don Mann (Auckland)	2	-	-	-	-
Mita Mohi (Canterbury)	1	-	-	-	-
Phil Orchard (Wellington)	3	2	-	-	6
John O'Sullivan (Auckland)	1	-	-	-	-
Bob Paul (Wellington)	2	-	-	-	-
Brian Tracey (Auckland)	3	-	-	-	-
Rod Walker (Canterbury)	2	-	-	-	-
John Whittaker (Wellington)	3	2	-	-	6
Dennis Williams (Auckland)	3	1	-	-	3
John Wilson (Auckland)	2	-	3	-	6

1975

FRANCE 14 ....**WALES 7**
At Toulouse, Sunday, March 2, 1975
Attendance: 7,563; **Referee:** Fred Lindop (England)
France: T - Curt, Terrats; G - Serrano 3;
FG - Imbert, Lacoste
Wales: T - Wilson; G - Coslett 2
France: Francis Tranier, Elie Bonal, Michel Molinier,
Rene Terrats, Bernard Curt, Jean-Pierre Lacoste, Jean-
Marie Imbert, Francis De Nadia, Fernand Kaminski,
Nestor Serrano, Serge Gleyzes, Didier Hermet, Michel
Anglade. Replacement: Jean-Louis Castel
Wales: Bill Francis, Roy Mathias, David Willicombe,
Frank Wilson, Maurice Richards, David Watkins, Peter
Banner, Mick Murphy, Richard Evans, Brian Butler, John
Mantle, Colin Dixon, Kel Coslett. Replacement: Richard
Wallace (for Watkins).

ENGLAND 20 ....**FRANCE 2**
At Headingley, Leeds, Sunday, March 16, 1975
Attendance: 10,842; **Referee:** Keith Page (Australia),
replaced by H Hunt (England) after 28 minutes.
England: T - Fielding 2, Millward, Morgan; G - Gray 4
France: G - Serrano
England: Paul Charlton, Keith Fielding, Derek Noonan,
Les Dyl, John Atkinson, Ken Gill, Roger Millward, Dave
Chisnall, John Gray, Phil Jackson, Tommy Martyn,
George Nicholls, Barry Philbin. Replacement: Mick
Morgan (for Philbin).
France: Francis Tranier, Elie Bonal, Michel Molinier,
Terrats, Bernard Curt, Jean-Pierre Lacoste, Jean-Marie
Imbert, Francis De Nadia, Fernand Kaminski, Nestor
Serrano, Serge Gleyzes, Didier Hermet, Michel Anglade.

AUSTRALIA 36 ....**NEW ZEALAND 8**
At Lang Park, Brisbane, Sunday, June 1, 1975
Attendance: 10,000; **Referee:** Francois Escande (France)
Australia: T - Cronin 2, Langlands 2, Fulton, Platz,
Randall, Branighan; G - Cronin 6
New Zealand: T - Stirling, Whittaker; G - Collicoat
Australia: Graeme Langlands (c), Chris Anderson, Bob
Fulton, Mick Cronin, Terry Fahey, Tim Pickup, Ross
Strudwick, Terry Randall, John Lang, David Wright,
Gary Stevens, Lew Platz, Ron Coote. Replacements:
Paul Sait (for Wright), Ray Branighan (for Fahey).
New Zealand: Warren Collicoat, Mocky Brereton, John
O'Sullivan, John Whittaker, Phil Orchard, Dennis
Williams, Ken Stirling, John Hibbs, Tom Conroy,
Graeme West, Tony Coll, Ray Baxendale, Murray Eade.

ENGLAND 7 ....**WALES 12**
At Lang Park, Brisbane, Tuesday, June 10, 1975
Attendance: 6,000; **Referee:** Don Lancashire (Australia)
England: T - Martyn; G - Fairbairn 2
Wales: T - Sullivan, Treasure; G - Watkins 3
England: George Fairbairn, Keith Fielding, Derek
Noonan, Les Dyl, John Atkinson, Roger Millward, Steve
Nash, Dave Chisnall, Mick Morgan, Mike Coulman, Eric
Chisnall, George Nicholls, Steve Norton. Replacements:
Ken Gill (for Millward), Tommy Martyn (for Coulman).
Wales: Bill Francis, Roy Mathias, David Watkins, David
Willicombe, Clive Sullivan, David Treasure, Peter
Banner, Jim Mills, Tony Fisher, Bobby Wanbon, Colin
Dixon, Eddie Cunningham, Kel Coslett. Replacements:
John Mantle (for Dixon), Frank Wilson (for Banner).

AUSTRALIA 30 ....**WALES 13**
At Sydney Cricket Ground, Saturday, June 14, 1975
Attendance: 25,386; **Referee:** Francois Escande (France)
Australia: T - Harris, Langlands, Raudonikis, Fulton;
G - Cronin 9
Wales: T - Fisher; G - Watkins 5
Australia: Graeme Langlands (c), Mark Harris, Bob
Fulton, Mick Cronin, John Rhodes, Tim Pickup, Tom
Raudonikis, Terry Randall, John Lang, John O'Neill,
Gary Stevens, Lew Platz, Paul Sait. Replacements: John
Donnelly (for Stevens).
Wales: Bill Francis, Roy Mathias, David Watkins, David
Willicombe, Clive Sullivan, Glyn Turner, David Treasure,
Jim Mills, Tony Fisher, Bobby Wanbon, John Mantle,
Eddie Cunningham, Kel Coslett. Replacements: Frank
Wilson (for Sullivan), Peter Rowe (for Treasure).

NEW ZEALAND 27 ....**FRANCE 0**
At Christchurch, Sunday, June 15, 1975
Attendance: 2,500; **Referee:** Laurie Bruyeres (Australia)
New Zealand: T - Jarvis 2, Stirling, Eade, Conroy;
G - Sorensen 6
New Zealand: John Whittaker, Don Munro, Dennis
Williams, John O'Sullivan, Phil Orchard, Bob Jarvis, Ken
Stirling, John Greengrass, Tom Conroy, Dane Sorensen,
Tony Coll, Ray Baxendale, Murray Eade. Replacements:
Warren Collicoat (for O'Sullivan), Lindsay Proctor (for
Greengrass).
France: Francis Tranier, Elie Bonal, Andre Ruiz, Rene
Terrats, Andre Dumas, Jose Calle, Jean-Marie Imbert,
Francis De Nadia, Antoine Gonzales, Charles Zalduendo,
Serge Gleyzes, Michel Cassin, Jean-Claude Mayorgas.

NEW ZEALAND 17 ....**ENGLAND 17**
At Carlaw Park, Auckland, Saturday, June 21, 1975
Attendance: 12,000; **Referee:** Laurie Bruyeres (Australia)
New Zealand: T - Williams 2, Orchard; G - Sorensen 4
England: T - Fairbairn 2, Atkinson; G - Fairbairn 4
New Zealand: John Whittaker, Don Munro, Dennis
Williams, John O'Sullivan, Phil Orchard, Bob Jarvis, Ken
Stirling, John Greengrass, Tom Conroy, Dane Sorensen,
Tony Coll, Ray Baxendale, Murray Eade. Replacements:
Warren Collicoat (for Whittaker), Lindsay Proctor (for
Greengrass).
England: George Fairbairn, Keith Fielding, John Walsh,
Les Dyl, John Atkinson, Ken Gill, Steve Nash, Dave
Chisnall, Keith Bridges, Eric Chisnall, George Nicholls,
Phil Cookson, Steve Norton. Replacement: Mick Morgan
(for Dave Chisnall).

AUSTRALIA 26 ....**FRANCE 6**
At Lang Park, Brisbane, Sunday, June 22, 1975
Attendance: 9,000; **Referee:** John Percival
(New Zealand)
Australia: T - Harris 2, Fulton 2, Pickup, Cronin;
G - Cronin 4
France: G - Calle 3
Australia: Graeme Langlands (c), Mark Harris, Bob
Fulton, Mick Cronin, John Rhodes, Tim Pickup, Tom
Raudonikis, John Donnelly, John Lang, Arthur Beetson,
Lew Platz, Terry Randall, Ron Coote. Replacements:
Chris Anderson, John Quayle.
France: Francis Tranier, Bernard Curt, Andre Ruiz, Rene
Terrats, Andre Dumas, Jose Calle, Jean-Marie Imbert,
Francis De Nadia, Fernand Kaminski, Michel Cassin,
Serge Gleyzes, Michel Maique, Michel Anglade.
Replacements: Charles Zalduendo.

AUSTRALIA 10 ....**ENGLAND 10**
At Sydney Cricket Ground, Saturday, June 28, 1975
Attendance: 33,858; **Referee:** John Percival
(New Zealand)
Australia: T - Coote, Anderson; G - Cronin 2
England: T - Dunn, Gill; G - Fairbairn 2
Australia: Graeme Langlands (c), Mark Harris, Bob
Fulton, Mick Cronin, John Rhodes, Tim Pickup, Tom
Raudonikis, Terry Randall, John Lang, Arthur Beetson,
Lew Platz, Gary Stevens, Ron Coote. Replacements:
Chris Anderson (for Harris), John Donnelly (for Pickup).
England: George Fairbairn, Keith Fielding, John Walsh,
Les Dyl, Ged Dunn, Roger Millward, Steve Nash, Mike
Coulman, Keith Bridges, Mick Morgan, George Nicholls,
Phil Cookson, Steve Norton. Replacements: Eric
Chisnall (for Cookson), Ken Gill (for Millward).

NEW ZEALAND 13 ....**WALES 8**
At Carlaw Park, Auckland, Saturday, June 28, 1975
Attendance: 9,368; **Referee:** Laurie Bruyeres (Australia)
New Zealand: T - Orchard; G - Collicoat 5
Wales: T- Mills, Francis; G - Watkins
New Zealand: Warren Collicoat, Don Munro, Dennis
Williams, John O'Sullivan, Phil Orchard, Bob Jarvis, Ken
Stirling, Lindsay Proctor, Tom Conroy, Dane Sorensen,
Tony Coll, Ray Baxendale, Murray Eade.
Wales: Bill Francis, Roy Mathias, David Watkins, David
Willicombe, Clive Sullivan, David Treasure, Peter
Banner, Jim Mills, Tony Fisher, Bobby Wanbon, John
Mantle, Col Dixon, Kel Coslett. Replacements: Brian
Butler (for Mantle).

ENGLAND 22 ....**WALES 16**
*At Wilderspool, Warrington, Saturday, September 20,
1975*
Attendance: 5,034; **Referee:** Marcel Caillol (France)
England: T- Fielding, Holmes, Hughes; G - Fairbairn 6;
FG - Bridges
Wales: T - Banner, Coslett; G -Watkins 5
England: George Fairbairn, Keith Fielding, Eric Hughes,
John Holmes, John Atkinson, Ken Gill, Roger Millward,
Brian Hogan, Keith Bridges, Colin Forsyth, Jeff
Grayshon, Bob Irving, Steve Norton. Replacements:
Dave Eckersley (for Holmes), George Nicholls (for Gill).

Wales: Bill Francis, John Bevan, David Watkins, Frank
Wilson, Clive Sullivan, David Treasure, Peter Banner,
Mel James, Tony Fisher, John Mantle, Eddie
Cunningham, Brian Gregory, Kel Coslett. Replacements:
Glyn Turner (for Treasure), Peter Rowe (for Gregory).

NEW ZEALAND 8 ....**AUSTRALIA 24**
*At Carlaw Park, Auckland, Saturday, September 28,
1975*
Attendance: 18,000; **Referee:** Fred Lindop (England)
New Zealand: G - Collicoat 4
Australia: T - Quayle, Higgs, Cronin, Schubert;
G - Cronin 6
New Zealand: Warren Collicoat, Phil Orchard, Paul
Matete, Dennis Williams, Fred Ah Kuoi, Bob Jarvis, Ken
Stirling, John Greengrass, Tom Conroy, Dane Sorensen,
Tony Coll, Ray Baxendale, Murray Eade. Replacements:
John Smith (for Jarvis), Kurt Sorensen (for Coll).
Australia: Graham Eadie, John Rhodes, Mick Cronin,
John Brass (c), Ian Schubert, John Peard, Johnny
Mayes, Greg Veivers, George Piggins, Ian Mackay, Lou
Platz, Ray Higgs, John Quayle. Replacements: Tom
Raudonikis (for Eadie), Denis Fitzgerald (for Platz).

FRANCE 2 ....**ENGLAND 48**
At Bordeaux, Saturday, October 11, 1975
Attendance: 1,581; **Referee:** John Percival
(New Zealand)
France: G - Calle
England: T - Fielding 4, Dunn 2, Holmes 2, Hogan,
Forsyth, Gill, Hughes; G - Fairbairn 4, Millward 2
France: Maurice De Matos, Jean-Francois Grechi,
Andre Ruiz, Rene Terrats, Michel Lafargue, Jose Calle,
Jean-Marie Imbert, Guy Garcia, Francis Duthil, Michel
Gonzales, Jean-Marie Bosc, Jean-Pierre Tremouille, Guy
Buchi. Replacements: Guy Vigouroux (for Bosc),
Charles Thenegal (for Garcia).
England: George Fairbairn, Keith Fielding, Eric Hughes,
John Holmes, Ged Dunn, Ken Gill, Roger Millward,
Brian Hogan, Keith Bridges, Colin Forsyth, Jeff
Grayshon, Bob Irving, Steve Norton.

FRANCE 12 ....**NEW ZEALAND 12**
At Marseille, Friday, October 17, 1975
Attendance: 8,000; **Referee:** Billy Thompson (England)
France: T - Chauvet 2; G - Guilhem 3
New Zealand: T - Jarvis, Proctor; G - Collicoat 3
France: Marcel Pillon, Jean-Francois Grechi, Andre
Ruiz, Bernard Guilhem, Patrick Chauvet, Jose Calle,
Jean-Marie Imbert, Charles Zalduendo, Antoine
Gonzales, Charles Thenegal , Jean-Pierre Tremouille,
Jean-Pierre Sauret, Rene Terrats. Replacement: Michel
Moussard (for Thenegal).
New Zealand: Warren Collicoat, Phil Orchard, Bruce
Dickison, Bob Jarvis, John Smith, Dennis Williams, Ken
Stirling, John Greengrass, Tom Conroy, Lindsay
Proctor, Ray Baxendale, Tony Coll, Peter Gurnick.
Replacement: Tony Gordon (for Dickison).

WALES 6 ....**AUSTRALIA 18**
At Vetch Field, Swansea, Sunday, October 19, 1975
Attendance: 11,112; **Referee:** John Percival
(New Zealand)
Wales: G - Watkins 3
Australia: T - Schubert 3, Peard; G - Cronin 3
Wales: David Watkins, Roy Mathias, Bill Francis, Frank
Wilson, John Bevan, Glyn Turner, Peter Banner, Jim
Mills, Tony Fisher, John Mantle, Eddie Cunningham, Col
Dixon, Kel Coslett. Replacement: Peter Rowe (for Dixon).
Australia: Graham Eadie, Allan McMahon, Mick Cronin,
Steve Rogers, Ian Schubert, John Peard, Johnny Mayes,
Greg Veivers, George Piggins, Arthur Beetson (c), Terry
Randall, Ray Higgs, John Quayle. Replacements: Ian
Mackay (for Quayle), Jim Porter (for Mayes).

Rugby League World Cup Statistics

ENGLAND 27 ....**NEW ZEALAND 12**
At Odsal Stadium, Bradford, Saturday, October 25, 1975
Attendance: 5,937; **Referee:** Andre Lacaze (France)
England: T - Gill 3, Norton, Wright, Dunn, Hughes;
G - Fairbairn 3
New Zealand: T - Gordon, Smith;
G - Collicoat 2, Gordon
England: George Fairbairn, Stuart Wright, Eric Hughes,
John Holmes, Ged Dunn, Ken Gill, Roger Millward,
Brian Hogan, Keith Bridges, Colin Forsyth, Mick Adams,
Jeff Grayshon, Steve Norton. Replacements: George
Nicholls (for Adams), Les Dyl (for Wright).
New Zealand: Warren Collicoat, Phil Orchard, John
Smith, Dennis Williams, Bruce Dickison, Bob Jarvis,
Ken Stirling, John Greengrass, Tom Conroy, Lindsay
Proctor, Ray Baxendale, Tony Coll, Murray Eade.
Replacements: Tony Gordon (for Stirling), Peter Gurnick
(for Baxendale).

FRANCE 2 ....**AUSTRALIA 41**
At Perpignan, Sunday, October 26, 1975
Attendance: 10,440; **Referee:** Bill Thompson (England)
France: G - Guilhem
Australia: T - Rogers 2, Rhodes, Peard, Platz, Higgs,
Randall, Raudonikis, Eadie; G - Eadie 7
France: Marcel Pillon, Jean-Francois Grechi, Andre
Ruiz, Bernard Guilhem, Patrick Chauvet, Jose Calle,
Jean-Marie Imbert, Charles Zalduendo, Antoine
Gonzales, Charles Thenegal, Jean-Pierre Tremouille,
Jean-Pierre Sauret, Rene Terrats. Replacements:
Philippe Clergeau (for Ruiz), Michel Moussand (for
Zalduendo).
Australia: Graham Eadie, John Rhodes, Steve Rogers,
John Brass, Jim Porter, John Peard, Tom Raudonikis,
Arthur Beetson (c), John Lang, Terry Randall, Lew Platz,
Ray Higgs, Greg Pierce. Replacement: Ian Schubert (for
Rhodes)

ENGLAND 16 ....**AUSTRALIA 13**
At Central Park, Wigan, Saturday, November 1, 1975
Attendance: 9,393; **Referee:** John Percival
(New Zealand)
England: T - Grayshon, Holmes; G - Fairbairn 5
Australia: T - Schubert 3; G - Cronin 2
England: George Fairbairn, Dave Redfearn, John
Holmes, Les Dyl, Ged Dunn, Ken Gill, Roger Millward,
Brian Hogan, Keith Bridges, Jimmy Thompson, Bob
Irving, Jeff Grayshon, Steve Norton. Replacements:
Mick Adams (for Bridges), Eric Hughes (for Redfearn).
Australia: Graham Eadie, John Rhodes, Mick Cronin,
John Brass, Ian Schubert, John Peard, Johnny Mayes,
Ian Mackay, George Piggins, Arthur Beetson (c), Terry
Randall, Ray Higgs, Greg Pierce. Replacement: Steve
Rogers (for Peard).

WALES 25................................**NEW ZEALAND 24**
At Vetch Field, Swansea, Sunday, November 2, 1975
Attendance: 2,645; **Referee:** Georges Jameau (France)
Wales: T - Francis 2, Bevan, Willicombe, Mantle;
G - Watkins 5
New Zealand: T - Coll, Orchard, Gordon, Greengrass;
G - Gordon 5, Collicoat
Wales: David Watkins, Roy Mathias, Roy Mathias,
Frank Wilson, David Willicombe, John Bevan, Bill
Francis, Peter Banner, Jim Mills, Tony Fisher, Mick
Murphy, John Mantle, Stuart Gallacher, Brian Gregory.
Replacement: Clive Jones (for Gregory).
New Zealand: Warren Collicoat, Phil Orchard, Fred Ah
Kuoi, Dennis Williams, Tony Gordon, Bob Jarvis, John
Smith, John Greengrass, Tom Conroy, Dane Sorensen,
Kurt Sorensen, Tony Coll, Peter Gurnick. Replacements:
Bruce Dickison (for Collicoat), Lindsay Proctor (for
Jarvis).

WALES 23 ....**FRANCE 2**
At The Willows, Salford, Thursday, November 6, 1975
Attendance: 2,247; **Referee:** Fred Lindop (England)
Wales: T - Francis, Gregory, Willicombe, Bevan,
Banner; G - Watkins 4
France: G - Guilhem

Wales: David Watkins, Roy Mathias, Frank Wilson,
David Willicombe, John Bevan, Bill Francis, Peter
Banner, John Mantle, Graham Evans, Mick Murphy,
Stuart Gallacher, Brian Gregory, Clive Jones.
Replacements: Glyn Turner (for Francis), John Butler
(for Mantle).
France: Jose Calle, Jean-Francois Grechi, Rene Terrats,
Bernard Guilhem, Bernard Curt, Jean-Pierre Lacoste,
Jean-Marie Imbert, Yves Alvernhe, Antoine Gonzales,
Michel Moussand, Jean-Pierre Tremouille, Jean-Pierre
Sauret, Jean-Claude Mayorgas. Replacement: Michel
Maique (for Tremouille).

FINAL TABLE

	P	W	D	L	F	A	Pts
Australia	8	6	1	1	198	69	13
England	8	5	2	1	167	84	12
Wales	8	3	0	5	110	130	6
New Zealand	8	2	2	4	121	149	6
France	8	1	1	6	40	204	3

No Final required. Australia won the Cup.

CHALLENGE MATCH *(Held after World Championship)*

ENGLAND 0...................................**AUSTRALIA 25**
At Headingley, Leeds, Wednesday, November 12, 1975
Attendance: 7,727; **Referee:** Fred Lindop (England)
Australia: T - Lang 2, Peard, Randall, Cronin; G - Eadie 5
England: Ray Dutton, Mike Smith, Nigel Stephenson,
Eric Hughes, Ged Dunn, Ken Gill, Roger Millward, Harry
Beverley, Keith Bridges, Jimmy Thompson, Jeff
Grayshon, Mick Adams, Stanley Fearnley.
Replacements: David Topliss (for Fearnley), Richard
Stone (for Adams).
Australia: Graham Eadie, John Rhodes, Mick Cronin,
Steve Rogers, Ian Schubert, John Peard, Tom
Raudonikis, Greg Veivers, John Lang, Arthur Beetson
(c), Terry Randall, Ray Higgs, Greg Pierce.

THE 1975 SQUADS

AUSTRALIA *(Captain-coach: Graeme Langlands)*

	M	T	G	FG	Pts
Chris Anderson (Canterbury-Bankstown)	3	1	-	-	3
Arthur Beetson (Eastern Suburbs)	5	-	-	-	-
Ray Branighan (Manly-Warringah)	1	1	-	-	3
John Brass (Eastern Suburbs)	3	-	-	-	-
Ron Coote (Eastern Suburbs)	3	1	-	-	3
Mick Cronin (Gerringong)	7	4	32	-	76
John Donnelly (Western Suburbs)	3	-	-	-	-
Graham Eadie (Manly-Warringah)	4	1	7	-	17
Terry Fahey (Wellington)	1	-	-	-	-
Denis Fitzgerald (Parramatta)	1	-	-	-	-
Bob Fulton (Manly-Warringah)	4	4	-	-	12
Mark Harris (Eastern Suburbs)	3	3	-	-	9
Ray Higgs (Parramatta)	4	2	-	-	6
John Lang (Brisbane Easts)	5	-	-	-	-
Graeme Langlands (St George)	4	3	-	-	9
Ian Mackay (Eastern Suburbs)	3	-	-	-	-
Allan McMahon (Balmain)	1	-	-	-	-
Johnny Mayes (Eastern Suburbs)	3	-	-	-	-
John O'Neill (South Sydney)	1	-	-	-	-
Tim Pickup (Canterbury-Bankstown)	4	1	-	-	3
Lew Platz (Wynnum-Manly)	6	2	-	-	6
John Peard (Eastern Suburbs)	4	2	-	-	6
Greg Pierce (Cronulla-Sutherland)	2	-	-	-	-
George Piggins (South Sydney)	3	-	-	-	-
Jim Porter (Parramatta)	2	-	-	-	-
John Quayle (Parramatta)	3	1	-	-	3
Terry Randall (Manly-Warringah)	7	2	-	-	6
Tom Raudonikis (Western Suburbs)	5	2	-	-	6
John Rhodes (Wynnum-Manly)	6	1	-	-	3
Steve Rogers (Cronulla-Sutherland)	3	2	-	-	6
Paul Sait (South Sydney)	2	-	-	-	-
Ian Schubert (Eastern Suburbs)	4	7	-	-	21
Gary Stevens (South Sydney)	3	-	-	-	-
Ross Strudwick (Brisbane Easts)	1	-	-	-	-
Greg Veivers (Brisbane Souths)	2	-	-	-	-
David Wright (Brisbane Brothers)	1	-	-	-	-

ENGLAND *(Coach: Alex Murphy)*

	M	T	G	FG	Pts
Mick Adams (Widnes)	2	-	-	-	-
John Atkinson (Leeds)	4	1	-	-	3
Keith Bridges (Featherstone Rovers)	6	-	-	1	1
Paul Charlton (Salford)	1	-	-	-	-
Dave Chisnall (Warrington)	3	-	-	-	-
Eric Chisnall (St Helens)	3	-	-	-	-
Phil Cookson (Leeds)	2	-	-	-	-
Mike Coulman (Salford)	2	-	-	-	-
Ged Dunn (Hull Kingston Rovers)	4	4	-	-	12
Les Dyl (Leeds)	6	-	-	-	-
Dave Eckersley (St Helens)	1	-	-	-	-
George Fairbairn (Wigan)	7	2	26	-	58
Keith Fielding (Salford)	6	7	-	-	21
Colin Forsyth (Bradford Northern)	3	1	-	-	3
Ken Gill (Salford)	8	5	-	-	15
Parry Gordon (Warrington)	-	-	-	-	-
John Gray (Wigan)	1	-	4	-	8
Jeff Grayshon (Dewsbury)	4	1	-	-	3
Brian Hogan (Wigan)	4	1	-	-	3
John Holmes (Leeds)	4	3	-	-	9
Eric Hughes (Widnes)	4	5	-	-	15
Bob Irving (Wigan)	3	-	-	-	-
Phil Jackson (Bradford Northern)	1	-	-	-	-
Tommy Martyn (Warrington)	2	1	-	-	-
Roger Millward (Hull Kingston Rovers)	7	1	2	-	7
Mick Morgan (Wakefield Trinity)	4	1	-	-	3
Steve Nash ((Featherstone Rovers)	3	-	-	-	-
George Nicholls (St Helens)	6	-	-	-	-
Derek Noonan (Warrington)	2	-	-	-	-
Steve Norton (Castleford)	6	1	-	-	3
Barry Philbin (Warrington)	1	-	-	-	-
Dave Redfearn (Bradford Northern)	1	-	-	-	-
Jimmy Thompson (Featherstone Rovers)	1	-	-	-	-
John Walsh (St Helens)	2	-	-	-	-
Stuart Wright (Wigan)	1	1	-	-	3

FRANCE *(Coach: Puig Aubert)*

	M	T	G	FG	Pts
Michel Anglade (Saint-Gaudens)	3	-	-	-	-
Yves Alvernhe (Albi)	1	-	-	-	-
Elie Bonal (Carcassonne)	3	-	-	-	-
Jean-Marie Bosc (Saint-Esteve)	1	-	-	-	-
Guy Bucchi (Marseille)	1	-	-	-	-
Jose Calle (Saint-Esteve)	6	-	4	-	8
Michel Cassin (Tonneins)	2	-	-	-	-
Jean-Louis Castel (Albi)	1	-	-	-	-
Patrick Chauvet (Carcassonne)	2	2	-	-	6
Philippe Clergeau (Bordeaux)	1	-	-	-	-
Bernard Curt (Bordeaux)	4	1	-	-	3
Maurice De Matos (Toulouse)	1	-	-	-	-
Francis De Nadia (Limoux)	4	-	-	-	-
Andre Dumas (Lezignan)	2	-	-	-	-
Francis Duthil (Bordeaux)	1	-	-	-	-
Guy Garcia (Carcassonne)	1	-	-	-	-
Serge Gleyzes (Carcassonne)	4	-	-	-	-
Antoine Gonzales (Pamiers)	4	-	-	-	-
Michel Gonzales (Pamiers)	1	-	-	-	-
Jean-Francois Grechi (Limoux)	4	-	-	-	-
Bernard Guilhem (Carcassonne)	3	-	5	-	10
Didier Hermet (Villeneuve)	2	-	-	-	-
Jean-Marie Imbert (Avignon)	8	-	-	1	1
Fernand Kaminski (Albi)	3	-	-	-	-
Jean-Pierre Lacoste (Villeneuve)	3	-	-	1	1
Michel Lafargue (Tonneins)	1	-	-	-	-
Gabriel Laskawiec (Albi)	-	-	-	-	-
Michel Maique (Lezignan)	2	-	-	-	-
Jean-Claude Mayorgas (Toulouse)	2	-	-	-	-
Michel Molinier (Saint-Gaudens)	2	-	-	-	-
Michel Moussaud (Albi)	3	-	-	-	-
Marcel Pillon (Saint-Esteve)	2	-	-	-	-
Andre Ruiz (Pau)	5	-	-	-	-
Jean-Pierre Sauret (XIII Catalan)	1	-	-	-	-
Nestor Serrano (Saint-Gaudens)	2	-	4	-	8
Rene Terrats (Saint-Esteve)	8	1	-	-	3
Charles Thenegal (Toulouse)	3	-	-	-	-
Francis Tranier (Villefranche)	4	-	-	-	-
Jean-Pierre Tremouille (Tonneins)	4	-	-	-	-
Guy Vigouroux (Tonneins)	1	-	-	-	-
Charles Zalduendo (Toulouse)	4	-	-	-	-

NEW ZEALAND *(Coach: George Menzies)*

	M	T	G	FG	Pts
Fred Ah Kuoi (Auckland)	2	-	-	-	-
Ray Baxendale (West Coast)	7	-	-	-	-
Mocky Brereton (Auckland)	1	-	-	-	-
Warren Collicoat (Auckland)	8	-	16	-	32
Tony Coll (West Coast)	8	1	-	-	3
Tom Conroy (Auckland)	8	1	-	-	3
Bruce Dickison (Canterbury)	3	-	-	-	-
Murray Eade (Auckland)	6	1	-	-	3
Tony Gordon (Auckland)	3	2	6	-	18
John Greengrass (Canterbury)	6	1	-	-	3
Peter Gurnick (Auckland)	3	-	-	-	-
John Hibbs (Wellington)	1	-	-	-	-
Bob Jarvis (Auckland)	7	3	-	-	9
Paul Matete (Auckland)	1	-	-	-	-
Don Munro (Wellington)	3	-	-	-	-
Phil Orchard (Wellington)	8	3	-	-	9
John O'Sullivan (Auckland)	4	-	-	-	-
Lindsay Proctor (Auckland)	6	1	-	-	3
John Smith (Auckland)	4	1	-	-	3
Dane Sorensen (Auckland)	5	-	10	-	20
Kurt Sorensen (Auckland)	2	-	-	-	-
Ken Stirling (Auckland)	7	2	-	-	6
Graeme West (Taranaki)	1	-	-	-	-
John Whittaker (Wellington)	3	1	-	-	3
Dennis Williams (Auckland)	8	2	-	-	6

WALES *(Coach: Les Pearce)*

	M	T	G	FG	Pts
Peter Banner (Salford)	7	2	-	-	6
John Bevan (Warrington)	4	2	-	-	6
Brian Butler (Swinton)	2	-	-	-	-
Kel Coslett (St Helens)	6	1	2	-	7
Eddie Cunningham (St Helens)	4	-	-	-	-
Colin Dixon (Salford)	4	-	-	-	-
Richard Evans (Swinton)	2	-	-	-	-
Tony Fisher (Leeds)	6	1	-	-	3
Bill Francis (Wigan)	8	4	-	-	12
Stuart Gallacher (Keighley)	2	-	-	-	-
Brian Gregory (Wigan)	3	1	-	-	3
Mel James (St Helens)	1	-	-	-	-
John Mantle (St Helens)	8	1	-	-	3
Roy Mathias (St Helens)	7	-	-	-	-
Jim Mills (Widnes)	5	1	-	-	3
Mick Murphy (Bradford Northern)	3	-	-	-	-
Mike Nicholas (Warrington)	-	-	-	-	-
Maurice Richards (Salford)	1	-	-	-	-
Peter Rowe (Blackpool Borough)	3	-	-	-	-
Clive Sullivan (Hull Kingston Rovers)	4	1	-	-	3
David Treasure (Oldham)	4	1	-	-	3
Glyn Turner (Hull Kingston Rovers)	4	-	-	-	-
Richard Wallace (York)	1	-	-	-	-
Bobby Wanbon (Warrington)	3	-	-	-	-
David Watkins (Salford)	8	-	26	-	52
David Willicombe (Wigan)	6	2	-	-	6
Frank Wilson (St Helens)	7	1	-	-	3

FRIENDLIES WHILE ON TOUR

AUSTRALIA

AUCKLAND 6 ....AUSTRALIA 17
Auckland: G - Collicoat 3
Australia: T - Raudonikis, Cronin, McMahon; G - Cronin 4

SALFORD 6 ....AUSTRALIA 44
Salford: T - Fiddler, Mayor
Australia: T - Rhodes 3, Quayle 2, Cronin, Brass, McMahon, Mayes, Platz; G - Cronin 7

ST HELENS 7 ....AUSTRALIA 32
St Helens: T - Hull; G - Pimblett 2
Australia: T - Pierce 2, Schubert 2, Brass, Rogers; G - Eadie 7

OLDHAM 10 ....AUSTRALIA 20
Oldham: T - Murphy, Brown; G - Larder 2
Australia: T - Rogers 2, Rhodes, Raudonikis; G - Eadie 4

211

YORK 4 ....**AUSTRALIA 45**
York: G - Hetherington 2
Australia: T - McMahon 2, Rogers 2, Raudonikis 2,
Schubert, Lang, Porter, Mackay; G - Cronin 6

ENGLAND

WESTERN AUSTRALIA 2 ....**ENGLAND 40**
WA: G - Gush
England: T - Atkinson 2, Fielding 2, Dyl 2, Gill,
Millward, Walsh; G - Fairbairn 6; FG - Nash

TOOWOOMBA 16 ....**ENGLAND 25**
Toowoomba: T - Connell, Smith, Collins, Crisp;
G - Collins 2
England: T - Fielding 2, Norton, Millward, Noonan;
G - Fairbairn 5

SOUTHERN DIVISION 8 ....**ENGLAND 19**
Southern Division: T - Harris, Stuart; G - Cronin
England: T - Dyl, Martyn, Cookson; G - Walsh 5

WAIKATO 2 ....**ENGLAND 40**
Waikato: G - Moru
England: T - Dyl 3, Fielding 3, Atkinson 2, Gill,
Fairbairn; G - Walsh 3, Fairbairn 2

ILLAWARRA 15..............................**ENGLAND 12**
Illawarra: T - Fitzgibbon, Fogarty, Renno;
G - Ayliffe 3, Milthorpe
England: T - E Chisnall, Dyl; G - Fairbairn 3

BRISBANE 21.................................**ENGLAND 10**
Brisbane: T - Richardson, Smith, Veivers; G - Stewart 6
England: T - Dyl, Noonan; G - Fairbairn 2

PAPUA NEW GUINEA 12 ....**ENGLAND 40**
PNG: T - Eko, Patalui; G - Wartove 3
England: T - Fairbairn 2, Fielding 2, Coulman, Nash,
D Chisnall; G - Fairbairn 8

FRANCE

AUCKLAND 9.....................................**FRANCE 3**
Auckland: T - Dyer; G - Jordan 3
France: T -Bonal

NEW ZEALAND

SOUTH-WEST FRANCE 4 ....**NEW ZEALAND 39**
SW France: G - Cazadei
NZ: T - Dickison 3, Ah Kuoi 2, Williams, Smith,
Greengrass, Proctor; G - Collicoat 4, Gordon 2

BARROW 0 ....**NEW ZEALAND 24**
NZ: T - Ah Kuoi 2, Smith 2, D Sorensen, Gordon;
G - D Sorensen 2, Gordon

KEIGHLEY 8 ....**NEW ZEALAND 20**
Keighley: T - Roe; G - Moncrieff 2; FG - Moncrieff
NZ: T - Dickison 2, Ah Kuoi, Orchard: G - Gordon 4

WALES

IPSWICH 13 ....**WALES 35**
Ipswich: T - Richards 2, Dionysius; G - Dionysius 2
Wales: T - Mathias 4, Francis, Coslett, Fisher, Mills,
Watkins; G - Coslett 2, Watkins, Treasure

WELLINGTON 8 ....**WALES 52**
Wellington: T - Farrel, Whare Henry; G - Fox
Wales: T - Cunningham 2, Dixon 2, Mathias 2,
Sullivan 2, Treasure, Rowe, Nicholas; G - Watkins 8

WEST COAST 5 ....**WALES 35**
West Coast: T - Low; G - Crestani
Wales: T - Sullivan 3, Wanbon, Mantle, Turner,
Mathias;
G - Coslett 7

CANTERBURY 18 ....**WALES 25**
Canterbury: Cooksley, Dickison;
G - Brereton 5, Lawrence
Wales: Mathias 2, Willicombe, Rowe, Nicholas;
G - Watkins 5

AUCKLAND 31 ....**WALES 5**
Auckland: T - Hansen 2, Collicoat, O'Sullivan, Ah Kuoi;
G - Collicoat 8
Wales: T - Dixon; G - Coslett

MAORIS 12.......................................**WALES 18**
Maoris: T - P Orchard, Williams; G - Wilson 3
Wales: Wilson 2, Banner, Mathias; G - Watkins 3

1977

NEW ZEALAND 12 ....**AUSTRALIA 27**
At Carlaw Park, Sunday, May 29, 1977
Attendance: 20,019; **Referee:** Billy Thompson (England)
New Zealand: T - Smith, Rushton; G - Collicoat 6
Australia: T - Harris, Thomas, McMahon 2, Peard;
G - Cronin 6
New Zealand: Warren Collicoat, Dane O'Hara, Olsen
Filipaina, Chris Jordan, Kevin Fisher, Dennis Williams,
John Smith, Whetu Henry, Alan Rushton, Dane
Sorensen, Kurt Sorensen, Tony Coll, Whare Henry.
Replacements: John Whittaker (for Jordan), Ray
Baxendale (for Whare Henry).
Australia: Graham Eadie, Mark Harris, Mick Cronin,
Mark Thomas, Allan McMahon; John Peard, Tommy
Raudonikis, Greg Veivers (c), Nick Geiger, Denis
Fitzgerald, Terry Randall, Ray Higgs, Greg Pierce

GREAT BRITAIN 23 ....**FRANCE 4**
At Carlaw Park, Auckland, Sunday, June 5, 1977
Attendance: 10,000; **Referee:** Bob Cooper
(New Zealand)
Great Britain: T - Wright, Millward, Dyl; G - Fairbairn 7
France: G - Calle 2
Great Britain: George Fairbairn, Keith Fielding, John
Holmes, Les Dyl, Stuart Wright, Roger Millward (c),
Steve Nash, Steve Pitchford, David Ward, Jim
Thompson, Eddie Bowman, George Nicholls, Phil
Hogan. Replacements: Ken Gill (for Millward), Len
Casey (for Hogan).
France: Jacques Guigue, Jose Moya, Christian
Laskawiec, Andre Ruiz, Patrick Chauvet, Jose Calle (c),
Guy Alard, Michel Cassin, Herve Bonnet, Henri Daniel,
Jean-Pierre Sauret, Jean-Jaques Cologni, Joel
Roosebrouck. Replacement: Guy Rodriguez (for Bonnet).

AUSTRALIA 21....................................**FRANCE 9**
At Sydney Cricket Ground, Saturday, June 11, 1977
Attendance: 13,231; **Referee:** Billy Thompson (England)
Australia: T - Eadie 2, McMahon, Fitzgerald, Veivers;
G - Cronin 3
France: T - Moya; G - Calle 3
Australia: Graham Eadie, Terry Fahey, Mick Cronin,
Mark Thomas, Allan McMahon, John Peard, Tom
Raudonikis, Denis Fitzgerald, Nick Geiger, Greg Veivers,
Terry Randall, Arthur Beetson (c), Rod Reddy.
Replacements: Ray Higgs (for Beetson), Russel Gartner
(for Thomas).
France: Jacques Guigue, Jose Moya, Jean-Marc
Bourret, Rene Terrats, Christian Laskawiec, Jose Calle
(c), Guy Alard, Michel Cassin, Guy Garcia, Max Chantal,
Jean-Pierre Sauret, Manuel Caravaca, Joel
Roosebrouck. Replacements: Jean-Marie Imbert (for
Bourret), Guy Rodriguez (for Caravaca).

NEW ZEALAND 12 ....**GREAT BRITAIN 30**
*At Addington Showgrounds, Christchurch,
Sunday, June 12, 1977*
Attendance: 5,342; **Referee:** Marcel Caillol (France)
New Zealand: T - Fisher, Whittaker; G - Collicoat 3
Great Britain: T - Wright 2, Francis, Nicholls, Bowman,
Millward; G - Fairbairn 6

New Zealand: Warren Collicoat, John Whittaker, Olsen Filipaina, Fred Ah Kuoi, Kevin Fisher, Dennis Williams, John Smith, Whetu Henry, Alan Rushton, Lindsay Proctor, Tony Coll, Kurt Sorensen, Whare Henry. Replacements: Chris Jordan, Mark Graham.
Great Britain: George Fairbairn, Bill Francis, John Holmes, Les Dyl, Stuart Wright, Roger Millward (c), Steve Nash, Steve Pitchford, David Ward, Jim Thompson, Eddie Bowman, George Nicholls, Phil Hogan. Replacements: Ken Gill, Len Casey.

AUSTRALIA 19 ....GREAT BRITAIN 5
At Lang Park, Saturday, June 18, 1977
Attendance: 25,200; **Referee:** Marcel Caillol (France)
Australia: T - Eadie 2, Randall; G - Cronin 5
Great Britain: T - Millward; G - Fairbairn
Australia: Graham Eadie, Terry Fahey, Mick Cronin, Mark Thomas, Allan McMahon, John Peard, Tom Raudonikis, Denis Fitzgerald, Nick Geiger, Greg Veivers, Terry Randall, Arthur Beetson (c), Greg Pierce. Replacements: Ray Higgs (for Raudonikis).
Great Britain: George Fairbairn, Keith Fielding, Bill Francis, Les Dyl, Stuart Wright, Roger Millward (c), Steve Nash, Steve Pitchford, David Ward, Jim Thompson, Eddie Bowman, George Nicholls, Phil Hogan. Replacements: John Holmes (for Fielding), Peter Smith (for Ward).

NEW ZEALAND 28 ....FRANCE 20
At Carlaw Park, Auckland, Sunday, July 19, 1977
Attendance: 8,000; **Referee:** Billy Thompson (England)
New Zealand: T - Fisher, Jordan, Smith, Graham; G - Jordan 8
France: T - Cologni 2, Roosebrouck, Guigue; G - Moya 4
New Zealand: Michael O'Donnell, John Whittaker, Dennis Williams, Fred Ah Kuoi, Kevin Fisher, Chris Jordan, John Smith, Whetu Henry, Alan Rushton, Lindsay Proctor, Tony Coll (c), Kurt Sorensen, Mark Graham. Replacements: Olsen Filipaina, Ray Baxendale.
France: Jose Calle (c), Jacques Guigue, Rene Terrats, Andre Ruiz, Jose Moya, Guy Alard, Jean-Marie Imbert, Michel Cassin, Guy Garcia, Jean-Pierre Sauret, Manuel Caravaca, Jean-Jacques Cologni, Joel Roosebrouck. Replacements: Jackie Imbert, Michel Moussard.

FINAL TABLE

	P	W	D	L	F	A	Pts
Australia	3	3	0	0	67	26	6
Great Britain	3	2	0	1	58	35	4
New Zealand	3	1	0	2	52	77	2
France	3	0	0	3	33	72	0

FINAL

AUSTRALIA 13 ....GREAT BRITAIN 12
At Sydney Cricket Ground, Saturday, June 25, 1977
Attendance: 24,457; **Referee:** Billy Thompson (England)
Australia: T - McMahon, Gartner, Kolc; G - Cronin 2
Great Britain: T - Pitchford, Gill; G - Fairbairn 3
Australia: Graham Eadie, Mark Harris, Mick Cronin, Russel Gartner, Allan McMahon, John Peard, John Kolc, Terry Randall, Nick Geiger, Greg Veivers, Arthur Beetson (c), Ray Higgs, Greg Pierce. Replacement: Denis Fitzgerald (for Veivers).
Great Britain: George Fairbairn, Bill Francis, John Holmes, Les Dyl, Stuart Wright, Roger Millward (c), Steve Nash, Steve Pitchford, Keith Elwell, Jim Thompson, Eddie Bowman, George Nicholls, Phil Hogan. Replacements: Ken Gill (for Wright), Len Casey (for Hogan).

THE 1977 SQUADS

AUSTRALIA *(Coach: Terry Fearnley)*

	M	T	G	FG	Pts
Arthur Beetson (Eastern Suburbs) (c)	3	-	-	-	-
Steve Crear (Brisbane Wests)	-	-	-	-	-
Mick Cronin (Parramatta)	4	-	16	-	32
Graham Eadie (Manly-Warringah)	4	4	-	-	12
Terry Fahey (South Sydney)	2	-	-	-	-
Denis Fitzgerald (Parramatta)	4	1	-	-	3

Russel Gartner (Manly-Warringah)	2	1	-	-	3
Nick Geiger (Brisbane Norths)	4	-	-	-	-
Mark Harris (Eastern Suburbs)	2	1	-	-	3
Ray Higgs (Parramatta)	4	-	-	-	-
John Kolc (Parramatta)	1	1	-	-	3
Allan McMahon (Balmain)	4	4	-	-	12
Rod Morris (Brisbane Easts)	-	-	-	-	-
Graham Olling (Parramatta)	-	-	-	-	-
John Peard (Parramatta)	4	1	-	-	3
Greg Pierce (Cronulla-Sutherland)	3	-	-	-	-
Terry Randall (Manly-Warringah)	4	1	-	-	3
Tom Raudonikis (Western Suburbs)	3	-	-	-	-
Rod Reddy (St George)	1	-	-	-	-
Mark Thomas (Brisbane Brothers)	3	1	-	-	3
Greg Veivers (Brisbane Souths)	4	1	-	-	3

FRANCE *(Coach: Yves Begou)*

	M	T	G	FG	Pts
Guy Alard (Carcassonne)	3	-	-	-	-
Christian Baile (Carcassonne)	-	-	-	-	-
Herve Bonnet (Saint-Esteve)	1	-	-	-	-
Jean-Marc Bourret (XIII Catalan)	1	-	-	-	-
Jean-Louis Brial (XIII Catalan)	-	-	-	-	-
Jose Calle (Saint-Esteve) (c)	3	-	5	-	10
Manuel Caravaca (Carcassonne)	2	-	-	-	-
Michel Cassin (Toulouse)	3	-	-	-	-
Max Chantal (Villeneuve)	1	-	-	-	-
Patrick Chauvet (Carcassonne)	1	-	-	-	-
Jean-Jacques Cologni (XIII Catalan)	2	2	-	-	6
Henri Daniel (XIII Catalan)	1	-	-	-	-
Guy Garcia (Carcassonne)	2	-	-	-	-
Jacques Guigue (Avignon)	3	1	-	-	3
Jackie Imbert (Avignon)	1	-	-	-	-
Jean-Marie Imbert (Avignon)	2	-	-	-	-
Christian Laskawiec (Albi)	2	-	-	-	-
Gerard Lepine (Bordeaux)	-	-	-	-	-
Jean-Claude Mayorgas (Toulouse)	-	-	-	-	-
Michel Moussard (Albi)	1	-	-	-	-
Jose Moya (Carcassonne)	3	1	4	-	11
Guy Rodriguez (Toulouse)	2	-	-	-	-
Joel Roosebrouck (Villeneuve)	3	1	-	-	3
Andre Ruiz (Carcassonne)	2	-	-	-	-
Pierre Saboureau (XIII Catalan)	-	-	-	-	-
Jean-Pierre Sauret (XIII Catalan)	3	-	-	-	-
Rene Terrats (Saint-Esteve)	2	-	-	-	-

GREAT BRITAIN *(Coach: David Watkins)*

	M	T	G	FG	Pts
Eddie Bowman (Workington Town)	4	1	-	-	3
Len Casey (Hull Kingston Rovers)	3	-	-	-	-
Les Dyl (Leeds)	4	1	-	-	3
Keith Elwell (Widnes)	1	-	-	-	-
George Fairbairn (Wigan)	4	-	17	-	34
Keith Fielding (Salford)	2	-	-	-	-
Bill Francis (Wigan)	3	1	-	-	3
Ken Gill (Salford)	3	1	-	-	3
Alan Hodgkinson (Rochdale Hornets)	-	-	-	-	-
Phil Hogan (Barrow)	4	-	-	-	-
John Holmes (Leeds)	4	-	-	-	-
Sammy Lloyd (Castleford)	-	-	-	-	-
Roger Millward (Hull Kingston Rovers) (c)	4	3	-	-	9
Steve Nash (Salford)	4	-	-	-	-
George Nicholls (St Helens)	4	1	-	-	3
Steve Pitchford (Leeds)	4	1	-	-	3
Peter Smith (Featherstone Rovers)	1	-	-	-	-
Jim Thompson (Featherstone Rovers)	4	-	-	-	-
David Ward (Leeds)	4	-	-	-	-
Stuart Wright (Widnes)	4	3	-	-	9

Chosen to tour but withdrew: Eddie Cunningham (St Helens) (replaced by Thompson); Phil Lowe (Hull Kingston Rovers) (Hogan); Tommy Martyn (Warrington) (Pitchford); Jim Mills (Widnes) (Smith)

NEW ZEALAND *(Coach: Ron Ackland)*

	M	T	G	FG	Pts
Fred Ah Kuoi (Auckland)	2	-	-	-	-
Ray Baxendale (West Coast)	2	-	-	-	-
Tony Coll (West Coast) (c)	3	-	-	-	-
Warren Collicoat (Wellington)	2	-	6	-	12
Tom Conroy (Auckland)	-	-	-	-	-
Olsen Filipaina (Auckland)	3	-	-	-	-
Kevin Fisher (Waikato)	3	2	-	-	6
Mark Graham (Auckland)	2	1	-	-	3
Whare Henry (Wellington)	2	-	-	-	-
Whetu Henry (Wellington)	3	-	-	-	-
Chris Jordan (Auckland)	3	1	8	-	19
Michael O'Donnell (Canterbury)	1	-	-	-	-
Dane O'Hara (Auckland)	1	-	-	-	-
Lindsay Proctor (Auckland)	2	-	-	-	-
Alan Rushton (Canterbury)	3	1	-	-	3
John Smith (Auckland)	3	2	-	-	6
Dane Sorensen (Cronulla-Sutherland)	1	-	-	-	-
Kurt Sorensen (Auckland)	3	-	-	-	-
John Whittaker (Wellington)	3	1	-	-	3
Dennis Williams (Auckland)	3	-	-	-	-

FRIENDLIES

AUSTRALIA

SOUTH ISLAND 5 .... **AUSTRALIA 68**

AUCKLAND 19 .... **AUSTRALIA 15**

FRANCE

PAPUA NEW GUINEA 37 .... **FRANCE 6**
At Boroko Oval, Port Moresby, Sunday, May 29, 1975
Attendance: 14,000
PNG: T - P Tore, D Boge, P Pais, J Meta, G Kora,
B Karavu, A Rero; G - J Lenix 7, D Boge
France: T- C Baile, J-M Bourret

BRISBANE 14 .... **FRANCE 12**

WELLINGTON 0 .... **FRANCE 8**

NEWCASTLE 19 .... **FRANCE 12**

TOOWOOMBA 14 .... **FRANCE 10**

GREAT BRITAIN

NORTHERN MAORIS 14 .... **GREAT BRITAIN 18**

AUCKLAND 14 .... **GREAT BRITAIN 10**

MONARO 33 .... **GREAT BRITAIN 12**

NORTH QUEENSLAND 17 .... **GREAT BRITAIN 14**

QUEENSLAND 13 .... **GREAT BRITAIN 18**
Queensland: T - J Ribot 2, B Gardiner; G - J Ribot,
D Brohman
Gt Britain: T - K Fielding 2, B Francis, P Hogan;
G - G Fairbairn 3

NEW SOUTH WALES 35 .... **GREAT BRITAIN 5**
At Sydney Cricket Ground, Saturday, July 2, 1977
Attendance: 7,244
NSW: B Hetherington 2, R McGregor, R Reddy,
M Krilich; G - Cronin 9, Rogers
Gt Britain: T - Millward; G - D Watkins

1985-88

NEW ZEALAND 18 .... **AUSTRALIA 0**
At Carlaw Park, Auckland, Sunday, July 7, 1985
Attendance: 15,327; **Referee:** Julien Rascagneres
(France)
New Zealand: T - Friend 2, Leuluai; G - Filipaina 3
New Zealand: Gary Kemble, Dean Bell, Gary Prohm,
James Leuluai, Dane O'Hara, Olsen Filipaina, Clayton
Friend, Owen Wright, Howie Tamati, Kevin Tamati, Mark
Graham (c), Kurt Sorensen, Hugh McGahan.
Replacements: Joe Ropati, Ricky Cowan.
Australia: Garry Jack, John Ribot, Mal Meninga, Steve
Ella, John Ferguson, Wally Lewis (c), Des Hasler, Peter
Tunks, Ben Elias, Steve Roach, Paul Vautin, Peter
Wynn, Wayne Pearce. Replacements: Chris Close, Greg
Dowling.

GREAT BRITAIN 6 .... **NEW ZEALAND 6**
At Elland Road, Leeds, Sunday, November 9, 1985
Attendance: 22,209; **Referee:** Barry Gomersall
(Australia)
Great Britain: G - Crooks 3
New Zealand: T - Graham; G - Dane Sorensen
Great Britain: Mick Burke, Des Drummond, Garry
Schofield, Shaun Edwards, Joe Lydon, Ellery Hanley,
Deryck Fox, Jeff Grayshon, David Watkinson, John
Fieldhouse, Andy Goodway, Ian Potter, Harry Pinner (c).
Replacements: Chris Arkwright, Lee Crooks.
New Zealand: Gary Kemble, Darrell Williams, Dean
Bell, James Leuluai, Dane O'Hara, Fred Ah Kuoi,
Clayton Friend, Kevin Tamati, Wayne Wallace, Dane
Sorensen, Mark Graham (c), Kurt Sorensen, Gary
Prohm. Replacements: Olsen Filipaina, Hugh McGahan.

FRANCE 0 .... **NEW ZEALAND 22**
At Stade Gilbert Brutus, Perpignan,
Saturday, December 7, 1985
Attendance: 5,000; **Referee:** Ronnie Campbell
(Great Britain)
New Zealand: T - McGahan 2, Kemble, Kurt Sorensen;
G - Filipaina 3
France: Serge Pallares, Hugues Ratier, Denis Berge,
Roger Palisses, Didier Couston, Dominique Espugna,
Bruno Guasch, Max Chantal, Thierry Bernabe, Serge
Titeux, Pierre Montgaillard, Marc Palanque, Guy Laforgue
(c). Replacements: Andre Perez, Jean-Luc Rabot.
New Zealand: Gary Kemble, Dean Bell, James Leuluai,
Fred Ah Kuoi, Dane O'Hara, Olsen Filipaina, Clayton
Friend, Kurt Sorensen, Wayne Wallace, Dane Sorensen,
Hugh McGahan (c), Owen Wright, Ron O'Regan.
Replacements: Mark Elia, Brent Todd.

FRANCE 10 .... **GREAT BRITAIN 10**
At Parc de Sports, Avignon, Sunday, February 16, 1986
Attendance: 6,000; **Referee:** Kevin Roberts (Australia)
France: T - Dumas; G - Dumas 3
Great Britain: T - Hanley; G - Crooks 3
France: Gilles Dumas, Pascal Laroche, Philippe
Fourquet, Alain Maury, Didier Couston, Dominique
Espugna, Patrick Entat, Max Chantal, Patrick Baco,
Serge Titeux, Marc Palanque, Guy Laforgue (c), Thierry
Bernabe. Replacements: Denis Berge (for Laroche),
Jean-Luc Rabot (for Titeux).
Great Britain: Mick Burke, Des Drummond, Garry
Schofield, Ellery Hanley, Henderson Gill, Tony Myler,
Deryck Fox, Lee Crooks, David Watkinson, Shaun
Wane, John Fieldhouse, Ian Potter, Harry Pinner (c).

AUSTRALIA 32 .... **NEW ZEALAND 12**
At Lang Park, Brisbane, Tuesday, July 29, 1986
Attendance: 22,811; **Referee:** Robin Whitfield (England)
Australia: T - Kenny 2, Sterling, Lewis, Miles,
O'Connor; G - O'Connor 4
New Zealand: T - Williams 2; G - Filipaina 2
Australia: Garry Jack, Michael O'Connor, Gene Miles,
Brett Kenny, Les Kiss, Wally Lewis (c), Peter Sterling,
Steve Roach, Royce Simmons, Peter Tunks, Noel Cleal,
Steve Folkes, Wayne Pearce. Replacements: Terry
Lamb, Bryan Niebling.

New Zealand: Gary Kemble, Darrell Williams, Joe Ropati, Gary Prohm, Dane O'Hara, Olsen Filipaina, Gary Freeman, Brent Todd, Barry Harvey, Kurt Sorensen, Mark Graham (c), Hugh McGahan, Ron O'Regan. Replacements: Shane Cooper, Owen Wright.

PAPUA NEW GUINEA 24 ....NEW ZEALAND 22
At Lloyd Robson Oval, Port Moresby,
Sunday, August 17, 1986
Attendance: 15,000; **Referee:** Kevin Roberts (Australia)
Papua New Guinea: T - Haili 2, Ako, Atoi; G - Kovae 4
New Zealand: T - Brown, Wallace, McGahan, Ropati; G - Brown 3
Papua New Guinea: Dairi Kovae, J Katsir, Lauta Atoi, Bal Nupampo, M Kerekere, Darius Haili, Tony Kila (c), Joe Tep, Roy Heni, Ati Lomutopa, Bobby Ako, Bernard Waketsi, Arebo Taumaku. Replacements: Kepi Saea, Nick Andy.
New Zealand: Gary Kemble, Marty Crequer, Darrell Williams, Joe Ropati, Dane O'Hara, Shane Cooper, Gary Freeman, Adrian Shelford, Wayne Wallace, Peter Brown, Owen Wright, Hugh McGahan (c), Ron O'Regan. Replacements: James Leuluai, Sam Stewart.

PAPUA NEW GUINEA 12 ....AUSTRALIA 62
At Lloyd Robson Oval, Port Moresby, October 4, 1986
Attendance: 17,000; **Referee:** Neville Kesha (New Zealand)
Papua New Guinea: T - Numapo 2; G - Kovae 2
Australia: T - Kiss 2, O'Connor 2, Cleal 2, Mortimer, Jack, Lindner, Roach, Hasler, Lewis; G - O'Connor 7
Papua New Guinea: Dairi Kovae, J Katsir, Lauta Atoi, Bal Nupampo, M Kerekere, Darius Haili, Tony Kila (c), Joe Tep, Roy Heni, Ati Lomutopa, Bobby Ako, Bernard Waketsi, Arebo Taumaku. Replacements: Kepi Saea, Nick Andy.
Australia: Garry Jack, Michael O'Connor, Gene Miles, Chris Mortimer, Les Kiss, Wally Lewis (c), Des Hasler, Steve Roach, Royce Simmons, Bryan Niebling, Noel Cleal, Paul Dunn, Bob Lindner. Replacements: Mal Meninga, Paul Sironen.

GREAT BRITAIN 15 ....AUSTRALIA 24
At Central Park, Wigan, Saturday, November 22, 1986
Attendance: 20,169; **Referee:** Julien Rascagneres (France)
Great Britain: T - Schofield 2; G - Lydon 2, Gill; FG - Schofield
Australia: T - Miles, Lindner, Shearer, Lewis; G - O'Connor 4
Great Britain: Joe Lydon, Henderson Gill, Garry Schofield, David Stephenson, John Basnett, Tony Myler, Andy Gregory, Kevin Ward, David Watkinson (c), Lee Crooks, Chris Burton, Andy Goodway (Wigan), Harry Pinner (Widnes). Replacements: Ian Potter (for Burton).
Australia: Garry Jack, Dale Shearer, Brett Kenny, Gene Miles, Michael O'Connor, Wally Lewis (c), Peter Sterling, Greg Dowling, Royce Simmons, Paul Dunn, Mal Meninga, Bryan Neibling, Bob Lindner. Replacements: Terry Lamb (for Meninga), Les Davidson (for Dunn).

FRANCE 0 ....AUSTRALIA 52
At Stade Albert Domec, Carcassonne,
Saturday, December 13, 1986
Attendance: 3,000; **Referee:** Fred Lindop (Great Britain)
Australia: T - Shearer 4, Jack 3, Folkes, Niebling, O'Connor; G - O'Connor 6
France: Patrick Wozniack, Sebastien Rodriguez, Phillipe Fourquet, Francis Laforgue, Hughes Ratier, Roger Palisses, Christian Scicchitano, Max Chantal, Thierry Bernabe, Serge Titeux, Guy Laforgue (c), Daniel Verdes, Philippe Gestas. Replacements: Gilles Dumas (for Rodriguez), Yves Storer (for Chantal).
Australia: Garry Jack, Dale Shearer, Brett Kenny, Gene Miles, Michael O'Connor, Wally Lewis (c), Peter Sterling, Greg Dowling, Royce Simmons, Paul Dunn, Steve Folkes, Bryan Niebling, Bob Lindner. Replacements: Terry Lamb (for Dowling), Les Davidson (for Folkes).

GREAT BRITAIN 52 ....FRANCE 4
At Headingley, Leeds, Saturday, January 24, 1987
Attendance: 6,567; **Referee:** Mick Stone (Australia)
Great Britain: T - Edwards 2, Hanley 2, Gregory 2, Lydon, Forster, Goodway; G - Lydon 8
France: G - Perez 2
Great Britain: Joe Lydon, Mark Forster, Garry Schofield, David Stephenson, Henderson Gill, Ellery Hanley (c), Shaun Edwards, David Hobbs, Kevin Beardmore, Lee Crooks, Andy Goodway, Roy Haggerty, Mike Gregory. Replacements: David Creasser, Keith England.
France: Andre Perez, Didier Couston, Roger Palisses, Hugues Ratier, Cyrille Pons, Dominique Espugna, Gilles Dumas, Yves Storer, Yannik Mantese, Jean-Luc Rabot, Daniel Verdes, Marc Palanque (c), Thierry Bernabe. Replacements: Patrick Rocci, Serge Titeux.

GREAT BRITAIN 42 ....PAPUA NEW GUINEA 0
At Central Park, Wigan, Saturday. October 24, 1987
Attendance: 9,121; **Referee:** Francis Desplas (France)
Great Britain: T - Edwards 2, Ford, Medley, Hanley, Lydon, Gregory; G - Stephenson 7
Great Britain: Steve Hampson, Des Drummond, David Stephenson, Joe Lydon, Phil Ford, Shaun Edwards, Andy Gregory, Kevin Ward, Paul Groves, Brian Case, Andy Goodway, Paul Medley, Ellery Hanley (c). Replacements: John Woods, Karl Fairbank.
Papua New Guinea: Dairi Kovae, Arnold Krewanty, Lauta Atoi, Bal Numapo (c), Kepi Saea, Darius Haili, Tony Kila, Joe Tep, Roy Heni, Ati Lomutopa, Mathius Kombra, Bernard Waketsi, Arebo Taumaku. Replacements: Mathius Kitimon, David Gaius.

FRANCE 21 ....PAPUA NEW GUINEA 4
At Stade Albert Domec, Carcassonne,
Sunday, November 15, 1987
Attendance: 3,500; **Referee:** John Holdsworth (Great Britain)
France: T - Fraisse 2, Pons, Ratier; G - Bourrel 2; FG - Bourrel
Papua New Guinea: T - Kovae
France: Jean-Philippe Pougeau, Hugues Ratier (c), Guy Delaunay, David Fraisse, Cyrille Pons, Jacques Moliner, Frederic Bourrel, Jean-Luc Rabot, Matthieu Khedimi, Pierre Alleres, Pierre Montgaillard, Daniel Divet, Guy Laforgue. Replacements: Daniel Verdes, Gilles Dumas.
Papua New Guinea: Dairi Kovae, Arnold Krewanty, Lauta Atoi, Kepi Saea, Mea Morea, Bal Numapo (c), Tony Kila, Arebo Taumaku, Roy Heni, Ati Lomutopa, Bernard Waketsi, Bobby Ako, Gideon Kouoru. Replacements: Darius Haili, Mathius Kombra.

PAPUA NEW GUINEA 22.............GREAT BRITAIN 42
At Lloyd Robson Oval, Port Moresby, Sunday, May 22,
1988
Attendance: 12,107; **Referee:** Greg McCallum (Australia)
Papua New Guinea: T - Kovae 2, Krewanty, Rop; G - Numapo 3
Great Britain: T - Schofield 2, Gill 2, Medley, M Gregory, Stephenson; G - Loughlin 7
Papua New Guinea: Dairi Kovae, Arnold Krewanty, Mea Morea, Bal Numapo (c), Kepi Saea, Darius Haili, Tony Kila, Yer Bom, Michael Matmillo, Isaac Rop, Tuiyo Evei, Mathius Kombra, Haoda Kouoru. Replacements: Ngala Lapan, Thomas Rombuk.
Great Britain: Paul Loughlin, Phil Ford, Garry Schofield, David Stephenson, Henderson Gill, Shaun Edwards, Andy Gregory, Kevin Ward, Kevin Beardmore, Brian Case, Paul Medley, Mike Gregory, Ellery Hanley (c). Replacements: David Hulme, Paul Dixon.

AUSTRALIA 12 ....GREAT BRITAIN 26
At Sydney Football Stadium, Saturday, July 9, 1988
Attendance: 15,994; **Referee:** Francis Desplas (France)
Australia: T - Lewis, Backo; G - O'Connor 2
Great Britain: T - Gill 2, Offiah, Ford, M Gregory; G - Loughlin 3

215

Rugby League World Cup Statistics

Australia: Garry Jack, Andrew Ettingshausen, Michael O'Connor, Peter Jackson, Tony Currie, Wally Lewis (c), Peter Sterling, Martin Bella, Greg Conescu, Sam Backo, Wally Fullerton Smith, Paul Vautin, Wayne Pearce. Replacements: Gary Belcher (for Sterling), Bob Lindner (for Fullerton Smith).
Great Britain: Phil Ford, Henderson Gill, Paul Loughlin, David Stephenson, Martin Offiah, David Hulme, Andy Gregory, Kevin Ward, Paul Hulme, Hugh Waddell, Mike Gregory, Roy Powell, Ellery Hanley (c). Replacements: Brian Case (for Waddell).

NEW ZEALAND 66 ....PAPUA NEW GUINEA 14
At Carlaw Park, Auckland, Sunday, July 10, 1988
Attendance: 8,392; **Referee:** Greg McCallum (Australia)
New Zealand: T - S Horo 3, Iro 3, Mercer 2, Graham, Shelford, Wallace, Williams; G - Brown 9
Papua New Guinea: T - Matmillo, Kovae; G - Numapo 3
New Zealand: Darrell Williams, Shane Horo Dean Bell (c), Kevin Iro, Gary Mercer, Shane Cooper, Clayton Friend, Peter Brown, Wayne Wallace, Adrian Shelford, Mark Graham (c), Sam Stewart, Mark Horo. Replacements: Gary Freeman, Esene Faimalo.
Papua New Guinea: Dairi Kovae, Arnold Krewanty, Bal Numapo (c), Louta Atoi, Mea Morea, Darius Haili, Tony Kila, Yer Bom, Michael Matmillo, Daroa Ben Moide, Tuiyo Evei, Mathius Kombra, Gideon Kouoru. Replacements: Ipisa Wanega, Haoda Kouoru.

NEW ZEALAND 12 ....GREAT BRITAIN 10
At Addington Showgrounds, Christchurch, Sunday, July 17, 1988
Attendance: 8,525; **Referee:** Mick Stone (Australia)
New Zealand: T - Freeman 2; G - Brown 2
Great Britain: T - Loughlin, D Hulme; G - Loughlin
New Zealand: Darrell Williams, Shane Horo Dean Bell (c), Kevin Iro, Gary Mercer, Shane Cooper, Clayton Friend, Peter Brown, Wayne Wallace, Adrian Shelford, Mark Graham (c), Sam Stewart, Mark Horo. Replacements: Gary Freeman.
Great Britain: Phil Ford, Henderson Gill, Paul Loughlin, David Stephenson, Martin Offiah, David Hulme, Andy Gregory, Kevin Ward, Kevin Beardmore, Hugh Waddell, Mike Gregory, Roy Powell, Ellery Hanley (c). Replacements: Paul Hulme.

AUSTRALIA 70 ....PAPUA NEW GUINEA 8
At Eric Weissel Oval, Wagga Wagga, Wednesday, July 20, 1988
Attendance: 11,685; **Referee:** Neville Kesha (New Zealand)
Australia: T - O'Connor 4, Langer 2, Meninga 2, Jack, Currie, Lewis, Fullerton Smith, Miller, Conescu; G - O'Connor 7
Papua New Guinea: T - Morea; G - Numapo 2
Australia: Garry Jack, Michael O'Connor, Mal Meninga, Peter Jackson, Tony Currie, Wally Lewis (c), Allan Langer, Paul Dunn, Greg Conescu, Phil Daley, Wally Fullerton Smith, Gavin Miller, Wayne Pearce. Replacements: Des Hasler (for Lewis), Paul Vautin (for Fullerton Smith).
Papua New Guinea: Ipisa Wanega, Arnold Krewanty, Darai Kovae, Bal Numapo (c), Mea Morea, Lauto Atoi, Darius Haili, Thomas Rombuk, Michael Matmillo, Daroa Ben Moide, Mathius Kombra, Tuiyo Evei, Joe Gispe. Replacements: Sam Karara (for Gispe), Andrew Kuno (for Kombra).

FINAL TABLE

	P	W	D	L	F	A	Pts
Australia *	7	5	0	2	252	91	12
New Zealand *	7	4	1	2	158	86	11
Great Britain	8	4	2	2	203	90	10
Papua New Guinea *	7	1	0	6	84	325	4
France	5	1	1	3	35	140	3

(Australia, New Zealand and Papua New Guinea each received two points when France forfeited its Southern Hemisphere away games)*

FINAL
AUSTRALIA 25 ....NEW ZEALAND 12
At Eden Park, Auckland, Sunday, October 9, 1988
Attendance: 46,000; **Referee:** Graham Ainui (Papua New Guinea)
Australia: T - Langer 2, Miller, Shearer; G - O'Connor 4; FG - Elias
New Zealand: T - T Iro, K Iro; G - Brown 2
Australia: Garry Jack, Dale Shearer, Andrew Farrar, Mark McGaw, Michael O'Connor, Wally Lewis (c), Allan Langer, Paul Dunn, Ben Elias, Steve Roach, Paul Sironen, Gavin Miller, Wayne Pearce. Replacements: Terry Lamb (for Lewis), David Gillespie (for Roach).
New Zealand: Gary Mercer, Tony Iro, Kevin Iro, Dean Bell (c), Mark Elia, Gary Freeman, Clayton Friend, Adrian Shelford, Wayne Wallace, Peter Brown, Kurt Sorenson, Mark Graham (c), Mark Horo. Replacements: Shane Cooper (for Mercer), Sam Stewart (for Shelford).

THOSE WHO PLAYED (1985-88)

AUSTRALIA

	M	T	G	FG	Pts
Sam Backo (Canberra)	1	1	-	-	4
Gary Belcher (Canberra)	1	-	-	-	-
Martin Bella (North Sydney)	1	-	-	-	-
Chris Close (Manly-Warringah)	1	-	-	-	-
Noel Cleal (Manly-Warringah)	2	2	-	-	8
Greg Conescu (Brisbane)	2	1	-	-	4
Tony Currie (Canterbury-Bankstown)	2	1	-	-	4
Phil Daley (Manly-Warringah)	1	-	-	-	-
Les Davidson (South Sydney)	2	-	-	-	-
Greg Dowling (Wynnum-Manly)	3	-	-	-	-
Paul Dunn (Canterbury-Bankstown)	5	-	-	-	-
Ben Elias (Balmain)	2	-	-	1	1
Steve Ella (Parramatta)	1	-	-	-	-
Andrew Ettingshausen (Cronulla-Sutherland)	1	-	-	-	-
Andrew Farrar (Canterbury-Bankstown)	1	-	-	-	-
John Ferguson (Eastern Suburbs)	1	-	-	-	-
Steve Folkes (Canterbury-Bankstown)	2	1	-	-	4
Wally Fullerton Smith (St George)	2	1	-	-	4
David Gillespie (Canterbury-Bankstown)	1	-	-	-	-
Des Hasler (Manly-Warringah)	3	1	-	-	4
Garry Jack (Balmain)	8	5	-	-	20
Peter Jackson (Canberra)	2	-	-	-	-
Brett Kenny (Parramatta)	3	2	-	-	8
Les Kiss (North Sydney)	2	2	-	-	8
Terry Lamb (Canterbury-Bankstown)	4	-	-	-	-
Allan Langer (Brisbane)	2	4	-	-	16
Wally Lewis (Wynnum-Manly)	8	5	-	-	20
Bob Lindner (Wynnum-Manly)	4	2	-	-	8
Mark McGaw (Cronulla-Sutherland)	1	-	-	-	-
Mal Meninga (Canberra)	4	2	-	-	8
Gene Miles (Wynnum-Manly)	4	2	-	-	8
Gavin Miller (Cronulla-Sutherland)	2	2	-	-	8
Chris Mortimer (Canterbury-Bankstown)	1	1	-	-	4
Bryan Niebling (Redcliffe)	4	1	-	-	4
Michael O'Connor (St George, Manly-Warringah)	7	8	34	-	100
Wayne Pearce (Balmain)	5	-	-	-	-
John Ribot (Manly-Warringah)	1	-	-	-	-
Steve Roach (Balmain)	5	1	-	-	4
Dale Shearer (Manly-Warringah)	3	6	-	-	24
Royce Simmons (Penrith)	4	-	-	-	-
Paul Sironen (Balmain)	2	-	-	-	-
Peter Sterling (Parramatta)	4	1	-	-	4
Peter Tunks (Canterbury-Bankstown)	2	-	-	-	-
Paul Vautin (Manly-Warringah)	3	-	-	-	-
Peter Wynn (Parramatta)	1	-	-	-	-

FRANCE

	M	T	G	FG	Pts
Pierre Ailleres (Toulouse)	1	-	-	-	-
Patrick Baco (XIII Catalan)	1	-	-	-	-
Denis Berge (Le Pontet)	2	-	-	-	-
Thierry Bernabe (Le Pontet)	4	-	-	-	-
Frederic Bourrel (Limoux)	1	-	2	1	5
Max Chantal (Villeneuve)	3	-	-	-	-
Didier Couston (Le Pontet)	3	-	-	-	-
Guy Delaunay (Saint-Esteve)	1	-	-	-	-
Daniel Divet (Limoux)	1	-	-	-	-
Gilles Dumas (Saint-Gaudens)	4	1	3	-	10
Patrick Entat (Avignon)	1	-	-	-	-
Dominique Espugna (Lezignan)	3	-	-	-	-
David Fraisse (Le Pontet)	1	2	-	-	8
Philippe Fourquet (Toulouse)	2	-	-	-	-
Philippe Gestas (Saint-Gaudens)	1	-	-	-	-
Bruno Guasch (Saint-Esteve)	1	-	-	-	-
Matthieu Khedimi (Saint-Esteve)	1	-	-	-	-
Francis Laforgue (XIII Catalan)	1	-	-	-	-
Guy Laforgue (XIII Catalan)	4	-	-	-	-
Pascal Laroche (Villeneuve)	1	-	-	-	-
Yannik Mantese (Albi)	1	-	-	-	-
Alain Maury (Villeneuve)	1	-	-	-	-
Jacques Moliner (Lezignan)	1	-	-	-	-
Pierre Montgaillard (XIII Catalan)	2	-	-	-	-
Marc Palanque (Le Pontet)	3	-	-	-	-
Roger Palisses (Saint-Esteve)	3	-	-	-	-
Serge Pallares (XIII Catalan)	1	-	-	-	-
Andre Perez (XIII Catalan)	2	2	-	-	4
Cyrille Pons (Saint-Gaudens)	2	1	-	-	4
Jean-Philippe Pougeau (Saint-Esteve)	1	-	-	-	-
Jean-Luc Rabot (Villeneuve)	4	-	-	-	-
Hugues Ratier (Lezignan)	4	1	-	-	4
Patrick Rocci (Le Pontet)	1	-	-	-	-
Sebastien Rodriguez (XIII Catalan)	1	-	-	-	-
Christian Scicchitano (Carpentras)	1	-	-	-	-
Yves Storer (Saint-Gaudens)	2	-	-	-	-
Serge Titeux (Le Pontet)	4	-	-	-	-
Daniel Verdes (Villeneuve)	3	-	-	-	-
Patrick Wozniack (Villeneuve)	1	-	-	-	-

GREAT BRITAIN

	M	T	G	FG	Pts
Chris Arkwright (St Helens)	1	-	-	-	-
John Basnett (Widnes)	1	-	-	-	-
Kevin Beardmore (Castleford)	3	-	-	-	-
Chris Burton (Hull Kingston Rovers)	1	-	-	-	-
Mick Burke (Widnes)	2	-	-	-	-
Brian Case (Wigan)	3	-	-	-	-
David Creasser (Leeds)	1	-	-	-	-
Lee Crooks (Hull)	5	-	6	-	12
Paul Dixon (Halifax)	1	-	-	-	-
Des Drummond (Leigh, Warrington)	3	-	-	-	-
Shaun Edwards (Wigan)	4	4	-	-	16
Keith England (Castleford)	1	-	-	-	-
Karl Fairbank (Halifax)	1	-	-	-	-
John Fieldhouse (Widnes)	2	-	-	-	-
Phil Ford (Bradford Northern)	3	2	-	-	8
Mark Forster (Warrington)	1	1	-	-	4
Deryck Fox (Featherstone Rovers)	2	-	-	-	-
Henderson Gill (Wigan)	6	4	1	-	18
Andy Gregory (Warrington)	5	3	-	-	12
Mike Gregory (Warrington)	4	2	-	-	8
Andy Goodway (Oldham)	5	1	-	-	4
Jeff Grayshon (Leeds)	1	-	-	-	-
Paul Groves (St Helens)	1	-	-	-	-
Roy Haggerty (St Helens)	1	-	-	-	-
Steve Hampson (Wigan)	1	-	-	-	-
Ellery Hanley (Bradford Northern)	7	4	-	-	16
David Hobbs (Oldham)	1	-	-	-	-
David Hulme (Widnes)	3	1	-	-	4
Paul Hulme (Widnes)	2	-	-	-	-
Paul Loughlin (St Helens)	3	1	11	-	26
Joe Lydon (Widnes)	4	2	10	-	28
Paul Medley (Widnes)	2	2	-	-	8
Tony Myler (Widnes)	2	-	-	-	-
Martin Offiah (Widnes)	2	1	-	-	4
Harry Pinner (St Helens)	3	-	-	-	-
Ian Potter (Wigan)	2	-	-	-	-
Roy Powell (Leeds)	2	-	-	-	-
Garry Schofield (Hull)	5	4	-	1	17

	M	T	G	FG	Pts
David Stephenson (Wigan)	6	1	7	-	18
Hugh Waddell (Oldham)	2	-	-	-	-
Shaun Wane (Wigan)	1	-	-	-	-
Kevin Ward (Castleford)	5	-	-	-	-
David Watkinson (Hull Kingston Rovers)	3	-	-	-	-
John Woods (Warrington)	1	-	-	-	-

PAPUA NEW GUINEA

	M	T	G	FG	Pts
Bobby Ako (Mt Hagen)	3	1	-	-	4
Nick Andy (Port Moresby)	2	-	-	-	-
Lauta Atoi (Bouganville)	6	1	-	-	4
Daroa Ben Moide	2	-	-	-	-
Yer Bom	3	-	-	-	-
Tuiyo Evei (Goroka)	3	-	-	-	-
David Gaius (Rabaul)	1	-	-	-	-
Joe Gispe (Rabaul)	1	-	-	-	-
Darius Haili (Kimbe)	7	2	-	-	8
Roy Heni (Port Moresby)	4	-	-	-	-
Sam Karara	1	-	-	-	-
Joe Katsir (Lae)	2	-	-	-	-
Mofu Kerekere (Port Moresby)	2	-	-	-	-
Tony Kila (Port Moresby)	6	-	-	-	-
Mathius Kitimon (Port Moresby)	1	-	-	-	-
Mathius Kombra (Mendi)	4	-	-	-	-
Gideon Kouoru (Port Moresby)	2	-	-	-	-
Haoda Kouoru (Port Moresby)	2	-	-	-	-
Dairi Kovae (Port Moresby)	7	4	6	-	28
Arnold Krewanty (Port Moresby)	5	1	-	-	4
Andrew Kuno	1	-	-	-	-
Ngala Lapan (Lae)	1	-	-	-	-
Ati Lomutopa (Goroka)	3	-	-	-	-
Michael Matmillo (Port Moresby)	3	1	-	-	4
Mea Morea (Port Moresby)	4	1	-	-	4
Bal Numapo (Kundiawa)	7	2	8	-	24
Thomas Rombuk (Lae)	1	-	-	-	-
Isaac Rop	1	-	-	-	4
Kepi Saea (Port Moresby)	6	-	-	-	-
Arebo Taumaku (Port Moresby)	5	-	-	-	-
Joe Tep (Port Moresby)	3	-	-	-	-
Bernard Waketsi (Port Moresby)	5	-	-	-	-
Ipisa Wanega (Kundiawa)	2	-	-	-	-

NEW ZEALAND

	M	T	G	FG	Pts
Fred Ah Kuoi (Hull)	2	-	-	-	-
Dean Bell (Eastern Suburbs)	6	-	-	-	-
Peter Brown (Auckland)	4	1	16	-	36
Shane Cooper (Auckland)	5	-	-	-	-
Ricky Cowan (Auckland)	1	-	-	-	-
Marty Crequer (Auckland)	1	-	-	-	-
Mark Elia (Auckland)	2	-	-	-	-
Esene Faimalo (Canterbury)	1	-	-	-	-
Olsen Filipaina (Eastern Suburbs, North Sydney)	4	-	8	-	16
Gary Freeman (Auckland)	5	2	-	-	8
Clayton Friend (Auckland)	6	2	-	-	8
Mark Graham (North Sydney)	6	2	-	-	8
Barry Harvey (Taranaki)	1	-	-	-	-
Mark Horo (Auckland)	3	-	-	-	-
Shane Horo (Waikato)	2	3	-	-	12
Kevin Iro (Wigan)	3	4	-	-	16
Tony Iro (Wigan)	1	1	-	-	4
Gary Kemble (Hull)	5	1	-	-	4
James Leuluai (Hull)	3	1	-	-	4
Hugh McGahan (Eastern Suburbs)	5	3	-	-	12
Gary Mercer (Bradford Northern)	4	2	-	-	8
Dane O'Hara (Hull)	5	-	-	-	-
Ron O'Regan (Auckland)	3	-	-	-	-
Gary Prohm (Hull Kingston Rovers)	3	-	-	-	-
Joe Ropati (Auckland)	3	1	-	-	4
Adrian Shelford (Canterbury)	4	-	-	-	-
Dane Sorensen (Cronulla-Sutherland)	2	-	1	-	2
Kurt Sorensen (Cronulla-Sutherland, Widnes)	5	1	-	-	4
Sam Stewart (Wellington)	4	-	-	-	-
Howie Tamati (Taranaki)	1	-	-	-	-
Kevin Tamati (Warrington)	2	-	-	-	-
Brent Todd (Canterbury)	3	-	-	-	-
Wayne Wallace (Canterbury)	6	2	-	-	8
Darrell Williams (Auckland)	5	4	-	-	16
Owen Wright (Auckland)	4	-	-	-	-

Rugby League World Cup Statistics

1989-92

NEW ZEALAND 14..........................**AUSTRALIA 22**
At Mt Smart Stadium, Auckland, Sunday, July 23, 1989
Attendance: 15,000; **Referee:** Robin Whitfield
(Great Britain)
New Zealand: T - Elia, Mercer; G - Shelford 3
Australia: T - Shearer, O'Connor, Meninga, Clyde;
G - O'Connor 2, Meninga
New Zealand: Darrell Williams, Gary Mercer, Kevin Iro,
Tony Kemp, Mark Elia, Kelly Shelford, Shane Cooper,
Gary Freeman, Brent Todd, Duane Mann, James
Goulding, Sam Stewart, Mark Horo, Hugh McGahan (c).
Replacements: Kurt Sherlock (for Kemp), Brendon
Tuuta (for Horo).
Australia: Gary Belcher, Michael Hancock, Dale
Shearer, Tony Currie, Michael O'Connor, Wally Lewis,
Des Hasler, Sam Backo, Kerrod Walters, Steve Roach,
Mal Meninga, Bradley Clyde, Paul Vautin. Replacement:
Bruce McGuire (for Backo).

GREAT BRITAIN 10...................**NEW ZEALAND 6**
At Central Park, Wigan, Saturday, November 11, 1989
Attendance: 20,346; **Referee:** Greg McCallum
(Australia)
Great Britain: T - Offiah, Tait; G - Loughlin
New Zealand: T - Shelford; G - Shelford
Great Britain: Alan Tait, Phil Ford, Paul Newlove, Paul
Loughlin, Martin Offiah, Shaun Edwards, David Hulme,
Kelvin Skerrett, Paul Hulme, Andy Platt, Andy Goodway,
Roy Powell, Mike Gregory (c). Replacements: Joe
Lydon (for Newlove), Keith England (for Edwards).
New Zealand: Tony Kemp, Kevin Iro, Dean Bell, Darrell
Williams, Gary Mercer, Kelly Shelford, Gary Freeman,
Brent Todd, Duane Mann, Esene Famailo, Kurt
Sorensen, Sam Stewart, Hugh McGahan (c).
Replacements: Dean Clark (for Shelford), Francis Leota
(for Faimalo).

FRANCE 0...............................**NEW ZEALAND 34**
At Stade Albert Domec, Sunday, December 3, 1989
Attendance: 4,208; **Referee:** Robin Whitfield
(Great Britain)
New Zealand: T - Watson 3, Kemp, Williams, Kuiti,
Bell; G - Sherlock 3
France: Jean-Philippe Pougeau, Philippe Chiron,
Philippe Fourquet, David Fraisse, Cyrille Pons, Gilles
Dumas (c), Patrick Entat, Jean-Luc Rabot, Mathieu
Khedimi, Yves Storer, Daniel Divet, Didier Cabestany,
Thierry Bernabe. Replacements: Denis Bienes (for
Storer), Regis Courty (for Chiron).
New Zealand: Tony Kemp, David Watson, Dean Bell,
Darrell Williams, Gary Mercer, Dean Clark, Gary
Freeman, Brent Todd, Duane Mann, George Mann, Mike
Kuiti, Sam Stewart, Hugh McGahan (c). Replacements:
Kurt Sherlock (for Mercer), Kelly Shelford (for Clark)

PAPUA NEW GUINEA 8..............**GREAT BRITAIN 40**
*At Lloyd Robson Oval, Port Moresby, Saturday, June 2,
1990.*
Attendance: 7,837; **Referee:** Dennis Hale
(New Zealand)
Papua New Guinea: T - Ongogo; G - Numapo 2
Great Britain: T - Gibson 2, Eastwood, Goulding,
Dixon, D Powell, Schofield; G - J Davies 6
Papua New Guinea: Ipisa Wanega, Arnold Krewanty,
Philip Boge, Bal Numapo, Mea Morea, Stanley Haru,
Gigmai Ongogo, Ati Lomutopa, Tuiyo Evei, Michael
Matmillo, Michael Angra, Arebo Taumaku (c), Joe
Gispe. Replacements: Max Tiri (for Lomutopa), Chris
Itam (for Morea)
Great Britain: Alan Tait, Paul Eastwood, Daryl Powell,
Jonathan Davies, Carl Gibson, Garry Schofield, Bobbie
Goulding, Roy Powell, Lee Jackson, Keith England,
Denis Betts, Paul Dixon, Mike Gregory (c).
Replacements: Deryck Fox (for Jackson), Phil Clarke
(for Gregory).

AUSTRALIA 34...................................**FRANCE 2**
At Pioneer Oval, Parkes, Wednesday, June 28, 1990.
Attendance: 12,384 *(Ground record)*
Referee: Graham Ainui (Papua New Guinea)
Australia: T - Mackay 3, McGaw 2, Daley, Meninga,
Shearer; G - Belcher
France: G - Dumas
Australia: Gary Belcher, Michael O'Connor, Mal
Meninga (c), Mark McGaw, Dale Shearer, Laurie Daley,
Allan Langer, Martin Bella, Kerrod Walters, Steve
Roach, Paul Sironen, David Gillespie, Brad Mackay.
Replacements: Mark Carroll (for Sironen), Andrew
Ettingshausen (for McGaw).
France: Eric Castel, Hugues Ratier (c), Jean-Bernard
Saumitou, Guy Delaunay, Cyrille Pons, Gilles Dumas,
Patrick Entat, Jean-Luc Rabot, Francis Lope, Thierry
Buttignol, Didier Cabestany, Daniel Divet, Thierry
Valero. Replacement: Jean Ruiz (for Buttignol)

NEW ZEALAND 21....................**GREAT BRITAIN 18**
*At Queen Elizabeth II Stadium, Christchurch,
Sunday, July 15, 1990.*
Attendance: 3,133; **Referee:** Bill Harrigan (Australia)
New Zealand: T - Kemp, Nikau; G - Ridge 6;
FG - McGahan
Great Britain: T - Schofield, Roy Powell, Offiah;
G - Davies 3
New Zealand: Matthew Ridge, Sam Panapa, Kevin Iro,
Darrell Williams, Tony Iro, Tony Kemp, Gary Freeman,
Brent Todd, Duane Mann, Peter Brown, Mark Horo,
Tawera Nikau, Hugh McGahan (c). Replacements:
Morvin Edwards (for Kevin Iro), Dean Lonergan (for
Todd).
Great Britain: Joe Lydon, Jonathan Davies, Daryl
Powell, Carl Gibson, Martin Offiah, Garry Schofield,
Bobbie Goulding, Kelvin Skerrett, Martin Dermott, Keith
England, Denis Betts, Roy Powell, Mike Gregory (c).
Replacements: Shaun Irwin, Paul Dixon.

PAPUA NEW GUINEA 10.............**NEW ZEALAND 18**
*At Lloyd Robson Oval, Port Moresby,
Saturday, August 11, 1990.*
Attendance: 4,478; **Referee:** Bill Harrigan (Australia)
Papua New Guinea: T - Waine, Soga; G - Numapo
New Zealand: T - Lonergan, Panapa, Watson;
G - Ridge 3
Papua New Guinea: Ipisa Wanega, Arnold Krewanty,
Philip Boge, Bal Numapo (c), Goie Waine, Stanley
Haru, Gigmai Ongogo, Kes Paglipari, Bobby Ako, Tuiyo
Evei, Michael Matmillo, Matthew Elara, Opai Soga.
Replacements: Max Tiri, Michael Angra.
New Zealand: Matthew Ridge, Tony Iro, David Watson,
Paddy Tuimavave, Sam Panapa, Tony Kemp, Gary
Freeman, Peter Brown, Duane Mann, Brent Todd, Dean
Lonergan, Tawera Nikau, Mark Horo. Replacements:
Mike Kuiti, Morvin Edwards, Mark Nixon, George
Mann.

GREAT BRITAIN 0...........................**AUSTRALIA 14**
At Elland Road, Leeds, Saturday, November 24, 1990.
Attendance: 32,500; **Referee:** Alain Sablayrolles
(France)
Australia: T - Ettingshausen, Meninga, Elias;
G - Meninga
Great Britain: Steve Hampson, Martin Offiah, Daryl
Powell, Carl Gibson, Paul Eastwood, Garry Schofield,
Andy Gregory, Karl Harrison, Lee Jackson, Andy Platt,
Denis Betts, Paul Dixon, Ellery Hanley (c).
Replacements: Jonathan Davies (for Gibson), Mike
Gregory (for Dixon), Roy Powell (for Harrison).
Australia: Gary Belcher, Andrew Ettingshausen, Mal
Meninga (c), Laurie Daley, Dale Shearer, Cliff Lyons,
Ricky Stuart, Glenn Lazarus, Ben Elias, Steve Roach,
Paul Sironen, Bob Lindner, Brad Mackay.
Replacements: David Gillespie (for Lazarus), Greg
Alexander (for Shearer), Des Hasler (for Mackay), Mark
Sargent (for Sironen).

FRANCE 10 ....**AUSTRALIA 34**
At Stade Gilbert Brutus, Perpignan,
Sunday, December 9, 1990.
Attendance: 3,428; **Referee:** John Holdsworth
(Great Britain)
France: T - Pons, Entat; G - Tisseyre
Australia: T - Mackay 2, Shearer, Alexander,
Ettingshausen, Meninga, Roach; G - Alexander 3
France: David Fraisse, Cyrille Pons, Serge Bret, Guy
Delaunay, Alain Bouzer, Jacques Moliner, Patrick Entat
(c), Thierry Buttignol, Thierry Valero, Marc Tisseyre,
Francis Lope, Daniel Divet, Daniel Verdes. Replacements:
Denis Bienes (for Bret), Patrick Marginet (for Fraisse).
Australia: Gary Belcher, Greg Alexander, Dale Shearer,
Mal Meninga (c), Andrew Ettingshausen, Cliff Lyons,
Ricky Stuart, Glenn Lazarus, Ben Elias, Steve Roach,
Paul Sironen, Bob Lindner, Brad Mackay.
Replacements: David Gillespie (for Lindner), Chris
Johns (for Alexander), Des Hasler (for Stuart), Mark
Sargent (for Lazarus).

FRANCE 10 ....**GREAT BRITAIN 45**
At Stade Gilbert Brutus, Perpignan,
Sunday, January 27, 1991.
Attendance: 3,965; **Referee:** Greg McCallum (Australia)
France: T - Auroy, Fraisse; G - Tisseyre
Great Britain: T - Schofield 2, Offiah 2, Edwards 2,
Betts, Platt; G - Eastwood 6; FG - Schofield
France: Christophe Auroy, Eric Remirez, David Fraisse,
Guy Delaunay, Cyrille Pons, Gilles Dumas (c), Patrick
Entat, Marc Tisseyre, Thierry Valero, Thierry Buttignol,
Jean-Pierre Magnac, Daniel Verdes, Jacques Moliner.
Replacements: Denis Bienes (for Dumas), Pierre
Chamorin (for Verdes), Abderazach Baba (for Valero).
Great Britain: Steve Hampson, Paul Eastwood, Carl
Gibson, Daryl Powell, Martin Offiah, Garry Schofield,
Shaun Edwards, Ian Lucas, Lee Jackson, Andy Platt,
Denis Betts, Les Holliday, Ellery Hanley (c).
Replacements: Mark Aston (for Schofield), St John Ellis
(for Hampson), Richie Eyres (for Jackson), Karl
Fairbank (for Holliday).

NEW ZEALAND 32 ....**FRANCE 10**
At Addington Showgrounds, Christchurch,
Sunday, June 23, 1991.
Attendance: 2,000; **Referee:** Graham Ainui
(Papua New Guinea)
New Zealand: T - Shelford, Blackmore, Watson, Friend,
Panapa; G - Botica 6
France: T - Verdes; G - Dumas 3
New Zealand: Frano Botica, Sam Panapa, Jarrod
McCracken, David Watson, Richie Blackmore, Kelly
Shelford, Gary Freeman (c), Peter Brown, Duane Mann,
Brent Todd, Emosi Koloto, Dean Lonergan, Tawera
Nikau. Replacements: Clayton Friend, George Mann,
Mike Patton, Gary Mercer.
France: Pascal Fages, Jean-Marc Garcia, David Despin,
Denis Bienes, Cyrille Pons, Gilles Dumas (c), Patrick
Entat, Thierry Buttignol, Thierry Valero, Yves Storer,
Didier Cabestany, Gerard Boyals, Daniel Verdes.
Replacements: Robert Viscay, Franck Romano, Roger
Palisses, Thierry Bernabe.

PAPUA NEW GUINEA 18 ....**FRANCE 20**
At Danny Leahy Oval, Goroka, Sunday, July 7, 1991.
Attendance: 11,485; **Referee:** Colin Morris
(Great Britain)
Papua New Guinea: T - Gela, Naipao; G - Wanega 5
France: T - Despin 2, Garcia; G - Torreilles 4
Papua New Guinea: Ipisa Wanega, Arnold Krewanty,
Paul Gela, Elias Kamiak, Joe Rema, Stanley Haru (c),
Gigmai Ongogo, James Naipao, Bernard Bate, John
Unagi, Thomas Daki, Max Tiri, Joe Gispe.
Replacements: Joshua Kouoru, Johannes Kola, Opai
Soga, Kes Pagliari.
France: Christophe Auroy, Jean-Marc Garcia, David
Despin, Denis Bienes, Cyrille Pons, Pascal Fages,
Patrick Entat, Gerard Boyals, Patrick Torreilles, Thierry
Buttignol (c), Bertrand Plante, Didier Cabestany, Daniel
Verdes. Replacements: Robert Viscay, Marc Tisseyre,
Guy Delpeche, Pierre Chamorin.

AUSTRALIA 40 ....**NEW ZEALAND 12**
At Lang Park, Brisbane, Wednesday, July 31, 1991.
Attendance: 29,139; **Referee:** John Holdsworth
(Great Britain)
Australia: T - Carne, Meninga, Walters, Wishart, Clyde,
Ettingshausen, Daley; G - Meninga 6
New Zealand: T - McCracken, Blackmore; G - Botica 2
Australia: Andrew Ettingshausen, Willie Carne, Mal
Meninga (c), Laurie Daley, Rod Wishart, Peter Jackson,
Allan Langer, Martin Bella, Steve Walters, Craig
Salvatori, Mark Geyer, David Gillespie, Bradley Clyde.
Replacements: Chris Johns (for Jackson), Ian Roberts
(for Bella), John Cartwright (for Gillespie), Des Hasler
(for Clyde).
New Zealand: Frano Botica, David Watson, Jarrod
McCracken, Kevin Iro, Richie Blackmore, Gary Freeman
(c), Clayton Friend, Peter Brown, Duane Mann, Brent
Todd, George Mann, Gary Mercer, Tawera Nikau.
Replacements: Emosi Koloto (for Mercer), Esene
Faimalo (for Brown), Jason Williams (for McCracken),
Mike Patton (for George Mann).

PAPUA NEW GUINEA 6 ....**AUSTRALIA 40**
At Lloyd Robson Oval, Port Moresby,
Sunday, October 31, 1991.
Attendance: 14,500; **Referee:** Denis Hale (New Zealand)
Papua New Guinea: T - Haru; G - Boge
Australia: T - Carne 3, Belcher, Ettingshausen, Jackson,
Meninga, Wishart, Clyde; G - Meninga 2
Papua New Guinea: Philip Boge, Lipirin Palangat, Korul
Sinemau, Richard Wagambie, Joshua Kouoru, Stanley
Haru (c), Sam Karara, John Unagi, Danny Moi, James
Naipao, Thomas Daki, Kes Pagliari, Joe Gispe.
Replacements: Kera Ngaffin (for Moi), Jack Uradok (for
Palangat), Ngala Lapan (for Daki), Leslee Hoffman (for
Gispe).
Australia: Gary Belcher, Rod Wishart, Andrew
Ettingshausen, Mal Meninga (c), Willie Carne, Peter
Jackson, Geoff Toovey, Martin Bella, Kerrod Walters,
Glenn Lazarus, Bradley Clyde, Ian Roberts, Brad Fittler.
Replacements: Gary Coyne (for Bella), Chris Johns (for
Wishart), Cliff Lyons (for Jackson), Kevin Walters (for
Kerrod Walters).

GREAT BRITAIN 56 ....**PAPUA NEW GUINEA 4**
At Central Park, Wigan, Saturday, November 9, 1991.
Attendance: 4,193; **Referee:** Bill Harrigan (Australia)
Great Britain: T - Schofield 2, Moriarty 2, Jackson 2,
Sullivan, Newlove, Betts, Harrison; G - Davies 8
Papua New Guinea: T - Karu
Great Britain: Steve Hampson, Paul Newlove, Jonathan
Davies, Daryl Powell, Anthony Sullivan, Garry Schofield
(c), Shaun Edwards, Karl Harrison, Martin Dermott,
Andy Platt, Paul Moriarty, Denis Betts, Michael
Jackson. Replacements: Gary Connolly (for Hampson),
Karl Fairbank (for Platt), Deryck Fox (for Edwards), Gary
Price (for Moriarty).
Papua New Guinea: Ipisa Wanega, Joshua Kouoru,
Richard Wagambie, Philip Boge, Chris Itam, Tuksy
Karu, Stanley Haru (c), John Unagi, Kes Pagliari, Kera
Ngaffin, James Naipao, Leslee Hoffman, Joe Gispe.
Replacements: Max Tiri (for Naipo), Ngala Lapan (for
Karu), Thomas Daki (for Ngaffin), Lipirin Palangat (for
Wanega).

FRANCE 28 ....**PAPUA NEW GUINEA 14**
At Stade Albert Domec, Carcassonne,
Sunday, November 24, 1991.
Attendance: 1,440; **Referee:** Colin Morris (Great Britain)
France: T - Divet, Bonnafous, Garcia, Pons, Dumas;
G - Dumas 4
Papua New Guinea: T - Haru, Itam; G - Karu 2, Haru
France: Marc Balleroy, Jean-Marc Garcia, David Despin,
Denis Bienes, Cyrille Pons, Gilles Dumas, Patrick Entat,
Yves Villoni, Francis Lope, Pierre Ailleres, Daniel Divet,
Pierre Montgaillard, Christophe Bonnafous.
Replacements: Pascal Fages (for Balleroy), Yves Storer
(for Bonnafous), Abderazach Baba (for Ailleres),
Adolphe Alesina (for Bienes).

Rugby League World Cup Statistics

Papua New Guinea: Ipisa Wanega, Joshua Kouoru, Richard Wagambie, Philip Boge, Chris Itam, Tuksy Karu, Stanley Haru (c), Kera Ngaffin, Michael Matmillo, James Naipao, Kes Paglipari, Max Tiri, Joe Gispe. Replacements: Ngala Lapan (for Karu), Leslee Hoffman (for Naipao), Lipirin Palangat (for Kouoru), Michael Angra (for Paglipari).

GREAT BRITAIN 36 ....**FRANCE 0**
At The Boulevard, Hull, Saturday, March 7, 1992.
Attendance: 5,250; **Referee:** Eddie Ward (Australia)
Great Britain: T - Holliday, Eastwood, Platt, Hunte, Dermott, Fox; G - Eastwood 6
Great Britain: Graham Steadman, Paul Eastwood, Gary Connolly, Allan Bateman, Alan Hunte, Daryl Powell, Shaun Edwards (c), Lee Crooks, Martin Dermott, Kelvin Skerrett, Denis Betts, Karl Fairbank, Les Holliday. Replacements: Andy Platt (for Skerrett), Deryck Fox (for Bateman), Steve McNamara (for Fairbank).
France: Patrick Limongi, Claude Sirvent, Pierre Chamorin, Pascal Fages, Cyrille Pons, Gilles Dumas (c), Patrick Entat, Yves Villoni, Thierry Valero, Pierre Ailleres, Bernard Llong, Christophe Bonnafous, Jacques Pech. Replacements: Patrick Torreilles (for Bonnafous), Francis Lope (for Llong), Pascal Bomati (for Pons).

AUSTRALIA 16 ....**GREAT BRITAIN 10**
At Lang Park, Brisbane, Friday, July 3, 1992.
Attendance: 33,313; **Referee:** Dennis Hale (New Zealand)
Australia: T - Daley, Meninga; G - Meninga 4
Great Britain: T - Offiah; G - Eastwood 3
Australia: Andrew Ettingshausen, Willie Carne, Mal Meninga (c), Brad Fittler, Michael Hancock, Laurie Daley, Allan Langer, Glenn Lazarus, Steve Walters, Paul Harragon, Paul Sironen, Bob Lindner, Bradley Clyde. Replacements: David Gillespie (for Sironen), Chris Johns (for Carne), Kevin Walters (for Ettingshausen), John Cartwright (for Lindner).
Great Britain: Graham Steadman, Paul Eastwood, Daryl Powell, Paul Newlove, Martin Offiah, Garry Schofield (c), Shaun Edwards, Kelvin Skerrett, Martin Dermott, Andy Platt, Denis Betts, Billy McGinty, Phil Clarke. Replacements: Paul Hulme (for McGinty), Karl Harrison (for Skerrett), Gary Connolly (for Newlove), Joe Lydon (for Schofield).

NEW ZEALAND 66 ....**PAPUA NEW GUINEA 10**
At Carlaw Park, Auckland, Sunday July 5, 1992.
Attendance: 3,000; **Referee:** Greg McCallum (Australia)
New Zealand: T - Blackmore 3, Clark 2, Ridge, Hoppe, Iro, Kemp, Freeman, Stuart, Mann, Hill; G - Ridge 4, Halligan 3
Papua New Guinea: T - Uradok 2; G - Boge
New Zealand: Matthew Ridge, Sean Hoppe, Kevin Iro, Tony Kemp, Richie Blackmore, Dean Clark, Gary Freeman (c), Brent Stuart, Duane Mann, Brent Todd, Gavin Hill, Quentin Pongia, Tawera Nikau. Replacements: Daryl Halligan, Brendon Tuuta, Tea Ropati, Mark Woods.
Papua New Guinea: Philip Boge, Kini Tani, August Joseph, Richard Wagambie (c), Jack Uradok, Tuksy Karu, Aquila Emil, Ben Bire, Michael Matmillo, Kera Ngaffin, Nande Yer, James Naipao, Joe Gispe. Replacements: Ngala Lapan, John Piel, Korul Sinemau, Michael Angra.

AUSTRALIA 36 ....**PAPUA NEW GUINEA 14**
At Townsville Sports Reserve,
Wednesday, July 15, 1992.
Attendance: 12,470; **Referee:** Dennis Hale (New Zealand)
Australia: T - G Mackay 2, Carne, Fittler, Daley, Sargent, Johns; G - Meninga 4
Papua New Guinea: T - Joseph, Babago, Emil; G - Boge
Australia: Willie Carne, Graham Mackay, Mal Meninga (c), Brad Fittler, Michael Hancock, Laurie Daley, Allan Langer, Glenn Lazarus, Steve Walters, David Gillespie, Bob Lindner, Paul Sironen, Brad Mackay. Replacements: Kevin Walters, Chris Johns, John Cartwright, Mark Sargent.

Papua New Guinea: Philip Boge, Jack Uradok, August Joseph, Korul Sinemau, Richard Wagambie, Tuksy Karu, Aquila Emil, Ben Bire, Michael Matmillo, Kera Ngaffin (c), James Naipao, Daroa Ben Moide, Joe Gispe. Replacements: Sauna Babago, Nande Yer, James Kapai, Nere Launa.

FINAL TABLE

	P	W	D	L	F	A	Pts
Australia	8	8	0	0	236	68	16
Great Britain	8	5	0	3	215	79	10
New Zealand	8	5	0	3	203	120	10
France	8	2	0	6	80	247	4
Papua New Guinea	8	0	0	8	84	304	0

FINAL

GREAT BRITAIN 6 ....**AUSTRALIA 10**
At Wembley Stadium, London, Saturday, October 24, 1992.
Attendance: 73,631
(World record for international match)
Referee: Dennis Hale (New Zealand)
Great Britain: G - Fox 3
Australia: T - Renouf; G - Meninga 3
Great Britain: Joe Lydon, Alan Hunte, Gary Connolly, Garry Schofield (c), Martin Offiah, Shaun Edwards, Deryck Fox, Kevin Ward, Martin Dermott, Andy Platt, Denis Betts, Phil Clarke, Ellery Hanley. Replacements: John Devereux (for Connolly), Alan Tait (for Lydon), Kelvin Skerrett (for Ward), Richie Eyres (for Hanley).
Australia: Tim Brasher, Michael Hancock, Steve Renouf, Mal Meninga (c), Willie Carne, Brad Fittler, Allan Langer, Glenn Lazarus, Steve Walters, Mark Sargent, Paul Sironen, Bob Lindner, Bradley Clyde. Replacements: David Gillespie (for Sironen), Kevin Walters (for Clyde), John Cartwright (for Sargent).

THOSE WHO PLAYED (1989-92)

AUSTRALIA

	M	T	G	FG	Pts
Greg Alexander (Penrith)	2	1	3	-	10
Sam Backo (Brisbane)	1	-	-	-	-
Martin Bella (Manly-Warringah)	3	-	-	-	-
Gary Belcher (Canberra)	5	1	1	-	6
Tim Brasher (Balmain)	1	-	-	-	-
Willie Carne (Brisbane)	5	5	-	-	20
Mark Carroll (South Sydney)	1	-	-	-	-
John Cartwright (Penrith)	4	-	-	-	-
Bradley Clyde (Canberra)	5	3	-	-	12
Gary Coyne (Canberra)	1	-	-	-	-
Tony Currie (Brisbane)	1	-	-	-	-
Laurie Daley (Canberra)	5	4	-	-	16
Ben Elias (Balmain)	2	1	-	-	4
Andrew Ettingshausen (Cronulla-Sutherland)	6	4	-	-	16
Brad Fittler (Penrith)	4	1	-	-	4
Mark Geyer (Penrith)	1	-	-	-	-
David Gillespie (Canterbury-Bankstown)	7	-	-	-	-
Michael Hancock (Brisbane)	4	-	-	-	-
Paul Harragon (Newcastle)	1	-	-	-	-
Des Hasler (Manly-Warringah)	4	-	-	-	-
Peter Jackson (North Sydney)	2	1	-	-	4
Chris Johns (Brisbane)	5	1	-	-	4
Allan Langer (Brisbane)	5	-	-	-	-
Glenn Lazarus (Canberra)	6	-	-	-	-
Wally Lewis (Brisbane)	1	-	-	-	-
Bob Lindner (Western Suburbs)	5	-	-	-	-
Cliff Lyons (Manly-Warringah)	3	-	-	-	-
Mark McGaw (Cronulla-Sutherland)	1	2	-	-	8
Bruce Mcllan (Balmain)	1	-	-	-	-
Brad Mackay (St George)	4	5	-	-	20
Graham Mackay (Penrith)	1	2	-	-	8
Mal Meninga (Canberra)	9	7	21	-	70
Michael O'Connor (Manly-Warringah)	2	1	2	-	8
Steve Renouf (Brisbane)	1	1	-	-	4
Steve Roach (Balmain)	4	1	-	-	-
Ian Roberts (Manly-Warringah)	2	-	-	-	-
Craig Salvatori (Eastern Suburbs)	1	-	-	-	-
Mark Sargent (Newcastle)	4	1	-	-	4

	M	T	G	FG	Pts
Dale Shearer (Manly-Warringah)	4	3	-	-	12
Paul Sironen (Balmain)	6	-	-	-	-
Ricky Stuart (Canberra)	2	-	-	-	-
Geoff Toovey (Manly-Warringah)	1	-	-	-	-
Paul Vautin (Manly-Warringah)	1	-	-	-	-
Kerrod Walters (Brisbane)	3	-	-	-	-
Kevin Walters (Brisbane)	4	-	-	-	-
Steve Walters (Canberra)	4	1	-	-	4
Rod Wishart (Illawarra)	2	2	-	-	8

FRANCE

	M	T	G	FG	Pts
Adolphe Alesina (Pamiers)	1	-	-	-	-
Pierre Ailleres (Toulouse)	2	-	-	-	-
Christophe Auroy (XIII Catalan)	2	1	-	-	4
Abderazach Baba (XIII Catalan)	2	-	-	-	-
Marc Balleroy (Avignon)	1	-	-	-	-
Thierry Bernabe (Carcassonne)	2	-	-	-	-
Denis Bienes (Saint-Gaudens)	6	-	-	-	-
Christophe Bonnafous (Albi)	2	1	-	-	4
Alain Bouzer (Toulouse)	1	-	-	-	-
Gerard Boyals (Saint-Gaudens)	2	-	-	-	-
Serge Bret (XIII Catalan)	1	-	-	-	-
Thierry Buttignol (Avignon)	5	-	-	-	-
Didier Cabestany (Saint-Esteve)	4	-	-	-	-
Eric Castel (Albi)	1	-	-	-	-
Pierre Chamorin (Saint-Esteve)	3	-	-	-	-
Philippe Chiron (Carpentras)	1	-	-	-	-
Regis Courty (XIII Catalan)	1	-	-	-	-
Guy Delaunay (XIII Catalan)	3	-	-	-	-
Guy Delpeche (Pamiers)	1	-	-	-	-
David Despin (Villeneuve)	3	2	-	-	8
Daniel Divet (Carcassonne)	4	1	-	-	4
Gilles Dumas (Saint-Gaudens)	6	1	8	-	20
Pascal Fages (Pia)	4	-	-	-	-
Patrick Entat (Avignon, Hull)	8	1	-	-	4
Philippe Fourquet (Saint-Gaudens)	1	-	-	-	-
David Fraisse (Carcassonne)	3	1	-	-	4
Jean-Marc Garcia (Saint-Esteve)	3	2	-	-	8
Mathieu Khedimi (Saint-Esteve)	1	-	-	-	-
Bernard Llong (XII Catalan)	1	-	-	-	-
Francis Lope (Toulouse)	4	-	-	-	-
Jean-Pierre Magnac (XIII Catalan)	1	-	-	-	-
Patrick Marginet (Saint-Esteve)	1	-	-	-	-
Jacques Moliner (XIII Catalan)	2	-	-	-	-
Pierre Montgaillard (XIII Catalan)	1	-	-	-	-
Roger Palisses (Saint-Esteve)	1	-	-	-	-
Bertrand Plante (Villeneuve)	1	-	-	-	-
Cyrille Pons (Saint-Gaudens)	8	2	-	-	8
Jean-Philippe Pougeau (Saint-Esteve)	1	-	-	-	-
Jean-Luc Rabot (Villeneuve)	2	-	-	-	-
Hugues Ratier (Lezignan)	1	-	-	-	-
Eric Remirez (Carcassonne)	1	-	-	-	-
Franck Romano (Carpentras)	1	-	-	-	-
Jean Ruiz (Saint-Esteve)	1	-	-	-	-
Jean-Bernard Saumitou (Villeneuve)	1	-	-	-	-
Yves Storer (Saint-Gaudens)	3	-	-	-	-
Marc Tisseyre (Pamiers)	3	-	2	-	4
Patrick Torreilles (Pia)	2	-	4	-	8
Thierry Valero (Lezignan)	5	-	-	-	-
Daniel Verdes (Villeneuve)	4	1	-	-	4
Yves Villoni (Avignon)	2	-	-	-	-
Robert Viscay (Saint-Gaudens)	2	-	-	-	-

GREAT BRITAIN

	M	T	G	FG	Pts
Mark Aston (Sheffield)	1	-	-	-	-
Allan Bateman (Warrington)	1	-	-	-	-
Denis Betts (Wigan)	8	2	-	-	8
Phil Clarke (Wigan)	3	-	-	-	-
Gary Connolly (St Helens)	4	-	-	-	-
Lee Crooks (Castleford)	1	-	-	-	-
Jonathan Davies (Widnes)	4	-	17	-	34
Martin Dermott (Wigan)	5	1	-	-	4
John Devereux (Widnes)	1	-	-	-	-
Paul Dixon (Hull, Leeds)	3	1	-	-	4
Paul Eastwood (Hull)	5	2	15	-	38
Shaun Edwards (Wigan)	6	2	-	-	8
St John Ellis (Castleford)	1	-	-	-	-
Keith England (Castleford)	3	-	-	-	-

	M	T	G	FG	Pts
Richie Eyres (Widnes)	2	-	-	-	-
Karl Fairbank (Bradford Northern)	3	-	-	-	-
Phil Ford (Leeds)	1	-	-	-	-
Deryck Fox (Featherstone Rovers)	4	1	3	-	10
Carl Gibson (Leeds)	4	2	-	-	8
Andy Goodway (Wigan)	1	-	-	-	-
Bobbie Goulding (Wigan)	2	1	-	-	4
Andy Gregory (Wigan)	1	-	-	-	-
Mike Gregory (Warrington)	4	-	-	-	-
Steve Hampson (Wigan)	3	-	-	-	-
Ellery Hanley (Wigan)	3	-	-	-	-
Karl Harrison (Hull, Halifax)	3	1	-	-	4
Les Holliday (Widnes)	2	1	-	-	4
David Hulme (Widnes)	1	-	-	-	-
Paul Hulme (Widnes)	2	-	-	-	-
Alan Hunte (St Helens)	2	1	-	-	4
Shaun Irwin (Castleford)	1	-	-	-	-
Lee Jackson (Hull)	3	-	-	-	-
Michael Jackson (Wakefield Trinity)	1	2	-	-	8
Paul Loughlin (St Helens)	1	-	1	-	2
Ian Lucas (Wigan)	1	-	-	-	-
Joe Lydon (Wigan)	4	-	-	-	-
Billy McGinty (Wigan)	1	-	-	-	-
Steve McNamara (Hull)	1	-	-	-	-
Paul Moriarty (Widnes)	1	2	-	-	8
Paul Newlove (Featherstone Rovers)	3	1	-	-	4
Martin Offiah (Widnes, Wigan)	6	5	-	-	20
Andy Platt (Wigan)	7	2	-	-	8
Daryl Powell (Sheffield Eagles)	7	1	-	-	4
Roy Powell (Leeds)	4	1	-	-	4
Gary Price (Wakefield Trinity)	1	-	-	-	-
Garry Schofield (Leeds)	7	6	-	1	25
Kelvin Skerrett (Bradford Northern, Wigan)	5	-	-	-	-
Graham Steadman (Castleford)	2	-	-	-	-
Anthony Sullivan (St Helens)	1	1	-	-	4
Alan Tait (St Helens)	3	1	-	-	4
Kevin Ward (St Helens)	1	-	-	-	-

NEW ZEALAND

	M	T	G	FG	Pts
Dean Bell (Wigan)	2	1	-	-	4
Richie Blackmore (Auckland)	3	5	-	-	20
Frano Botica (Auckland)	2	-	8	-	16
Peter Brown (Auckland, Halifax)	4	-	-	-	-
Dean Clark (Auckland)	3	2	-	-	8
Shane Cooper (St Helens)	1	-	-	-	-
Morvin Edwards (Wellington)	2	-	-	-	-
Mark Elia (Canterbury-Bankstown)	1	1	-	-	4
Esene Faimalo (Canterbury, Widnes)	2	-	-	-	-
Gary Freeman (Balmain)	8	1	-	-	4
Clayton Friend (Carlisle)	2	1	-	-	4
James Goulding (Newcastle)	1	-	-	-	-
Daryl Halligan (North Sydney)	1	-	3	-	6
Gavin Hill (Canterbury-Bankstown)	1	1	-	-	4
Sean Hoppe (Canberra)	1	1	-	-	4
Mark Horo (Parramatta)	3	-	-	-	-
Kevin Iro (Wigan, Manly-Warringah)	5	1	-	-	4
Tony Iro (Manly-Warringah)	2	-	-	-	-
Tony Kemp (Newcastle)	6	3	-	-	12
Emosi Koloto (Widnes)	2	-	-	-	-
Mike Kuiti (Wellington)	2	1	-	-	4
Francis Leota (Auckland)	1	-	-	-	-
Dean Lonergan (Auckland)	3	1	-	-	4
Jarrod McCracken (Canterbury-Bankstown)	2	1	-	-	4
Hugh McGahan (Eastern Suburbs)	4	-	-	1	1
Duane Mann (Auckland, Warrington)	8	1	-	-	4
George Mann (Auckland)	4	-	-	-	-
Gary Mercer (Bay of Plenty, Warrington)	5	1	-	-	4
Tawera Nikau (Auckland)	5	1	-	-	4
Sam Panapa (Auckland)	3	2	-	-	8
Mike Patton (Auckland)	2	-	-	-	-
Quentin Pongia (Canterbury)	1	-	-	-	-
Matthew Ridge (Manly-Warringah)	3	1	13	-	30
Tea Ropati (Auckland)	1	-	-	-	-
Kelly Shelford (Auckland)	4	2	4	-	16
Kurt Sherlock (Eastern Suburbs)	2	-	3	-	6
Kurt Sorensen (Widnes)	1	-	-	-	-
Sam Stewart (Newcastle)	3	-	-	-	-

	M	T	G	FG	Pts
Brent Stuart (Canterbury)	1	1	-	-	4
Brent Todd (Canberra)	8	-	-	-	-
Paddy Tuimavave (Auckland)	1	-	-	-	-
Brendon Tuuta (Western Suburbs)	2	-	-	-	-
David Watson (Auckland)	4	5	-	-	20
Darrell Williams (Manly-Warringah)	4	1	-	-	4
Jason Williams (South Sydney)	1	-	-	-	-
Mark Woods (Wellington)	1	-	-	-	-

PAPUA NEW GUINEA

	M	T	G	FG	Pts
Bobby Ako (Mt Hagen Eagles)	1	-	-	-	-
Michael Angra (Mt Hagen Eagles)	4	-	-	-	-
Sauna Babago (Port Moresby Vipers)	1	1	-	-	4
Bernard Bate (Rabaul Island Gurias)	1	-	-	-	-
Daroa Ben Moide	1	-	-	-	-
Ben Bire (Port Moresby Vipers)	2	-	-	-	-
Philip Boge (Port Moresby Vipers)	7	-	3	-	6
Thomas Daki (Lae Bombers)	3	-	-	-	-
Matthew Elara (Port Moresby Vipers)	1	-	-	-	-
Aquila Emil (Port Moresby Vipers)	2	1	-	-	4
Tuiyo Evei (Goroka Lahinis)	2	-	-	-	-
Paul Gela (Goroka Lahinis)	1	1	-	-	4
Joe Gispe (Port Moresby Vipers)	7	-	-	-	-
Stanley Haru (Port Moresby Vipers)	6	2	1	-	10
Leslee Hoffman (Mt Hagen Eagles)	3	-	-	-	-
Chris Itam (Mt Hagen Eagles)	3	1	-	-	4
August Joseph (Rabaul Island Gurias)	2	1	-	-	4
Elias Kamiak (Mt Hagen Eagles)	1	-	-	-	-
James Kapai (Rabaul Island Gurias)	1	-	-	-	-
Sam Karara (Kundiawa Warriors)	1	-	-	-	-
Tuksy Karu (Port Moresby Vipers)	4	1	2	-	8
Johannes Kola (Port Moresby Vipers)	1	-	-	-	-
Joshua Kouoru (Port Moresby Vipers)	4	-	-	-	-
Arnold Krewanty (Port Moresby Vipers)	3	-	-	-	-
Ngala Lapan (Lae Bombers)	4	-	-	-	-
Nere Launa (Mt Hagen Eagles)	1	-	-	-	-
Ati Lomutopa (Goroka Lahinis)	1	-	-	-	-
Michael Matmillo (Lae Bombers)	5	-	-	-	-
Danny Moi (Port Moresby Vipers)	1	-	-	-	-
Mea Morea (Port Moresby Vipers)	1	-	-	-	-
James Naipao (Port Moresby Vipers)	6	1	-	-	4
Kera Ngaffin (Port Moresby Vipers)	5	-	-	-	-
Bal Numapo (Kundiawa Warriors)	2	-	3	-	6
Gigmai Ongogo (Mt Hagen Eagles)	3	1	-	-	4
Kes Paglipari (Port Moresby Vipers)	5	-	-	-	-
Lipirin Palangat (Rabaul Island Gurias)	3	-	-	-	-
John Piel (Lae Bombers)	1	-	-	-	-
Joe Rema (Mendi Muruks)	1	-	-	-	-
Korul Sinemau (Lae Bombers)	3	-	-	-	-
Opai Soga (Goroka Lahinis)	2	1	-	-	4
Kini Tani (Port Moresby Vipers)	1	-	-	-	-
Arebo Taumaku (Port Moresby Vipers)	1	-	-	-	-
Max Tiri (Mt Hagen Eagles)	5	-	-	-	-
John Unagi (Kundiawa Warriors)	3	-	-	-	-
Jack Uradok (Port Moresby Vipers)	3	2	-	-	8
Richard Wagambie (Port Moresby Vipers)	5	-	-	-	-
Goie Waine (Kundiawa Warriors)	1	1	-	-	4
Ipisa Wanega (Kundiawa Warriors)	5	-	5	-	10
Nande Yer (Lae Bombers)	2	-	-	-	-

1995

GROUP ONE

ENGLAND 20 ....AUSTRALIA 16
At Wembley, Saturday 7 October 1995
Attendance: 41,271; **Referee:** Stuart Cummings (England)
England: T - Robinson, Newlove, Farrell, Joynt; G - Farrell 2
Australia: T - Menzies 2, Coyne; G - Wishart 2
England: Kris Radlinski, Jason Robinson, Barrie-Jon Mather, Paul Newlove, John Bentley, Daryl Powell, Shaun Edwards, Karl Harrison, Lee Jackson, Andy Platt, Denis Betts, Phil Clarke, Andrew Farrell. Subs: Bobby Goulding, Nick Pinkney, Chris Joynt, Simon Haughton
Australia: Tim Brasher, Rod Wishart, Mark Coyne, Terry Hill, John Hopoate, Brad Fittler, Geoff Toovey, David Gillespie, Wayne Bartrim, Mark Carroll, Steve Menzies, Dean Pay, Jim Dymock. Subs: Robbie O'Davis, Matthew Johns, Jason Smith, Paul Harragon

FIJI 52 .... SOUTH AFRICA 6
At Cougar Park, Keighley, Sunday 8 October 1995
Attendance: 4,845; **Referee:** David Manson (Australia)
Fiji: T - Sovatabua 2, Dakuitoga, Seru 2, Nadruku, Taga, Sagaitu, Marayawa, Naisoro; G - Nayacakalou 3, Taga 3
South Africa: G - van Wyk 3
Fiji: Waisale Sovatabua, Joe Dakuitoga, Livai Nalagilagi, Filemoni Seru, Noa Nadruku, Noa Nayacakalou, Save Taga, Malakai Yasa, Iane Sagaitu, Pio Nakubuwai, Apisalome Degei, Iliesa Toga, Sam Marayawa. Subs: Kajava Salusalu, George Vatubua, Ulaiasi Wainidroa, Kalaveti Naisoro.
South Africa: Pierre van Wyk, Guy Coombe, Andrew Ballot, Willem Boshoff, Mark Johnson, Francois Cloete, Berend Alkema, Gideon Watts, Kobus van Deventer, Jaco Booysen, Gerald Williams, Tim Fourie, Jaco Alberts. Subs: Ernest Ludick, Eugene Powell, Koot Human, Jaco van Niekerk

AUSTRALIA 86 ....SOUTH AFRICA 6
At Gateshead International Stadium, Tuesday 10 October 1995
Attendance: 9,191; **Referee:** Russell Smith (England)
Australia: T - O'Davis 2, Moore 2, McGregor 2, Hopoate 3, A Johns 2, Raper, Smith, Kosef, Brasher, Dymock; G - A Johns 11
South Africa: T - Watts; G - van Wyk
Australia: Robbie O'Davis, Brett Dallas, Danny Moore, Paul McGregor, John Hopoate, Matthew Johns, Andrew Johns, Adam Muir, Aaron Raper, Paul Harragon, Billy Moore, Jason Smith, Nik Kosef. Subs: Tim Brasher, Jim Dymock, Wayne Bartrim, Mark Carroll
South Africa: Pierre van Wyk, Guy Coombe, Andrew Ballot, Willem Boshoff, Mark Johnson, Berend Alkema, Kobus van Deventer, Gideon Watts, Francois Cloete, Jaco Booysen, Gerald Williams, Koot Human, Tim Fourie. Subs: Ernest Ludick, Eugene Powell, Nico Serfontein, Jaco van Niekerk

ENGLAND 46...FIJI 0
At Central Park, Wigan, Wednesday 11 October 1995
Attendance: 26,263; **Referee:** Dennis Hale (New Zealand)
England: T - Radlinski, Robinson 2, Newlove, Bentley, Smith, Broadbent, Haughton; G - Farrell 4, Goulding 3
England: Kris Radlinski, Jason Robinson, Nick Pinkney, Paul Newlove, John Bentley, Tony Smith, Bobbie Goulding, Paul Broadbent, Lee Jackson, Dean Sampson, Denis Betts, Mick Cassidy, Andrew Farrell. Subs: Shaun Edwards, Paul Cook, Simon Haughton, Steve McCurrie
Fiji: Waisale Sovatabua, Joe Dakuitoga, Livai Nalagilagi, Filemoni Seru, Noa Nadruku, Noa Nayacakalou, Save Taga, Malakai Yasa, Iane Sagaitu, Pio Nakubuwai, Apisalome Degei, Iliesa Toga, Sam Marayawa. Subs: Niumaia Korovata, Ulaiasi Wainidroa, George Vatubua, Kalaveti Naisoro

AUSTRALIA 66 ....**FIJI 0**
At Alfred McAlpine Stadium, Huddersfield,
Saturday 14 October 1995
Attendance: 7,127; **Referee:** Eddie Ward (Australia)
Australia: T - Brasher, Dallas 3, Hill 2, O'Davis 3,
Menzies 2, Larson; G - A Johns 9
Australia: Tim Brasher, Brett Dallas, Mark Coyne, Terry
Hill, Robbie O'Davis, Brad Fittler, Geoff Toovey, Dean
Pay, Andrew Johns, Mark Carroll, Steve Menzies, Gary
Larson, Jim Dymock. Subs: Paul McGregor, Matthew
Johns, Jason Smith, Nik Kosef
Fiji: Waisale Sovatabua, Orisi Cavuilati, Livai Nalagilagi,
Filemoni Seru, Noa Nadruku, Noa Nayacakalou, Save
Taga, Malakai Yasa, Iane Sagaitu, Pio Nakubuwai, Joe
Dakuitoga, Samuela Davetawalu, Niumaia Korovata.
Subs: Kalaveti Naisoro, George Vatubua, Waisake
Vatubua, Kini Koroibuleka

ENGLAND 46 ....**SOUTH AFRICA 0**
At Headingley, Leeds, Saturday 14 October 1995
Attendance: 14,041; **Referee:** David Manson (Australia)
England: T - Pinkney 2, Goulding, Haughton, Radlinski,
Broadbent, Smith, Sampson; G - Goulding 7
England: Paul Cook, John Bentley, Nick Pinkney, Barrie-
Jon Mather, Martin Offiah, Daryl Powell, Bobbie
Goulding, Karl Harrison, Mick Cassidy, Andy Platt,
Simon Haughton, Chris Joynt, Phil Clarke. Subs: Kris
Radlinski, Paul Broadbent, Tony Smith, Dean Sampson
South Africa: Pierre van Wyk, Guy Coombe, Tim Fourie,
Willem Boshoff, Andrew Ballot, Mark Johnson, Berend
Alkema, Gideon Watts, Kobus van Deventer, Jaco
Booysen, Gerald Williams, Jaco Alberts, John
Mudgeway. Subs: Justin Jennings, Elmar Lubbe,
Francois Cloete, Jaco Visser

GROUP ONE TABLE

	P	W	D	L	F	A	Pts
England	3	3	0	0	112	16	6
Australia	3	2	0	1	168	26	4
Fiji	3	1	0	2	52	118	2
South Africa	3	0	0	3	12	184	0

GROUP TWO

NEW ZEALAND 25 ....**TONGA 24**
At Wilderspool Stadium, Warrington,
Sunday 8 October 1995
Attendance: 8,083; **Referee:** David Campbell (England)
New Zealand: T - Hoppe, Blackmore 2, Kemp, Okesene;
G - Ridge 2; FG - Ridge
Tonga: T - Taufa, Veikoso, W Wolfgramm, Finau;
G - Amone 4
New Zealand: Matthew Ridge, Sean Hoppe, Richard
Blackmore, Ruben Wiki, Richard Barnett, Gene Ngamu,
Stacey Jones, Quentin Pongia, Syd Eru, Jason Lowrie,
Tony Iro, Stephen Kearney, Tony Kemp. Subs: Henry
Paul, Hitro Okesene, Kevin Iro, Mark Horo
Tonga: Asa Amone, Una Taufa, Tevita Vaikona, Phil
Howlett, Jimmy Veikoso, Angelo Dymock, Willie
Wolfgramm, Martin Masella, Duane Mann, Lee Hansen,
George Mann, Solomon Haumono, Awen Guttenbeil.
Subs: Salesi Finau, Talite Liava'a, Luke Leilua, Taukolo
Tonga

PAPUA NEW GUINEA 28 ....**TONGA 28**
At The Boulevard, Hull, Tuesday 10 October 1995
Attendance: 5,121; **Referee:** Claude Alba (France)
Papua New Guinea: Buko, Gene, Lam, Paiyo, Solbat;
G - Paiyo 4
Tonga: T - Taufa, Howlett, W Wolfgramm, Guttenbeil 2,
Liku; G - Amone 2
Papua New Guinea: David Buko, James Kops, David
Gomia, John Okul, Joshua Kouoru, Stanley Gene,
Adrian Lam, Tuiyo Evei, Elias Paiyo, David Westley, Max
Tiri, Nande Yer, Bruce Mamando. Subs: Robert Tela,
Lucas Solbat, Marcus Bai, David Reeka
Tonga: Asa Amone, Una Taufa, Tevita Vaikona, Phil
Howlett, Jimmy Veikoso, Angelo Dymock, Willie
Wolfgramm, Martin Masella, Duane Mann, Lee Hansen,
George Mann, Solomon Haumono, Awen Guttenbeil.
Subs: Salesi Finau, Tau'alupe Liku, Luke Leilua, Taukolo
Tonga

NEW ZEALAND 22 ....**PAPUA NEW GUINEA 6**
At Knowsley Road, St Helens, Friday 13 October 1995
Attendance: 8,679; **Referee:** Stuart Cummings
(England)
New Zealand: T - Ridge, Hoppe, Blackmore;
G - Ridge 4, Ngamu
Papua New Guinea: T - Bai; G - Paiyo
New Zealand: Matthew Ridge, Sean Hoppe, Richard
Blackmore, Ruben Wiki, Jason Williams, Henry Paul,
Stacey Jones, Quentin Pongia, Gary Freeman, Jason
Lowrie, Stephen Kearney, Mark Horo, Tony Kemp. Subs:
Gene Ngamu, Hitro Okesene, Kevin Iro, Tony Iro
Papua New Guinea: David Buko, James Kops, David
Gomia, John Okul, Joshua Kouoru, Stanley Gene,
Adrian Lam, Nande Yer, Elias Paiyo, David Westley, Max
Tiri, Michael Angra, Bruce Mamando. Subs: Robert Tela,
Lucas Solbat, Marcus Bai, Ben Biri

GROUP TWO TABLE

	P	W	D	L	F	A	Pts
New Zealand	2	2	0	0	47	30	4
Tonga	2	0	1	1	52	53	1
Papua New Guinea	2	0	1	1	34	50	1

GROUP THREE

WALES 28 ....**FRANCE 6**
At Ninian Park, Cardiff, Monday 9 October 1995
Attendance: 10,250; **Referee:** Eddie Ward (Australia)
Wales: T - Harris, Devereux, Sullivan 3;
G - Davies 3, Harris
France: T - Torreilles; G - Banquet
Wales: Iestyn Harris, John Devereux, Allan Bateman,
Scott Gibbs, Anthony Sullivan, Jonathan Davies, Kevin
Ellis, Kelvin Skerrett, Martin Hall, David Young, Paul
Moriarty, Mark Perrett, Richie Eyres. Subs: Mark Jones,
Adrian Hadley, Keiron Cunningham, Rowland Phillips
France: David Despin, Frederic Banquet, David Fraisse,
Pierre Chamorin, Jean-Marc Garcia, Pascal Fages,
Patrick Entat, Didier Cabestany, Patrick Torreilles,
Frederic Teixido, Gael Tallec, Pascal Jampy, Thierry
Valero. Subs: Vincent Banet, Karl Jaavuo, Brian Coles,
Lilian Hebert

WESTERN SAMOA 56 ....**FRANCE 10**
At Ninian Park Cardiff, Thursday 12 October 1995
Attendance: 2,173; **Referee:** Kelvin Jeffs (Australia)
Western Samoa: T - P Tuimavave, Laumatia, Tuigamala
2, W Swann, Tatupu 2, Matautia 2, Perelini;
G - Schuster 8
France: T - Chamorin, Cabestany; G - Banquet
Western Samoa: Paki Tuimavave, Brian Laumatia, John
Schuster, Va'aiga Tuigamala, Lolani Koko, Tea Ropati,
Willie Swann, Se'e Solomona, Willie Poching, Fa'ausu
Afoa, Tony Tatupu, Vila Matautia, Tony Tuimavave. Subs:
Mark Elia, Sam Panapa, Apollo Perelini, Joe Vagana
France: Frederic Banquet, Brian Coles, Jean-Marc
Garcia, Pierre Chamorin, Pascal Mons, Pascal Fages,
Patrick Entat, Hadj Boudebza, Patrick Torreilles, Karl
Jaavuo, Cyril Baudouin, Didier Cabestany, Thierry
Valero. Subs: Vincent Banet, Pascal Jampy, Frederic
Teixido, Marc Tisseyre

WALES 22 ....**WESTERN SAMOA 10**
At Vetch Field, Swansea, Sunday 15 October 1995
Attendance: 15,385; **Referee:** Russell Smith (England)
Wales: T - Harris, Sullivan, Ellis; G - Davies 4:
FG - Davies, Harris
Western Samoa: T - Matautia; G - Schuster 3
Wales: Iestyn Harris, Anthony Sullivan, Allan Bateman,
John Devereux, Adrian Hadley, Jonathan Davies, Kevin
Ellis, Kelvin Skerrett, Martin Hall, David Young, Paul
Moriarty, Scott Quinnell, Richie Eyres. Subs: Neil Cowie,
Keiron Cunningham, Rowland Phillips, Paul Atcheson
Western Samoa: Paki Tuimavave, John Schuster, Tea
Ropati, Va'aiga Tuigamala, Brian Laumatia, Sam
Panapa, Willie Swann, Se'e Solomona, Willie Poching,
Fa'ausu Afoa, Tony Tatupu, Vila Matautia, Tony
Tuimavave. Subs: Mark Elia, Des Maea, Apollo Perelini,
Joe Vagana

Rugby League World Cup Statistics

GROUP THREE TABLE

	P	W	D	L	F	A	Pts
Wales	2	2	0	0	50	16	4
Western Samoa	2	1	0	1	66	32	2
France	2	0	0	2	16	84	0

SEMI-FINALS

ENGLAND 25 ....**WALES 10**
At Old Trafford, Manchester, Saturday 21 October 1995
Attendance: 30,042; **Referee:** Eddie Ward (Australia)
England: T - Newlove, Offiah 2, Betts, Clarke; G - Goulding, Farrell; FG - Goulding
Wales: T - Phillips; G - Davies 3
England: Kris Radlinski, Jason Robinson, Nick Pinkney, Paul Newlove, Martin Offiah, Tony Smith, Bobbie Goulding, Karl Harrison, Lee Jackson, Andy Platt, Denis Betts, Phil Clarke, Andrew Farrell. Subs: Barrie-Jon Mather, Mick Cassidy, Simon Haughton, Dean Sampson.
Wales: Iestyn Harris, John Devereux, Allan Bateman, Scott Gibbs, Anthony Sullivan, Jonathan Davies, Kevin Ellis, Kelvin Skerrett, Martin Hall, David Young, Paul Moriarty, Scott Quinnell, Richie Eyres. Subs: Mark Jones, Keiron Cunningham, Rowland Phillips, Adrian Hadley.

AUSTRALIA 30 ....**NEW ZEALAND 20** *(AET)*
At Alfred McAlpine Stadium, Huddersfield, Sunday 22 October 1995
Attendance: 16,608; **Referee:** Russell Smith (England)
Australia: T - Brasher, Coyne, Hill, Fittler, Menzies 2; G - A Johns 3
New Zealand: T - K Iro, Barnett, T Iro; G - Ridge 4
Australia: Tim Brasher, Rod Wishart, Mark Coyne, Terry Hill, Brett Dallas, Brad Fittler, Geoff Toovey, Dean Pay, Andrew Johns, Mark Carroll, Steve Menzies, Gary Larson, Jim Dymock. Subs: Robbie O'Davis, Matthew Johns, Jason Smith, Nik Kosef
New Zealand: Matthew Ridge, Sean Hoppe, Kevin Iro, Richard Blackmore, Richard Barnett, Tony Kemp, Stacey Jones, John Lomax, Henry Paul, Jason Lowrie, Stephen Kearney, Quentin Pongia, Mark Horo. Subs: Gene Ngamu, Ruben Wiki, Tony Iro, Hitro Okesene.

CENTENARY WORLD CUP FINAL

ENGLAND 8 ....**AUSTRALIA 16**
At Wembley, Saturday 28 October, 1995
Attendance: 66,540; **Referee:** Stuart Cummings (England)
England: T - Newlove; G - Goulding 2
Australia: T - Brasher, Wishart; G - A Johns 4
England: Kris Radlinski, Jason Robinson, Gary Connolly, Paul Newlove, Martin Offiah, Tony Smith, Bobbie Goulding, Karl Harrison, Lee Jackson, Andy Platt, Denis Betts, Phil Clarke, Andrew Farrell. Subs: Mick Cassidy, Chris Joynt, Barrie-Jon Mather, Nick Pinkney
Australia: Tim Brasher, Rod Wishart, Mark Coyne, Terry Hill, Brett Dallas, Brad Fittler, Geoff Toovey, Dean Pay, Andrew Johns, Mark Carroll, Steve Menzies, Gary Larson, Jim Dymock. Subs: Jason Smith, Robbie O'Davis, Matthew Johns, Nik Kosef.

THE 1995 SQUADS

AUSTRALIA *(Coach: Bob Fulton)*

	M	T	G	FG	Pts
Wayne Bartrim (St George)	2	0	0	0	0
Tim Brasher (Sydney Tigers)	5	4	0	0	16
Mark Carroll (Manly)	5	0	0	0	0
Mark Coyne (St George)	4	2	0	0	8
Brett Dallas (Sydney Bulldogs)	4	3	0	0	12
Jim Dymock(Sydney Bulldogs)	5	1	0	0	4
Brad Fittler (Penrith)	4	1	0	0	4
David Gillespie (Manly)	1	0	0	0	0
Paul Harragon (Newcastle Knights)	2	0	0	0	0
Terry Hill (Manly)	4	3	0	0	12
John Hopoate (Manly)	2	3	0	0	12
Andrew Johns (Newcastle Knights)	4	2	27	0	62
Matthew Johns (Newcastle Knights)	5	0	0	0	0

Nik Kosef (Manly)	4	1	0	0	4
Gary Larson (North Sydney) *	3	1	0	0	4
Paul McGregor (Illawarra)	2	2	0	0	8
Steve Menzies (Manly)	4	6	0	0	24
Billy Moore (North Sydney)	1	0	0	0	0
Danny Moore (Manly)	1	2	0	0	8
Adam Muir (Newcastle Knights)	1	0	0	0	0
Robbie O'Davis (Newcastle Knights)	5	5	0	0	20
Dean Pay (Sydney Bulldogs)	4	0	0	0	0
Aaron Raper (Cronulla)	1	1	0	0	4
Jason Smith (Sydney Bulldogs)	5	1	0	0	4
Geoff Toovey (Manly)	4	0	0	0	0
Rod Wishart (Illawarra)	3	1	2	0	8

* Larson replaced injured Harragon after two matches

ENGLAND *(Coach: Phil Larder)*

	M	T	G	FG	Pts
John Bentley (Halifax)	3	1	0	0	4
Denis Betts (Auckland Warriors)	4	1	0	0	4
Paul Broadbent (Sheffield Eagles)	2	2	0	0	8
Mick Cassidy (Wigan)	4	0	0	0	0
Phil Clarke (Sydney City Roosters)	4	1	0	0	4
Gary Connolly (Wigan)	1	0	0	0	0
Paul Cook (Leeds)	2	0	0	0	0
Shaun Edwards (Wigan)	2	0	0	0	0
Andrew Farrell (Wigan)	4	1	7	0	18
Bobbie Goulding (St Helens)	5	1	13	1	31
Karl Harrison (Halifax)	4	0	0	0	0
Simon Haughton (Wigan)	4	2	0	0	8
Lee Jackson (Sheffield Eagles)	4	0	0	0	0
Chris Joynt (St Helens)	3	1	0	0	4
Barrie-Jon Mather (Wigan)	4	0	0	0	0
Steve McCurrie (Widnes)	1	0	0	0	0
Paul Newlove (Bradford Bulls)	4	4	0	0	16
Martin Offiah (Wigan)	3	2	0	0	8
Nick Pinkney (Keighley Cougars)	5	2	0	0	8
Andy Platt (Auckland Warriors/Widnes)	4	0	0	0	0
Daryl Powell (Keighley Cougars)	2	0	0	0	0
Kris Radlinski (Wigan)	5	2	0	0	8
Jason Robinson (Wigan)	4	3	0	0	12
Dean Sampson (Castleford)	3	1	0	0	4
Tony Smith (Castleford)	4	2	0	0	8

FIJI *(Coach: Graham Murray)*

	M	T	G	FG	Pts
Orisi Cavuilati (Bulldogs)	1	0	0	0	0
Joe Dakuitoga (Penrith)	3	1	0	0	4
Samuela Davetawalu (Fiji Fish Nadi)	1	0	0	0	0
Apisalome Degei (Parramatta)	2	0	0	0	0
Kini Koroibuleka (Yanco)	1	0	0	0	0
Niumaia Korovata (Yanco)	2	0	0	0	0
Sam Marayawa (Tumbarumba)	2	0	0	0	4
Noa Nadruku (Canberra Raiders)	3	1	0	0	4
Kalaveti Naisoro(Lautoka Foodtown)	3	1	0	0	4
Pio Nakubuwai (Yanco)	3	0	0	0	0
Livai Nalagilagi (Penrith)	3	0	0	0	0
Noa Nayacakalou (Penrith)	3	0	3	0	6
Inoke Ratudina (Carpenters Motors)	0	0	0	0	0
Kiniviliame Ratukana (Fiji Bitter Army)	0	0	0	0	0
Freddie Robarts (Waitakere Raiders)	0	0	0	0	0
Iane Sagaitu (North Sydney)	3	1	0	0	4
Kaiava Salusalu (Lautoka Foodtown)	1	0	0	0	0
Filemoni Seru (S Queensland Crushers)	3	2	0	0	8
Waisale Sovatabua (Carpenters Motors)	3	2	0	0	8
Save Taga (Fiji Fish Nadi)	3	1	3	0	10
Iliesa Toga (Narrabeean)	2	0	0	0	0
Vonivate Toga (Fiji Fish Nadi)	0	0	0	0	0
George Vatubua (Lautoka Foodtown)	3	0	0	0	0
Waisake Vatubua (Hyundai Bulldogs)	1	0	0	0	0
Ulaiasi Wainidroa (Fiji Fish Nadi)	2	0	0	0	0
Malakai Yasa (Lautoka Foodtown)	3	0	0	0	0

FRANCE *(Coach: Ivan Gresesque)*

	M	T	G	FG	Pts
Patrick Acroue (Avignon)	0	0	0	0	0
Ezzedine Attia (Cannes)	0	0	0	0	0
Vincent Banet (Limoux)	2	0	0	0	0
Frederic Banquet (Sheffield Eagles)	2	0	2	0	4

	M	T	G	FG	Pts
Cyril Baudouin (Carpentras)	1	0	0	0	0
Hadj Boudebza (St Esteve)	1	0	0	0	0
Didier Cabestany (Catalan)	2	1	0	0	4
Pierre Chamorin (St Esteve)	2	1	0	0	4
Brian Coles (Catalan)	2	0	0	0	0
David Despin (Villeneuve-sur-Lot)	1	0	0	0	0
Patrick Entat (Avignon)	2	0	0	0	0
Pascal Fages (Pia)	2	0	0	0	0
David Fraisse (Workington Town)	1	0	0	0	0
Jean-Marc Garcia (St Esteve)	2	0	0	0	0
Lilian Hebert (Pia)	1	0	0	0	0
Karl Jaavuo (Pia)	2	0	0	0	0
Pascal Jampy (St Esteve)	2	0	0	0	0
Stephan Millet (St Gaudens)	0	0	0	0	0
Pascal Mons (Carcassonne)	1	0	0	0	0
Gael Tallec (Wigan)	1	0	0	0	0
Frederic Teixido (Limoux)	2	0	0	0	0
Marc Tisseyre (Limoux)	1	0	0	0	0
Patrick Torreilles (Pia)	2	1	0	0	4
Thierry Valero (FC Lezignan)	2	0	0	0	0

NEW ZEALAND (Coach: Frank Endacott)

	M	T	G	FG	Pts
Richard Barnett (Cronulla)	2	1	0	0	4
Richard Blackmore (Auckland Warriors)	3	3	0	0	12
Syd Eru (Auckland Warriors)	1	0	0	0	0
Gary Freeman (Penrith)	1	0	0	0	0
Daryl Halligan (Sydney Bulldogs)	0	0	0	0	0
Sean Hoppe (Auckland Warriors)	3	2	0	0	8
Mark Horo (Western Suburbs)	3	0	0	0	0
Kevin Iro (Leeds)	3	1	0	0	4
Tony Iro (Sydney City Roosters)	3	1	0	0	4
Stacey Jones (Auckland Warriors)	3	0	0	0	0
Stephen Kearney (Auckland Warriors)	3	0	0	0	0
Tony Kemp (Leeds)	3	1	0	0	4
John Lomax (Canberra Raiders)	1	0	0	0	0
Jason Lowrie (Sydney City Roosters)	3	0	0	0	0
Gene Ngamu (Auckland Warriors)	3	0	1	0	2
Hitro Okesene (Auckland Warriors)	3	1	0	0	4
Henry Paul (Wigan)	3	0	0	0	0
Quentin Pongia (Canberra Raiders)	3	0	0	0	0
Matthew Ridge (Manly)	3	1	10	1	25
Brent Stuart (Western Suburbs)	0	0	0	0	0
John Timu (Sydney Bulldogs)	0	0	0	0	0
Brendon Tuuta (Castleford)	0	0	0	0	0
Ruben Wiki (Canberra Raiders)	3	0	0	0	0
Jason Williams (Sydney Bulldogs)	1	0	0	0	0

PAPUA NEW GUINEA (Coach: Joe Tokam)

	M	T	G	FG	Pts
Michael Angra (Hagen Eagles)	1	0	0	0	0
Marcus Bai (Port Moresby Vipers)	2	1	0	0	4
Ben Biri (Port Moresby Vipers)	1	0	0	0	0
David Buko (Goroka Lahanis)	2	1	0	0	4
Aquila Emil (Port Moresby Vipers)	0	0	0	0	0
Tuiyo Evei (Goroka Lahanis)	1	0	0	0	0
Stanley Gene (Goroka Lahanis)	2	1	0	0	4
David Gomia (Goroka Lahanis)	2	0	0	0	0
August Joseph (Rabaul Gurias)	0	0	0	0	0
James Kops (Hagen Eagles)	2	0	0	0	0
Joshua Kouoru (Rabaul Gurias)	2	0	0	0	0
Adrian Lam (Sydney City Roosters)	2	1	0	0	4
Bruce Mamando (Canberra Raiders)	2	0	0	0	0
Billy Noi Jnr (Hagen Eagles)	0	0	0	0	0
John Okul (Moorebank Bulldogs)	2	0	0	0	0
Elias Paiyo (Port Moresby Vipers)	2	1	5	0	14
Samuel Pinpin (Mendi Muruks)	0	0	0	0	0
David Reeka (Lae Bombers)	1	0	0	0	0
Lucas Solbat (Rabaul Gurias)	2	1	0	0	4
Robert Tela (Lae Bombers)	2	0	0	0	0
Petrus Thomas (Mendi Muruks)	0	0	0	0	0
Max Tiri (Hagen Eagles)	2	0	0	0	0
David Westley (Canberra Raiders)	2	0	0	0	0
Nande Yer (Mendi Muruks)	2	0	0	0	0

SOUTH AFRICA (Coach: Tony Fisher)

	M	T	G	FG	Pts
Jaco Alberts (South Queensland Crushers)	2	0	0	0	0
Berend Alkema	3	0	0	0	0
Andrew Ballot (Bay of Plenty)	3	0	0	0	0
Jaco Booysen (St Helens Devils)	3	0	0	0	0
Willem Boshoff (Eastern Reds)	3	0	0	0	0
Francois Cloete (Barea Students)	3	0	0	0	0
Guy Coombe (Durban Sharks)	3	0	0	0	0
Tim Fourie (City Scorpions)	3	0	0	0	0
Pierre Grobbelaar (Vaal Buffaloes)	0	0	0	0	0
Koot Human (South Queensland Crushers)	2	0	0	0	0
Justin Jennings (South Queensland Crushers)	1	0	0	0	0
Mark Johnson (Workington Town)	3	0	0	0	0
Elmar Lubbe (Eastern Reds)	1	0	0	0	0
Ernest Ludick	2	0	0	0	0
Warren McCann	0	0	0	0	0
John Mudgeway (Durban Sharks)	1	0	0	0	0
Eugene Powell (City Scorpions)	2	0	0	0	0
Nico Serfontein	1	0	0	0	0
Kobus van Deventer (Germiston Warriors)	3	0	0	0	0
Jaco van Niekerk (Eastern Reds)	2	0	0	0	0
Pierre van Wyk (Eastern Reds)	3	0	4	0	8
Jaco Visser	1	0	0	0	0
Gideon Watts	3	1	0	0	4
Gerald Williams (Durban Sharks)	3	0	0	0	0

TONGA (Coach: Mike McClennan)

	M	T	G	FG	Pts
Peri Amato (Mua Saints)	0	0	0	0	0
Asa Amone (Halifax)	2	0	6	0	12
Angelo Dymock (Moorepark)	2	0	0	0	0
Salesi Finau (Canberra Raiders)	2	1	0	0	4
Awen Guttenbeil (Manly)	2	2	0	0	8
Lee Hansen (Widnes)	2	0	0	0	0
Solomon Haumono (Manly)	2	0	0	0	0
Phil Howlett (Parramatta)	2	1	0	0	4
Luke Leilua (Otahuhu)	2	0	0	0	0
Talite Liava'a (Litchfield)	1	0	0	0	0
Tau'alupe Liku (Leigh)	1	1	0	0	4
Mateaki Mafi (Kolomua)	0	0	0	0	0
Duane Mann (Auckland Warriors)	2	0	0	0	0
George Mann (Leeds)	2	0	0	0	0
Martin Masella (Illawarra)	2	0	0	0	0
Andrew Tangata-Toa (Newcastle Knights)	0	0	0	0	0
Una Taufa (Canberra Raiders)	2	2	0	0	8
Taukolo Tonga (Kolomua Warriors)	2	0	0	0	0
Tevita Vaikona (Hull)	2	0	0	0	0
Jimmy Veikoso (Belconen)	2	1	0	0	4
Frank Watene (Auckland Warriors)	0	0	0	0	0
Willie Wolfgramm (Narrendera)	2	2	0	0	8

WALES (Coach: Clive Griffiths)

	M	T	G	FG	Pts
Paul Atcheson (Oldham)	1	0	0	0	0
Allan Bateman (Warrington)	3	0	0	0	0
Dean Busby (St Helens)	0	0	0	0	0
Neil Cowie (Wigan)	1	0	0	0	0
Keiron Cunningham (St Helens)	3	0	0	0	0
Jonathan Davies (Warrington)	3	0	10	1	21
John Devereux (Widnes)	3	1	0	0	4
Kevin Ellis (Warrington)	3	1	0	0	4
Richie Eyres (Leeds)	3	0	0	0	0
Phil Ford (Salford)	0	0	0	0	0
Scott Gibbs (St Helens)	2	0	0	0	0
Jonathan Griffiths (St Helens)	0	0	0	0	0
Adrian Hadley (Widnes)	2	0	0	0	0
Martin Hall (Wigan)	3	0	0	0	0
Iestyn Harris (Warrington)	3	2	1	1	11
Mark Jones (Warrington)	2	0	0	0	0
Paul Moriarty (Halifax)	3	0	0	0	0
Mark Perrett (Halifax)	1	0	0	0	0
Rowland Phillips (Workington)	3	1	0	0	4
Scott Quinnell (Wigan)	2	0	0	0	0
Kelvin Skerrett (Wigan)	3	0	0	0	0
Gareth Stephens (Castleford)	0	0	0	0	0
Anthony Sullivan (St Helens)	3	4	0	0	16
Richard Webster (Salford)	0	0	0	0	0
David Young (Salford)	3	0	0	0	0

WESTERN SAMOA *(Coach: Graham Lowe)*

	M	T	G	FG	Pts
Fa'ausu Afoa (Penrith)	2	0	0	0	0
Mark Elia (Albi)	2	0	0	0	0
Lolani Koko (Narrendera)	1	0	0	0	0
Brian Laumatia (Cronulla)	2	1	0	0	4
Des Maea (Auckland Warriors)	1	0	0	0	0
Gus Malietoa-Brown (Auckland Warriors)	0	0	0	0	0
Vila Matautia (St Helens)	2	3	0	0	12
Sam Panapa (Salford)	2	0	0	0	0
Apollo Perelini (St Helens)	2	1	0	0	4
Robert Piva (Queensland Cowboys)	0	0	0	0	0
Willie Poching (Auckland Warriors)	2	0	0	0	0
Tea Ropati (Auckland Warriors)	2	0	0	0	0
John Schuster (Halifax)	2	0	11	0	22
Mike Setefano (North Harbour)	0	0	0	0	0
Se'e Solomona (Auckland Warriors)	2	0	0	0	0
Henry Suluvale (Sydney City Roosters)	0	0	0	0	0
Willie Swann (Auckland Warriors)	2	1	0	0	4
Tony Tatupu (Auckland Warriors)	2	2	0	0	8
Setu Tuilaepa (Narrendera)	0	0	0	0	0
Va'aiga Tuigamala (Wigan)	2	2	0	0	8
Paki Tuimavave (North Harbour)	2	1	0	0	4
Tony Tuimavave (Auckland Warriors)	2	0	0	0	0
Earl Va'a (Wellington Dukes)	0	0	0	0	0
Joe Vagana (Auckland Warriors)	2	0	0	0	0
Nigel Vagana (Auckland Warriors)	0	0	0	0	0

EMERGING NATIONS 1995

GROUP ONE

COOK ISLANDS 64.................................**USA 6**
At Featherstone, Monday 16 October, 1995;
Attendance: 3,133
Cook Islands: T - Cuthers 3, Hunter 2, Noovao 2, Johnston 2, Bowen, Toa; G - Noovao 10
USA: T - Preston; G- Niu

SCOTLAND 34 ....**RUSSIA 9**
At Featherstone, Monday 16 October, 1995;
Attendance: 3,133
Scotland: T - Blee 2, Tait 2, How, Waddell; G- McAlister 4, Thompson
Russia: T - Netchaev, Otradnov; FG - Scheglov

COOK ISLANDS 58............................**RUSSIA 20**
At Leigh, Wednesday 18 October, 1995;
Attendance: 1,921
Cook Islands: Tariu 4, Cuthers 2, Tuaru 2, Shepherd, Noovao, Bowen, Toa; G - Noovao 4, Piakura
Russia: T - Kiryakov 2, Sirgeev, Romanov; G - Kozlov, Vinokhodov

SCOTLAND 38 ....**USA 16**
At Northampton, Wednesday 18 October, 1995;
Attendance: 2,088
Scotland: T - Shelford 3, Thompson, Ketteridge, How, M Smith; G - Thompson 5
USA: T - Niu 2, Lewis; G - Niu 2

COOK ISLANDS 21..........................**SCOTLAND 10**
At Castleford, Friday 20 October, 1995;
Attendance: 2,889
Cook Islands: T - Tariu 2, Shepherd 2; G - Noovao 2; FG - Davys
Scotland: T - A Tait 2; G - Thompson

RUSSIA 28 ....**USA 26**
At Warrington, Friday 20 October, 1995;
Attendance: 1,950
Russia: T- Gavriline 3, Kiryakov, Romanov, Netchaev; G - Scheglov, Netchaev
USA: T- Preston 2, Maffie, Wallace, Broussard; G - Niu 3

GROUP TWO

IRELAND 48 ....**MOLDOVA 26**
At Rochdale, Monday 16 October, 1995;
Attendance: 1,235
Ireland: T - Gordon 3, Crompton, Foy, Casey, Grainey, Smith, McElhatton; G - Comerford 6
Moldova: T - Piskunov 2, Olar, Krivtsov, Benkowskiy; G - Olar 3

MOLDOVA 24 ....**MORROCCO 19**
At Northampton, Wednesday 18 October, 1995;
Attendance: 2,008
Moldova: T - Piskunov 3, Strakh, V Sapega; G: Olar, Piskunov
Morocco: T - Katir 2, Mahabi; G - Echalouki 2, Mahabi; FG - Katir

IRELAND 42.....................................**MOROCCO 6**
At Dewsbury, Friday 20 October, 1995;
Attendance: 1,756
Ireland: T - Ricky Smith, Horrigan, Grainey, Gordon, Comerford, Foy, Browne, Sullivan; G - Comerford 5
Morocco: T - Bibarss; G - Amar

GROUP ONE TABLE

	P	W	D	L	F	A	Pts
Cook Islands	3	3	0	0	143	36	6
Scotland	3	2	0	1	82	46	2
Russia	3	1	0	2	57	118	2
USA	3	0	0	3	48	130	0

GROUP TWO TABLE

	P	W	D	L	F	A	Pts
Ireland	2	2	0	0	90	32	4
Moldova	2	1	0	1	50	67	2
Morocco	2	0	0	2	25	66	0

EMERGING NATIONS FINAL

COOK ISLANDS 22 ....**IRELAND 6**
At Gigg Lane, Bury, Tuesday 24 October, 1995;
Attendance: 4,147; **Referee:** Dennis Hale (New Zealand)
Cook Islands: T - Cuthers, Bowen, Kermonde, Shepherd; G - Noovao 3
Ireland: T - Comerford; G - Comerford
Cook Islands: Tiri Toa, Sonny Shepherd, Andrew Paita, Allan Tuaru, Ngere Tariu, Craig Bowen (c), Ali Davys, Bob Hunter, James Cuthers, Jason Temu, Alex Kermonde, Tama Henry, Meti Noovao, Subs, Tangi Tangimeta played, Tungane Tini played, Lloyd Matapo not used, Lefou Jack not used.
Ireland: Gavin Gordon, Phelim Comerford, Richard Smith, Ricky Smith, Eugene McEntaggert, Craig McElhatton, Martin Crompton, Bryan Smyth, Seamus McCallion, Leo Casey, Gary Grainey, Tony Nuttall, Paul Owens, (c), Subs, Conor O'Sullivan played, Des Foy played, Sean Casey played, Eric Boyle not used.

2000

GROUP ONE

ENGLAND 2 ....AUSTRALIA 22
At Twickenham, Saturday 28 October 2000
Attendance: 33,758; **Referee:** David Pakieto
(New Zealand)
England: G - Farrell
Australia: T - Sailor (4, 79), Gidley (32),
MacDougall (66); G - Rogers 3
England: 1 Kris Radlinski (Wigan Warriors); 2 Leon
Pryce (Bradford Bulls); 3 Scott Naylor (Bradford Bulls); 4
Keith Senior (Leeds Rhinos); 5 Chev Walker (Leeds
Rhinos); 6 Tony Smith (Wigan Warriors); 7 Sean Long
(St Helens); 8 Harvey Howard (Bradford Bulls); 9 Paul
Rowley (Halifax Blue Sox); 10 Stuart Fielden (Bradford
Bulls); 11 Adrian Morley (Leeds Rhinos); 12 Mike
Forshaw (Bradford Bulls); 13 Andrew Farrell (C) (Wigan
Warriors). Subs (all used): 14 Paul Wellens (St Helens);
15 Kevin Sinfield (Leeds Rhinos); 16 Darren Fleary
(Leeds Rhinos); 17 Paul Anderson (Bradford Bulls).
On report: Tony Smith (20) – high tackle,
no case to answer
Australia: 1 Darren Lockyer (Brisbane Broncos); 2 Mat
Rogers (Cronulla); 3 Ryan Girdler (Penrith Panthers); 4
Matthew Gidley (Newcastle Knights); 5 Wendell Sailor
(Brisbane Broncos); 6 Brad Fittler (C) (Sydney
Roosters); 7 Brett Kimmorley (Melbourne Storm); 8
Shane Webcke (Brisbane Broncos); 9 Andrew Johns
(Newcastle Knights); 10 Robbie Kearns (Melbourne
Storm); 11 Gorden Tallis (Brisbane Broncos); 12 Bryan
Fletcher (Sydney Roosters); 13 Scott Hill (Melbourne
Storm). Subs (all used): 14 Adam MacDougall
(Newcastle Knights); 15 Jason Croker (Canberra
Raiders); 16 Darren Britt (Sydney Bulldogs); 17 Jason
Stevens (Cronulla).

FIJI 38 ....RUSSIA 12
At Craven Park, Barrow, Sunday 29 October 2000
Attendance: 2,187; **Referee:** Russell Smith (England)
Fiji: T - Tuqiri (5, 23), Kuruduadua (17), Vunivalu
(42,58,61), Sovatabua (80); G - Tuqiri 5
Russia: T - Iliassov (37), Rullis (46);
G - Jiltsov, Mitrofanov
Fiji: 1 Lote Tuqiri (C) (Brisbane Broncos); 2 Jone
Kuruduadua (Bellingen-Dorrigo); 3 Waisale Sovatabua
(Huddersfield-Sheffield Giants); 4 Eparama Navale
(Northern Eagles); 5 Semi Tadulala (Brisbane Wests); 6
Stephen Smith (Otahuhu); 7 Kalaveti Naisoro
Tuiabayaba (Bounty Rum Crushers); 8 Tabua Cakacaka
(Cootamundra); 9 Fred Robart (Te Atatu); 10 Etuate
Vakatawa (Tumbarumba); 11 Josese Tamani
(Cabramatta); 12 Samu Marayawa (Ourimbah); 13
Atunaisa Vunivalu (Serua Dragons). Subs (all used): 14
Farasiko Tokarei (Nadi Steelers); 15 Josefa Lasagavibau
(Nadera Panthers); 16 Amani Takayawa (Nadi Steelers);
17 Peceli Vuniyayawa (Queanbeyan).
Russia: 1 Robert Iliassov (Kazan Arrows); 2 Mikhail
Mitrofanov (Kazan Arrows); 3 Matthew Donovan
(Western Suburbs); 4 Craig Cygler (Cairns Brothers); 5
Maxim Romanov (Kazan Arrows); 6 Andre Olar
(Toulouse); 7 Igor Gavriline (Lokomotiv Moscow); 8 Ian
Rubin (C) (Sydney Roosters); 9 Alexander Lysenkov
(Lokomotiv Moscow); 10 Robert Campbell (Redcliffe);
11 Petr Sokolov (Lokomotiv Moscow); 12 Aaron Findlay
(Canterbury Bulldogs); 13 Joel Rullis (Western
Suburbs). Subs (all used): 14 Pavel Kalachkine (Kazan
Arrows); 15 Victor Netchaev (Lokomotiv Moscow); 16
Igor Jiltsov (Lokomotiv Moscow); 17 Vadim Postnikov
(Lokomotiv Moscow).

AUSTRALIA 66 ....FIJI 8
At Gateshead International Stadium,
Wednesday 1 November 2000
Attendance: 4,197; **Referee:** Robert Connolly (England)
Australia: T - Rogers (6, 21,65,78), Kennedy (11,62),
Girdler (35, 42), Barrett (13), Hindmarsh (16),
MacDougall (30), Gidley (50); G - Rogers 9
Fiji: T - Cakacaka (24), Tuqiri (52)

Australia: 1 Darren Lockyer (Brisbane Broncos); 2 Mat
Rogers (Cronulla); 3 Ryan Girdler (Penrith Panthers); 4
Matthew Gidley (Newcastle Knights); 5 Adam
MacDougall (Newcastle Knights); 6 Trent Barrett (St
George-Illawarra Dragons); 7 Andrew Johns (Newcastle
Knights); 8 Jason Stevens (Cronulla); 9 Craig Gower
(Penrith Panthers); 10 Michael Vella (Parramatta Eels);
11 Ben Kennedy (Newcastle Knights); 12 Nathan
Hindmarsh (Parramatta Eels); 13 Brad Fittler (C)
(Sydney Roosters). Subs (all used): 14 Scott Hill
(Melbourne Storm); 15 Jason Croker (Canberra
Raiders); 16 Robbie Kearns (Melbourne Storm); 17
Shane Webcke (Brisbane Broncos).
Fiji: 1 Lote Tuqiri (C) (Brisbane Broncos); 2 Jone
Kuruduadua (Bellingen-Dorrigo); 3 Waisale Sovatabua
(Huddersfield-Sheffield Giants); 4 Eparama Navale
(Northern Eagles); 5 Semi Tadulala (Brisbane Wests); 6
Stephen Smith (Otahuhu); 7 Kalaveti Naisoro
Tuiabayaba (Bounty Rum Crushers); 8 Tabua Cakacaka
(Cootamundra); 9 Fred Robart (Te Atatu); 10 Etuate
Vakatawa (Tumbarumba); 11 Josese Tamani
(Cabramatta); 12 Sam Marayawa (Ourimbah); 13
Atunaisa Vunivalu (Serua Dragons).
Subs (all used): 14 Farasiko Tokarei (Nadi Steelers); 15
Mesake Navugona (Bounty Rum Crushers); 16 Amani
Takayawa (Nadi Steelers); 17 Peceli Wawavanua
(Wallangarra).

ENGLAND 76 ....RUSSIA 4
At Knowsley Road, St Helens,
Wednesday 1 November 2000
Attendance: 5,736; **Referee:** Bill Shrimpton
(New Zealand)
England: T - Sinfield (10,40,78), Rowley (12,52),
Peacock (45, 54), Long (59,76), Hay (14), Walker (30),
Pryce (41), Stephenson (67), Deacon (72); G - Farrell
5, Long 5
Russia: G - Mitrofanov 2
England: 1 Paul Wellens (St Helens); 2 Leon Pryce
(Bradford Bulls); 3 Chev Walker (Leeds Rhinos); 4
Keith Senior (Leeds Rhinos); 5 Darren Rogers
(Castleford Tigers); 6 Tony Smith (C) (Wigan
Warriors) ; 7 Paul Deacon (Bradford Bulls); 8 Francis
Stephenson (Wakefield Trinity Wildcats); 9 Paul Rowley
(Halifax Blue Sox); 10 Darren Fleary (Leeds Rhinos); 11
Jamie Peacock (Bradford Bulls); 12 Andy Hay (Leeds
Rhinos); 16 Kevin Sinfield (Leeds Rhinos). Subs (all
used): 14 Sean Long (St Helens); 15 Stuart Spruce
(Bradford Bulls); 16 Stuart Fielden (Bradford Bulls); 17
Harvey Howard (Brisbane Broncos).
Russia: 1 Robert Iliassov (Kazan Arrows); 2 Mikhail
Mitrofanov (Kazan Arrows); 3 Andrei Doumalkine
(Lokomotiv Moscow); 4 Craig Cygler (Cairns Brothers);
5 Maxim Romanov (Kazan Arrows); 6 Andre Olar
(Toulouse); 7 Igor Gavriline (Lokomotiv Moscow); 8 Ian
Rubin (C) (Sydney Roosters); 9 Alexander Lysenkov
(Lokomotiv Moscow); 10 Robert Campbell (Redcliffe);
11 Petr Sokolov (Lokomotiv Moscow); 12 Aaron
Findlay (Canterbury Bulldogs); 13 Joel Rullis (Western
Suburbs). Subs (all used): 14 Pavel Kalachkine (Kazan
Arrows); 15 Victor Netchaev (Lokomotiv Moscow); 16
Igor Jiltsov (Lokomotiv Moscow); 17 Vadim Postnikov
(Lokomotiv Moscow)

AUSTRALIA 110 ....RUSSIA 4
At The Boulevard, Hull, Saturday 4 November 2000
Attendance: 3,044; **Referee:** Stuart Cummings
(England)
Australia: T - Girdler (4, 33, 68), MacDougall (7),
Sailor (10, 38, 46, 79), Barrett (16, 40), Fletcher (24),
Webcke (30), Tallis (50), Croker (52, 55), Hindmarsh
(59, 76), Johns (74), Gidley (80); G - Girdler 17
Russia: T - Donovan (19)
Australia: 1 Adam MacDougall (Newcastle Knights); 5
Wendell Sailor (Brisbane Broncos); 4 Matthew Gidley
(Newcastle Knights); 3 Ryan Girdler (Penrith Panthers);
2 Jason Croker (Canberra Raiders); 6 Trent Barrett (St
George-Illawarra Dragons); 7 Brett Kimmorley
(Melbourne Storm); 8 Shane Webcke (Brisbane
Broncos); 9 Andrew Johns (Newcastle Knights); 10

Robbie Kearns (Melbourne Storm); 11 Gorden Tallis (C) (Brisbane Broncos); 12 Bryan Fletcher (Sydney Roosters); 13 Scott Hill (Melbourne Storm). Subs (all used): 14 Craig Gower (Penrith Panthers); 15 Nathan Hindmarsh (Parramatta Eels); 16 Michael Vella (Parramatta Eels); 17 Ben Kennedy (Newcastle Knights).
Russia: 1 Mikhail Mitrofanov (Kazan Arrows); 5 Rinat Chamsoutdinov (Kazan Arrows); 3 Maxim Romanov (Kazan Arrows); 4 Robert Iliassov (Kazan Arrows); 2 Matthew Donovan (Western Suburbs); 6 Andre Olar (Toulouse); 7 Igor Gavriline (Lokomotiv Moscow); 8 Ian Rubin (C) (Sydney Roosters); 9 Alexander Lysenkov (Lokomotiv Moscow); 10 Robert Campbell (Redcliffe); 11 Kirillin Koulemine (Lokomotiv Moscow); 12 Roustem Garifoulline (Kazan Arrows); 13 Joel Rullis (Western Suburbs). Subs (all used): 14 Pavel Kalachkine (Kazan Arrows); 15 Michael Giorgas (Logan City); 16 Andrei Kuchumov (Moscow Magicians); 17 Viatcheslav Artachine (Kazan Arrows).

ENGLAND 66 ....FIJI 10
At Headingley, Leeds, Saturday 4 November 2000
Attendance: 10,052; **Referee:** Thierry Alibert (France)
England: T - Peacock (17,39,78), Wellens (10,47), Rogers (35,58), Hay (5), Smith (61), Farrell (26), Naylor (26), Radlinski (31); G - Farrell 9
Fiji: T - Navale (21), Tuqiri (75; G - Vunivalu
England: 1 Stuart Spruce (Bradford Bulls); 2 Paul Wellens (St Helens); 3 Scott Naylor (Bradford Bulls); 4 Kris Radlinski (Wigan Warriors); 5 Darren Rogers (Castleford Tigers); 6 Sean Long (St Helens); 7 Paul Deacon (Bradford Bulls); 8 Francis Stephenson (Wakefield Trinity Wildcats); 9 Tony Smith (Wigan Warriors); 10 Paul Anderson (Bradford Bulls); 11 Jamie Peacock (Bradford Bulls); 12 Andy Hay (Leeds Rhinos); 13 Andrew Farrell (C) (Wigan Warriors). Subs (all used): 14 Kevin Sinfield (Leeds Rhinos); 15 Chev Walker (Leeds Rhinos); 16 Stuart Fielden (Bradford Bulls); 17 Harvey Howard (Brisbane Broncos).
Fiji: 1 Lote Tuqiri (C) (Brisbane Broncos); 2 Niko Vakararawa (Lismore Workers); 3 Seteriki Rakabula (Bounty Rum Crushers); 4 Eparama Navale (Northern Eagles); 5 Jimi Bolakoro (Bounty Rum Crushers); 6 Waisale Sovatabua (Huddersfield-Sheffield Giants); 7 Kalaveti Naisoro Tuiabayaba (Bounty Rum Crushers); 8 Etuate Vakatawa (Tumbarumba); 9 Fred Robart (Te Atatu); 10 Tabua Cakacaka (Cootamundra); 11 Peceli Wawavanua (Wallangarra); 12 Samu Marayama (Ourimbah); 13 Atunaisa Vunivalu (Serua Dragons). Subs (all used): 14 Farasiko Tokarei (Nadi Steelers); 15 Josefa Lasagavibau (Nadera Panthers); 16 Roger Matakamikamica (Whitsunday); 17 Peceli Vuniyayawa (Queanbeyan).

GROUP ONE TABLE

	P	W	D	L	F	A	D	Pts
Australia	3	3	0	0	198	14	184	6
England	3	2	0	1	144	36	108	4
Fiji	3	1	0	2	56	144	-88	2
Russia	3	0	0	3	20	224	-204	0

GROUP TWO

LEBANON 0 ....NEW ZEALAND 64
At Kingsholm, Gloucester, Sunday 29 October 2000
Attendance: 2,496; **Referee:** Bill Harrigan (Australia)
New Zealand: T - Talau (11,69), Barnett (15,46), Carroll (23,52), Jellick (34), Vainikolo (37,66), Swann (60), Jones (76,78); G - Jones 6, H Paul 2
Lebanon: 1 Hazem El Masri (Sydney Bulldogs); 2 Najjarin Bilal (St George-Illawarra Dragons); 3 George Katrib (Canterbury Bulldogs); 4 Travis Touma (Sydney Bulls); 5 Hassan Saleh (Canterbury Bulldogs); 6 Jason Stanton (Sydney Bulls); 7 Paul Khoury (Canterbury Bulldogs); 8 Darren Maroon (C) (Sydney Bulls); 9 Anthony Semrani (Canterbury Bulldogs); 10 Moneh Elahmad (Cabramatta); 11 Sami Chamoun (Sydney Bulls); 12 Michael Coorey (Balmain); 13 Joe Lichaa (Sydney Roosters). Subs (all used): 14 Christopher

Salem (St Gaudens); 15 Charlie Nohra (The Oaks); 16 Kandy Tamer (Sydney Bulls); 17 Samer El Masri (Sydney Roosters).
New Zealand: 1 Richie Barnett (C) (Sydney Roosters); 2 Lesley Vainikolo (Canberra Raiders); 3 Tonie Carroll (Brisbane Broncos); 4 Willie Talau (Sydney Bulldogs); 5 Brian Jellick (N Queensland Cowboys); 6 Henry Paul (Bradford Bulls); 7 Stacey Jones (Auckland Warriors); 8 Craig Smith (St George-Illawarra Dragons); 9 Richard Swain (Melbourne Storm); 10 Quentin Pongia (Sydney Roosters); 11 Logan Swann (Auckland Warriors); 12 Stephen Kearney (Melbourne Storm); 13 Ruben Wiki (Canberra Raiders). Subs (all used): 14 Joe Vagana (Auckland Warriors); 15 Robbie Paul (Bradford Bulls); 16 Matt Rua (Melbourne Storm); 17 Nathan Cayless (Parramatta Eels).

WALES 38 ....COOK ISLANDS 6
At the Racecourse Ground, Wrexham,
Sunday 29 October 2000
Attendance: 5,017; **Referee:** Thierry Alibert (France)
Wales: T - Briers (6), Tassell (43, 70, 76), Jenkins (56), Cunningham (68); G - Harris 7
Cook Islands: T - Temata (22); G - Piakura
Wales: 1 Paul Atcheson (St Helens); 2 Paul Sterling (Leeds Rhinos); 3 Jason Critchley (unattached); 3 Kris Tassell (Salford City Reds); 4 Anthony Sullivan (St Helens); 6 Iestyn Harris (C) (Leeds Rhinos); 7 Lee Briers (Warrington Wolves); 8 Anthony Farrell (Leeds Rhinos); 9 Keiron Cunningham (St Helens); 10 Dave Whittle (Leigh Centurions); 11 Justin Morgan (Canberra Raiders); 12 Mick Jenkins (Hull FC); 13 Dean Busby (Warrington Wolves). Subs (all used): 14 Ian Watson (Swinton Lions); 15 Wes Davies (Wigan Warriors); 16 Paul Highton (Salford City Reds); 17 Garreth Carvell (Leeds Rhinos).
Cook Islands: 1 Richard Piakura (Ngatangiia/Matavera); 2 Tangiia Tongia (Canterbury Bulls); 3 Steve Berryman (Wainuimata); 4 Kevin Iro (C) (St Helens); 5 Karl Temata (Hibiscus Coast Raiders); 6 Craig Bowen (Brisbane Wests); 7 Leroy Joe (Hull KR); 8 George Tuakura (Mangere East); 9 Zane Clarke (Cessnock Goannas); 10 Jason Temu (Newcastle Knights); 11 Patrick Kuru (Tumbarumba); 12 Tyrone Pau (Ponsonby Ponies); 13 Anthony Samuel (Workington Town). Subs (all used): 14 Michael Andersson (Caloundra); 15 Peter Lewis (Auckland Warriors); 16 Tere Glassie (Newtown Jets); 17 Adam Cook (Wynnum Manly).
On report: George Tuakura (60) - high tackle, no case to answer

COOK ISLANDS 10 ....NEW ZEALAND 84
At Madejski Stadium, Reading,
Thursday 2 November 2000
Attendance: 3,982; **Referee:** Tim Mander (Australia)
Cook Islands: T - Noovao (33), Iro (74); G - Piakura
New Zealand: T - Barnett (3,65), Vagana (42), Vaealiki (52,79), Vainikolo (48), Lavea (21,24), Robbie Paul (11,16), Cayless (55), Lauitiiti (27), Puletua (36), Wiki (14), Pongia (78); G - Lavea 12
Cook Islands: 1 Richard Piakura (Ngatangiia/Matavera); 2 Tangiia Tongia (Canterbury Bulls); 3 Peter Lewis (Auckland Warriors); 4 Kevin Iro (C) (St Helens); 5 Karl Temata (Hibiscus Coast Raiders); 6 Leroy Joe (Hull KR); 7 Michael Andersson (Caloundra); 8 George Tuakura (Mangere East); 9 Zane Clarke (Cessnock Goannas); 10 Jason Temu (Newcastle Knights); 11 Anthony Samuel (Workington Town); 12 Tere Glassie (Newtown Jets); 13 Meti Noovao (Burleigh Bears). Subs (all used): 14 Craig Bowen (Brisbane Wests); 15 Vaine Kino (Sydney Bulls); 16 Patrick Kuru (Tumbarumba); 17 Sonny Shepherd (Ngatangiia)
New Zealand: 1 Richie Barnett (C) (Sydney Roosters); 2 Nigel Vagana (Auckland Warriors); 3 Richie Blackmore (Leeds Rhinos); 4 David Vaealiki (Parramatta Eels); 5 Lesley Vainikolo (Canberra Raiders); 6 Tasesa Lavea (Melbourne Storm); 7 Robbie Paul (Bradford Bulls); 8 Joe Vagana (Auckland Warriors); 9 Richard Swain (Melbourne Storm); 10 Nathan Cayless (Parramatta Eels); 11 Ali Lauitiiti (Auckland Warriors);

12 Tony Puletua (Penrith Panthers); 13 Ruben Wiki (Canberra Raiders). Subs (all used): 14 Stacey Jones (Auckland Warriors); 15 Craig Smith (St George-Illawarra); 16 Quentin Pongia (Sydney Roosters); 17 Stephen Kearney (Melbourne Storm).

WALES 24 ....LEBANON 22
At Stradey Park, Llanelli, Thursday 2 November 2000
Attendance: 1,497; **Referee:** David Pakieto (New Zealand)
Wales: T - Harris (7, 19), Sterling (13), Cunningham (28), Davies (62); G - Harris 2
Lebanon: T - Coorey (35), S El Masri (43), Saleh (78, 80); G - H El Masri 3
Wales: 1 Paul Atcheson (St Helens); 2 Paul Sterling (Leeds Rhinos); 4 Paul Critchley (unattached); 3 Kris Tassell (Salford City Reds); 5 Anthony Sullivan (St Helens); 6 Iestyn Harris (C) (Leeds Rhinos) ; 7 Lee Briers (Warrington Wolves); 8 Anthony Farrell (Leeds Rhinos); 9 Keiron Cunningham (St Helens); 10 Dave Whittle (Leigh Centurions); 11 Mick Jenkins (Hull FC); 12 Justin Morgan (Canberra Raiders); 13 Dean Busby (Warrington Wolves). Subs (all used): 14 Wes Davies (Wigan Warriors); 15 Chris Morley (Sheffield Eagles); 16 Paul Highton (Salford City Reds); 17 Garreth Carvell (Leeds Rhinos)
Lebanon: 1 Hazem El Masri (C) (Sydney Bulldogs); 2 Samer El Masri (Sydney Roosters); 4 Hassan Saleh (Canterbury Bulldogs); 3 Michael Coorey (Balmain); 5 Mohammed (Wally) Abbas (Canterbury Bulldogs); 6 Fady El Chab (Sydney Bulls); 7 Paul Khoury (Canterbury Bulldogs); 8 Darren Maroon (Sydney Bulls); 9 Anthony Semrani (Canterbury Bulldogs); 10 Moneh Elahmad (Cabramatta); 11 Sami Chamoun (Sydney Bulls); 12 Eben Goddard (St George-Illawarra Dragons); 13 Raymond Daher (Cabramatta). Subs (all used): 14 Christopher Salem (Sydney Bulls); 15 Joe Lichaa (Sydney Roosters); 16 Travis Touma (Sydney Bulls); 17 Kandy Tamer (Sydney Bulls).

COOK ISLANDS 22 ....LEBANON 22
At Millennium Stadium, Cardiff,
Sunday 5 November 2000
Attendance: 5,500; **Referee:** Bill Shrimpton (New Zealand)
Cook Islands: T - Joe (7), Berryman (23,74), Toa (36); G - Berryman 2, Piakura
Lebanon: T - Touma (19), H El Masri (42,78), H Saleh (76); G - H El Masri 3
Cook Islands: 1 Richard Piakura (Ngatangiia/Matavera); 2 Tiri Toa (Manukau); 3 Peter Lewis (Auckland Warriors); 4 Kevin Iro (C) (St Helens); 5 Karl Temata (Hibiscus Coast Raiders); 6 Craig Bowen (Brisbane Wests); 7 Leroy Joe (Hull KR); 8 George Tuakura (Mangere East); 9 Zane Clarke (Cessnock Goannas); 10 Jason Temu (Newcastle Knights); 11 Anthony Samuel (Workington Town); 12 Tyrone Pau (Ponsonby Ponies); 13 Steve Berryman (Wainuiomata). Subs (all used): 14 Michael Andersson (Caloundra); 15 Sonny Shepherd (Ngatangiia); 16 Raymond Ruapuro (Tupapa Marrarenga); 17 Adam Cook (Wynnum Manly).
Lebanon: 1 Muhamed Chahal (Sydney Bulls); 2 Mohammed (Wally) Abbas (Canterbury Bulldogs); 3 Hassan Saleh (Canterbury Bulldogs); 4 Hazem El Masri (C) (Sydney Bulldogs); 5 Travis Touma (Sydney Bulls); 6 Jason Stanton (Sydney Bulls); 7 Samer El Masri (Sydney Roosters); 8 Darren Maroon (Sydney Bulls); 9 Nedol Saleh (Western Suburbs); 10 Sami Chamoun (Sydney Bulls); 11 Chris Salem (St Gaudens); 12 Kandy Tamer (Sydney Bulls); 13 Raymond Daher (Cabramatta). Subs (all used): 14 Paul Khoury (Canterbury Bulldogs); 15 Joe Lichaa (Sydney Roosters); 16 George Katrib (Bulldogs); 17 Charlie Nohra (The Oaks).

WALES 18................................NEW ZEALAND 58
At Millennium Stadium, Cardiff,
Sunday 5 November 2000
Attendance: 17,612; **Referee:** Russell Smith (England)
Wales: T - Briers (31), Atcheson (70), Farrell (74); G - Harris 3

New Zealand: T - Vainikolo (9, 51, 79), Talau (22), Paul (26), Barnett (36, 67), Wiki (40), Carroll (62), Lautiiti (64), N Vagana (77); G - H Paul 5, Lavea 2
Wales: 1 Wes Davies (Wigan Warriors); 2 Paul Sterling (Leeds Rhinos); 3 Hefin O'Hare (Leeds Rhinos); 4 Jason Critchley (unattached); 5 Anthony Sullivan (St Helens); 6 Iestyn Harris (C) (Leeds Rhinos); 7 Lee Briers (Warrington Wolves); 8 Anthony Farrell (Leeds Rhinos); 9 Ian Watson (Swinton Lions); 10 Dave Whittle (Leigh Centurions); 11 Mick Jenkins (Hull FC); 12 Justin Morgan (Canberra Raiders); 13 Chris Morley (Sheffield Eagles). Subs (all used): 14 Barry Eaton (Dewsbury Rams); 15 Paul Atcheson (St Helens); 16 Paul Highton (Salford City Reds); 17 Chris Smith (St Helens).
New Zealand: 1 Richard Barnett (Sydney Roosters); 2 Nigel Vagana (Auckland Warriors); 3 Tonie Carroll (Brisbane Broncos); 4 Willie Talau (Canterbury Bulldogs); 5 Lesley Vainikolo (Canberra Raiders); 6 Henry Paul (Bradford Bulls); 7 Stacey Jones (Auckland Warriors); 8 Craig Smith (St George-Illawarra Dragons); 9 Richard Swain (Melbourne Storm); 10 Nathan Cayless (Parramatta Eels); 11 Matt Rua (Melbourne Storm); 12 Stephen Kearney (Melbourne Storm); 13 Ruben Wiki (Canberra Raiders). Subs (all used): 14 Tasesa Lavea (Melbourne Storm); 15 Joe Vagana (Auckland Warriors); 16 Tony Puletua (Penrith Panthers); 17 Ali Lautiiti (Auckland Warriors)

GROUP TWO TABLE

	P	W	D	L	F	A	D	Pts
New Zealand	3	3	0	0	206	28	178	6
Wales	3	2	0	1	80	86	-6	4
Lebanon	3	0	1	2	44	110	-66	1
Cook Islands	3	0	1	2	38	144	-106	1

GROUP THREE

FRANCE 20 ....PAPUA NEW GUINEA 23
At Charlety Stadium, Paris, Saturday 28 October 2000
Attendance: 7,498; **Referee:** Steve Ganson (England)
France: T - Benausse (14), Dekkiche (27), Hechiche (46, 80); G - Banquet 2
Papua New Guinea: T - Bai (53), Krewanty (56), Buko (70), Lam (77); G - Wilshere 2, Buko; FG - Lam
France: 1 Freddie Banquet (Villeneuve); 2 Yacine Dekkiche (Avignon); 3 Arnaud Dulac (St Gaudens); 4 Jean-Emmanuel Cassin (Toulouse); 5 Patrice Benausse (Toulouse); 6 Laurent Frayssinous (Villeneuve); 7 Fabien Devecchi (C) (Avignon); 8 Rachid Hechiche (Lyon); 9 Vincent Wulf (Villeneuve); 10 Frederic Teixido (Limoux); 11 Jerome Guisset (Warrington Wolves); 12 Gael Tallec (Halifax Blue Sox); 13 Pascal Jampy (UTC). Subs (all used): 14 Abderazak El Khalouki (Toulouse); 15 Laurent Carrasco (Villeneuve); 16 Jason Sands (Limoux); 17 David Despin (Villeneuve).
Papua New Guinea: 1 David Buko (Wagga Wagga); 2 John Wilshere (Brisbane Easts); 3 Eddie Aila (Brisbane Souths); 4 Alfred Songoro (Mackay Souths); 5 Marcus Bai (Melbourne Storm); 6 Stanley Gene (Hull FC); 7 Adrian Lam (C) (Sydney Roosters); 8 Raymond Karl (Enga Mioks); 9 Michael Marum (Port Moresby Vipers); 10 Lucas Solbat (Rabaul Gurias); 11 Duncan Naawi (Redcliffe); 12 Bruce Mamando (N Queensland Cowboys); 13 Tom O'Reilly (Oldham). Subs (all used): 14 Mark Mom (Brisbane Easts); 15 Alex Krewanty (Sydney Bulls); 16 Andrew Norman (Burdekin Roosters); 17 Michael Mondo (Yanco).

SOUTH AFRICA 18 ....TONGA 66
At Charlety Stadium, Paris, Saturday 28 October 2000
Attendance: 7,498; **Referee:** Darren Hopewell (New Zealand)
South Africa: T - Breytenbach (17), Barnard (60), Best (70); G - Bloem 2, O'Shea
Tonga: T - Vaikona (5, 19, 46), W Wolfgramm (54), D Mann (7, 75), Liava'a (26), Masella (36), Moala (40), E Mann (44), Lomi (51), L Kaufusi (63), Mason (80); G - Moala 6, D Mann

South Africa: 1 Tim O'Shea (Johannesburg); 2 Brian Best (Centurion Lions); 3 Leon Barnard (Centurion Lions); 4 Mark Johnson (Salford City Reds); 5 Archer Dames (Pretoria Bulls); 6 Conrad Breytenbach (Pretoria Bulls); 7 Jamie Bloem (C) (Halifax Blue Sox); 8 Jaco Booysen (Centurion Lions); 9 Sean Skelton (Marist, Aus); 10 Eugene Powell (Johannesburg Scorpions); 11 Sean Rutgerson (Canberra Raiders); 12 Quinton de Villiers (Pretoria Bulls); 13 Hercules Erasmus (Centurion Lions). Subs (all used): 14 Justin Jennings (Pretoria Bulls); 15 Corne Nel (Pretoria Bulls); 16 Hendrik Mulder (Centurion Lions); 17 Francois Cloete (Pretoria Bulls).

Tonga: 1 Paul Koloi (South Mackay); 2 Fifita Moala (Melbourne Storm); 3 Tevita Vaikona (Bradford Bulls); 4 Greg Wolfgramm (Canberra Raiders); 5 Lipina Kaufusi (Wests Magpies); 6 Phil Howlett (N Queensland Cowboys); 7 Willie Wolfgramm (Queanbeyan); 8 Martin Masella (C) (Wakefield Trinity Wildcats); 9 Esau Mann (Otahuhu); 10 Talite Liava'a (Auckland Warriors); 11 Willie Mason (Sydney Bulldogs); 12 Andrew Lomu (Sydney Roosters); 13 Duane Mann (Glenora). Subs (all used): 14 David Fisi'iahi (Eastern Tornadoes); 15 Willie Manu (Wests Magpies); 16 Nelson Lomi (Sydney Roosters); 17 Brent Kite (Canberra Raiders)

FRANCE 28 ....**TONGA 8**
At Stade Albert Domec, Carcassonne,
Wednesday 1 November 2000
Attendance: 10,288; **Referee:** Steve Clark (Australia)
France: T - Banquet (26), Sirvent (36), Dulac (66), Garcia (79), Jampy (80)
G - Banquet 4
Tonga: T - D Fisi'iahi (11), P Fisi'iahi (61)
France: 1 Freddie Banquet (Villeneuve); 2 Jean-Marc Garcia (UTC); 3 Jean Emmanuel Cassin (Toulouse); 4 Arnaud Dulac (St Gaudens); 5 Claude Sirvent (St Gaudens); 6 Fabien Devecchi (Avignon); 7 Julien Rinaldi (Villeneuve); 8 Rachid Hechiche (Lyon); 9 Vincent Wulf (Villeneuve); 10 Jason Sands (Villeneuve); 11 Jerome Guisset (Warrington Wolves); 12 Gael Tallec (Halifax Blue Sox); 13 Pascal Jampy (UTC). Subs (all used): 14 David Despin (Villeneuve); 15 Laurent Carrasco (Villeneuve); 16 Romain Sort (Villeneuve); 17 Frederic Teixido (Limoux).
Tonga: 1 Paul Koloi (South Mackay); 2 Fifita Moala (Melbourne Storm); 3 Tevita Vaikona (Bradford Bulls); 4 David Fisi'iahi (Eastern Tornadoes); 5 Lipina Kaufusi (Wests Magpies); 6 Phil Howlett (N Queensland Cowboys); 7 Nuko Hifo (Griffith); 8 Martin Masella (C) (Wakefield Trinity Wildcats); 9 Esau Mann (Otahuhu); 10 Talite Liava'a (Auckland Warriors); 11 Willie Mason (Sydney Bulldogs); 12 Brent Kite (Canberra Raiders); 13 Duane Mann (Glenora). Subs all used: 14 Paul Fisi'iahi (Eastern Tornadoes); 15 Willie Manu (Wests Magpies); 16 Nelson Lomi (Sydney Roosters); 17 Alfons Masella (St George Illawarra Dragons).
Sin bin: Lomi (25) - flop. **On report:** Lomi (74) - alleged late tackle, no case to answer

PAPUA NEW GUINEA 16 ....**SOUTH AFRICA 0**
At Stade Sept Derniers, Toulouse,
Thursday 2 November 2000
Attendance: 4,313; **Referee:** Darren Hopewell (New Zealand)
Papua New Guinea: T - Aila (25), Wilshere (31), Paiyo (52); G - Wilshere 2
Papua New Guinea: 1 David Buko (Wagga Wagga); 2 John Wilshere (Brisbane Easts); 3 Eddie Aila (Brisbane Souths); 4 Alfred Songoro (Mackay Souths); 5 Marcus Bai (Melbourne Storm); 6 Stanley Gene (Hull FC); 7 Adrian Lam (C) (Sydney Roosters); 8 Raymond Karl (Enga Mioks); 9 Mark Mom (Port Moresby Vipers); 10 Michael Mondo (Yanco); 11 Duncan Naawi (Redcliffe); 12 Bruce Mamando (N Queensland Cowboys); 13 Tom O'Reilly (Oldham). Subs (all used): 14 Elias Paiyo (Kellyville); 15 Alex Krewanty (Sydney Bulls); 16 Andrew Norman (Burdekin Roosters); 17 Makali Aizue (Goroka Lahanis).

South Africa: 1 Brian Best (Centurion Lions); 2 Archer Dames (Pretoria Bulls); 3 Mark Johnson (Salford City Reds); 4 Leon Barnard (Centurion Lions); 5 Ian Noble (Northwest Leopards); 6 Pierre Van Wyk (Centurion Lions); 7 Jamie Bloem (C) (Halifax Blue Sox); 8 Jaco Booysen (Centurion Lions); 9 Chris Hurter (Centurion Lions); 10 Eugene Powell (Johannesburg Scorpions); 11 Sean Rutgerson (Canberra Raiders); 12 Quinton de Villiers (Pretoria Bulls); 13 Hercules Erasmus (Centurion Lions). Subs (all used): 14 Justin Jennings (Pretoria Bulls); 15 Corne Nel (Pretoria Bulls); 16 Hendrik Mulder (Centurion Lions); 17 Francois Cloete (Pretoria Bulls).

FRANCE 56 ....**SOUTH AFRICA 6**
At Stade Municipale, Albi, Sunday 5 November 2000
Attendance: 7,969; **Referee:** Steve Clark (Australia)
France: T - Cassin (8, 35), Banquet (21), Guisset (40), Jampy (42, 45, 53), Sirvent (65), Tallec (72);
G - Banquet 10
South Africa: T - de Villiers (79); G - Bloem
France: 1 Freddie Banquet (Villeneuve); 2 Jean-Marc Garcia (UTC); 3 Jean-Emmanuel Cassin (Toulouse); 4 Arnaud Dulac (St Gaudens); 5 Claude Sirvent (St Gaudens); 6 Fabien Devecchi (C) (Avignon); 7 Julien Rinaldi (Villeneuve); 8 Rachid Hechiche (Lyon); 9 Vincent Wulf (Villeneuve); 10 Frederic Teixido (Limoux); 11 Jerome Guisset (Warrington Wolves); 12 Gael Tallec (Halifax Blue Sox); 13 Pascal Jampy (UTC). Subs (all used): 14 David Despin (Villeneuve); 15 Laurent Carrasco (Villeneuve); 16 Romain Sort (Villeneuve); 17 Jason Sands (Limoux).
Sin bin: Hechiche (58) - interference
South Africa: 1 Brian Best (Centurion Lions); 2 Ian Noble (Northwest Leopards); 3 Leon Barnard (Centurion Lions); 4 Mark Johnson (Salford City Reds); 5 Archer Dames (Pretoria Bulls); 6 Pierre Van Wyk (Centurion Lions); 7 Jamie Bloem (C) (Halifax Blue Sox); 8 Jaco Booysen (Centurion Lions); 9 Justin Jennings (Pretoria Bulls); 10 Eugene Powell (Johannesburg Scorpions); 11 Quinton de Villiers (Pretoria Bulls); 12 Sean Rutgerson (Canberra Raiders); 13 Hercules Erasmus (Centurion Lions). Subs (all used): 14 Chris Hurter (Centurion Lions); 15 Jaco Webb (Blue Bulls); 16 Hendrik Mulder (Centurion Lions); 17 Richard Louw (Kempton).
Sin bin: Bloem (31) - interference
Dismissal: Bloem (31) - dissent

PAPUA NEW GUINEA 30 ....**TONGA 22**
At Stade Municipale, St Esteve,
Monday 6 November 2000
Attendance: 3,666; **Referee:** Steve Ganson (England)
Papua New Guinea: T - Mondo (19), Gene (23,66), Buko (34), Karl (51); G - Wilshere 5
Tonga: T - Moala (10, 56), Mason (39), Vaikona (59); G - Moala 3
Papua New Guinea: 1 David Buko (Wagga Wagga); 2 John Wilshere (Brisbane Easts); 3 Eddie Aila (Brisbane Souths); 4 Alfred Songoro (Mackay Souths); 5 Marcus Bai (Melbourne Storm); 6 Stanley Gene (Hull FC); 7 Adrian Lam (C) (Sydney Roosters); 8 Raymond Karl (Enga Mioks); 9 Mark Mom (Port Moresby Vipers); 10 Michael Mondo (Yanco); 11 Duncan Naawi (Redcliffe); 12 Bruce Mamando (N Queensland Cowboys); 13 Tom O'Reilly (Oldham). Subs (all used): 14 Elias Paiyo (Kellyville); 15 Alex Krewanty (Sydney Bulls); 16 Andrew Norman (Burdekin Roosters); 17 Makali Aizue (Goroka Lahanis).
Tonga: 1 Lipina Kaufusi (Wests Magpies); 2 Fifita Moala (Melbourne Storm); 3 Paul Koloi (South Mackay); 4 Greg Wolfgramm (Canberra Raiders); 5 Tevita Vaikona (Bradford Bulls); 6 Phil Howlett (N Queensland Cowboys); 7 Duane Mann (Glenora); 8 Martin Masella (C) (Wakefield Trinity Wildcats); 9 Esau Mann (Otahuhu); 10 Alfons Masella (St George-Illawarra Dragons); 11 Malupo Kaufusi (Wests Magpies); 12 Willie Mason (Canterbury Bulldogs); 13 Willie Manu (Wests Magpies). Subs (all used): 14 David Fisi'iahi (Eastern Tornadoes); 15 Willie Wolfgramm (Queanbeyan); 16 Nelson Lomi (Sydney Roosters); 17 Andrew Lomu (Sydney Roosters).

GROUP THREE TABLE

	P	W	D	L	F	A	D	Pts
Papua New Guinea	3	3	0	0	69	42	27	6
France	3	2	0	1	104	37	67	4
Tonga	3	1	0	2	96	76	20	2
South Africa	3	0	0	3	24	138	-114	0

GROUP FOUR

IRELAND 30 ....SAMOA 16
At Windsor Park, Belfast, Saturday 28 October 2000
Attendance: 3,207; **Referee:** Tim Mander (Australia)
Ireland: T - Joynt (3), Ricketsen (24), Eagar (43), Carney (47), Prescott (57); G - Prescott 5
Samoa: T - Leauma (7), Milford (28), Betham (66); G - Geros 2
Ireland: 1 Steve Prescott (Wakefield Trinity Wildcats); 2 Brian Carney (Hull FC); 6 Michael Withers (Bradford Bulls); 4 Michael Eagar (Castleford Tigers); 5 Mark Forster (Warrington Wolves); 3 Tommy Martyn (St Helens); 7 Ryan Sheridan (Leeds Rhinos); 8 Terry O'Connor (C) (Wigan Warriors); 9 Danny Williams (Melbourne Storm); 10 Barrie McDermott (Leeds Rhinos); 11 Chris Joynt (St Helens); 12 Kevin Campion (Brisbane Broncos); 13 Luke Ricketson (Sydney Roosters). Subs (all used): 14 Liam Bretherton (Leigh Centurions); 15 Johnny Lawless (Huddersfield-Sheffield Giants); 16 David Barnhill (Leeds Rhinos); 17 Paul Southern (Salford City Reds).
On report: McDermott (66) – butting, no case to answer
Samoa: 1 Loa Milford (Balmain Tigers); 2 Bryan Leauma (Penrith Panthers); 3 Anthony Swann (Canberra Raiders); 4 Joe Galuvao (Auckland Warriors); 5 Francis Meli (Auckland Warriors); 6 Simon Geros (Burleigh Bears); 7 Willie Swann (Hunslet Hawks); 8 Frank Puletua (Penrith Panthers); 9 Monty Betham (Auckland Warriors); 10 Jerry Seuseu (Auckland Warriors); 11 David Solomona (Sydney Roosters); 12 Fred Petersen (Penrith Panthers); 13 Willie Poching (Wakefield Trinity Wildcats). Subs: 14 Tony Tatupu (Wakefield Trinity Wildcats); 15 Farvae Kalolo (Auckland Warriors); 16 Mark Leafa (Sydney Bulldogs); 17 Henry Aau Fa'afili (Auckland Warriors) not used.

SCOTLAND 16 ....AOTEAROA MAORI 17
At Firhill Park, Glasgow, Sunday 29 October 2000
Attendance: 2,008; **Referee:** Stuart Cummings (England)
Scotland: T - Penny (18), Maiden (68), Bell (71); G - Mackay, Crowther
Aotearoa Maori: T - Toopi (12, 55), Kidwell (50); G - Ngamu 2; FG - Ngamu
Scotland: 1 Lee Penny (Warrington Wolves); 2 Matt Daylight (Hull FC); 3 Graham Mackay (Leeds Rhinos); 4 Geoff Bell (N Queensland Cowboys); 5 Lee Gilmour (Wigan Warriors) 6 Andrew Purcell (Castleford Tigers); 7 Richard Horne (Hull FC); 8 Daniel Heckenberg (St George-Illawarra Dragons); 9 Danny Russell (C) (Huddersfield-Sheffield Giants); 10 Dale Laughton (Huddersfield-Sheffield Giants); 11 Scott Logan (Sydney Roosters); 12 Scott Cram (London Broncos); 13 Adrian Vowles (Castleford Tigers). Subs (all played): 14 David Maiden (Hull FC); 15 Matt Crowther (Huddersfield-Sheffield Giants); 16 Wayne McDonald (Hull FC); 17 Darren Shaw (Castleford Tigers).
Sin bin: McDonald (40) - fighting
Aotearoa Maori: 1 Clinton Toopi (Auckland Warriors); 2 Odell Manuel (Auckland Warriors); 3 Toa Kohe-Love (Warrington Wolves); 4 David Kidwell (Parramatta Eels); 5 Sean Hoppe (St Helens); 6 Gene Ngamu (Huddersfield-Sheffield Giants); 7 Hare Te Rangi (Otahuhu Leopards); 8 Paul Rauhihi (Newcastle Knights); 9 Henry Perenara (Auckland Warriors); 10 Terry Hermansson (Auckland Warriors); 11 Wairangi Koopu (Auckland Warriors); 12 Tyran Smith (Wests Tigers); 13 Tawera Nikau (Warrington Wolves). Subs (all played): 14 Martin Moana (Halifax Blue Sox); 15 Kylie Leuluai (Wests Tigers); 16 Chris Nahi (Brisbane Easts); 17 Tahi Reihana (Brisbane Souths).
Sin bin: Nikau (40) - fighting

IRELAND 18 ....SCOTLAND 6
At Tolka Park, Dublin, Wednesday 1 November 2000
Attendance: 1,782; **Referee:** Russell Smith (England)
Ireland: T - Sheridan (2), Withers (68); G - Prescott 5
Scotland: T - Arnold (37); G - Crowther
Ireland: 1 Steve Prescott (Wakefield Trinity Wildcats); 2 Brian Carney (Hull FC); 6 Michael Withers (Bradford Bulls); 4 Michael Eagar (Castleford Tigers); 5 Ian Herron (Hull FC); 3 Tommy Martyn (St Helens); 7 Ryan Sheridan (Leeds Rhinos); 8 Terry O'Connor (C) (Wigan Warriors); 9 Johnny Lawless (Huddersfield-Sheffield Giants); 10 Barrie McDermott (Leeds Rhinos); 11 Chris Joynt (St Helens); 12 Kevin Campion (Brisbane Broncos); 13 Luke Ricketson (Sydney Roosters). Subs (all used): 14 Danny Williams (Melbourne Storm); 15 Jamie Mathiou (Leeds Rhinos); 16 David Barnhill (Leeds Rhinos); 17 Dave Bradbury (Huddersfield-Sheffield Giants)
Scotland: 1 Danny Arnold (Huddersfield-Sheffield Giants); 2 Matt Daylight (Hull FC); 3 Lee Gilmour (Wigan Warriors); 4 Geoff Bell (N Queensland Cowboys); 5 Matt Crowther (Huddersfield-Sheffield Giants); 6 Richard Horne (Hull FC); 7 Scott Rhodes (Leeds Rhinos); 8 Daniel Heckenberg (St George-Illawarra Dragons); 9 Danny Russell (Huddersfield-Sheffield Giants) (C); 10 Dale Laughton (Huddersfield-Sheffield Giants); 11 Scott Logan (Sydney Roosters); 12 Scott Cram (London Broncos); 13 Adrian Vowles (Castleford Tigers). Subs (all played): 14 David Maiden (Hull FC); 15 Nathan Graham (Dewsbury Rams); 16 Wayne McDonald (Hull FC); 17 Darren Shaw (Castleford Tigers)
Sin bin: Vowles (59) - persistent offside

SAMOA 21 ....AOTEAROA MAORI 16
At Derwent Park, Workington, Wednesday 1 November 2000
Attendance: 4,107; **Referee:** Bill Harrigan (Australia)
Samoa: T - Fa'afili (42, 54), W Swann (57), Milford (79); G - Poching 2; FG - W Swann
Maori: T - Matthews (2), Nelson (49), Rauhihi (70); G - Goodwin 2
Samoa: 1 Loa Milford (Balmain Tigers); 2 Francis Meli (Auckland Warriors); 3 Anthony Swann (Canberra Raiders); 4 Joe Galuvao (Auckland Warriors); 5 Bryan Leauma (Penrith Panthers); 6 Henry Aau Fa'afili (Auckland Warriors); 7 Willie Swann (Hunslet Hawks); 8 Frank Puletua (Penrith Panthers); 9 Monty Betham (Auckland Warriors); 10 Jerry Seuseu (Auckland Warriors); 11 David Solomona (Sydney Roosters); 12 Mark Leafa (Sydney Bulldogs); 13 Willie Poching (C) (Wakefield Trinity Wildcats). Subs (all used): 14 Tony Tatupu (Wakefield Trinity Wildcats); 15 Philip Leuluai (Auckland Warriors); 16 Simon Geros (Burleigh Bears); 17 Max Fala (Northcote Tigers).
Aotearoa Maori: 1 Clinton Toopi (Auckland Warriors); 2 Jarred Mills (Newtown); 3 Paul Whatuira (Auckland Warriors); 4 Boycie Nelson (Glenora Bears); 5 Steve Matthews (Glenora Bears); 6 Luke Goodwin (Newtown); 7 Jeremy Smith (Sydney Roosters); 8 Paul Rauhihi (Newcastle Knights); 9 James Cook (Northcote Tigers); 10 Tahi Reihana (Brisbane Souths); 11 Kylie Leuluai (Wests Tigers); 12 Tyran Smith (Wests Tigers); 13 Tawera Nikau (Warrington Wolves). Subs (all played): 14 Toa Kohe-Love (Warrington Wolves); 15 Martin Moana (Halifax Blue Sox); 16 David Kidwell (Parramatta Eels); 17 Terry Hermansson (Auckland Warriors).

IRELAND 30 ....AOTEAROA MAORI 16
At Tolka Park, Dublin, Saturday 4 November 2000
Attendance: 3,164; **Referee:** Bill Harrigan (Australia)
Ireland: T - Forster (34), Carney (40), Barnhill (47), Withers (61), Sheridan (80); G - Prescott 5
Maori: T - Nelson (52), Te Rangi (69), Koopu (78); G - Perenara, Ngamu
Ireland: 1 Steve Prescott (Wakefield Trinity Wildcats); 2 Brian Carney (Hull FC); 3 Michael Withers (Bradford Bulls); 4 Luke Ricketson (Sydney City Roosters); 5 Mark Forster (Warrington Wolves); 6 Gavin Clinch (Huddersfield-Sheffield Giants); 7 Ryan Sheridan (Leeds

231

Rugby League World Cup Statistics

Rhinos); 8 Terry O'Connor (C) (Wigan Warriors); 9 Danny Williams (Melbourne Storm); 10 Barrie McDermott (Leeds Rhinos); 11 Chris Joynt (St Helens); 12 David Barnhill (Leeds Rhinos); 13 Kevin Campion (Brisbane Broncos). Subs (all used): 14 Liam Bretherton (Leigh Centurions); 15 Johnny Lawless (Huddersfield-Sheffield Giants); 16 Liam Tallon (Brisbane Norths); 17 Paul Southern (Salford City Reds).

Aotearoa Maori: 1 Clinton Toopi (Auckland Warriors); 2 Odell Manuel (Auckland Warriors); 3 Toa Kohe-Love (Warrington Wolves); 4 David Kidwell (Parramatta Eels); 5 Sean Hoppe (St Helens); 6 Gene Ngamu (Huddersfield-Sheffield Giants); 7 Hare Te Rangi (Otahuhu Leopards); 8 Paul Rauhihi (Newcastle Knights); 9 Henry Perenara (Auckland Warriors); 10 Terry Hermansson (Auckland Warriors); 11 Wairangi Koopu (Auckland Warriors); 12 Tyran Smith (Wests Tigers); 13 Tawera Nikau (Warrington Wolves). Subs (all used): 14 Martin Moana (Halifax Blue Sox); 15 Boycie Nelson (Glenora Bears); 16 Chris Nahi (Brisbane Easts); 17 Tahi Reihana (Brisbane Souths).

SCOTLAND 12 ....SAMOA 20
At Tynecastle, Edinburgh, Sunday 5 November 2000
Attendance: 1,579; **Referee:** David Pakieto (New Zealand)
Scotland: T - Vowles (44), Rhodes (47); G - Crowther 2
Samoa: T - Leauma (17, 58), Solomona (21), Milford (31); G - Laloata 2
Scotland: 1 Danny Arnold (Huddersfield-Sheffield Giants); 5 Matt Crowther (Huddersfield-Sheffield Giants); 3 Lee Gilmour (Wigan Warriors); 4 Geoff Bell (North Queensland Cowboys); 2 Matt Daylight (Hull FC); 6 Andrew Purcell (Castleford Tigers); 7 Richard Horne (Hull FC); 8 Daniel Heckenberg (St George-Illawarra Dragons); 9 Danny Russell (C) (Huddersfield-Sheffield Giants); 10 Dale Laughton (Huddersfield-Sheffield Giants); 11 Scott Logan (Sydney Roosters); 12 Scott Cram (London Broncos); 13 Adrian Vowles (Castleford Tigers). Subs (all played): 14 Scott Rhodes (Leeds Rhinos); 15 David Maiden (Hull FC); 16 Wayne McDonald (Hull FC); 17 Darren Shaw (Castleford Tigers).
Samoa: 1 Loa Milford (Wests Tigers); 5 Bryan Leauma (Penrith Panthers); 3 Anthony Swann (Canberra Raiders); 4 Shane Laloata (Nelson Bay); 2 Peter Lima (Toulouse); 6 Henry Aau Fa'afili (Auckland Warriors); 7 Albert Talapeau (Sydney Roosters); 8 Frank Puletua (Penrith Panthers); 9 Monty Betham (Auckland Warriors); 10 Jerry Seuseu (Auckland Warriors); 11 David Solomona (Sydney Roosters); 12 Tony Tatupu (Wakefield Trinity Wildcats); 13 Willie Poching (C) (Wakefield Trinity Wildcats). Subs (all used): 14 Willie Swann (Hunslet Hawks); 15 Philip Leuluai (Auckland Warriors); 16 Mark Leafa (Canterbury Bulldogs); 17 Max Fala (Northcote Tigers).

GROUP FOUR TABLE

	P	W	D	L	F	A	D	Pts
Ireland	3	3	0	0	78	38	40	6
Samoa	3	2	0	1	57	58	-1	4
Maori	3	1	0	2	49	67	-18	2
Scotland	3	0	0	3	34	55	-21	0

AUSTRALIA 66 ....SAMOA 10
At Vicarage Road, Watford, Saturday 11 November 2000
Attendance: 5,404; **Referee:** Stuart Cummings (England)
Australia: T - Girdler (5), Fittler (24), Fletcher (27, 70, 73), Sailor (40), Johns (42, 80), Hill (50, 78), MacDougall (57, 75); G - Rogers 9
Samoa: T - Solomona (33), Leauma (63); G - Laloata
Australia: 1 Darren Lockyer (Brisbane Broncos); 5 Wendell Sailor (Brisbane Broncos); 4 Matthew Gidley (Newcastle Knights); 3 Ryan Girdler (Penrith Panthers); 2 Mat Rogers (Cronulla Sharks); 6 Brad Fittler (C) (Sydney Roosters); 7 Brett Kimmorley (Melbourne Storm); 8 Shane Webcke (Brisbane Broncos); 9 Andrew Johns (Newcastle Knights); 10 Robbie Kearns (Melbourne Storm); 11 Gorden Tallis (Brisbane Broncos); 12 Bryan Fletcher (Sydney Roosters); 13 Scott Hill (Melbourne Storm). Subs (all used): 14 Adam MacDougall (Newcastle Knights); 15 Jason Croker (Canberra Raiders); 16 Darren Britt (Sydney Bulldogs); 17 Jason Stevens (Cronulla Sharks).
Samoa: 1 Laloa Milford (Wests Tigers); 2 Bryan Leauma (Penrith Panthers); 3 Anthony Swann (Canberra Raiders); 4 Shane Laloata (Nelson Bay); 5 Peter Lima (Toulouse); 6 Henry Aau Fa'afili (Auckland Warriors); 7 Willie Swann (Hunslet Hawks); 8 Frank Puletua (Penrith Panthers); 9 Monty Betham (Auckland Warriors); 10 Jerry Seuseu (Auckland Warriors); 11 David Solomona (Sydney Roosters); 12 Philip Leuluai (Auckland Warriors); 13 Willie Poching (C) (Wakefield Trinity Wildcats). Subs (all used): 14 Tony Tatupu (Wakefield Trinity Wildcats); 15 Mark Leafa (Canterbury Bulldogs); 16 Max Fala (Northcote Tigers); 17 Francis Meli (Auckland Warriors).

ENGLAND 26 ....IRELAND 16
At Headingley, Leeds, Saturday 11 November 2000
Attendance: 15,405; **Referee:** Tim Mander (Australia)
England: T - Senior (4), Peacock (39), Smith (59), Walker (69); G - Farrell 5
Ireland: T - Withers (8,78), Martyn (12); G - Prescott 2
England: 1 Paul Wellens (St Helens); 2 Chev Walker (Leeds Rhinos); 4 Kris Radlinski (Wigan Warriors); 4 Keith Senior (Leeds Rhinos); 5 Darren Rogers (Castleford Tigers); 6 Sean Long (St Helens); 7 Paul Deacon (Bradford Bulls); 8 Stuart Fielden (Bradford Bulls); 9 Paul Rowley (Halifax Blue Sox); 10 Paul Anderson (Bradford Bulls); 11 Adrian Morley (Leeds Rhinos); 12 Mike Forshaw (Bradford Bulls); 13 Andrew Farrell (C) (Wigan Warriors). Subs (all used): 14 Tony Smith (Wigan Warriors); 15 Scott Naylor (Bradford Bulls); 16 Jamie Peacock (Bradford Bulls); 17 Harvey Howard (Bradford Broncos).
Ireland: 1 Steve Prescott (Wakefield Trinity Wildcats); 2 Brian Carney (Hull FC); 6 Michael Withers (Bradford Bulls); 4 Michael Eagar (Castleford Tigers); 5 Mark Forster (Warrington Wolves); 3 Tommy Martyn (St Helens); 7 Ryan Sheridan (Leeds Rhinos); 8 Terry O'Connor (C) (Wigan Warriors); 9 Danny Williams (Melbourne Storm); 10 Barrie McDermott (Leeds Rhinos); 11 Chris Joynt (St. Helens); 12 Kevin Campion (Brisbane Broncos); 13 Luke Ricketson (Sydney Roosters). Subs (all used): 14 Gavin Clinch (Huddersfield-Sheffield Giants); 15 David Barnhill (Leeds Rhinos); 16 Jamie Mathiou (Leeds Rhinos); 17 Paul Southern (Salford City Reds).
Sin bin: Steve Prescott (52) – holding down.
On report: Barrie McDermott (45) – high tackle

NEW ZEALAND 54................................FRANCE 6
At The Jungle, Castleford, Sunday 12 November 2000
Attendance: 5,158; **Referee:** Bill Harrigan (Australia)
New Zealand: T - Rua (3), Pongia (18), Smith (20), R Paul (31, 43, 65), Kearney (39), Jellick (48), Talau (50), Blackmore (62); G - H Paul 7
France: T - Sirvent (59); G - Banquet
New Zealand: 1 Richie Barnett (C) (Sydney Roosters); 2 Brian Jellick (North Queensland Cowboys); 3 Richie

Blackmore (Leeds Rhinos); 4 Willie Talau (Canterbury Bulldogs); 5 Nigel Vagana (Auckland Warriors); 6 Henry Paul (Bradford Bulls); 7 Robbie Paul (Bradford Bulls); 8 Craig Smith (St George-Illawarra Dragons); 9 Richard Swain (Melbourne Storm); 10 Quentin Pongia (Sydney City Roosters); 11 Matt Rua (Melbourne Storm); 12 Stephen Kearney (Melbourne Storm); 13 Logan Swann (Auckland Warriors). Subs (all used): 14 Nathan Cayless (Parramatta Eels); 15 Joe Vagana (Auckland Warriors); 16 Ruben Wiki (Canberra Raiders); 17 Tonie Carroll (Brisbane Broncos).
France: 1 Freddie Banquet (Villeneuve); 5 Claude Sirvent (St-Gaudens); 4 Arnaud Dulac (St-Gaudens); 3 Jean-Emmanuel Cassin (Toulouse); 2 Jean-Marc Garcia (UTC); 6 Fabien Devecchi (C) (Avignon); 7 Julien Rinaldi (Villeneuve); 8 Rachid Hechiche (Lyon); 9 Vincent Wulf (Villeneuve); 10 Jason Sands (Limoux); 11 Jerome Guisset (Warrington Wolves); 12 Gael Tallec (Halifax Blue Sox); 13 Pascal Jampy (UTC). Subs (all used): 14 David Despin (Villeneuve); 15 Laurent Carrasco (Villeneuve); 16 Romain Sort (Villeneuve); 17 Frederic Teixido (Limoux)

WALES 22 ....PAPUA NEW GUINEA 8
At Auto Quest Stadium, Widnes,
Sunday 12 November 2000
Attendance: 5,211; **Referee:** David Pakieto (New Zealand)
Wales: T - Critchley (21), Briers (25), Davies (38); G - Harris 5
Papua New Guinea: T - Wilshere (70); G - Wilshere 2
Wales: 1 Paul Atcheson (St Helens); 2 Paul Sterling (Leeds Rhinos); 4 Jason Critchley (unattached); 3 Kris Tassell (Salford City Reds); 5 Anthony Sullivan (St Helens); 6 Iestyn Harris (C) (Leeds Rhinos); 7 Lee Briers (Warrington Wolves); 8 Anthony Farrell (Leeds Rhinos); 9 Keiron Cunningham (St Helens); 10 Justin Morgan (Canberra Raiders); 11 Mick Jenkins (Hull FC); 12 Paul Highton (Salford City Reds); 13 Dean Busby (Warrington Wolves). Subs (all used): 14 Wes Davies (Wigan Warriors); 15 Chris Morley (Sheffield Eagles); 16 John Devereux (unattached); 17 Paul Moriarty (unattached).
Papua New Guinea: 1 David Buko (Wagga Wagga); 2 John Wilshere (Brisbane Easts); 3 Eddie Aila (Brisbane Souths); 4 Alfred Songoro (Mackay Souths); 5 Marcus Bai (Melbourne Storm); 6 Stanley Gene (Hull FC); 7 Adrian Lam (C) (Wigan Warriors); 8 Raymond Karl (Enga Mioks); 9 Mark Mom (Port Moresby Vipers); 10 Michael Mondo (Yanco); 11 Duncan Naawi (Redcliffe); 12 Bruce Mamando (N Queensland Cowboys); 13 Tom O'Reilly (Oldham). Subs (all used): 14 Elias Paiyo (Kellyville); 15 Alex Krewanty (Sydney Bulls); 16 Andrew Norman (Burdekin Roosters); 17 Makali Aizue (Goroka Lahanis).
On report: Mondo (78) - dangerous tackle

SEMI-FINALS

AUSTRALIA 46 ....WALES 22
At McAlpine Stadium, Huddersfield,
Sunday 19 November 2000
Attendance: 8,124; **Referee:** Russell Smith (England)
Australia: T - Kimmorley (5), Sailor (11), Fittler (28, 61), Fletcher (54), Lockyer (57, 64), Gower (70), Kennedy (80); G - Lockyer 4; Girdler
Wales: T - Watson (14), Tassell (18), Briers (23); G - Harris 4; FG - Briers 2
Australia: 1 Darren Lockyer (Brisbane Broncos); 5 Wendell Sailor (Brisbane Broncos); 4 Matthew Gidley (Newcastle Knights); 3 Ryan Girdler (Penrith Panthers); 2 Adam MacDougall (Newcastle Knights); 6 Brad Fittler (C) (Sydney Roosters); 7 Brett Kimmorley (Melbourne Storm); 8 Shane Webcke (Brisbane Broncos); 9 Craig Gower (Penrith Panthers); 10 Michael Vella (Parramatta Eels); 11 Gorden Tallis (Brisbane Broncos); 12 Bryan Fletcher (Sydney Roosters); 13 Scott Hill (Melbourne Storm). Subs (all used): 14 Trent Barrett (St George-Illawarra Dragons); 15 Robbie Kearns (Melbourne Storm); 16 Ben Kennedy (Newcastle Knights); 17 Nathan Hindmarsh (Parramatta Eels).

On report: Webcke (77) - striking, no case to answer
Wales: 1 Iestyn Harris (C) (Leeds Rhinos); 2 Chris Smith (St Helens); 4 Jason Critchley (unattached); 3 Kris Tassell (Salford City Reds); 5 Anthony Sullivan (St Helens); 6 Lee Briers (Warrington Wolves); 7 Ian Watson (Widnes Vikings); 8 Anthony Farrell (Leeds Rhinos); 9 Keiron Cunningham (St Helens); 10 Paul Moriarty (unattached); 11 Justin Morgan (Canberra Raiders); 12 Paul Highton (Salford City Reds); 13 Chris Morley (Sheffield Eagles). Subs (all used): 14 Wes Davies (Wigan Warriors); 15 Paul Atcheson (St Helens); 16 John Devereux (unattached); 17 David Luckwell (Batley Bulldogs).

ENGLAND 6 ....NEW ZEALAND 49
At Reebok Stadium, Bolton,
Saturday 18 November 2000
Attendance: 16,032; **Referee:** Referee: Tim Mander (Australia)
England: T - Smith (44); G - Farrell
New Zealand: T - Vainikolo (33,56), Talau (48,62), Kearney (2), Wiki (36), N. Vagana (53), Swann (75); Goals: H Paul 8; G - H Paul 8; FG - H Paul
England: 1 Kris Radlinski (Wigan Warriors); 2 Chev Walker (Leeds Rhinos); 3 Scott Naylor (Bradford Bulls); 4 Keith Senior (Leeds Rhinos); 5 Paul Wellens (St Helens); 7 Sean Long (St Helens); 6 Paul Deacon (Bradford Bulls); 8 Stuart Fielden (Bradford Bulls); 9 Tony Smith (Wigan Warriors); 10 Harvey Howard (Brisbane Broncos); 11 Paul Sculthorpe (St Helens); 12 Mike Forshaw (Bradford Bulls); 13 Andrew Farrell (C) (Wigan Warriors). Subs (all used): 14 Jamie Peacock (Bradford Bulls); 15 Andy Hay (Leeds Rhinos); 16 Darren Fleary (Leeds Rhinos); 17 Paul Anderson (Bradford Bulls).
On report: Darren Fleary (39) – late, high tackle
New Zealand: 1 Richie Barnett (C) (Sydney City Roosters); 2 Nigel Vagana (Auckland Warriors); 3 Tonie Carroll (Brisbane Broncos); 4 Willie Talau (Canterbury Bulldogs); 5 Lesley Vainikolo (Canberra Raiders); 6 Henry Paul (Bradford Bulls); 7 Stacey Jones (Auckland Warriors); 8 Craig Smith (St George-Illawarra); 9 Richard Swain (Melbourne Storm); 10 Quentin Pongia (Sydney City Roosters); 11 Matt Rua (Melbourne Storm); 12 Stephen Kearney (Melbourne Storm); 13 Ruben Wiki (Canberra Raiders). Subs (all used): 14 Robbie Paul (Bradford Bulls); 15 Joe Vagana (Auckland Warriors); 16 Nathan Cayless (Parramatta Eels); 17 Logan Swann (Auckland Warriors).

FINAL

AUSTRALIA 40 ....NEW ZEALAND 12
At Old Trafford, Manchester,
Saturday 25 November 2000
Attendance: 44,329; **Referee:** Stuart Cummings (England)
Australia: T - Gidley (26), Hindmarsh (46), Lockyer (53), Sailor (66, 69), Fittler (74), Barrett (76); G - Rogers 6
New Zealand: T - Vainikolo (50), Carroll (57); G - H Paul 2
Australia: 1 Darren Lockyer (Brisbane Broncos); 5 Wendell Sailor (Brisbane Broncos); 4 Matthew Gidley (Newcastle Knights); 3 Adam MacDougall (Newcastle Knights); 2 Mat Rogers (Cronulla Sharks); 6 Brad Fittler (C) (Sydney Roosters); 7 Brett Kimmorley (Melbourne Storm); 8 Shane Webcke (Brisbane Broncos); 9 Andrew Johns (Newcastle Knights); 10 Robbie Kearns (Melbourne Storm); 11 Gorden Tallis (Brisbane Broncos); 12 Bryan Fletcher (Sydney Roosters); 13 Scott Hill (Melbourne Storm). Subs (all used): 17 Jason Stevens (Cronulla Sharks) for Webcke (13); 16 Darren Britt (Sydney Bulldogs) for Kearns (20); 15 Nathan Hindmarsh (Parramatta Eels) for Fletcher (20); Fletcher for Tallis (27); Webcke for Stevens (57); Tallis for Fletcher (62); 14 Trent Barrett (St George-Illawarra Dragons) for MacDougall (64); Kearns for Hindmarsh (78)

Rugby League World Cup Statistics

New Zealand: 1 Richie Barnett (C) (Sydney City Roosters); 2 Nigel Vagana (Auckland Warriors); 3 Tonie Carroll (Brisbane Broncos); 4 Willie Talau (Canterbury Bulldogs); 5 Lesley Vainikolo (Canberra Raiders); 6 Henry Paul (Bradford Bulls); 7 Stacey Jones (Auckland Warriors); 8 Craig Smith (St George-Illawarra Dragons); 9 Richard Swain (Melbourne Storm); 10 Quentin Pongia (Sydney City Roosters); 11 Matt Rua (Melbourne Storm); 12 Stephen Kearney (Melbourne Storm); 13 Ruben Wiki (Canberra Raiders). Subs (all played): 16 Nathan Cayless (Parramatta Eels) for Smith (14); 15 Joe Vagana (Auckland Warriors) for Pongia (14); 17 Logan Swann (Auckland Warriors) for Rua (20); Pongia for J Vagana (31); Smith for Cayless (31); Rua for Wiki (41); 14 Robbie Paul (Bradford Bulls) for Swain (58); J Vagana for Smith (58); Cayless for Pongia (58); Wiki for Kearney (70); Smith for J Vagana (75); Pongia for Cayless (75).

THE 2000 SQUADS

AUSTRALIA *(Coach: Chris Anderson)*

	M	T	G	FG	Pts
Trent Barrett (St George Illawarra)	4	4	0	0	16
Darren Britt (Sydney Bulldogs)	3	0	0	0	0
Jason Croker (Canberra Raiders)	4	2	0	0	8
Brad Fittler (Sydney Roosters)	5	4	0	0	16
Bryan Fletcher (Sydney Roosters)	5	5	0	0	20
Matthew Gidley (Newcastle Knights)	6	4	0	0	16
Ryan Girdler (Penrith Panthers)	5	6	18	0	60
Craig Gower (Penrith Panthers)	3	1	0	0	4
Scott Hill (Melbourne Storm)	6	2	0	0	8
Nathan Hindmarsh (Parramatta Eels)	4	4	0	0	16
Andrew Johns (Newcastle Knights)	5	3	0	0	12
Robbie Kearns (Melbourne Storm)	6	0	0	0	0
Ben Kennedy (Newcastle Knights)	3	3	0	0	12
Brett Kimmorley (Melbourne Storm)	5	1	0	0	4
Darren Lockyer (Brisbane Broncos)	5	3	4	0	20
Adam MacDougall (Newcastle Knights)	6	5	0	0	20
Mat Rogers (Cronulla Sharks)	4	4	27	0	70
Wendell Sailor (Brisbane Broncos)	5	10	0	0	40
Jason Stevens (Cronulla Sharks)	4	0	0	0	0
Gorden Tallis (Brisbane Broncos)	5	1	0	0	4
Michael Vella (Parramatta Eels)	3	0	0	0	0
Shane Webcke (Brisbane Broncos)	6	1	0	0	4

COOK ISLANDS *(Coach: Stan Martin)*

	M	T	G	FG	Pts
Michael Andersson (Caloundra)	3	0	0	0	0
Steve Berryman (Wainuimata)	2	2	2	0	12
Craig Bowen (Brisbane Wests)	3	0	0	0	0
Zane Clarke (Cessnock Goannas)	3	0	0	0	0
Adam Cook (Wynnum Manly)*	2	0	0	0	0
Tere Glassie (Newtown Jets)	2	0	0	0	0
Kevin Iro (St Helens)	3	1	0	0	4
Leroy Joe (Hull KR)	3	1	0	0	4
Vaine Kino (Sydney Bulls)	1	0	0	0	0
Patrick Kuru (Tumbarumba)	2	0	0	0	0
Peter Lewis (Auckland Warriors)	3	0	0	0	0
Meti Noovao (Burleigh Bears)	1	1	0	0	4
Tyrone Pau (Ponsonby Ponies)	2	0	0	0	0
Richard Piakura (Ngatangiia/Matavera)	3	0	3	0	6
Raymond Ruapuro (Tupapa Marrarenga)	1	0	0	0	0
Anthony Samuel (Workington Town)	3	0	0	0	0
Sonny Shepherd (Ngatangiia)	2	0	0	0	0
Karl Temata (Hibiscus Coast Raiders)	3	1	0	0	4
Jason Temu (Newcastle Knights)	3	0	0	0	0
Tiri Toa (Manukau)	1	1	0	0	4
Tangiia Tongia (Canterbury Bulls)	2	0	0	0	0
George Tuakura (Mangere East)	3	0	0	0	0

* later known as Adam Watene

ENGLAND *(Coach: John Kear)*

	M	T	G	FG	Pts
Paul Anderson (Bradford Bulls)	4	0	0	0	0
Paul Deacon (Bradford Bulls)	4	1	0	0	4
Andy Farrell (Wigan Warriors)	5	1	21	0	46
Stuart Fielden (Bradford Bulls)	5	0	0	0	0
Darren Fleary (Leeds Rhinos)	3	0	0	0	0

Mike Forshaw (Bradford Bulls)	3	0	0	0	0
Andy Hay (Leeds Rhinos)	3	2	0	0	8
Harvey Howard (Brisbane Broncos)	5	0	0	0	0
Sean Long (St Helens)	5	2	5	0	18
Adrian Morley (Leeds Rhinos)	2	0	0	0	0
Scott Naylor (Bradford Bulls)	4	1	0	0	4
Jamie Peacock (Bradford Bulls)	4	6	0	0	24
Leon Pryce (Bradford Bulls)	2	1	0	0	4
Kris Radlinski (Wigan Warriors)	4	1	0	0	4
Darren Rogers (Castleford Tigers)	3	2	0	0	8
Paul Rowley (Halifax Blue Sox)	3	2	0	0	8
Paul Sculthorpe (St Helens)	1	0	0	0	0
Keith Senior (Leeds Rhinos)	4	1	0	0	4
Kevin Sinfield (Leeds Rhinos)	3	3	0	0	12
Tony Smith (Wigan Warriors)	4	3	0	0	12
Stuart Spruce (Bradford Bulls)	2	0	0	0	0
Francis Stephenson (Wakefield Trinity Wildcats)	2	1	0	0	4
Chev Walker (Leeds Rhinos)	5	2	0	0	8
Paul Wellens (St Helens)	5	2	0	0	8

FIJI *(Coach: Don Furner)*

	M	T	G	FG	Pts
Jim Bolokaro (Bounty Rum Crushers)	1	0	0	0	0
Tabua Cakacaka (Cootamundra)	3	1	0	0	4
Jone Kuruduadua (Bellingen-Dorrigo)	2	1	0	0	4
Josefa Lasagavibau (Nadera Panthers)	2	0	0	0	0
Sam Marayawa (Ourimba)	3	0	0	0	0
Roger Matakamikamica (Whitsunday)	1	0	0	0	0
Kalaveti Naisoro Tuiabayaba (Bounty Rum Crushers)	3	0	0	0	0
Mesake Navugona (Bounty Rum Crushers)	1	0	0	0	0
Eparama Navale (Northern Eagles)	3	1	0	0	4
Setareki Rakabula (Bounty Rum Crushers)	1	0	0	0	0
Fred Robart (Te Atatu)	3	0	0	0	0
Stephen Smith (Otahuhu)	2	0	0	0	0
Waisale Sovatabua (Huddersfield-Sheffield Giants)	3	1	0	0	4
Semi Tadulala (Brisbane Wests)	2	0	0	0	0
Amani Takayawa (Nadi Steelers)	2	0	0	0	0
Josese Tamani (Cabramatta)	2	0	0	0	0
Farasiko Tokarei (Nadi Steelers)	3	0	0	0	0
Lote Tuqiri (Brisbane Broncos)	3	4	5	0	26
Niko Vakararawa (Lismore Workers)	1	0	0	0	0
Etuate Vakatawa (Tumbarumba)	3	0	0	0	0
Atunaisa Vunivalu (Serua Dragons)	3	3	1	0	14
Peceli Vuniyayana (Queanbeyan)	2	0	0	0	0
Peceli Wawavanua (Wallangarra)	2	0	0	0	0

FRANCE *(Coach: Gilles Dumas)*

	M	T	G	FG	Pts
Freddie Banquet (Villeneuve)	4	2	17	0	42
Patrice Benausse (Toulouse)	1	1	0	0	4
Laurent Carrasco (Villeneuve)	4	0	0	0	0
Jean-Emmanuel Cassin (Toulouse)	4	2	0	0	8
Yacine Dekkiche (Avignon)	1	1	0	0	4
David Despin (Villeneuve)	4	0	0	0	0
Fabien Devecchi (Avignon)	4	0	0	0	0
Arnaud Dulac (St Gaudens)	4	1	0	0	4
Abderazak El Khalouki (Toulouse)	1	0	0	0	0
Laurent Frayssinous (Villeneuve)	1	0	0	0	0
Jean-Marc Garcia (UTC)	3	1	0	0	4
Jerome Guisset (Warrington Wolves)	4	1	0	0	4
Rachid Hechiche (Lyon)	4	2	0	0	8
Pascal Jampy (UTC)	4	4	0	0	16
Julien Rinaldi (Villeneuve)	3	0	0	0	0
Jason Sands (Limoux)	4	0	0	0	0
Claude Sirvent (St Gaudens)	3	3	0	0	12
Romain Sort (Villeneuve)	3	0	0	0	0
Gael Tallec (Halifax Blue Sox)	4	1	0	0	4
Frederic Teixido (Limoux)	4	0	0	0	0
Vincent Wulf (Villeneuve)	4	0	0	0	0

IRELAND *(Coaches: Steve O'Neill & Andy Kelly)*

	M	T	G	FG	Pts
David Barnhill (Leeds Rhinos)	4	1	0	0	4
David Bradbury (Huddersfield-Sheffield Giants)	1	0	0	0	0

	M	T	G	FG	Pts
Liam Bretherton (Leigh Centurions)	2	0	0	0	0
Kevin Campion (Brisbane Broncos)	4	0	0	0	0
Brian Carney (Hull FC)	4	2	0	0	8
Gavin Clinch (Huddersfield-Sheffield Giants)	2	0	0	0	0
Michael Eagar (Castleford Tigers)	3	1	0	0	4
Mark Forster (Warrington Wolves)	3	1	0	0	4
Ian Herron (Hull FC)	1	0	0	0	0
Chris Joynt (St Helens)	4	1	0	0	4
Johnny Lawless (Huddersfield-Sheffield Giants)	3	0	0	0	0
Tommy Martyn (St Helens)	3	1	0	0	4
Jamie Mathiou (Leeds Rhinos)	2	0	0	0	0
Barrie McDermott (Leeds Rhinos)	4	0	0	0	0
Terry O'Connor (Wigan Warriors)	4	0	0	0	0
Steve Prescott (Wakefield Trinity Wildcats)	4	1	17	0	38
Luke Ricketson (Sydney Roosters)	4	1	0	0	4
Ryan Sheridan (Leeds Rhinos)	4	2	0	0	8
Paul Southern (Salford City Reds)	3	0	0	0	0
Liam Tallon (Brisbane Norths)	1	0	0	0	0
Danny Williams (Melbourne Storm)	4	0	0	0	0
Michael Withers (Bradford Bulls)	4	4	0	0	16

LEBANON *(Coach: John Elias)*

	M	T	G	FG	Pts
Mohammed Abbas (Canterbury Bulldogs)	2	0	0	0	0
Najjarin Bilal (St George Illawarra)	1	0	0	0	0
Muhammed Chahal (Sydney Bulls)	1	0	0	0	0
Sami Chamoun (Sydney Bulls)	3	0	0	0	0
Michael Coorey (Balmain)	2	1	0	0	4
Raymond Daher (Cabramatta)	2	0	0	0	0
Fady El Chab (Sydney Bulls)	1	0	0	0	0
Hazem El Masri (Sydney Bulldogs)	3	2	6	0	20
Samer El Masri (Sydney Roosters)	3	1	0	0	4
Moneh Elahmad (Cabramatta)	2	0	0	0	0
Eben Goddard (St George Illawarra)	1	0	0	0	0
George Katrib (Canterbury Bulldogs)	2	0	0	0	0
Paul Khoury (Canterbury Bulldogs)	3	0	0	0	0
Joe Lichaa (Sydney Roosters)	3	0	0	0	0
Darren Maroon (Sydney Bulls)	3	0	0	0	0
Charlie Nohra (The Oaks)	2	0	0	0	0
Hassan Saleh (Canterbury Bulldogs)	3	3	0	0	12
Nedol Saleh (Western Suburbs)	1	0	0	0	0
Christopher Salem (St Gaudens)	3	0	0	0	0
Anthony Semrani (Sydney Bulldogs)	2	0	0	0	0
Jason Stanton (Sydney Bulls)	2	0	0	0	0
Kandy Tamer (Sydney Bulls)	3	0	0	0	0
Travis Touma (Sydney Bulls)	3	1	0	0	4

AOTEAROA MAORI *(Coach: Cameron Bell)*

	M	T	G	FG	Pts
James Cook (Northcote Tigers)	1	0	0	0	0
Luke Goodwin (Newtown)	1	0	2	0	4
Terry Hermansson (Auckland Warriors)	3	0	0	0	0
Sean Hoppe (St Helens)	2	0	0	0	0
David Kidwell (Parramatta Eels)	3	1	0	0	4
Toa Kohe-Love (Warrington Wolves)	3	0	0	0	0
Wairangi Koopu (Auckland Warriors)	2	1	0	0	4
Kylie Leuluai (Wests Tigers)	2	0	0	0	0
Odell Manuel (Auckland Warriors)	2	0	0	0	0
Steve Matthews (Glenora Bears)	1	1	0	0	4
Jarred Mills (Newtown)	1	0	0	0	0
Martin Moana (Halifax Blue Sox)	3	0	0	0	0
Chris Nahi (Brisbane Easts)	2	0	0	0	0
Boycie Nelson (Glenora Bears)	2	2	0	0	8
Gene Ngamu (Huddersfield-Sheffield Giants)	2	0	3	1	7
Tawera Nikau (Warrington Wolves)	3	0	0	0	0
Henry Perenara (Auckland Warriors)	2	0	1	0	2
Paul Rauhihi (Newcastle Knights)	3	1	0	0	4
Tahi Reihana (Brisbane Souths)	3	0	0	0	0
Jeremy Smith (Sydney Roosters)	1	0	0	0	0
Tyran Smith (Wests Tigers)	3	0	0	0	0
Hare Te Rangi (Otahuhu)	2	1	0	0	4
Clinton Toopi (Auckland Warriors)	3	2	0	0	8
Paul Whatuira (Auckland Warriors)	1	0	0	0	0

NEW ZEALAND *(Coach: Frank Endacott)*

	M	T	G	FG	Pts
Richie Barnett (Sydney Roosters)	6	6	0	0	24
Richie Blackmore (Leeds Rhinos)	2	1	0	0	4
Tonie Carroll (Brisbane Broncos)	5	4	0	0	16
Nathan Cayless (Parramatta Eels)	6	1	0	0	4
Brian Jellick (N Queensland Cowboys)	2	2	0	0	8
Stacey Jones (Auckland Warriors)	5	2	6	0	20
Stephen Kearney (Melbourne Storm)	6	2	0	0	8
Ali Lauitiiti (Auckland Warriors)	2	2	0	0	8
Tasesa Lavea (Melbourne Storm)	2	2	14	0	36
Henry Paul (Bradford Bulls)	5	1	24	1	53
Robbie Paul (Bradford Bulls)	5	5	0	0	20
Quentin Pongia (Sydney Roosters)	5	2	0	0	8
Tony Puletua (Penrith Panthers)	2	1	0	0	4
Matt Rua (Melbourne Storm)	5	1	0	0	4
Craig Smith (St George Illawarra)	6	1	0	0	4
Richard Swain (Melbourne Storm)	6	0	0	0	0
Logan Swann (Auckland Warriors)	4	2	0	0	8
Willie Talau (Sydney Bulldogs)	5	6	0	0	24
Joe Vagana (Auckland Warriors)	6	0	0	0	0
Nigel Vagana (Auckland Warriors)	5	3	0	0	12
Lesley Vainikolo (Canberra Raiders)	5	9	0	0	36
David Vaealiki (Parramatta Eels)	1	2	0	0	8
Ruben Wiki (Canberra Raiders)	6	3	0	0	12

PAPUA NEW GUINEA *(Coach: Bob Bennett)*

	M	T	G	FG	Pts
Eddie Aila (Brisbane Souths)	4	1	0	0	4
Makali Aizue (Goroka Lahanis)	3	0	0	0	0
Marcus Bai (Melbourne Storm)	4	1	0	0	4
David Buko (Wagga Wagga)	4	2	1	0	10
Stanley Gene (Hull FC)	4	2	0	0	8
Raymond Karl (Enga Mioks)	4	1	0	0	4
Alex Krewanty (Sydney Bulls)	4	1	0	0	4
Adrian Lam (Sydney Roosters)	4	1	0	1	5
Bruce Mamando (North Queensland Cowboys)	4	0	0	0	0
Michael Marum (Port Moresby Vipers)	1	0	0	0	0
Mark Mom (Brisbane Easts)	4	0	0	0	0
Michael Mondo (Yanco)	4	1	0	0	4
Duncan Naawi (Redcliffe)	4	0	0	0	0
Andrew Norman (Burdekin Roosters)	4	0	0	0	0
Tom O'Reilly (Oldham)	3	1	0	0	4
Elias Paiyo (Kellyville)	1	0	0	0	0
Lucas Solbat (Rabaul Gurias)	1	0	0	0	0
Alfred Songoro (Mackay Souths)	4	0	0	0	0
John Wilshere (Brisbane Easts)	4	2	11	0	30

RUSSIA *(Coach: Evgani Klebanov)*

	M	T	G	FG	Pts
Viatcheslav Artachine (Kazan Arrows)	1	0	0	0	0
Robert Campbell (Redcliffe)	3	0	0	0	0
Rinat Chamsoutdinov (Kazan Arrows)	1	0	0	0	0
Craig Cygler (Cairns Brothers)	2	0	0	0	0
Matthew Donovan (Western Suburbs)	2	1	0	0	4
Andrei Doumalkine (Lokomotiv Moscow)	1	0	0	0	0
Arron Findlay (Canterbury Bulldogs)	2	0	0	0	0
Roustem Garifoulline (Kazan Arrows)	1	0	0	0	0
Igor Gavriline (Lokomotiv Moscow)	3	0	0	0	0
Michael Giorgas (Logan City)	1	0	0	0	0
Robert Iliassov (Kazan Arrows)	3	1	0	0	4
Igor Jiltsov (Lokomotiv Moscow)	2	0	1	0	2
Pavel Kalachkine (Kazan Arrows)	3	0	0	0	0
Kirillin Koulemine (Lokomotiv Moscow)	1	0	0	0	0
Andrei Kuchumov (Moscow Magicians)	1	0	0	0	0
Alexander Lysenkov (Lokomotiv Moscow)	3	0	0	0	0
Mikhail Mitrofanov (Kazan Arrows)	3	0	3	0	6
Victor Netchaev (Lokomotiv Moscow)	2	0	0	0	0
Andre Olar (Toulouse)	3	0	0	0	0
Vadim Postnikov (Lokomotiv Moscow)	2	0	0	0	0
Maxim Romanov (Kazan Arrows)	3	0	0	0	0
Ian Rubin (Sydney Roosters)	3	0	0	0	0
Joel Rullis (Western Suburbs)	3	1	0	0	4
Petr Sokolov (Lokomotiv Moscow)	2	0	0	0	0

SAMOA (Coach: Darrell Williams)

	M	T	G	FG	Pts
Henry Aau Fa'afili (Auckland Warriors) *	3	2	0	0	8
Monty Betham (Auckland Warriors)	4	1	0	0	4
Max Fala (Northcote Tigers)	3	0	0	0	0
Joe Galuvao (Auckland Warriors)	2	0	0	0	0
Simon Geros (Burleigh Bears)	2	0	2	0	4
Farvae Kalolo (Auckland Warriors)	1	0	0	0	0
Shane Laloata (Nelson Bay)	2	0	3	0	6
Mark Leafa (Sydney Bulldogs)	4	0	0	0	0
Bryan Leauma (Penrith Panthers)	4	4	0	0	16
Philip Leuluai (Auckland Warriors)	3	0	0	0	0
Peter Lima (Toulouse)	2	0	0	0	0
Francis Meli (Auckland Warriors)	3	0	0	0	0
Loa Milford (Balmain)	4	3	0	0	12
Fred Petersen (Penrith Panthers)	1	0	0	0	0
Willie Poching (Wakefield Trinity Wildcats)	4	0	2	0	4
Frank Puletua (Penrith Panthers)	4	0	0	0	0
Jerry Seuseu (Auckland Warriors)	4	0	0	0	0
David Solomona (Sydney Roosters)	4	2	0	0	8
Anthony Swann (Canberra Raiders)	4	0	0	0	0
Willie Swann (Hunslet Hawks)	4	1	0	1	5
Albert Talapeau (Sydney Roosters)	1	0	0	0	0
Tony Tatupu (Wakefield Trinity Wildcats)	4	0	0	0	0

* one as unused sub

SCOTLAND (Coach: Shaun McRae)

	M	T	G	FG	Pts
Danny Arnold (Huddersfield-Sheffield Giants)	2	1	0	0	4
Geoff Bell (North Queensland Cowboys)	3	1	0	0	4
Scott Cram (London Broncos)	3	0	0	0	0
Matt Crowther (Huddersfield-Sheffield Giants)	3	0	4	0	8
Matt Daylight (Hull FC)	3	0	0	0	0
Lee Gilmour (Wigan Warriors)	3	0	0	0	0
Nathan Graham (Dewsbury Rams)	1	0	0	0	0
Daniel Heckenberg (St George Illawarra)	3	0	0	0	0
Richard Horne (Hull FC)	3	0	0	0	0
Dale Laughton (Huddersfield-Sheffield Giants)	3	0	0	0	0
Scott Logan (Sydney Roosters)	3	0	0	0	0
Graham Mackay (Leeds Rhinos)	1	0	1	0	2
David Maiden (Hull FC)	3	1	0	0	4
Wayne McDonald (Hull FC)	3	0	0	0	0
Lee Penny (Warrington Wolves)	1	1	0	0	4
Andrew Purcell (Castleford Tigers)	2	0	0	0	0
Scott Rhodes (Leeds Rhinos)	2	1	0	0	4
Danny Russell (Huddersfield-Sheffield Giants)	3	0	0	0	0
Darren Shaw (Castleford Tigers)	3	0	0	0	0
Adrian Vowles (Castleford Tigers)	3	1	0	0	4

SOUTH AFRICA (Coach: Paul Matete)

	M	T	G	FG	Pts
Leon Barnard (Centurion Lions)	3	1	0	0	4
Brian Best (Centurion Lions)	3	1	0	0	4
Jamie Bloem (Halifax Blue Sox)	3	0	3	0	6
Jaco Booysen (Centurion Lions)	3	0	0	0	0
Conrad Breytenbach (Pretoria Bulls)	1	1	0	0	4
Francois Cloete (Pretoria Bulls)	2	0	0	0	0
Archer Dames (Pretoria Bulls)	3	0	0	0	0
Quinton de Villiers (Pretoria Bulls)	3	1	0	0	4
Hercules Erasmus (Centurion Lions)	3	0	0	0	0
Chris Hurter (Centurion Lions)	2	0	0	0	0
Justin Jennings (Pretoria Bulls)	3	0	0	0	0
Mark Johnson (Salford City Reds)	3	0	0	0	0
Richard Louw (Kempton)	1	0	0	0	0
Hendrik Mulder (Centurion Lions)	3	0	0	0	0
Corne Nel (Pretoria Bulls)	2	0	0	0	0
Ian Noble (Northwest Leopards)	2	0	0	0	0
Tim O'Shea (Johannesburg)	1	0	1	0	2
Eugene Powell (Johannesburg)	3	0	0	0	0
Sean Rutgerson (Canberra Raiders)	3	0	0	0	0
Sean Skelton (Marist, Aus)	1	0	0	0	0
Pierre Van Wyk (Centurion Lions)	2	0	0	0	0
Jaco Webb (Blue Bulls)	1	0	0	0	0

TONGA (Coach: Murray Hurst)

	M	T	G	FG	Pts
David Fisi'iahi (Eastern Tornadoes)	3	1	0	0	4
Paul Fisi'iahi (Eastern Tornadoes)	1	1	0	0	4
Nuko Hifo (Griffith)	1	0	0	0	0
Phil Howlett (N Queensland Cowboys)	3	0	0	0	0
Lipina Kaufusi (Wests Magpies)	3	1	0	0	4
Malupo Kaufusi (Wests Magpies)	1	0	0	0	0
Brent Kite (Canberra Raiders)	2	0	0	0	0
Paul Koloi (South Mackay)	3	0	0	0	0
Talite Liava'a (Auckland Warriors)	2	1	0	0	4
Nelson Lomi (Sydney Roosters)	3	1	0	0	4
Andrew Lomu (Sydney Roosters)	2	0	0	0	0
Duane Mann (Glenora Bears)	3	2	1	0	10
Esau Mann (Otahuhu)	3	1	0	0	4
Willie Manu (Wests Magpies)	3	0	0	0	0
Alfons Masella (St George Illawarra)	2	0	0	0	0
Martin Masella (Wakefield Trinity Wildcats)	3	1	0	0	4
Willie Mason (Sydney Bulldogs)	3	2	0	0	8
Fifita Moala (Melbourne Storm)	3	3	9	0	30
Tevita Vaikona (Bradford Bulls)	3	4	0	0	16
Greg Wolfgramm (Canberra Raiders)	2	0	0	0	0
Willie Wolfgramm (Queanbeyan)	2	1	0	0	4

WALES (Coach: Clive Griffiths)

	M	T	G	FG	Pts
Paul Atcheson (St Helens)	5	1	0	0	4
Lee Briers (Warrington Wolves)	5	4	0	2	18
Dean Busby (Warrington Wolves)	3	0	0	0	0
Garreth Carvell (Leeds Rhinos)	2	0	0	0	0
Jason Critchley (unattached)	5	1	0	0	4
Keiron Cunningham (St Helens)	4	2	0	0	8
Wes Davies (Wigan Warriors)	5	2	0	0	8
John Devereux (unattached)	2	0	0	0	0
Barry Eaton (Dewsbury Rams)	1	0	0	0	0
Anthony Farrell (Leeds Rhinos)	5	1	0	0	4
Iestyn Harris (Leeds Rhinos)	5	2	21	0	50
Paul Highton (Salford City Reds)	5	0	0	0	0
Mick Jenkins (Hull FC)	4	1	0	0	4
David Luckwell (Batley Bulldogs)	1	0	0	0	0
Justin Morgan (Canberra Raiders)	5	0	0	0	0
Paul Moriarty (unattached)	2	0	0	0	0
Chris Morley (Sheffield Eagles)	4	0	0	0	0
Hefin O'Hare (Leeds Rhinos)	1	0	0	0	0
Chris Smith (St Helens)	2	0	0	0	0
Paul Sterling (Leeds Rhinos)	4	1	0	0	4
Anthony Sullivan (St Helens)	5	0	0	0	0
Kris Tassell (Salford City Reds)	4	4	0	0	16
Ian Watson (Swinton Lions)	3	1	0	0	4
David Whittle (Leigh Centurions)	3	0	0	0	0

EMERGING NATIONS 2000

GROUP ONE

USA 52 ....CANADA 10
At Court Place Farm, Oxford, Monday 13 November 2000
Attendance: 500
USA: T - Balachandran, Vassilakopoulos, Duncan 2, Niu, Warren 2, Broussard, Fabri, Sheridan, G - Simon 6
Canada: T - Whale, Van der Hoek, G - De Snayer

CANADA 6 ....ITALY 66
At Cougar Park, Keighley, Wednesday 15 November 2000
Attendance: 1,028
Canada: T - Coussons; G - Weiler
Italy: T - Trimboli 2, Schifilitti 2, D'Arro, Barbaro, Ienco 2, Napolitano 2, Di Paoli, Frare, A Dal Santo; G - Frare 7

ITALY 40 ....USA 16
At the New Shay, Halifax, Friday 17 November 2000
Attendance: 1,487
Italy: T - Riolo, Frare 2, Ienco 2, Mancuso, A Capovilla; G - Albertini 4, Ienco 2.
USA: T - O'Neill, Duncan, Retchless; G - Duncan

GROUP ONE TABLE

	P	W	D	L	F	A	Pts
Italy	2	2	0	0	106	22	4
USA	2	1	0	1	68	50	2
Canada	2	0	0	2	16	118	0

GROUP TWO

BARLA GB & IRELAND 60 ....MOROCCO 2
At Lionheart Stadium, Featherstone,
Monday 13 November 2000
Attendance: 769
BARLA: T - Jackson 2, Cooper, 2, Davidson, Morton 2, Innes 2, O'Neill, Shaw, Halmshaw, G - Jackson 4, Innes 2.
Morocco: G - Martinez

MOROCCO 12 ....JAPAN 8
At New Craven Park, Hull,
Wednesday 15 November 2000
Attendance: 1,488
Morocco: T- El Arf, G - Martinez 4
Japan: T - Kunemura, G - Inose 2

BARLA GB & IRELAND 54 ....JAPAN 0
At Copeland Stadium, Whitehaven,
Friday 17 November 2000
Attendance: 1,007
BARLA: T - Lynn 2, Newby, Jones, Innes 2, G Fletcher 2, Shaw, McHugh, O'Neil, G - Newby 5

GROUP TWO TABLE

	P	W	D	L	F	A	Pts
BARLA GB & Ireland	2	2	0	0	114	2	4
Morocco	2	1	0	1	14	68	2
Japan	2	0	0	2	8	66	0

PLAY-OFFS

CANADA 28..JAPAN 12
At Robin Park, Wigan, Monday 20 November 2000
Attendance: 500
Canada: T - Demetriou 2, Whale, McKenzie;
G - Weiler 2, De Snayer 2
Japan: T - Williamson, Nakashima; G - Okamura 2
(Canada finished 5th)

UNITED STATES 50..........................MOROCCO 10
At Robin Park, Wigan, Monday 20 November 2000
Attendance: 500
USA: T - Sheridan 2, Broussard, O'Neill, Retchless 2, Duncan 2, Hollingsworth; G - Duncan 6, Niu
Morocco: T - El Arf, Fakir; G - Martinez
(USA finished 3rd)

FINAL

BARLA GB & IRELAND 20 ....ITALY 14
At Ram Stadium, Dewsbury, Monday 20 November 2000
Attendance: 1,601; **Referee:** Robert Connolly (England)
BARLA: T - Fletcher, McHugh, Birdsall; G - Jackson 4
Italy: T - Riolo, A Capovilla, Bulgarelli; G - Albertini
BARLA: Dave Hedgecock, Steve Morton, Phil O'Neil (c), Darrell Cooper, Wayne McHugh, Darren Jones, Terry Lynn, Stuart Dancer, Marc Jackson, Terry Halmshaw, Brian Newby, Ian Devlin, Scott Fletcher. Subs: Rob Shaw, Paul Davidson, Phil Sherwen, Paul Birdsall.
Italy: Darren Albertini, Charlie Ienco, Ian Schifilitti, Dainan Mancuso, David Riolo, John Frare, Michael Mantelli, Paul Dalsanto, Darren Capovilla, Brendan Di Paoli, Mark Sessarago, Adam Capovilla. Subs: Patrick Trimboli, Carlo Napolitano, Anthony Dalsanto, Pete Magnone

WOMENS WORLD SERIES 2000

GREAT BRITAIN & IRELAND 12 ....NEW ZEALAND 22
At Orrell, Tuesday, November 7 2000
Great Britain: T - Gilmour, Land; G - Dobek 2
New Zealand: T - Witehera, Te Amo 2, Niha, Wrigley; G Hina

AUSTRALIA 6 ....NEW ZEALAND 10
At South Leeds Stadium, Hunslet,
Friday, November 10 2000
Australia: T - Norris; G - Shaw
New Zealand: T - Johnstone, Witehera; G - Hina

GREAT BRITAIN & IRELAND 14 ....AUSTRALIA 10
At Ram Stadium, Dewsbury,
Tuesday, November 14 2000
Great Britain: T - Banks, Gilmour, Dobek; G - Dobek
Australia: T - Jarrett, Murphy; G - Shaw

PLAY-OFFS

NEW ZEALAND 50 ....AUSTRALIA 6
At Ram Stadium, Dewsbury, Friday November 17 2000
New Zealand: T - O'Carroll 2, Mariu 2, Howard, Logopati, Driscoll, Te Amo, Presland, White; G - Hina 4, Mariu
Australia: T - Fanning; G - Shaw

GREAT BRITAIN & IRELAND 4 ....AUSTRALIA 0
At The Jungle, Castleford, Tuesday November 21 2000
Great Britain: G - Dobek 2

FINAL

NEW ZEALAND 26........GREAT BRITAIN & IRELAND 4
At Wilderspool Stadium, Warrington,
Friday 24 November 2000
New Zealand: T - Hina 2, Te Amo 2, Presland.
G - Hina 2, Mariu
Great Britain: T - Land
New Zealand: Kat Howard, Sharlene Johnson, Michelle Driscoll, Selena Te Amo, Stacey O'Carroll, Trish Hina, Laura Mariu , Nicole Presland, Tracy Wrigley, Louise Avaiki, Rachel White, Nadene Conlon, Tasha Davie. Subs: Miriama Niha, Leah Witehira, Somma Te Kahu, Hanu Wainohu
Great Britain: Joanne Hewson, Dani Titterington, Allison Kitchin, Natalie Gilmour, Teresa Bruce, Brenda Dobek, Wendy Charnley, Paula Tunnicliffe, Shelley Land, Lisa Macintosh, Jane Bank, Rebecca Stevens, Sally Milburn. Subs: Sam Bailey, Michelle Handley, Sarah Roper, Gemma Walsh

WORLD CUP 2000 - QUALIFYING TOURNAMENT

MEDITERRANEAN GROUP

ITALY 16 ....LEBANON 36
at Stade Jean Laffon, Perpignan,
Thursday 11th November, 1999
Italy: T - Riolo, Barbaro, Salafia; G - Salafia 2
Lebanon: T - Coorey, Lambert, Salem 2, Chalal, Daher; G - H El Masri 6

ITALY 34...MOROCCO 0
at Stade de Minimes, Toulouse,
Sunday 14th November, 1999
Italy: T - Riolo 3, Margheritini, Napoli, Di Paolo; G - Margheritini 5

LEBANON 104 ....MOROCCO 0
at Parc Des Sports, Avignon,
Wednesday 17th November, 1999
Lebanon: T - Salem 5, H El Masri 4, Lambert, Chalal 3, Khoury, Touma, N Saleh, Coorey, Chehade; G - H El Masri 16

MEDITERRANEAN GROUP TABLE

	P	W	D	L	F	A	Pts
Lebanon	2	2	0	0	140	16	4
Italy	2	1	0	1	50	36	2
Morocco	2	0	0	2	0	138	0

PACIFIC GROUP

UNITED STATES 54 ....JAPAN 0
at Disney's Wide World of Sports, Orlando,
Tuesday 9th November, 1999
United States: T- Craig, Balachandran, Broussard 3,
Mains, Matautia, Niu, Sheridan, Fabri, Faimalo;
G - Niu 4, David Bowe

JAPAN 14 ....CANADA 0
at Disney's Wide World of Sports, Orlando,
Thursday 11th November, 1999
Japan: T - Bannister, Ueda, Kanemura; G - Tateyama

UNITED STATES 68 ....CANADA 0
at Disney's Wide World of Sports, Orlando,
Monday 15th November, 1999
United States: T - Fabri, Sheridan 3, Broussard 3,
Warren 2, Mains, Matautia 2, Faimalo; G - Niu 7, Bowe

PACIFIC GROUP TABLE

	P	W	D	L	F	A	Pts
USA	2	2	0	0	122	0	4
Japan	2	1	0	1	14	54	2
Canada	2	0	0	2	0	82	0

FINAL

UNITED STATES 8 ....LEBANON 62
at Disney's Wide World of Sports, Orlando,
Sunday 21st November, 1999
United States: T - Mains; G - Niu 2
Lebanon: T - Coorey 3, Khoury 2, Chehade, Chalal,
Lambert, Touma, H El Masri, Salem; G - H El Masri 9

WORLD CUP RECORDS

Trophy wins:
9 by Australia; 3 by Great Britain; New Zealand 1

Highest score and widest margin:
Australia 110 v Russia 4
at Hull, 4 November 2000

Biggest attendance:
73,631 - Great Britain v Australia
at Wembley (Final), 24 October 1992

Most tries in a match:
4 by Keith Fielding (England) v France
at Bordeaux, 11 October 1975
by Dale Shearer (Australia) v France
at Carcassonne, 13 December 1986
by Michael O'Connor (Australia) v Papua New Guinea
at Wagga, 20 July 1988
by Mat Rogers (Australia) v Fiji
at Gateshead, 1 November 2000
by Wendell Sailor (Australia) v Russia
at Hull, 4 November 2000
by Manu Vatuvei (New Zealand) v England
at Newcastle, 8 November 2008

Most goals in a match:
17 Ryan Girdler (Australia) v Russia
at Hull, 4 November 2000

Most points in a match:
46 by Ryan Girdler (Australia) v Russia
at Hull, 4 November 2000